ARISTOTLE, *DE MOTU ANIMALIUM*

Aristotle, *De Motu Animalium*

A New Critical Edition of the Greek Text

by

OLIVER PRIMAVESI

with an English Translation by
BENJAMIN MORISON

and

an Introduction by
CHRISTOF RAPP AND OLIVER PRIMAVESI

OXFORD
UNIVERSITY PRESS

OXFORD
UNIVERSITY PRESS

Great Clarendon Street, Oxford, OX2 6DP,
United Kingdom

Oxford University Press is a department of the University of Oxford.
It furthers the University's objective of excellence in research, scholarship,
and education by publishing worldwide. Oxford is a registered trade mark of
Oxford University Press in the UK and in certain other countries

Published in the United States of America by Oxford University Press
198 Madison Avenue, New York, NY 10016, United States of America

British Library Cataloguing in Publication Data
Data available

Library of Congress Control Number: 2022947450

ISBN 978–0–19–887446–1

Printed and bound in the UK by
TJ Books Limited

CONTENTS

FOREWORD

In 2020, the Press published the Proceedings of the 19th *Symposium Aristotelicum*, devoted to Aristotle's *De Motu Animalium* (*MA*). Apart from the discussions of individual chapters of *MA*, these proceedings also contain an introduction in two parts—part I, by C. Rapp, on the argument of *MA*; part II, by O. Primavesi, on the text of *MA*—and a new critical edition of the Greek text by O. Primavesi with a facing English translation by B. Morison. The Press kindly suggested republishing the introduction, the edition, and the translation as a book on its own. That suggestion, which we gratefully accepted, has yielded the present volume.

It is, of course, true that there is already the excellent separate edition of *MA* with introduction, Greek text, English translation, interpretative essays, and commentary by Martha Nussbaum. Yet since that edition came out, in 1978, there have been more than four decades of scholarly debate on *MA* and on the philosophical issues concerned. The controversial issues include, for instance, the difficult relationship between the 'cardiocentrism' of *MA*'s picture of the soul and the theory of the soul as expounded in *De Anima*. There is also the methodological question as to why Aristotle discusses, in *MA*, the function of external resting points not only with regard to animal self-motion but also with regard to the movement of the heavens. Furthermore, we may single out the 'practical syllogism' and the interaction of *phantasia* and desire in the causation of animal self-motion, the coexistence of internal and external unmoved movers, and, last not least, the connate *pneuma*. Thus, we confidently hope that an overview of those debates, as the one offered by C.R. in the first part of the introduction to the present volume, will be of use for the student of *MA* and of Aristotle's psychology in general.

As to the Greek text, our picture of the transmission of *MA* changed dramatically when the late Pieter De Leemans brought out, in 2011, his excellent edition of William of Moerbeke's mediaeval Latin translation of the treatise. For De Leemans had hit upon a small group of comparatively young Greek manuscripts that come surprisingly close to William's mysterious 'second source'— postulated but deemed irretrievably lost by Nussbaum. Meanwhile, both O.P.'s work on the text of *MA* and more recent investigations into the transmission of the first part of the *Parva Naturalia* (of which *MA* is part and parcel not only in the mind of Aristotle but also in the Greek manuscripts) have shown that we are dealing here with a second, independent branch of the transmission; on its contribution to the text of *Parva Naturalia* I see Isépy/Prapa 2018,

Primavesi 2022, and the present volume, pp. 100–103 and 146–156. O.P. has named the new branch **β**, whereas **α** designates the branch of manuscripts on which all previous editions of *MA*, from Immanuel Bekker (1831) to Martha Nussbaum (1978), had to rely almost exclusively. Among the 47 extant Greek *MA* manuscripts (see the list in Appendix I on pp. 136–140), only two— Berolinensis Phillippicus 1507/I (Bᶜ) and Erlangensis UB A 4 (Eʳ)—have preserved a complete and uncontaminated **β**-text. Yet the **β**-readings, most of which were unknown to previous editors, carry, in principle, as much weight for the constitution of the text as the **α**-readings—a basic fact illustrated by the new *stemma codicum* on p. 133. Therefore, we think that there is room for a volume that makes accessible to a larger public both the new picture of the transmission and the new edition of the Greek text together with its translation into English.

The Greek text offered in the present volume differs from Nussbaum's text in 120 passages, which the reader will find listed in Appendix III on pp. 142–146. It seems unlikely, however, that in every passage where **α**-text and **β**-text diverge, every user of the present volume will share O.P.'s views on the relative merits of the **α**- and of the **β**-reading in question. All the less so since O.P. has himself changed his mind in two passages since the publication of the *Symposium Aristotelicum* volume: from **α** to **β** in one case and from **β** to **α** in the other. In 702ᵇ8, he now thinks that the apparently smooth **α**-reading (τοῦ μὲν τῆς βακτηρίας ἐσχάτου) is just a superficial correction of the **β**-reading (τοῦ μὲν τῆς βακτηρίας τοῦ ἐσχάτου) which, albeit ungrammatical, points the way to restoring the much more satisfactory reading τοῦ ἐσχάτου τοῦ μὲν τῆς βακτηρίας. As to the quotation from *Iliad* VIII in ch. 4., by contrast, he now believes that we should ascribe the presence of the dubious, un-Homeric πάνυ in the new **β**-reading of 700ᵃ1, i.e. of *Iliad* VIII, 22, to scribal error and not, as he had done previously, to the fact that Aristotle is likely to be quoting from memory. Filippomaria Pontani (Venice), a renowned expert on the transmission of Homer, has convinced him that Aristotle, the author of a monograph on *Homeric Problems* in six volumes, would simply not write such a thing in a Homeric quotation, not even when quoting from memory. Therefore, O.P. has returned to the Homeric μάλα in 700ᵃ1, i.e. to the **α**-reading that all manuscripts of the *Iliad* confirm.

Anyhow, what matters most is that one is now in the position to judge for oneself all cases of **α/β**-divergence by weighing the **α**-readings known since Bekker 1831 against the **β**-readings documented—in most cases for the first time—in the *apparatus criticus* of the present edition. The new picture of the transmission also implies that it must count as methodologically flawed to defend a reading transmitted just by *one half* of **α**—be it Parisinus E or the **γ**-branch—against a reading *shared* by the other half of **α** and by the new **β**-branch.

The reader will find further thoughts on the argument, the text, and the translation of *MA* in the reviews of the *Symposium Aristotelicum* volume by Daniel Coren, Andrea Falcon, Robert Mayhew, Marco Zingano, and Diego Zucca, which we have inserted into the bibliography.

It is a pleasure to thank Mr. M. Neidhart (LMU) for his help in preparing the book for the publisher and Mr. E. Saraswathi for the excellent typesetting performed by the firm of Straive.

Munich and Princeton, December 2022
O. Primavesi
C. Rapp
B. Morison

Introduction Part I

The Argument of De Motu Animalium

CHRISTOF RAPP

1. Aristotle's *De Motu Animalium*: Its Topic and Purpose

The treatise that has come down to us under the title *De Motu Animalium* (*MA*) holds a peculiar place within the Aristotelian *oeuvre*.[1] It treats the phenomenon of animal self-motion—that animals, both human and non-human, are capable of moving themselves. Although animals do so in several different ways—e.g. by walking, flying, swimming, crawling, creeping, and hopping—there is a common cause of this movement that *MA* means to uncover.[2] This general topic seems to align the treatise with the common project of Aristotle's zoological writings. And, indeed, there is substantial common ground between *MA* and the zoological treatise *De Incessu Animalium* (usually translated as 'On the Progression of Animals') as well as those chapters of *De Partibus Animalium* that inquire into the extremities and all other motion-enabling parts of animals. At the same time, it is remarkable that the argument of *MA* dwells for almost two chapters on the movement of the universe as a whole. In a similar vein, the treatise includes references to the unmoved mover, to the eternal movement of celestial bodies, and to 'first philosophy'. In general, there is a tendency

---

[1] I would like to thank Andreas Anagnostopoulos, David Charles, Klaus Corcilius, James G. Lennox, and Christopher Shields for written comments on earlier versions of this text.

[2] At the beginning of the treatise, at 698ᵃ4, Aristotle announces that he will speak 'about the common cause (περὶ τῆς κοινῆς αἰτίας)' of all kinds of movements; in the treatise's closing lines, at 704ᵇ2, he concludes that he has now dealt with the causes 'regarding motion in general (περὶ [...] τῆς κοινῆς κινήσεως)'.

throughout the treatise to show that the principles that are invoked to explain the movement of sublunary animals instantiate, or at least align with, certain more comprehensive kinetic principles.

This remarkably *synoptic* perspective notwithstanding, *MA* also carries out a very precise task that connects it with Aristotle's psychological and/or psycho-physical writings, namely *De Anima* on the one hand and the short treatises contained in the collection *Parva Naturalia* on the other: from *MA* 6 onwards the overarching project of identifying the common cause of all animal motion is recast as the more specific question of how it is that the soul moves an animal's body. That the soul is partly constituted by the capacity to originate loco-motion is the central thesis of *De Anima* III 9–11. At the end of *De Anima* III 10, after having assessed the role of thinking and desiring in initiating locomotion, Aristotle points out that 'the instrument by which desire initiates motion is already something bodily' and that it is necessary to examine it among the functions common to body and soul (433^{b}19–21). Considering things that are 'common to body and soul' is a characterization that Aristotle also applies to the project carried out in the *Parva Naturalia*: in *De Sensu* 1 (436^{a}6–9), he mentions as examples of such common functions 'sense-perception, memory, spirit, appetite, and desire in general'—though none of the treatises of the *Parva Naturalia* has 'spirit, appetite, and desire in general (θυμὸς καὶ ἐπιθυμία καὶ ὅλως ὄρεξις)' as its topic,[3] whereas *MA* has a lot to say about desiring and its somatic-physiological side. Moreover, chapter 10 of *MA* concludes the meticulously developed account of how the soul moves the body by saying that 'it has now been stated by which moved part the soul imparts movement' (703^{a}28–9). Since this refers to the moved *bodily* part *by which* the soul imparts movement, the formulation suggests itself as answering to the announcement made at the end of *De Anima* III 10. Such a correspondence would render essential parts of *MA* a psycho-physical or psychosomatic project designed to explore the bodily instruments and preconditions for the soul's initiation of movement.[4]

It is obvious, then, that the project of *MA* is connected with many different aspects of Aristotle's philosophical and scientific thought. These connections are reflected in numerous allusions and cross-references[5] to other Aristotelian works. Though dedicated to a relatively precise and well-defined question, the treatise *MA* thus stands out by its tendency to treat the explanation of animal

---

[3] As Jaeger 1913a, 39, observed, the project of *MA*, consisting in the search for a *common* cause of animal motion, is similar to the project of the *Parva Naturalia* also in that the latter treatises treat phenomena like sleeping, waking, breathing as *common*, and not as peculiar to different species. On the relation of the *MA* to the *Parva Naturalia*, see now Rashed 2004, 191–202.

[4] For a full discussion of questions of this kind, see Laks 2020.

[5] Düring 1966, 296, nn. 37 and 38, offers a collection of such cross-references and formulations reminiscent of the wording in other Aristotelian works.

motion almost as the missing link between different strands of Aristotelian philosophy and by shedding light on a variety of exegetically controversial and philosophically challenging issues.

Martha C. Nussbaum's book on *De Motu Animalium*—first submitted as a PhD thesis in 1975, then published in the first edition in 1978 and in a second revised edition in 1985—is the first full modern commentary on the *MA* and, thus, became a landmark publication. Although some of Nussbaum's specific claims were received with reluctance by the scholarly community, and although some of her discussions seem to be recognizably influenced by philosophical tendencies of these years, her book as a whole managed to establish an agenda of philosophical issues that continue to be discussed in connection with this treatise down to the present day. Since the publication of Nussbaum's book a German (Kollesch 1985) and a French (Morel 2013) commentary of Aristotle's *MA* have been released; also, an English translation of Michael of Ephesus' Greek commentary on *De Motu Animalium* has been published (Preus 1981). A collection of ten essays on the *MA* has been edited by Marwan Rashed and André Laks (Laks/Rashed 2004). Apart from commentaries and collections, several monographs have been dedicated to the *MA* as a whole, most notably Labarrière 2004, Morel 2007, and Corcilius 2008a. Other studies such as Lorenz 2006 have focused in part on the thematically related chapters III 9–11 of *De Anima*.[6]

2. The Structure of *De Motu Animalium*

The treatise is structured, at the macro level, by two different—though related—guiding questions. The first of them is given at the beginning of **chapter 1**. What needs investigation, Aristotle says, is the 'common cause'[7] of animal motion (698^a4) pertaining to all particular types of movement. Apparently, this formulation is meant to demarcate the project of *MA* from the related but distinct project of *De Incessu Animalium*, which focuses more on the different types of animal motion and the different anatomies of the various genera of animals. The next five chapters deal with certain preconditions of animal self-motion, but they also dwell on the question of whether the same conditions hold for other cases of movement—in particular, that of the universe as a whole. Hence, the second guiding question, formulated at the beginning of chapter 6,

---

[6] Cf. also the recent commentaries on *De Anima*, Polansky 2007 and Shields 2016, as well as Johansen 2012.

[7] I stick to this established rendering, although I agree, of course, that Aristotle aims at a 'common explanation' of animal motion; cf. Nussbaum 1983, n. 2.

marks the transition to a more focused discussion of animal motion; strictly speaking, there are two such questions: 'it remains to consider how the soul moves the body and what the principle/origin of animal motion is' (700^{b}9–11). The first question is straightforward and seems to take up an issue that has been prepared for by *De Anima* III 9–11; for saying that the soul imparts movement by desiring (in combination with perceiving, *phantasia*, or thinking), leaves open the question of how the psychic capacity to desire can actually make the animal's limbs move and set the entire animal into motion. The second question refers to a principle of animal motion, and is thus reminiscent of the initially formulated quest for the 'common cause' of animal motion. We can expect, then, that any full account of such a common cause will mention the soul or particular capacities of the soul, but will also identify certain bodily instruments through which movement is imparted to the locomotion-enabling parts of an animal's body. Since the sought-after cause is a common one, the somatic or physiological explanation must also be one that abstracts from the anatomic peculiarities of different genera of animals.

Two main parts of the treatise? The first part of the treatise thus spans **chapters 1 to 5**, the second part **chapters 6 to 10** (or 11—depending on whether one sees the last chapter as an appendix or as more intimately connected with the main argument of chapters 6 to 10).[8] In principle one could say, then, that the first part deals with certain conditions of movement in general, while the second part focuses on animal motion more specifically. This seems to be right, but it is not the entire story, for chapters 1–2 are already dedicated to animal motion in particular and chapter 6 follows the first part of the treatise in comparing animal motion to cosmic or celestial movement. Nevertheless, it seems convenient to subdivide the treatise into these two main parts.[9]

The entire first part of the treatise is held together by a quite general claim stated early in the first chapter (698^{a}7–10), that what moves itself by itself—a self-mover—is the origin or principle (*archē*) of the movement of other things, while the principle of *its own* movement, i.e. the principle of the movement of self-movers, is unmoved (*akinēton*). This claim is not meant to be peculiar to animal motion; on the contrary, it is stressed that the claim is imported from another context related to the discussion of eternal motion. The transition to the discussion of animals is made by the announcement that one must apply this general claim to particular cases and the particular case to be discussed above all is animal motion.

The case of animal motion. This latter announcement is substantiated in **the rest of chapter 1** and in **chapter 2**, first by showing that there must be something

---

[8] Morel 2020 argues that chapter 11 is an important part of the overall project.

[9] On some implications of this subdivision of the treatise, see section 3 (iii), below.

within the animal that is at rest (*MA* 1, from 698ª14), then again by showing that there must be something unmoved external to the animal, by pressing against which the animal moves (*MA* 2). In other words, the general *akinēton*-requirement stated at the outset applies to the locomotion of animals in at least two different ways, first in that they need an internal resting point and second in that they need an external resting point or platform that offers resistance (for otherwise they would have the same experience as people trying to walk on sand that always gives way). The internal resting point gets immediately correlated with joints, for when the animal bends or straightens its limbs one point within the joint moves, while another point must remain at rest (the joint or a point within the joint is, as Aristotle says, sometimes potentially one, while actually two, and sometimes actually one, while potentially two); joints are thus origins of movement, especially the unmoved region or point within them. As for the external resting point, *MA* 2 shows that this unmoved thing must, as a whole, be different from, and thus no part of, the moving thing as a whole.[10]

The akinēton-*requirement and the motion of the whole.* When introducing the external resting point at the beginning of *MA* 2, Aristotle notes that it is worthwhile to pause for more general reflection at this juncture, since this idea makes the present study relevant not only to animal motion, but also to the motion of the universe (698ᵇ9–12). And, indeed, **chapter 3 and the first part of chapter 4** consider *aporiai*, difficulties,[11] deriving from the attempt to apply the *akinēton*-requirement, as it was specified for animals, to the movement of the universe as a whole: is there something unmoved that bears the same relation to the whole of nature that the surface of the earth bears to self-moving terrestrial animals? Would that mean that there is something unmoved which is neither in nor of the universe? If the mover of the universe is itself moved it must at least touch and lean on something that is unmoved and must not be a part of the universe. Or is the mover of the universe itself unmoved? The two poles of the universe, which some might suggest, cannot do this job of the mover. Nor could the mythical Atlas, who is said to twirl the heavens around the poles while keeping his feet on the earth. Moreover, all models that introduce an interior mover, like Atlas, that makes use of the earth's state of rest, would face the problem of excessive powers; for if the mover exerts disproportionate power on the earth, the earth could be moved from its central position. Scenarios like this, if they are possible, threaten to make the universe destructible. For Aristotle, however, the *MA* is not the right place to fully resolve this sort of difficulty.[12] Nor is it

---

[10] Cf. Coope 2020, sections 2–3.

[11] There are above all two such difficulties that are flagged as *aporiai*: 3, 699ª12–ᵇ11 and 4, 699ᵇ12–31; cf. Coope 2020 and Morison 2020.

[12] Or so he says a few lines later in *MA* 4, 700ª20–1: 'But whether there is something higher and a first mover is unclear, and such a principle is a topic for another discussion.'

clear and uncontroversial how the digression on the movement of the whole universe is meant to contribute to the overall argument.[13] At any rate, the brief passage that rounds off the discussion of the two *aporiai*[14] approvingly quotes Homer saying that Zeus cannot be dragged from heaven to earth however hard one toils. Aristotle interprets these lines as implying that what is absolutely (and by its nature) unmoved could never be moved and that the assumption of such an (entirely unmoved) principle could also avoid the above-mentioned threat of the universe's destructibility.

The akinēton-*requirement in its broader context.* **The rest of chapter 4 and the whole of chapter 5** seem to resume the original agenda and repeat the uncontested result of *MA* 1 and 2—namely, that in order to move, living beings need both internal and external unmoved points. This result is now embedded into two broader perspectives. First it is asked whether the same requirements also hold for inanimate beings or whether it is enough if they hold for the animate beings, which, as was already stated in *MA* 1, set inanimate beings in motion. Next the question is raised whether these requirements hold only for locomotion or for all kinds of change and growth. In answer, Aristotle refers the reader to the primacy of locomotion both in the universe and in the generation of individual animals. One can say that by the end of *MA* 5, the very generally formulated *akinēton*-requirements from the beginning of *MA* 1 have been in some way probed with regard to several particular cases (as proposed at 698ª12–14): with regard to living beings, the universe as a whole, inanimate beings, and several types of movement/change (*kinēsis*).

[13] Several commentators are unsatisfied by regarding these difficulties as 'merely digressing' from the main topic; thus Nussbaum 1978 tries to integrate them into the 'interdisciplinary' project that she diagnosed (see below, section 7), while Coope 2020 and Morison 2020 develop a reading according to which the discussion of these difficulties is meant to show 'that the analysis of the self-motion of animals he gives in chapters 1 and 2 gave us only an incomplete picture of the immobile causal factors involved in motion' (Morison 2020, 274). And, indeed, the fact that at the end of *MA* 4 Aristotle speaks of unmoved *principles* of motion and not just of unmoved *preconditions* of motion (like the joint and the external springboard) deserves attention; cf. Coope 2020, 241: 'Thus, though it is true that the movement of the spheres, like animal self-movement, depends upon the existence of an unmoved external thing, in the case of the spheres this external thing is an unmoved mover, and hence has a role very different from that of the external springboard, the necessary condition for animal self-movement that we learn about in *MA* 2.' By the end of *MA* 4 the insufficiency of physical platforms or springboards has only been shown for the movement of the universe, not for the case of animal motion. One might argue, though, that the new approach in *MA* 6—which immediately refers to final causes both for cosmic movement and intentional animal motion—was indirectly motivated by the result of the puzzles. Alternatively, or as an addition to the view developed by Coope and Morison, one could stress that it is in response to the cosmic puzzles (see especially *MA* 4, 699ᵇ34 sqq.) that Aristotle for the first time in this treatise alludes to the idea of an unmoved mover that is unmoved by its nature and is not just unmoved as a matter of fact. Essentially the same idea will recur in the discussion of *MA* 9, where Aristotle assumes that the soul too is a mover of this kind, i.e. a mover that is per se unmoved, as opposed to resting parts of the body, which only happen to be unmoved.

[14] *MA* 4, 699ᵇ32–700ª6.

Transition to the second part of the treatise. The second main part of the treatise, starting with **chapter 6**, can thus turn to a different agenda. Since inanimate beings have been dealt with (partly elsewhere, partly by saying that their movement depends on self-movers), and since the discussion of the first mover and the first moved thing (i.e. the first heaven) has been addressed in the context of 'first philosophy', it remains to discuss *animal* self-motion. More specifically, it remains to discuss how the soul moves the body and what the principle/origin of animal motion is. These two questions provide the common thread of the argument until the end of *MA* 10. Remarkably, the new approach of *MA* 6 immediately mentions final causes for both cosmic movement and intentional animal motion.

The psychic factors of animal motion. The first step towards answering the guiding question of how the soul moves the body seems to make use of ideas like those put forward in *De Anima* III 9–11.[15] Animals move themselves for the sake of an end or goal. If we want to know how they do that and what the moving factors are, we can easily see that they are moved by discursive thought (*dianoia*), imagination or appearance (*phantasia*), choice (*prohairesis*), wish (*boulēsis*), and appetite (*epithumia*). This extensive list—which might even be extended to include sense-perception and spirit (*thumos*)[16]—can quickly be reduced to a short-list of two generic moving factors, namely thought (*nous*) and desire; for wish, spirit, and appetite are just kinds of desire, while sense-perception and *phantasia*, just like thought, involve discernment (*krinein*) and can thus, as Aristotle puts it, hold the same place as thought. Choice, the final candidate on the list, includes elements of both discursive thought and desire. The first mover can therefore be said to be the object of desire (*to orekton*) and the object of thought (*to dianoēton*)[17]—however, not just any object of discursive thought, but only a goal achievable by action. In *De Anima* III 9–11, after reaching a similar stage in the inquiry, Aristotle discusses which of them—desire or thought—is the decisive mover, while in *MA* 6 this discussion does not seem to play a role—perhaps because the model of the 'practical syllogism' in *MA* 7 will imply a more differentiated account of how desire and thought (or, in the case of non-human animals, perception and *phantasia*) must come together in order to initiate motion. Instead, *MA* 6

---

[15] Cf. the discussion in Corcilius 2020.

[16] This list is given in lines 700^{b}17–18; it seems easy to import the two missing candidates, sense-perception and spirit, from the following lines 700^{b}20 and ^{b}22. It is, however, a different question whether these words should be *printed* in the text, as in Torraca. In light of the new textual evidence Nussbaum seems to be even more justified in resisting this possibility and sticking to the majority reading (see Nussbaum 1976, 143–4, and Nussbaum 1983, 136, n. 42). This question is also discussed by Corcilius 2020, n. 40.

[17] 700^{b}23–4. On the eventful history of transmission of these lines, see Part II of this introduction; '*noēton*' is Primavesi's emendation for the transmitted '*dianoēton*'.

repeats one other important result from *De Anima* III 9–11,[18] one that concerns the relation between desire (*orexis*) or the capacity to desire (*orektikon*) on the one hand, and the desired object (*orekton*) on the other: while the latter imparts movement without being moved, the former imparts movement (to the animal) by being moved (through the object of desire). The final moved element in this chain, the animal, does not necessarily move anything else.[19] We thus get the triplet of unmoved mover—moved mover—moved object that we know from *De Anima* III 10. That the object of desire is an unmoved mover recalls the first statement of the *akinēton*-requirement in *MA* 1, according to which the movement of self-movers depends on prior unmoved movers. Aristotle will apparently refer back to this threefold account at the beginning of *MA* 10, when he mentions 'the account that states the cause of motion'.[20]

The practical syllogism and the completion of the psychological explanation.[21] **The first part of chapter 7** introduces the famous 'practical syllogism' and it does so in more words and with many more details and variants than any other passage in the Aristotelian *oeuvre*.[22] Remarkably, it is motivated by a quite specific question: given the scenario sketched above—treating objects of thinking and desiring as movers of the animal—how is it that when one thinks (of certain objects) one sometimes acts and sometimes does not act?[23] The reconstruction of Aristotle's argument in this chapter is notoriously controversial; it is, however, safe to say that the model of the practical syllogism serves the purpose of answering this question, in that it distinguishes between several types of 'premise' among the psychic antecedents of any action or intentional locomotion and shows that in order to bring about an action (which is said to hold the place of the conclusion) specific pairs of premises are required—most notably, the one saying what is good, the other what is possible, or, as many interpreters assume, the former representing desire, the latter thought or perception. For example, my thinking that every man should walk and, in addition, that I myself am a man, makes me immediately walk. Thinking that one should drink and thinking, in addition, that this is a drink, one immediately drinks. If only one of these premises were given, no action would come about. In addition, the model of the practical syllogism allows Aristotle to explain why in some cases additional

---

[18] Cf. *De An.* III 10, 433ᵇ13–18; for a discussion of this passage and its relation to the *MA*, see Laks 2020, sections 3–5, and Rapp 2020b.

[19] *MA* 6, 700ᵇ35–701ᵃ2.   [20] *MA* 10, 703ᵃ4–5.

[21] The headings of 'psychological' and 'physiological' are convenient to indicate the difference between passages using psychological vocabulary (e.g. perceiving, thinking, desiring) and those that incorporate bodily changes described in somatic-physiological terms (e.g. heating, cooling, contracting, and expanding). They are not meant, though, to claim that Aristotle provides two different accounts of animal motion, as suggested by Nussbaum 1978 (e.g. 87–8, 188) (and retracted by Nussbaum 1983, 139 sqq.).

[22] Cf. Cooper 2020.

[23] For an alternative reading of this sentence, see Crubellier 2004, 9–11.

calculation is required, whereas in other cases one acts immediately. At any rate, this discussion, triggered by the question of why it is that agents sometimes act and sometimes do not, yields the more general result that animals have impulses to move and act, when desire for a particular object, deriving from perception, *phantasia,* or thought, is the last or proximate cause of movement.[24]

Transition to the physiological side of the sought-after explanation. **The second part of chapter 7**, starting from 701^{b}1, marks an important change of focus. Up to now, the discussion had used only the kind of psychological vocabulary that we know from *De Anima* III 9–11; from this point forward, however, Aristotle speaks of anatomical regions and parts, like joints, sinews, bones, connate *pneuma*,[25] and the like, and of physiological processes, like cooling and heating, contracting and expanding. The initiation and transformation of movement within the animal's body is first illustrated by a series of three analogies.[26] Aristotle first refers to the automatic theatre in which, when certain cables are released, the puppets start striking their swords or sabres against each other.[27] The iron and wooden parts in the automatic theatre as well as the cables that are unfastened resemble the bones and the sinews in the interior of an animal's body. The automatic theatre is meant to illustrate that a small initial movement can, in the end, lead to tremendous changes and differences. The same point is illustrated by the rudder: even a feeble shift of the rudder can amount to a considerable shift of the prow. In a further analogy Aristotle refers to small carts with unequal wheels: although the driver tries to move them in a straight line they move in a circle because the smaller wheels function like centre points. This shows that initial alterations can not only be amplified, but also transformed into diverse kinds of alteration.[28] Now, in animals' bodies, as opposed to carts and automatic theatres, there are organic parts which can change their size or take on different forms, so that animal bodies are even better suited for transmitting, amplifying, and transforming small impulses so as to bring about the movement of the animals' limbs and, ultimately, of the animal as a whole.

The sequence of psycho-physiological alterations. Perception, imagination, and thought, together with desire, set the animal in motion. But where exactly does the movement originate and how is the original alteration translated into

---

[24] *MA* 7, 701^{a}33–6.

[25] *MA* 7, 701^{b}15 (see Primavesi's text and apparatus); for the appearance of the connate *pneuma* in the *MA*, see below, section 6.

[26] For the implied mechanical principles of these comparisons, cf. de Groot 2014, ch. 5.

[27] The understanding of this example is impeded by a corrupt text; for a new reconstruction of this example, see Part II of this introduction, section 11 (iv).

[28] Cf. Furley 1967, 216: 'The point of comparison is a little obscure, but I think it is supposed to show that one small and simple movement can by purely automatic means bring about a complex series of *different* movements.'

locomotion?[29] The analogies of *MA* 7 (the automatic theatre, the rudder, the carts) have given us a first clue, but it remains to trace the entire sequence from the first alterations down to the resulting episode of locomotion. **The final part of chapter 7** and **the main chunk of chapter 8** attempt to fill in the missing steps of such a sequence. Everything starts with the well-known trio of perception, *phantasia*, and thought. Perceptions immediately are or involve certain alterations, while *phantasia* and thought at least have 'the power of their objects' (701[b]19), for an imagined or thought-of object, say a frightening one, can have the same effect as the frightening thing itself when it makes us shudder and get scared. An object (if it is among the things that can be achieved or avoided by action) that is to be pursued or avoided thus becomes the origin of motion. Depending on whether such a perceived, imagined, or thought-of object appears to be pleasant (and thus worth pursuing) or painful (and thus better avoided), warming or cooling, respectively, necessarily follows within the animal's body. These changes might be small and feeble ones in the beginning, so that the subject does not even notice them. At any rate, they are apt to affect, in the end, the inner regions around the origin of the instrumental parts (the tissue around the joints of an animal's extremities?), which again are suited to change from solid to liquid or from hard to soft and vice versa. The involved bodily parts, those playing active and passive roles in the above-mentioned processes, are by their nature suited, respectively, to act upon and to be acted upon, so that the relevant action results immediately (later, in *MA* 9 and 10, this picture is further differentiated and also involves contraction and expansion as the effects of cooling and heating).

The location of the psychic origin of movement. The picture just sketched, however, is incomplete as long as the origin of the movement within the animal's body has not been precisely located.[30] **From the middle of chapter 8** (702[a]21) **to the end of chapter 9**, Aristotle constructs a grand argument to the effect that the psychic principle/origin of movement (or 'the principle of the moving soul')[31] is in the middle of the body, where the heart (or its analogue in bloodless animals) is located. In a first step Aristotle argues for the requirement that what moves the animal first must be in an origin and, in particular, in an origin/starting point that is not the endpoint of anything else;[32] for, as he argues in *MA* 1, some origins/starting points of movement are also endpoints of something else, including, for example, ordinary joints. Thus, the wrist might be an origin of movement when the hand moves a stick; at the same time, it is an endpoint of

---

[29]   Cf. Hankinson 2020.

[30]   Cf. Gregoric 2020b, sections 2–3.

[31]   Cf. the following alternative formulations: 702[a]32: ἡ ἀρχὴ τῆς ψυχῆς ἡ κινοῦσα; 702[b]2: ἡ κινοῦσα ἀπὸ τῆς ψυχῆς ἀρχή; 702[b]16: τὴν ἀρχὴν τῆς ψυχῆς τῆς κινούσης.

[32]   *MA* 8, 702[b]6–7.

the forearm. The elbow too is an origin of movement, but is also the endpoint of the upper arm, and so forth. In this sense, what moves the animal first, Aristotle says, must be in an origin that is not the endpoint of anything else. Aristotle demonstrates this latter point with a thought experiment: if the forearm were the complete animal, the motion-imparting principle/origin of the soul would be in the elbow. In the next step he shows that such an origin must be in the middle part of the body, from where it can bring about the movement of the right-hand part and the movement of the left-hand part alike. This is a reasonable conclusion, Aristotle says, for this is also the region where the primary organ of perception is located, so that the alteration occurring through sensual perception can immediately be communicated to the adjacent parts. Just like the joint in *MA* 1, this middle part of the body is said to be potentially one, but actually many, when the right and the left sides of the animal are moved. It has also been shown in *MA* 1 that a geometrical point, strictly speaking, cannot be divided, so that the middle part of the body at issue here must be like an extended magnitude, not like a point. Now suppose that both sides of the body are moved simultaneously, so that, if *A* represents the origin and *B* and *Γ* the two sides of the body, both *AB* and *AΓ* are moved.

If only *AB* were moved, the extreme of *AΓ* in the origin would be at rest and would enable the movement of *AB*; similarly, if only *AΓ* were moved, the extreme of *AB* in the origin would be unmoved and would facilitate the movement of *AΓ*. But since both *AB* and *AΓ* are moved, there is nothing left which is at rest, and this seems to violate the *akineton*-requirement as we know it from the beginning of *MA* 1. Aristotle therefore concludes that there must be something else over and above these, something which imparts movement yet is not moved.[33] This something, he continues, must be a unity and must not be identical with the starting point of either *AB* or *AΓ*,[34] in order to provide the resting point for the movements of both sides of the body. Aristotle

---

[33] *MA* 9, 702^{b}34–5.

[34] Unfortunately, this crucial conclusion in 703^{a}1–2 is encumbered by a textual problem; Jaeger suggested adding the word ἀκίνητον (unmoved) to the transmitted, apparently incomplete text, which would yield the conclusion that there must be something *unmoved* that moves both sides. However, it has already been concluded in the previous lines (702^{b}34–5) that there must be something unmoved that is different from *AB* and *AΓ*. Farquharson, by contrast, completes the sentence by following William of Moerbeke, who translates it as 'necesse unum esse', presupposing the words ἀναγκαῖον <ἓν> εἶναι ('must be some *one* thing' or 'must be a *unity*') in the Greek model Γ1. This latter reading was accepted by Torraca, Nussbaum, Kollesch, Primavesi; compare, however, the arguments for reading the text without ἀκίνητον or ἓν in Gregoric 2020, 426.

concludes that this unmoved unity is the soul, which is different from the extended middle region of the body, but resides therein.[35]

The role of the connate pneuma.[36] Now that the origin of movement has been located, Aristotle is in a position to complete the picture in **chapter 10**. Within the general scheme of the unmoved mover, the moved mover, and the moved thing, desire holds a middle position, for it is moved by the desired object and it imparts movement to the moved animal. In the case of living animals there must be a body of 'that sort' (i.e. a body that imparts movement while being moved?).[37] It turns out that it is the connate aeriform stuff called *pneuma* which is naturally suited to cause motion and to confer strength. The *pneuma* seems to be responsive to the cooling and heating which results from an animal's desire to avoid or to pursue certain objects and it transforms these impulses into pushing and pulling, which can in turn set the extremities of an animal into motion, provided that there is something which is at rest. The chapter does not dwell on the particular characteristics of the connate *pneuma*, apparently because Aristotle assumes that they are well known from other treatises. He makes every effort, though, to elucidate the location of the connate *pneuma* within the animal's body. The *pneuma*, he says, must stand in a similar relation to the psychic origin of movement as the moved point within a joint stands to the unmoved one. And since this psychic origin (of movement) is in the middle of the body— i.e. in the heart or the analogous part—the connate *pneuma* must also be there, in order to confer the impulses originating there to the adjacent parts of the body and possibly also (if one takes the analogy to the moved and the unmoved point within the joint seriously) in order to support itself against something that is unmoved.

Involuntary and non-voluntary movements. While the main part of the treatise is dedicated to voluntary actions and movements that originate from perception, imagination, or thought on the one hand and desire on the other, the final chapter, **chapter 11**, addresses the movements of parts of animals that come about, as it were, against their will, i.e. independently of what they are actually and consciously striving for.[38] Among these non-voluntary motions are sleep, waking, breathing, and others; as examples of involuntary movements Aristotle mentions movements of the heart and the genitals that come

---

[35] *MA* 9, 703^{a}1–3.   [36] Cf. Gregoric 2020b, section 4.

[37] Looking for 'the body of that sort' seems to be equivalent to looking for the bodily instrument by which desire imparts movement (cf. *De Anima* III 10, 433^{b}9–10); this is also suggested by the conclusion of the main chunk of *MA* 10 in 703^{a}28–9: 'it has now been stated by which moved part the soul imparts movement.'

[38] Cf. Morel 2020. For the question of how these phenomena relate to the explanandum of the common cause, cf. below, section 8.

about contrary to what thought commands. These latter movements result from alterations that take place in other regions of the body; Aristotle reminds the reader that imagination and thought, by bringing along the forms of objects, have the power to cause alterations similar to the ones caused by such objects themselves. Also, Aristotle points out that alterations can proceed from the parts (e.g. limbs, sense-organs) to the origin (i.e. the soul in the centre of the body) and again from the origin to the parts, so that certain inadvertent alterations in one part may take place as the result of an alteration originating from a different part and being relayed *through* the origin without being *endorsed* by it.

3. Authenticity

Until the mid-nineteenth century authors commenting on the Aristotelian *oeuvre* were happy to accept *MA* as an authentic Aristotelian treatise and to associate the forward-reference in *De Anima* III 10, 433^{b}19–21, with *MA*;[39] it is only from the 1850s onwards that influential scholars—among them Brandis, Freudenthal, Zeller, and Hicks[40]—were impressed by the doubts that Valentin Rose[41] raised about Aristotle's authorship. Already in 1912 and 1913 Farquharson and Jaeger persuasively rebutted Rose's main concerns.[42] Still, some observations concerning alleged tensions between *MA* and other Aristotelian treatises[43] were taken up by the proponents of a developmental account of Aristotle's psychology, most notably François Nuyens and W.D. Ross.[44]

---

[39] Cf. Trendelenburg 1833, 535, and Barthélemy-Saint-Hilaire 1846, 336; Spengel 1849, 167, assigns *MA* to Aristotle's physiological writings.

[40] Cf. Brandis 1857, II b 2, 1271, n. 482; Freudenthal 1869, 82; Zeller 1879, II 2, 97, n. 2; Hicks 1907, 564.

[41] Cf. Rose 1854, 162–7. This is the same person who was commissioned by the Prussian Academy of Sciences in Berlin to edit the first modern collection of Aristotle's fragments. Curiously enough, his undisputed achievements as editor were clouded by his biased ambition to prove that all these fragments too are spurious.

[42] Cf. also Torraca 1958. Given the overwhelming evidence provided by Farquharson 1912, Jaeger 1913b, Torraca 1958a, Düring 1966, and, finally, Nussbaum 1978, it may strike one as odd that in 1981 the organizers of the ninth Symposium Aristotelicum still nominated *De Motu Animalium* as a possible candidate for the list of spurious works; it is telling, though, that they could not find any scholar volunteering to argue against its authenticity (as reported by Nussbaum in the preface to the paperback version of her edition, 1985, XXV–VI).

[43] Most notably the suspicion that the idea of the soul's residing in a particular region of the body cannot derive from genuinely Aristotelian doctrines. Cf. Poppelreuter 1891, 10, n. 2, who uses the cardiocentrism of *MA* 10 as a decisive case against the treatise's authenticity.

[44] Cf. Nuyens 1948, Ross 1957, Ross 1961; for a discussion of the Nuyens/Ross thesis, see below, section 5 (ii).

(i) A Misguided or Inserted Reference in *MA* 10?

In *MA* 10, 703ª10–11 Aristotle says, 'Well, what it takes to preserve the connate *pneuma* (τίς μὲν οὖν ἡ σωτηρία τοῦ συμφύτου πνεύματος) has already been stated in other works.' Curiously enough, the first sentence of the supposedly late and inauthentic treatise *De Spiritu* announces an agenda that would perfectly correspond to this remark, as it mentions the permanence (διαμονή) and augmentation (αὔξησις) of the connate *pneuma* (481ª1–2). Zeller was the first to allude to this correspondence,[45] insinuating that such a reference to a spurious treatise within a supposedly authentic Aristotelian work would render the *MA* itself spurious. Indeed, *De Spiritu* includes many theorems that derive, as has been argued since Jaeger's time, from post-Aristotelian anatomy; it is only recently that a few scholars have made a case for its authenticity,[46] but all such attempts have been conclusively refuted.[47] Hence it can be ruled out that Aristotle wished to refer to this particular treatise. Against this background, one reasonable move consists in checking whether the reference might have been a later insertion. Jaeger actually argues along these lines, showing that the sentence in question interrupts a continuous train of thought and that only a few lines later there is another reference to a discussion of the connate *pneuma*, which would strangely duplicate the message that the topic of the *pneuma* has been dealt with elsewhere.[48]

Most commentators, however, try to identify other treatises as the target of the *MA* 10 reference. Michael of Ephesus, for example, suspects that the reference is to the lost treatise *On Nourishment* (Περὶ Τροφῆς), and there are indeed references to such a project in several Aristotelian writings;[49] however, it is not clear whether Aristotle ever completed such a treatise so that all assumptions concerning its content remain rather speculative. Farquharson hints at the possibility that the reference is inverted, i.e. that the author of *De Spiritu* wanted to allude to a question stated in the Aristotelian treatise; he also mentions a number of alternative passages to which the sentence in *MA* 10 could refer, but none of them seems a perfect match. Torraca suggests a passage in *De Respiratione* (479ᵇ26–480ª15) as the target of our cross-reference; this was criticized by Düring,[50] who instead proposes *De Iuventute and Senectute* 470ª5–ᵇ5, where, however, not the preservation of the *pneuma*, but the preservation of the (related) vital heat is at stake. Nussbaum suggests, among other things, a passage in *De Generatione Animalium* II 6 (742ª14–16), and, indeed, whatever modern scholars

---

[45] Cf. Zeller 1879, II 2, 97, n. 2.   [46] Bos/Ferwerda 2008.
[47] Gregoric/Lewis 2015.   [48] Cf. Jaeger 1913a, 48.
[49] See *Mete.* IV 3, 381ᵇ13, *De An.* II 4, 416ᵇ30, *Somn. Vig.* 456ᵇ6, *PA* II 3, 650ᵇ9–10, II 7, 653ᵇ14, III 14, 674ª20, IV 4, 678a19–20, *GA* V 3, 784ᵇ3.
[50] Cf. Düring 1959, 416.

can draw on in order to answer the question raised here—i.e. how the connate *pneuma* is preserved and how it is generated in the first place—the best available evidence will most certainly include material from the *GA*.[51] The only problem is that, according to a widespread consensus, the *GA* was written after the *MA*;[52] this is why Nussbaum (who also accepts this chronology) adds the cautionary note that such a reference to the *GA* would probably be a later insertion on the basis of the *GA*'s elaboration of the *pneuma* theory—which brings us back to Jaeger's suggestion.

In spite of all scholarly efforts, then, the sentence in *MA* 10, 703ª10–11, seems to remain slightly puzzling. Still, the difficulty posed by this single sentence should not be exaggerated; after all, it is just one unclear reference alongside approximately ten unambiguous, substantial, well-embedded references to other Aristotelian works as well as many formulations that exactly or almost exactly echo formulations from other Aristotelian treatises.[53] Moreover the forward-reference to an inquiry into what is common to body and soul in *De Anima* III 10, 433ᵇ19–21, together with the preview of the main points of this inquiry (433ᵇ21–7), satisfactorily matches the central theses of *MA* and *MA* alone, not the topically related treatise *De Incessu Animalium*.[54]

(ii)   Sparse Evidence in Ancient Testimonies?

Commentators have been puzzled by the fact that the title *De Motu Animalium* only occurs in some ancient catalogues of Aristotle's writings;[55] and these catalogues, one might argue, provide the strongest evidence from antiquity that a particular work was known as a genuine part of the Aristotelian corpus. In the case of *MA* this may seem particularly worrying, since we also possess no commentary from pre-Byzantine times. The situation is this: *MA* is mentioned in the catalogue provided by Ptolemy-el-Garib; this catalogue is dependent on the first edition of the Aristotelian works by Andronicus of Rhodes. Of the two earlier, Hellenistic catalogues that predate the edition by Andronicus, the catalogue given by Diogenes Laertius does not mention *MA* at all, while the other, which is included in the *Vita Hesychii*, mentions the title, but only in an appendix and not in its main section. The total absence from the Diogenes catalogue and the occurrence only in the—probably later—appendix of the Hesychian catalogue may seem grounds for suspicion at first glance. However, other well-known

---

[51] Cf., for example, Freudenthal 1995, 119–26 and 137–44.

[52] See below section 4 on chronology.   [53] Cf. n. 5 above.

[54] As the supporters of the inauthenticity thesis, above all Rose (1854, 163), usually assume. That the main points of the preview given in *De An.* 433ᵇ21–7 are actually picked up—partly verbatim—by *MA* has already been shown by Jaeger 1913a, 41–2.

[55] For the ancient catalogues of Aristotle's works, see Moraux 1951.

Aristotelian works, such as all the biological writings (with the sole exception of the *Historia Animalium*), are also not mentioned in the Hellenistic catalogues; and of the *Metaphysics*' fourteen books Diogenes mentions only Book *Δ*. The most probable explanation for the absence of *MA* and other undisputedly Aristotelian works from the original Hellenistic catalogue seems to be that the common model of the two Hellenistic catalogues registers only the subset of Aristotelian works that happened to be available at a certain place at a certain time—perhaps in the library of Alexandria[56]—while another subset of works was temporarily unavailable and was added to the catalogue only after it became accessible again.

Moreover, the catalogues are not the only evidence from antiquity that a certain book was regarded as genuinely Aristotelian. At least as important is the mention of a work or title by ancient commentators. And the title of *MA* is mentioned in one or another version by Alexander, Simplicius, and Philoponus;[57] Alexander and Themistius give paraphrases of its content without signalling any doubts about its authenticity.[58] In addition to the material already mentioned by Nussbaum, a long passage in Alexander's *De Anima* (76,6–78,2 Bruns) has only recently been identified as a substantial paraphrase, with many quotations, of Aristotle's *MA* 7, 701^{b}13 – 8, 702^{a}10.[59] This summary of some key theses of *MA* is of particular importance for the question of authenticity in that it is immediately triggered by Alexander's paraphrase of the thought of Aristotle's *De Anima* III 10; we can hence conclude, not only that Alexander had access to the text of the *MA* and that he took it as a genuine work of Aristotle's, but also that Alexander regarded the project of *MA* as the natural place to look for the inquiry that was announced in *De Anima* III 10.

(iii) The Alleged Lack of Thematic Unity

As already noted in section 2 above, it is common to subdivide *MA* into two main parts, chapters 1–5 and chapters 6–10 (plus chapter 11); according to some characterizations of this division, however, it seems to amount to two almost

---

[56] On the temporary splitting of the Aristotelian *oeuvre* in the time after Theophrastus' death, see Primavesi 2007; for the Alexandria hypothesis, see Moraux 1973, 4–5.

[57] For the occurrences of the title of *MA*, see the critical apparatus to the Greek text in this volume.

[58] Alexander, *De Anima* 97,26 (Bruns) and *In Mete.* 3,34–4,6 (Hayduck); Themistius, *In de An.* 121,1–18 (Heinze) and *In Cael.* 97,20 (Landauer). See Nussbaum 1978, 6, n. 15, for a collection of the ancient commentators' references to *MA*.

[59] Cf. Donini 1968 and Accattino/Donini 1996. Prior to Donini's and Accattino's discovery Alexander's reference to *MA* 9 in his *DA* 97,26 seemed to be the most substantial evidence for Alexander's knowledge of *MA*.

separate projects, thus threatening the thematic unity of the treatise.[60] Due to observations like this, nineteenth-century scholars had a hard time finding an appropriate systematic place for the treatise within the Aristotelian *oeuvre*, so that some, most notably Rose, as already mentioned, ended up even denying its authenticity. In a similar vein, the intrusion of the cosmological difficulties in *MA* 3–4 that point to an unmoved mover of the universe—a genuine topic of first philosophy—was seen as threatening the topical unity of the project as a whole.[61] Finally, the seemingly unrelated appearance of the connate *pneuma* in *MA* 10 was seen as a problem for the unity of the treatise (because the *pneuma* was not mentioned before) and for its authenticity (because theories of the *pneuma* were popular among post-Aristotelian Peripatetic philosophers: see section 6, below).

In recent scholarship, new arguments in favour of the assumption that the *MA* consists of two more or less disjunct projects have been put forward by Fazzo.[62] She distinguishes between '*MA* 1' (= chapters 1–5) and '*MA* 2' (= chapters 6–10) and treats 698ᵃ1–7, 698ᵃ7–14, and 700ᵇ4–11 as three self-contained prologues that have the purpose of relating the separate projects '*MA* 1' and '*MA* 2' to each other. Given the long digressions in chapters 3–4, and given the 'fresh-start' scenario at the beginning of chapter 6, this reading has its attraction. Still, there is a number of reasons for stressing the unity of the treatise against such a separation into '*MA* 1' and '*MA* 2'. To begin with, there are signs of awareness on Aristotle's part that from time to time the treatise is digressing from a main line of argument.[63] All of these flagged digressions concern cosmological questions; and from what would Aristotle think he was digressing, if not from the exposition of the main topic, i.e. the common cause of animal movement? Next, the comparison with cosmic movement is not confined to chapters 1–5; in chapter 6, for example, from 700ᵇ29 on, Aristotle still finds it instructive to relate the mover of the animal to the cosmic mover. Last but not least, the identification of internal and external resting points for living self-movers in chapters 1–2 is highly relevant to the search for the common cause of animal motion, especially since the idea of an inner resting point paves the way for the argument unfolded in chapters 8–9 (leading to the conclusion concerning the central position of the soul within the body).

---

[60] For a more in-depth discussion of the unity of *MA*, see Laks 2020, section 2.

[61] Kollesch 1985, 27, e.g., argues that the transition from chapter 2 to chapter 3 (i.e. from the movement of animals to the movement of the universe) as well as the transition from chapter 5. to chapter 6 (i.e. from the more general discussion back to the narrow topic of animal motion) are not fully successful, thus questioning the unity of the treatise for the two mentioned reasons.

[62] Cf. Fazzo 2004, though Fazzo, to be sure, does not dispute the authenticity of the treatise.

[63] Cf. *MA* 2, 698ᵇ9–12; 3, 699ᵃ12; 4, 699ᵇ12–13, 699ᵇ31.

4. The Chronology of the *De Motu Animalium*

Since the *MA*, owing to its subject matter, does not mention historical events, historical figures, and the like, there are almost no hints for an absolute dating of the treatise. According to the new textual evidence, it seems not unlikely that in a passage of *MA* 7, Aristotle uses the dual form δυεῖν instead of δυοῖν,[64] which, according to Attic inscriptions, occurs only from the 330s BC onward, so that, on this basis, the treatise should be assigned to a relatively late stage of Aristotle's philosophical production.

Apart from that, we have to make do with hints for relative dating. According to the cross-references we find in the *MA*, the treatise seems to presuppose, e.g., parts of Aristotle's biological writings (*IA*, *HA* II, possibly *PA* IV),[65] the *Physics*—or at least *Physics* VIII—,[66] *Metaphysics* Λ,[67] *De Generatione et Corruptione*,[68] and *De Anima*.[69] Some of these titles refer to works that are themselves taken to be rather late or mature works.[70] If one considers, in addition, the reference in *De An.* III 10, 433b19–21, as a genuine, well-embedded *forward*-reference to *MA*, one is entitled to conclude that Aristotle, when writing the *De Anima*—a work that as a whole presupposes many other philosophical and conceptual achievements—was thinking of the *MA* as a not-yet-completed project. All these preliminary observations about cross-references clearly hint at the time of Aristotle's second stay in Athens (from 335 BC).

Cross-references are among the most important tools for fixing the relative chronology of Aristotle's works, but they can also be misleading.[71] However, in the case of *MA* most of these cross-references go hand in hand with substantial argumentative presuppositions. For example, the opening of the treatise inevitably presupposes a discussion of particular kinds of animal locomotion and it presupposes that self-movers and their relation to an unmoved principle have been discussed elsewhere; *MA* 6 clearly presupposes that the several ways of desiring and the differences between the several cognitive-discerning faculties have been elaborated elsewhere. Similarly, *MA* 10 takes certain discussions about the connate *pneuma* just for granted. From this perspective, it seems safe to conclude that the *MA* must be a relatively late work.

---

[64] *MA* 7, 701ª24: δυεῖν ὁδῶν (Primavesi). Admittedly, this is just a conjecture, but it is made likely by the reading of Bᶜ: δύ' εἰ ποδῶν; also, it might well be that the epigraphic data only reflect earlier patterns.

[65] *MA* 1, 698ª3.   [66] *MA* 1, 698ª9–10.   [67] *MA* 6, 700ᵇ8–9.

[68] *MA* 5, 700ª29.   [69] *MA* 6, 700ᵇ5–6, 21–2.

[70] For the *De An.*, e.g., cf. Shields 2016, xii sq.

[71] Thielscher 1948 takes this method to its extreme, thus demonstrating, involuntarily (through some rather bizarre results), the limited evidence that cross-references, taken at face value, can provide.

The concluding lines of *MA* (11, 704ᵃ3–ᵇ3) locate the project of our treatise within an entire research programme.[72] They place the *MA* in a sequence with the *De Partibus Animalium*, *De Anima*, *De Sensu*, those treatises of the *Parva Naturalia* that are concerned with sleep and dreams, and *De Memoria*. The project of *MA* is mentioned last in this sequence. Afterwards, we are told, it only remains to consider generation, thus referring the reader to the treatise *De Generatione Animalium*. One might of course suspect that these concluding lines have been added after the event and, perhaps not by Aristotle himself, but by an editor. Also, even if we take Aristotle to be the author of these lines, it is not clear whether the order of this research programme is actually meant to correspond to a chronological order. Such concerns aside, the picture suggested in these concluding lines—i.e. that the *MA* comes after all these other projects and that it predates, but is close to, the *GA*—goes well with other independently attested assumptions. Most notably, it is widely assumed that the *GA* is one of the latest treatises written by Aristotle[73] (e.g. it includes no forward-references, and presumably no other Aristotelian work includes explicit backward-references to it; it is also remarkable that *GA* includes many details on the heart and on the *pneuma*, like other biological writings and like the *Parva Naturalia*, but also assumes soul–body hylomorphism, like the middle books of the *Metaphysics* and *De Anima*).[74] If this assumption is right, it is most significant for the chronology, as Nussbaum already observed,[75] that our treatise shares several interests with this presumably late treatise *GA*. For example, the *GA* seems to provide[76] the kind of information we need for understanding the nature of the connate *pneuma* in *MA* 10; also, it twice mentions the same kind of *automata* that are prominent in *MA* 7.[77]

In sum, then, even if it is impossible to provide irrefutable evidence for the suggested chronology, there are no obstacles to thinking that the *MA* is a relatively late work of Aristotle's, written, at any rate, during his second stay in Athens, perhaps even towards the end of it; at the same time, there are several positive hints that the treatise presupposes a philosophical background that must be collected from a number of previous Aristotelian works, some of which are themselves rather late. The marked synoptic interest of the treatise[78] might be seen (although this is fairly speculative) as the mark of a mature author who is happy to see results from different angles of his widely ramified work converging.

---

[72] Cf. Morel 2020, appendix.

[73] Cf. Balme 1987, 17: '*GA* is generally felt to be more mature and to come after *PA*; while I share this feeling, I must say that I can put up no objective evidence for it.'

[74] Thus, it includes two lines of thought that have been regarded as incompatible; see below, section 5.

[75] Nussbaum 1978, 12.   [76] See below, section 6.

[77] *GA* II 1, 734ᵇ9–17 and *GA* II 5, 741ᵇ8–15.   [78] Cf. section 1, above.

5. Incompatibility of the *De Motu Animalium* with the Psychology of *De Anima*?

One of the issues that has been troubling commentators for a long time is the relation between the *MA* and the presumably most authoritative treatise on all psychological questions, *De Anima*.

(i) Cardiocentrism and Instrumentalism

Indeed, it has been argued that the cardiocentrism defended in *MA* or, more generally, the very idea that the soul can be located in a specific region of the body is incompatible with one of the main tenets of *De Anima* II 1–4, the thesis of soul–body hylomorphism, according to which the soul is the form of an organic body or an actuality (*entelecheia*) of a potentially living body. For if the soul is a form, one could argue, in the sense of a unifying, structuring principle of a body in virtue of which there is a determinate living being of a certain species equipped with the capacities typical for members of this species, shouldn't the soul thus conceived be the form *of the entire living being* instead of residing in just one or the other organ of it?[79] In *MA* the argument for the central position of the soul is developed in the second half of *MA* 8 (from 702ª21 on) and in *MA* 9, but the concern about incompatibility is often associated with the final part of *MA* 10 (703ª29–ᵇ2), where Aristotle points out that an animal is constituted like a well-governed city, in that there is no need for separate rulers in the different parts of a city and, similarly, no need for soul in each part of an animal.[80] In *MA*, then, the theorem of the central position of the soul is a crucial part of the theory. This tendency connects *MA* with several treatises from the *Parva Naturalia* and with passages in *De Partibus Animalium*,[81] where Aristotle assigns the perceptual or nutritive faculty of the soul to the heart or its analogue in bloodless animals, so that one might be concerned that the *MA* alongside the *Parva Naturalia* and parts of the biological writings could turn out to be incompatible with the body–soul hylomorphism of *De Anima*.

Related to the assumed tension between soul–body hylomorphism and cardiocentrism is the concern that soul–body hylomorphism might not be compatible with saying that *the soul moves the body*, that *soul uses the body as an instrument*, or that *body and soul act on one another*, since this could be understood as

---

[79] On this topic, see now also Shields 2016, xii, n. 3, and, more generally, for an exposition of Aristotle's soul–body hylomorphism, xvii–xxviii.

[80] Cf. Gregoric 2020b, section 5.

[81] Cf. Gregoric 2020b, n. 11.

implying that the soul, instead of being a unifying principle of the body, functions as an independent substance. In the second half of the twentieth century,
this concern was sometimes fuelled by the idea that through the use of such
instrumental language the Aristotelian soul would come close to the 'ghost in
the machine'—a formulation coined by Gilbert Ryle to discredit certain implications of Cartesian dualism, most notably its instrumental interactionism—
while Aristotle, owing to his hylomorphism, was expected to be an unwavering
ally against all versions of soul–body dualism and interactionism.[82] Seen from this
perspective, the MA could come under suspicion, since, after all, it addresses the
questions of 'how the soul moves the body' (6, 700^{b}10) and 'through which part
the soul imparts movement' (10, 703^{a}28–9).

The mentioned concerns cannot easily be dismissed, since they touch upon
notoriously controversial debates concerning the precise implications of Aristotle's
soul–body hylomorphism.[83] It seems clear and uncontroversial, though, that
they cannot be used as an argument against Aristotle's authorship, because the
worrying observations are equally true of the Parva Naturalia and significant
parts of the biological writings, which nobody, presumably, would claim are all
spurious (thus probably ending up with more spurious than non-spurious
works). However, it is legitimate to ask whether cardiocentrism and the above-
mentioned instrumental formulations can be part of the same theoretical
framework that is unfolded in De Anima II 1–4 or whether cardiocentrism and
instrumentalism on the one hand, and soul–body hylomorphism on the other
belong to different or even incompatible theories. For a long time, the preferred
scholarly method for dealing with such perceived differences and incompatibil-
ities was the developmental approach, by which allegedly inconsistent doctrines
are assigned to distinct stages in the philosopher's assumed development.

(ii) The Developmental Approach

With respect to Aristotle's psychology such a developmental account was first
given by the Belgian scholar Nuyens.[84] Not unlike Jaeger, with whose name the

---

[82] The idea that Aristotle, avant la lettre, would join Ryle's alliance against Cartesian dualism is often
associated with a particular passage in De Anima I 4 (408^{b}13–15), where Aristotle says that it is better not
to say that the soul grieves or learns or thinks but 'man with the soul' or 'man in respect of his soul'. These
lines have been dubbed the 'celebrated Rylean passage' (Barnes 1971/2, 103), because they seem to
anticipate what Ryle describes as the category mistake of treating mental facts just like facts about spatially movable objects. In the more recent discussion, however, the precise target of this passage has been
revisited (cf. Shields 2007, 155–60; 2009, 285–9; 2016, ad loc., Carter 2018). Menn 2002 takes issue with
the widespread assumption that Aristotle in De Anima aims at refuting soul–body dualism.

[83] For a useful survey of different current interpretations of Aristotle's hylomorphic psychology, see
Caston 2006, 318, nn. 6–9.

[84] Cf. Nuyens 1948; his study was first published in Dutch in 1939.

rise of the developmental method is most often connected, Nuyens assumes that the early stage of Aristotle's work is characterized by its philosophical kinship to Plato, while the later stages are characterized by an increasing distance from Plato; accordingly, he sees the earliest stage of Aristotle's thinking about the soul exhibited in the fragments taken from the dialogue *Eudemus*[85] which includes remarks that are reminiscent of Plato's *Phaedo* (saying, e.g., that it is natural for the soul to live without a body),[86] while he finds the latest, most mature stage, which again is furthest from Plato, presented in *De Anima*, where the soul is defined as the form or first *entelecheia* of a body and, thus, is no longer supposed to exist as a separate substance within or alongside the body. Between the early and the late stages Nuyens detects an intermediate or transitive phase that, he says, encompasses Aristotle's biological writings (except *GA*) and most of the *Parva Naturalia* (except *De Sensu* and *De Memoria*); Ross, who accepts Nuyens' tripartite model,[87] characterizes this intermediate period as follows: 'The soul is no longer the prisoner of the body, but it is still a distinct entity which inhabits the body, and has its seat in a particular organ, the heart; and soul and body are described as acting on one another.'[88] He also says that in this middle phase the soul is thought of as 'closely associated with heat, and with the hottest organ in the body, the heart'.[89] Most notably, Ross modifies Nuyens' account with respect to *De Anima*, for he thinks that the most mature point in Aristotle's psychology, the *entelecheia* account of the soul, can only be found in *De Anima* II and III 1–8; thinking that *MA* displays all the features of what he takes to be the intermediate period and accepting that *De Anima* III 10, 433[b]19–21, is a genuine reference to *MA*, he excludes the final part of *De Anima* III from the late, mature period. He also deviates from Nuyens in that he assigns *De Sensu* and *De Memoria* to the middle period on the ground that they show no sign of the *entelecheia* view.

The Nuyens/Ross account used to be quite influential.[90] More recently, one could have the impression that the developmental approach in general has gone out of fashion—especially insofar as it makes Aristotle's supposedly increasing distance from Plato the primary driving force within this development.[91] Scholars have come to emphasize more and more that differences and perceived inconsistencies between various Aristotelian works can occur not only due to the philosopher's psychological or intellectual development, but also due to different contexts, purposes, or addressees of these particular writings. As for

---

[85] Cf. Aristotle, *Eudemus*, fragments 37–48 (Rose³).

[86] Cf. 41 (Rose³).   [87] Cf. Ross 1955, 1–18; 1957, 65–7; and 1961, 9–12.

[88] Ross 1957, 65.   [89] Ross 1961, 10.

[90] For a list of affirmative or even enthusiastic appraisals in the mid-twentieth century, see Hardie 1964, 56.

[91] For a discussion of developmental approaches, see, for example, the essays collected in Wians 1996.

the psychological writings, it is a drawback of Ross' suggestion that it has to assume a break within *De Anima* itself (namely, between *De An.* II and the later chapters of *De An.* III) and that it clashes with some other, at least plausible, chronological assumptions (see above, section 4). In addition, Nuyens and Ross work with a quite limited repertoire of criteria; for example, the absence of *entelecheia* from the *Parva Naturalia* and *De Anima*'s lack of interest in the heart need not be taken to indicate doctrinal differences, but might just correspond to a different kind of agenda or even to a deliberate and thought-through division of labour. In addition, one might think that Ross overly dramatized the incompatibility between the middle and the late periods by associating the cardiocentric view of the middle, biological period with what he called a 'two-substance' theory,[92] since most of these biological passages remain neutral with respect to the ontological assessment of the soul.[93]

(iii) Integrating Cardiocentrism

More importantly, supporters of the developmental account might have been too quick to assume that cardiocentrism and instrumental language are necessarily incompatible with the main tenets of soul–body hylomorphism, thus dismissing the exploration of possible connections between them. In this respect, considerable progress has been made by the papers of Block and Hardie,[94] which, engaging with the Nuyens/Ross account, show that Aristotle did not regard cardiocentrism as incompatible with hylomorphism—the main idea being that the definition of the soul as form or entelechy of the body does not logically forbid us 'to emphasize a particular bodily organ above the others and single it out as the source of those activities whereby the body lives'.[95] Block and Hardie also draw attention to a passage in *Metaphysics* Z 10 ($1035^{b}25$–7)[96]—in a chapter that is clearly committed to the idea that the soul is the form of the body (cf. $1035^{b}14$–16). In the section of this chapter that is dedicated to the question of whether the parts belonging to the form are prior to the material compound or not, Aristotle mentions parts that are 'simultaneous' in the sense that they are neither prior nor posterior; these are, he says, the parts which are 'dominant and in which the formula and the *ousia* are primarily [lodged], such as, if this be it, heart, or brain—it makes no difference which of these is of this

---

[92] Cf. Ross 1961, 10.

[93] Block 1961, 54–6, gives a useful discussion of five passages from *De Sensu* that Ross takes to be indications of the two-substance theory.

[94] Cf. Block 1961 and Hardie 1964.   [95] Block 1961, 52.

[96] Block 1961, 57–8 (he was referred to this passage, he says, by Rogers Albritton), and Hardie 1964, 61. This was taken up by Nussbaum 1978, 152–3.

sort'.[97] According to this passage, Aristotle does not hesitate to accept the existence of certain primary parts of a compound that are more intimately connected with the compound's essential activity than other parts and that, hence, are said to be the parts in which the essence 'resides'—although being the essence of the whole compound.[98] This is also part of the background that suggests that, as Hardie points out, the claim of the city simile in *MA* 10, namely that there is no need for soul in each part of an animal's body, should not be pressed too hard: 'The fact which Aristotle is stating is that, once movement has been initiated, the consequential movements follow without further idea-guided activity.'[99]

(iv) Integrating or Mitigating Instrumentalism?

A related, but different question is what to make of the seemingly disturbing instrumental language that occurs not only in *MA*, but also in the *Parva Naturalia*. The main worry is that such language could be used to state that a non-material, non-corporeal entity like the soul—perhaps with the help of a mediating stuff like the connate *pneuma*—acts on a different kind of entity, the merely material body. This would seem to come close to a Cartesian scenario in which the intellect uses the pineal gland to act on the bodily substance.[100] Against that background, the last decades have seen a broad consensus that the instrumental language need not be seen as incompatible with soul–body hylomorphism. But even if so much is agreed upon, there is the question of whether a sort of instrumentalism can be integrated into Aristotle's soul–body hylomorphism or whether the instrumental language should be paraphrased in a mitigating way.

(a) Mitigating paraphrases. For the latter camp several moves seem to be available. For example, one might try to downplay the impact of the instrumental language by

---

[97] '... ὅσα κύρια καὶ ἐν ᾧ πρώτῳ ὁ λόγος καὶ ἡ οὐσία, οἷον εἰ τοῦτο καρδία ἢ ἐγκέφαλος· διαφέρει γὰρ οὐθὲν πότερον τοιοῦτον.' The translation is based on M. Furth's.

[98] Tracy 1983, 333–4, elaborated on the idea that this passage could be crucial for overcoming perceived tensions between hylomorphism and cardiocentrism: 'The soul must be thought of as informing the entire nutritive and sensory apparatus, i.e. all the organs of the body, but as doing so from its source of foundation in the primary and first-formed organ of the body, the heart. [...] to say that the soul has its source in the heart is not to deny its presence in the rest of the body, but only to affirm that it is present in a different way in the heart and in the other organs.' For a recent elaboration of Tracy's suggestion see Rapp 2022.

[99] Hardie 1964, 60.

[100] For an intriguing discussion of the question of whether Aristotle's connate *pneuma* can be compared to Descartes' pineal gland, cf. Buddensiek 2009. See also Gregoric (2020a, 30) who points out that the connate *pneuma*, far from being an ancient counterpart to the pineal gland 'that reacts to mental states in some mysterious way', is 'a material thing which reacts physically to subtle thermic alterations in the heart'.

taking it as a loose, non-committal way of speaking.[101] More substantially, it has been pointed out that for Aristotle, phenomena like perception and desire are inextricably psycho-physical entities, so that it is futile dwelling on the worry that a non-material soul could ever act on a material body: 'it is not the soul which is (properly speaking) that which moves the animal but the (psycho-physical) person.'[102] Another move consists in highlighting the difference between the processes in living beings and the processes in mechanical toys,[103] the first being physiological, the latter being merely mechanical.[104] This difference comes to the fore in *MA* 7 in the transition from the automatic theatres and carts to the case of living beings. Authors emphasizing the contrast between these mechanical examples and living agents[105] might have in mind that the problematic kind of instrumentalism is mostly associated with mechanics, while in the case of living beings, the described chain of events takes place between parts of a living (ensouled) organism which are by their nature apt to be responsive to certain impulses (among them 'intentional' ones) and thus to contribute to the animal's goal-directed motion, which again is part of the animal's natural activity.

(b) *Soul-compound ambiguity.* More generally, one might point out that Aristotle is not always fully clear or consistent in the way he refers to capacities of the soul on the one hand and capacities or activated capacities of the living animal on the other. For example, in *De An.* III 10, 433^{b}17–18, Aristotle first nominates the *orektikon* as the moved mover, although *orektikon* is his usual term for the soul's capacity to desire; but in the next line he makes clear that he is speaking of the activated capacity to desire, which is a *kinēsis* and clearly involves relevant parts of the body of the desiring animal. One might use this ambiguity to say that all instrumental formulations seemingly applying to the soul are actually meant to refer to (activated) capacities of the living being.

---

[101] Cf. Hardie 1964, 58: 'Among familiar facts about bodies and souls there are some which make it natural to speak of bodies producing bodily effects... Hence what purports to be a non-committal report of observed psycho-physical concomitances is apt to generate a theory that things of two different kinds act on each other.' A similar strategy seems to be adopted by Nussbaum 1978, 152, where she argues that the famous formulation from *MA* 700^{b}10, 'how the soul moves the body', states the problem 'in a familiar form'.

[102] Charles 2009a, 307. Hankinson 2020, n. 39, places himself within the same camp. Nussbaum 1978, in the course of her 'interpretive essay 3', makes use of several of the above-mentioned strategies. Connected with the current strategy are her remarks on pages 155–6 to the effect that both perception and desire are 'realized' or 'manifested' in certain physiological changes and that motion follows only if desire physiologically mediates between the original change brought about by the initial cognitive or perceptual change and the change that follows upon desiring.

[103] Cf. Hardie 1964, 59.

[104] Cf. Farquharson commenting on *MA* 7, 701^{b}13–17: 'i.e. the body's motions are produced physiologically (by alteration) and not mechanically.'

[105] This thought is also taken up by Nussbaum 1978, 155–6.

(c) Unmitigated integration. There are, however, other observations which might suggest that there is no need to downplay or mitigate the instrumental language used in certain works of Aristotle's—most notably the observation that such language can also be found in *De Anima* itself, for example in the same passage of *De An.* III 10, in which Aristotle refers his reader to the *MA*: 'The instrument by which desire initiates movement is already something bodily.'[106] One might reject this passage as evidence, as it is taken from the final chapters of *De An.* III that Ross excludes from the hylomorphic part of the treatise. Against this rebuttal one might point to the instrumental language used, as it were, in the heart of the hylomorphic theory, namely in the definition of the soul in *De An.* II 1 (412ᵇ5–6) as 'first entelechy of a natural *organic* body (σώματος φυσικοῦ ὀργανικοῦ)'; it is a matter of dispute, though, whether *organikon* here should be understood in the sense of *organic*, i.e. being *with organs* or *constituted of organs*, or whether it must be rendered as *instrumental*.[107] Still, there are other unambiguous formulations at the core of *De An.* II—e.g. II 4, 415ᵇ19–20, where Aristotle says that all natural bodies are *organa*, instruments, of the soul. One could take this as a basis for arguing that formulations like 'the soul moves the animal with a bodily instrument' can and should be taken literally. With respect to the question of whether the soul could act on the body or the body on the soul, one could argue, Aristotle's main concern in *De An.* is to exclude the possibility that the soul could ever be moved (unless in an accidental sense, cf. I 4, 408ᵇ30–1), whereas he is quite unconcerned about the soul's moving the body or the animal (in an unmitigated sense)—as long as the soul does so without itself being moved.[108]

6. The Seemingly Unrelated Appearance of the Connate *Pneuma* in *MA* 10

The seemingly unrelated appearance of the connate *pneuma* in *MA* 10 used to cause unease among scholars. First of all, it might seem to provide a problem for the unity of the treatise, as its appearance seems to be strictly confined to this particular chapter.[109] Next, its occurrence in *MA* was taken as indicating a

---

[106] *De An.* III 10, 433ᵇ19–20: 'ᾧ δὲ κινεῖ ὀργάνῳ ἡ ὄρεξις, ἤδη τοῦτο σωματικόν ἐστιν.'

[107] This is a suggestion by Menn 2002, 108–11. See also Everson 1997, 64, and Shields 2016, 171–3. In support of the view that the body as a whole can be seen as an instrument one could refer to the evidence of *PA* I 5, 645ᵇ15–20.

[108] This is what I take to be the main implication of Menn 2002 for the current question.

[109] Cf. Kollesch 1985, 27. Nussbaum 1978, 144–6, considers similar concerns, showing why one could conceive of the argument of *MA* 6–8 as complete, but, in the end, goes for a solution that considers *MA* 10 as an integral part of the *MA* argument.

tension within Aristotle's *oeuvre*, especially since *De Anima* does not mention such a stuff by name.[110] Finally, it was thought that the postulation of *pneuma* in *MA* 10 fits better within post-Aristotelian physiology, in which it is known to have had a meteoric career,[111] rather than with Aristotle's own method.[112]

Indeed, the concept of the connate *pneuma*, far from being self-explanatory, provides Aristotle scholars with notorious puzzles; on the one hand, it seems closely related to the vital heat—though it is distinct from it—on the other hand, it is also compared to the element of the celestial bodies, the so-called *aithēr*.[113] Even its brief occurrence in *MA* 10 makes it perfectly plain that the *pneuma*'s physical properties must be different from those of the four 'ordinary' elements.[114] Yet this does not make the *pneuma* a 'mysterious', 'obscure', or 'semi-miraculous' stuff;[115] in the context of the *MA* it is invoked to fulfil a well-defined function within the initiation of motion, namely to transform thermic alterations into contractions and expansions, thereby amplifying the feeble perceptive impulses into the movement of bodily limbs. Aristotle seems to postulate that the aeriform stuff known in certain contemporary medical theories as 'connate *pneuma*' must by its nature have the appropriate properties to fulfil this particular function. This function is already sketched in the second part of *MA* 7,[116] so that by the time we reach *MA* 10, the stage has been thoroughly set for the appearance of the *pneuma*. Therefore it is just not true to say that *MA* 10, with its focus on the connate *pneuma*, is not integrated into the rest of the treatise and hence poses a problem for the treatise's unity. And according to the new textual evidence,[117] the *pneuma* is mentioned not only in *MA* 10, but already in *MA* 7, 701ᵇ15–16—in the same passage in which Aristotle points out that certain parts of living beings can become bigger and smaller under the influence of heating and cooling.[118] The *pneuma* thus seems to be integrated well enough into the main argument of the *MA* and to be intimately connected with the answer to our treatise's central question of how, and by means of which bodily instrument, the soul moves the body.

As for the remaining *pneuma*-related concerns (tensions with the rest of the *oeuvre*, post-Aristotelian influences, etc.), the most severe have been dissolved by

---

[110] This is the kind of argument prevalent in Nuyens' and Ross' developmental accounts; see section 5 above.

[111] Cf. Coughlin/Leith/Lewis 2020.   [112] Cf. Rose 1854, 165–7.

[113] Cf. *GA* II 3, 736ᵇ30–737ᵃ1. See also Solmsen 1957 on the comparison of these three stuffs.

[114] Cf. *MA* 10, 703ᵃ22–8.

[115] For a collection of attributes like these, see Freudenthal 1995, 122, n. 16.

[116] As also observed by Berryman 2002, 93–5.

[117] Cf. the manuscripts BᶜEʳb and William's Greek model *Γ*2; see Part II of this introduction, sections 8–9.

[118] The introduction of *pneuma* in *MA* 7 and 10 makes it plausible that Aristotle expects his readers to be familiar with this terminus.

intensified research on this topic.[119] This research has helped to identify a sensible division of labour between the vital heat and the connate *pneuma*[120] as well as to demarcate the genuinely Aristotelian use of the latter from post-Aristotelian uses, such as in the pseudo-Aristotelian *De Spiritu*.[121] Most notably, it has been shown how thoroughly the theory of the connate *pneuma* pervades important parts of Aristotle's physiological studies.[122] According to the most charitable and most ambitious readings, the connate *pneuma* was even intended to figure within an 'integrated physiological account of *all soul functions* (except the specifically human intellect)'.[123] Against this background, it would be rather surprising *not* to encounter this stuff in Aristotle's account of the initiation of bodily movement. This is the general scholarly background that may help to diffuse the impression that the use of the connate *pneuma* has a somehow un-Aristotelian flavour to it. As for the alleged incompatibility with *De Anima* it should finally be mentioned that although this work does not mention *pneuma* by name, the forward-reference in *De Anima* III 10, 433^{b}19–27, makes room for the question of what the *bodily instrument* is.[124]

7. The *MA*: An Interdisciplinary Inquiry?

As already noted,[125] it is characteristic of *MA* that questions about the motion of animals and questions about the motion of celestial bodies are discussed in close proximity. To the extent that the former kind of question is taken to belong to biology and the latter to cosmology, one might even wonder whether the treatise fuses biological and cosmological issues. And once we describe *MA*'s project like this, it might be thought to violate important rules of Aristotle's

---

[119] Cf., for example, Beare 1908 (especially 331 sqq.), Jaeger 1913a, Rüsche 1930 (especially 188–239), Peck 1943, Peck 1953, Ross 1955, 40–3, Verbeke 1978, Balme 1992, 158–65, Freudenthal 1995, especially 106–48, Berryman 2002. See also Gregoric 2020b chapter VII.

[120] Cf. Solmsen 1957, Balme 1992, 160–4, and Freudenthal 1995, 114–30; according to the latter author, the *pneuma* serves as a substrate to the vital heat.

[121] Cf. Gregoric/Lewis 2015 and Gregoric 2020a.

[122] As already shown by Peck 1943 and 1953.

[123] This is the thesis of Freudenthal 1995, 120, who also admits that such a theory is not fully elaborated in the Aristotelian *oeuvre* as it has come down to us, but claims that Aristotle seems to 'grope toward' such a theory (136).

[124] James Lennox kindly referred me to *GA* V 8, 789^{b}8–15, where Aristotle makes the connection between *pneuma* and the role of an *organon* quite explicit, by pointing out that nature uses *pneuma* as an instrument for many operations.

[125] See above, section 3 (iii).

own picture of separate, sectoral sciences, as set out most notably in the *Posterior Analytic*; according to this picture it would be fallacious kind-crossing (what Aristotle calls a '*metabasis eis allo genos*') to cross from one discipline with its own distinct objects, phenomena, and principles, to another discipline with distinct ones. Against this background Nussbaum brought up the idea that the *MA* is a 'interdisciplinary study'[126] that manifests 'a deliberate and fruitful'[127] departure from the earlier views of the *Organon*. The relatively late treatise *MA* acknowledges, according to Nussbaum, that 'some vital conclusions in the single sciences cannot be secured independently of our findings in other areas'.[128] According to her view, the later Aristotle thus loosens the methodological restrictions of his earlier work in favour of a 'less departmental and more flexible picture of scientific study'.[129] From this allegedly mature perspective, it is no longer problematic that cosmological and biological questions are dealt with in one and the same treatise. Nussbaum's suggestion has several non-trivial presuppositions. For example: that the questions discussed in *MA* are distinctively 'biological' or 'cosmological' respectively; that *MA* is actually meant as the apodeictic presentation of scientific knowledge in the sense of the *Posterior Analytics* (and that it does not include in turn, say, heuristic, apodeictic, or dialectical[130] parts); that in the framework of Aristotle's early methodology the transition from animal motion to the motion of celestial bodies and back would qualify as a fallacious '*metabasis*'; and, last but not least, that biology and cosmology are mutually dependent in that the findings of the one must be confirmed by the other.[131]

---

[126] Nussbaum 1978, 109. Cf. Nussbaum 1978, 6: 'It is true that the *MA* is "interdisciplinary" to an extent probably unparalleled in the corpus.' In general, Nussbaum's 'interpretive essay 2' as a whole is dedicated to this interdisciplinarity aspect.

[127] Nussbaum 1978, 113.   [128] Nussbaum 1978, 113.   [129] Nussbaum 1978, 113.

[130] This latter view, i.e. that the discussions of *MA* are dialectical in a sense, is defended by Morison 2020, n. 13.

[131] Nussbaum's picture of a mutual dependency of the two disciplines can be represented as follows (the scheme is an extension of Kung 1982, 71–3; the replies are mine): (1) Biology is dependent on cosmology, since (a) the promised account of the motion of animals cannot be given without cosmology's findings about the constitution of animals' environments (*quick reply*: the kind of environment that Aristotle considers here includes little more than the firm ground under an animal's feet, which is not a matter of cosmology), (b) the account of the physiological realization of desire, involving the *pneuma*, must make use of the theory of heavenly motion (*quick reply*: even if the matter of celestial bodies is the paradigm for the functioning of the connate *pneuma*—which could be questioned—it does not follow that the biological account actually relies on the cosmological one). (2) Cosmology is dependent on biology, since (a) the theory of *Ph.* VIII must be tested by applications to particular cases (*quick reply*: what is tested in chapters 3–4 of the *MA* are not the general theorems mentioned in 698[a]7–14, but the more specific claim, formulated within the *MA* itself, that there must be internal and external resting points), (b) the biological study of animal motion must secure that animals are self-movers, albeit not in a sense that would undermine the arguments for the unmoved mover (*quick reply*: the *MA* is not concerned to restrict the sense in which animals are self-movers in such a way that would defuse the problem posed

Nussbaum's interdisciplinarity thesis has been met with reservation. Joan Kung published a crisp and conclusive reply to this suggestion;[132] Jutta Kollesch, who in her commentary follows Nussbaum's views on many counts, protests against this unnecessary and unjustified move, as she sees it.[133] In general, one can avoid the problems that Nussbaum attempts to cure by her developmental account, if one takes, e.g., the beginning of the treatise not, like Nussbaum does,[134] as a blend of biology and cosmology, but as an argumentative move from the more specific case of animal motion to quite general principles of movement (i.e. that self-movers depend on something unmoved and that the first mover is necessarily unmoved) and back.[135] And apart from the fact that neither are the general kinetic principles demonstrated by their application to the case of animal motion, nor the application to the case of animal motion by the general kinetic principles, even the *Posterior Analytics* allows that the theorems of one discipline can be demonstrated by principles of another, provided that the former is subordinate to the latter.[136] Moreover, the discussion of celestial motion in *MA* 3 and 4 is far from attempting to *demonstrate* phenomena of one discipline by principles of the other; one might rather think of these passages as giving instructive applications, analogies, or comparisons, and such procedures often play a role in the heuristic or zetetic[137]—not the apodeictic—part of an inquiry.

8. The Explanandum of the Common Cause

Clearly, the treatise is dedicated to the common cause or explanation of *animal motion*. The broad term 'motion' (*kinēsis*), however, might raise concerns about the demarcation of the explanandum.[138] To begin with, the explanandum that Aristotle has in mind is considerably broader than 'actions', for in several

in *Ph.* VIII 2 and 6; also, one could argue, as, e.g., Kung 1982 did, that this problem has sufficiently been solved within *Ph.* VIII—for a more extended reply, see section 13 (i) below.

[132] Cf. Kung 1982. Lennox 2010 undertakes to refute the assumption shared by both Nussbaum and Kung, namely that the various natural treatises (at least *MA*, *Cael.*, and *Ph.* VIII) are contributions to different sciences.

[133] Cf. Kollesch 1985, 28–9. For a more recent criticism, see Falcon 2017.

[134] See Nussbaum 1978, 108: 'In the methodological remarks at the opening of the treatise and in many of the specific discussions throughout, we find a blend of biological and cosmological speculation that might strike us as anomalous…'.

[135] This is the line taken by Rapp 2020a, section 3, and similarly by Falcon 2017; see also Kung 1982, 71–2, for the view that the *MA* should be seen as an application of general principles from the *Physics* to the subordinate case of animal motion.

[136] Cf. *APo.* I 7, 75ᵇ14–17.   [137] Cf. Bénatouïl 2004, 93–4, on this point.

[138] Cf., e.g., Nussbaum 1983, 145–56.

works Aristotle wants to confine actions in the proper sense to human agents.[139] *De Motu Animalium*, by contrast, is about motions of both human and non-human animals and emphasizes the commonality rather than the differences between human and non-human animals.[140] Whenever the treatise comes to speak about capacities that are distinctive of human beings, like *nous* or *boulēsis*, i.e. thought or wish, it also mentions less exclusive capacities shared by human and non-human animals alike. It is only in one part of *MA* 7, in the discussion of the practical syllogism, that Aristotle seems to shift the attention from animals in general to human beings in particular;[141] but even in this context he ultimately aims at a conclusion about all animals.

Still, animals—broadly conceived—perform and undergo motions of all kinds. Are all of them part of the explanandum of the treatise? At *De Anima* III 9, 432ª7, Aristotle says that the soul has the capacity to move the animal locally (κατὰ τόπον). Similarly, in *De Incessu* 1, 704ª5, the topic of the treatise is confined to those parts of animals that are useful for local motion (κατὰ τόπον). The aim of *MA*, by contrast, according to its first lines, is to inquire into the common cause of animal motion—without a restriction to locomotion. However, the particular examples of movement that the first chapter of *MA* mentions—flying, swimming, walking—are clear instantiations of locomotion.[142] Also, *MA* 5, 700ª26, distinguishes local (κατὰ τόπον) motion from other kinds of change in a way that seems to assume that only *locomotion* was at issue up to that point. For these reasons, animal locomotion seems to be the central and paradigmatic phenomenon that the treatise attempts to account for. In addition, the second paragraph of the treatise (698ª7 sqq.) makes it clear that the entire project is meant to be about self-movers; if we take these pieces of evidence together, the explanandum of the treatise seems to consist in 'self-propelled motions from one place to another of the animal as a whole'.[143] And, indeed, the explanation that will be given in the treatise primarily accounts for motions that animals perform in order to reach certain objects that they desire;

---

[139] *EE* II 6, 1222ᵇ18–20, *EN* VI 2, 1139ª19–20. Although in the biological writings 'πράξεις' can also be used for the activities of non-human animals (cf. *HA* I 1, 487a10–20, and VIII 1, 588ª18) and is sometimes close to the meaning of *ergon* (e.g. *PA* I 5, 645ᵇ15–646ª2).

[140] Accordingly, plants—though animate—are not within the scope of the treatise. A certain vagueness about *whose* motion is at stake might derive from the fact that, as Aristotle says in *Historia Animalium* VIII 1, 588ᵇ4 sqq., the transition from the inanimate to the animate and from plants to animals takes place in small steps and, thus, seems to be almost continuous. This vagueness need not concern us here; some border cases will be discussed below.

[141] Cf. Cooper 2020, especially n. 11.

[142] In fact *MA* 2, 698ᵇ17, speaks of 'moving forward' and 'proceeding' (πρόεισιν, πορεία). Similarly, the summary of *MA* 2 given in *MA* 4, 700ª7–8, refers to locomotion: 'but also, in those things which move in respect of place (κατὰ τόπον) ...'.

[143] This is the formulation of Corcilius 2020, n. 2; for a discussion of the same question, cf. also Cooper 2020, n. 1.

the initiation of the pertinent type of motion involves an animal's perceptual–cognitive and its conative–desiderative apparatuses. Only late in the treatise, in *MA* 11, are we explicitly told that this relevant type of motion is voluntary or intentional (*hekousion*) motion.[144] If this is the treatise's central theme, what does this mean, on the one hand, for motions that are not initiated as the result of coordinated activities of the animals' perceptual–cognitive and the conative–desiderative capacities, and on the other hand, for self-motions that involve these capacities but are not strictly speaking *loco*motions? Let us look into both cases.

(i) The Non-Locomotive Case

Imagine an elephant that uses its trunk to reach out for a tasty fruit; owing to the trunk's extraordinary length the elephant need not even change its position to grab the longed-for treat.[145] This is an example of goal-directed animal motion that, in the framework of *MA*, could only be explained by reference to the animal's perception or imagination plus a desire for this type of object. The *MA*'s full account could even explain how the elephant's desire leads, step by step, to the movement of a bodily limb, the trunk. It seems, then, that the elephant example can be fully accounted for by the common cause that is put forward in *MA*, even though it does not involve the animal changing its position from one place to another as a whole. The upshot of this example is that, although self-propelled animal locomotion is undoubtedly the central phenomenon the *MA* attempts to account for, the common cause offered can also apply to cases of goal-directed animal motions that are not proper cases of *loco*motion.

This extension of the scope of the *MA*'s common cause or explanation is not insignificant, for it allows the inclusion of the goal-directed behaviour of stationary animals.[146] Some lower water animals, as Aristotle reports, live by sticking fast to an object, e.g. sponges; others are sessile or semi-sessile, e.g. sea-anemones; and still others, though unattached, are unable to move themselves, e.g. oysters and sea cucumbers.[147] Aristotle also reports indications that sea-anemones and sponges have perception; for sea-anemones display defensive behaviour when, e.g., a hand approaches[148] and sponges tend to contract and thus become hard to dislodge, people say, once they notice that someone is

---

[144] For the translation of ἑκούσιον, cf. Charles 1984, 59, Meyer 1993, 9–14, and Morel 2020, n. 6.

[145] Admittedly, this is a construed example. However, Aristotle's example of drinking (701ᵃ32) could be used for the same purpose (provided that the drink is within the drinker's reach).

[146] The significance of sessile animals for our context has been pointed out by Lorenz 2006, ch. 10 (similarly in Lorenz 2008).

[147] The examples are taken from *HA* I 1; see also *De An.* III 9, 432ᵇ19–21, where Aristotle speaks of animals that have perception, but are stationary and unmoving throughout their life.

[148] Cf. *HA* IV 4, 531ᵇ2–3.

trying to detach them.[149] If these animals are said to have perception, they have the feelings of pleasure and pain; and if they feel pleasure or pain, they must also have the capacity for desire.[150] One might regard these animals' motions, then, as basic forms of desire-driven behaviour—for example, for the sake of avoiding pain or destruction. In principle, this seems to fall within the scope of the common cause unfolded in *MA*—although, again, these are not cases of proper local movement.

(ii) The Non-Intentional Case

What about motions of animals that are not self-motions in the sense that they do not come about as the result of a certain interaction of the animal's perceptual–cognitive and desiderative capacities? Such motions are the topic of *MA* 11, so they are clearly addressed by the treatise. But do they really fall within the scope of the common cause or is their treatment in *MA* 11 just an appendix meant to fill out the larger picture with the kinds of animal motion not yet treated? The answer to this question depends on the interpretation of this tricky chapter. In this chapter Aristotle mentions non-voluntary motions, such as sleep, waking, and breathing on the one hand, and involuntary motions, such as the leap of the heart (triggered, probably, by some sort of emotion) and the sudden erection of the genitals on the other. Neither group includes genuine cases of locomotion and both concern motions of *parts* of the animal alone. The motions included in the first group need not be intended or desired to come about, so that neither cognitive nor desiderative capacities will play a role in their proper explanation. The motions of the second group seem to be connected with certain thoughts or episodes of imagination, e.g. thoughts of frightening or stimulating objects, but do they involve desire too? This is controversial among commentators;[151] if not even desire is involved, the common cause or explanation does not seem to be directly applicable, except in a modified sense. Still, some of these motions might fall within the scope of the common cause if one assumes that, even though they cannot be accounted for by the ordinary role of cognition and desire, their proper explanation will make restricted use of *this* part of the common cause that explains, e.g., how

[149] Cf. *HA* I 1, 487^{b}10–12, and V 16, 548^{b}10–15. While the aforementioned passages treat sponges like animals, there are other passages (*HA* VIII 1, 588^{b}21; *PA* IV 5, 681^{a}16–18) that align sponges with plants. This is not as puzzling as it might seem, as Aristotle clearly treats sponges, sea cucumbers, and the like as border cases between plants and animals; therefore, he aligns sponges with animals insofar as they seem to have perception (given that perception is the distinguishing mark of animals: e.g. *De An.* II 2, 413^{b}1–3), and aligns them with plants insofar as they are stationary and share other characteristics with them.

[150] Cf. *De An.* II 3, 414^{b}1–6.

[151] Nussbaum 1983, 146–7, and Corcilius 2008a, 352, answer this question in the negative, Morel 2020, 456 in the affirmative—though with the qualification that basic desires are involved.

perceptions and episodes of imagination can be transformed into movements of bodily parts or how movements within the body derive from the heart or an unmoved region therein.[152]

9. Mechanical and Bio-Kinematical Assumptions

Since Aristotle's *MA* regards animal locomotion as a function that is common to body and soul, it includes substantial, though not always self-explanatory, considerations about how the psychic impulse for motion is processed through the animal's body—from the origin to the extremities or movement-enabling parts. More than once, these considerations appeal to mechanical functions, often specifically to leverage phenomena. Significantly, medium forms of the Greek word ἀπερείδω ('supporting oneself against, leaning against'), which bring in the idea of forces exerted upon a prop or base of support, occur ten times in the treatise.[153] *MA* 1 and 2 appeal to the internal and external resting points that serve as props, *MA* 3 and 4 to the proportion or balance of forces, *MA* 7 introduces the three mechanical examples or analogies (the automatic theatre, the rudder, the carts),[154] *MA* 9 uses the analogy of two people pressing their backs against each other in order to move their legs and *MA* 10 describes the effect of the connate *pneuma* as pushing and pulling. In addition, when Aristotle introduces the idea of an inner resting point in *MA* 1 he compares the unmoved region within a joint to the centre of a circle, which is exactly how the early mechanical treatises illustrate the idea of the fulcrum,[155] i.e. the point that must remain at rest when a lever is applied.[156] While *MA* 1 seems to take for granted that the centre of a circle remains at rest, the *Mechanics* actually demonstrate that this holds of different kinds of movement.[157] The Greek word for 'fulcrum' is ὑπομόχλιον; it does not occur in Aristotle's own works, but is found frequently in the (presumably)[158] pseudo-Aristotelian treatises *Mechanics*

---

[152] Morel 2020 does explore this possibility; in Corcilius 2008a, 352–3, the involuntary motions are, in a similar vein, traced back to certain perceptual contents without mediating desires.

[153] *MA* 698^{b}6, ^{b}14, 699^{a}3, 700^{a}9, ^{a}10, ^{a}20, ^{a}22, 701^{a}14, 702^{a}26, 702^{b}35. See also the forms of ἀντερείδω ('offering resistance') in *MA* 698^{b}18, 699^{b}2, 703^{a}1.

[154] Cf. Hankinson 2020.   [155] See *Mech.* 3, 850^{a}35 sq.   [156] Ibid.

[157] See *Mech.* 8, 851^{b}16–21.

[158] It is a widely shared consensus in Aristotle scholarship, that these treatises derive from a Peripatetic context, but were not written by Aristotle himself—although with respect to the *Mechanica* the arguments against Aristotle's authorship have recently been somewhat qualified (van Leeuwen 2016, 7–18: 'more or less based on a gut feeling that the character and style of the text are un-Aristotelian'); with respect to the *Problemata*, cf. the contributions to Mayhew 2014.

and *Problemata*. Against this background it seems worthwhile to explore to what extent the *MA* is indebted to ideas deriving from early mechanics.

(i) The Impact of Early Mechanics

Bodnár, e.g., shows how the two Aristotelian treatises *IA* and *MA* 'deploy some of the analytical and explanatory techniques available from the contemporary mechanics'.[159] Berryman similarly observes that Aristotle's account of animal movement draws parallels to the phenomenon of leverage: 'Aristotle's interest is in the contrast between the moved mover and the unmoved mover, taking the role of the fulcrum as unmoved to offer support for the idea that all sequences of motion begin from an unmoved first principle.'[160]

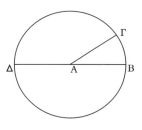

However, Berryman also draws attention to the limits of this comparison, as the fulcrum in mechanics, she says, 'hardly provides the origin of motion, merely playing a necessary role in the operation of leverage'.[161] De Groot undertakes an investigation of the impact of what she calls 'the principle of the moving radius' on Aristotle's explanation of animal motion. This principle says that points on a moving radius all move at different speeds, proportional to their distance from the centre; in its mechanical application the principle is meant to explain the lever and the amplification of effect involved in leverage.[162] She sees a hint of the moving radius principle in the diagram of *MA* 1 (see the figure above), in which Aristotle uses the centre of a circle to represent the unmoved point within a joint.

In this diagram the moving radius (moving from AB to $A\Gamma$) represents the bodily limb that is being bent, say the arm. De Groot sees here an example of leverage, for if A represents the elbow (serving as a fulcrum) and the radius the forearm, we can imagine a hand at B which moves a weight along the circumference up to Γ. More specifically, de Groot takes this to be an instance of what in modern terminology is called a 'third-class lever', 'where the fulcrum is located at one end of the beam of the lever but force is exerted *between* the fulcrum and the weight to be moved';[163] this presupposes that a force is exerted at a point close to the elbow where the muscles are attached to the forearm. Whether this interpretation is appropriate is difficult to decide, since Aristotle, as a matter of fact, does not speak in this context of loads and forces and, moreover, does not refer to muscles at all; what he refers to are sinews or

---

[159] Cf. Bodnár 2004, 137.   [160] Berryman 2009, 67.
[161] Berryman 2009, 67–8.   [162] Cf. De Groot 2008 and 2014, chs. 2 and 5.
[163] De Groot 2014, 33, and 2008, 55; for an interpretation of this diagram, see Rapp 2020a, 226–35.

tendons (see below), but the question of where they are attached to the bone plays no role. De Groot also argues that the same principle of the moving radius is used in *MA* 7 and provides the connection between the cart example and the automatic puppets in the theatre.[164] While de Groot thus concludes that Aristotle is familiar with the principle of the moving radius and the different manifestations of leverage,[165] Berryman sticks to the more cautious claim 'that Aristotle's somewhat scattered and piecemeal use of ideas that came to be characteristic of the mechanics tradition is best explained by the embryonic nature of the discipline in the fourth century'.[166]

(ii) Mechanistic Accounts and Intentional Movement

One might be reluctant, though, to speak of 'mechanics' and 'mechanical forces' in connection with the explanation of *intentional* movement. For doesn't the appeal to mechanical laws commit Aristotle to what we would call a 'mechanistic account'?[167] And isn't mechanics about *constrained* motion, while animal motion is supposed to belong to animals *naturally*?[168] Concerns like these may incline us to pursue large questions concerning mechanism and intentionality quite generally.[169] However, in the present context it seems both preferable and possible to take a more deflationary approach. After all, not each and every appeal to mechanical ideas immediately renders an account 'mechanistic'.[170] And in particular, the three mechanical examples in *MA* 7 have a well-defined and limited purpose[171] and are not at all meant to suggest that the animal as a whole works like a machine; Aristotle himself emphasizes the differences between animals and his technical examples.[172] Other ideas about forces and leverage seem to be borrowed from mechanics just for the purpose of under-standing certain functions of particular parts of the living body. Throughout the treatise, Aristotle says about bodily parts involved in the generation of locomotion

---

[164]   Cf. de Groot 2014, 114 sqq.; she makes this suggestion as an alternative to the common under-standing (expressed, e.g., by Nussbaum 1978, 347) according to which these examples are primarily meant to illustrate a *series* of movements caused, one after the other, by a sort of domino effect. Cf. also Hankinson 2020 on this topic.

[165]   Cf. De Groot 2014, 33.   [166]   Cf. Berryman 2009, 103.

[167]   'Mechanistic' in the sense that animal movement could be explained in merely or primarily mechanical terms, i.e. by the laws of mechanics; this notion of mechanistic is regularly associated with the threat of determinism.

[168]   This concern is raised by Bodnár 2004, 137 and 144–5; in response to this concern he refers to *Ph.* VIII 4, 254^{b}15–20, where Aristotle points out that natural motions of the animal as a whole are not necessarily the natural motions of the living body.

[169]   Cf. the headings 'L'Homme Machine' and 'The Phantom of Liberty?' Hankinson 2020 has given his sections 2 and 5.

[170]   As convincingly argued by Berryman 2003.   [171]   See above, section 2.

[172]   Cf. *MA* 7, 701^{b}13–16.

that they are *by their nature* apt to react in a certain way,[173] while motions that occur 'as the result of one thing striking against another'[174] are flagged as a separate class. Aristotle is also sensitive to the difference between the expansion or contraction of the *pneuma* which comes about *without force* owing to its nature and the pushing and pulling that results from the *pneuma's* expansion or contraction and is exerted *through force* to the adjacent parts.[175] Most notably, the process that leads to intentional action is always initiated and shaped by cognitive acts and is gone through for the purpose of reaching a certain goal or end, so that the intended explanation of the animal locomotion as a whole is teleological,[176] even if certain preconditions of this process or certain stretches of it require a mechanical explanation.

(iii) Bio-Kinematical Questions

It remains to take stock of the bio-kinematical applications of these ideas. In *MA* 7, after the discussion of the automatic theatre and the wagons, Aristotle concludes that animals are moved in the same way and he specifies the point of comparison as follows:[177] In the animal body sinews or tendons (νεῦρα, *neura*) correspond to cables that can be 'unfastened' and bones correspond to the iron or wooden parts. The core idea seems to be that the slackening (and pulling) of the stringy parts, i.e. the sinews or tendons that are attached to bones, move particular bones around the joints, of which one part remains at rest serving as a prop or fulcrum. Pavel Gregoric and Martin Kuhar[178] have added some pertinent observations. One concerns muscles, which the modern reader is surprised not to find in *MA*, since, as we now know, they move the bones through their contraction; this might be the reason why scholars have tacitly added muscles to the picture.[179] Gregoric and Kuhar, by contrast, argue that Aristotle ascribed this particular function to sinews and tendons (*neura*), not to muscles; since he described sinews as hard and solid, while identifying muscles with soft and supple flesh, he took sinews and muscles to be distinct in kind (even though he mistakenly identified certain muscles as sinews). Gregoric and Kuhar also connect the account of *MA* with passages where Aristotle clearly

---

[173] Cf. *MA* 701ᵇ8, 702ᵃ12, ᵃ21, ᵃ24, 703ᵃ22, ᵃ35, 703ᵇ2.

[174] Cf. *MA* 6, 700ᵇ12–3.   [175] Cf. *MA* 10, 703ᵃ22–3.

[176] The role of teleological explanation is constantly stressed by Nussbaum 1978, in particular throughout the 'interpretive essay 1', where a fictitious dialogue character by the name of Democritus serves as a mechanistic strawman against the teleological position. In Nussbaum 1986 she says about the historical Democritus that he depicts animals as puppets (269). Nussbaum's emphasis on the role of teleological explanation is, in principle, impeccable, though it is less clear that the rebuttal of mechanistic philosophers is a main aim of the *MA*.

[177] *MA* 7, 701ᵇ7–10.   [178] Cf. Gregoric/Kuhar 2014.

[179] Cf. Nussbaum 1978, 281 and 284, and Preus 1981, 81—quoted in Gregoric/Kuhar 2014.

registers the presence of certain small *neura* within the heart (which they identify as the *chordae tendineae*),[180] such that the connate *pneuma* within the heart
could directly act on these tendons. Given that these small *neura* do not form a
continuous system with the *neura* outside of the heart, however, it must still be
explained how their impulses are transmitted to those sinews that are actually
attached to the bones. This might be the reason why other commentators prefer
to rely on the continuity of the vascular system, which enable the connate
pneuma to reach throughout the body and to transmit motion from the origin
to all other parts of the body.[181]

Other details of the *MA*'s bio-kinematical picture concern a section in *MA* 8,
702a7–10, where Aristotle points out 'that the interior regions and the ones
around the origins of the instrumental parts are made as they are, so as to
change from solidified to liquid and from liquid to solidified, alternating
between soft and hard'. Obviously, the process described here is meant to be an
effect of the activity of desire and its concomitant thermic alterations. The
'instrumental/organic parts' are meant to refer to the limbs,[182] so that the 'origins' of them mentioned here are likely to be the joints. So much is widely
agreed upon, the rest is more controversial. What is 'around' these joints and
what is the subject undergoing these processes of solidification and rarefaction
(i.e. softening)? Aristotle is aware of the fact that there are ligaments (also: *neura*)
around the joints and that adjacent bones are connected through them.[183] In
MA 7 he says that stringy parts (including, probably, all sorts of *neura*) are slackened or pulled, which we took (in accordance with *MA* 10) to be the direct
effect of the contraction and expansion of the connate *pneuma*. Can *solidification*
and *softening* be taken as alternative descriptions of *the same* effect, i.e. of being
slackened or pulled, applied to the same subject (i.e. sinews, tendons, and, perhaps, ligaments)? Or are these terms meant to apply to another subject, such as
the homoiomerous tissue around the joint (perhaps including articular capsules
or cartilage)? In particular, it has been suggested that the flesh around the joints,
by alternating between solidity and softness, enables a single point within the
joint to be fixed at one time and moveable at another.[184] For those who assume,
then, that the solidification and softening of the flesh around the joints is different from the slackening and pulling of the sinew-like parts (and that the former
process is not just a continuation of the latter), the question arises whether
both processes are similarly thought to be coordinate effects of the thermic

---

[180] Gregoric/Kuhar 2014, 97–8.
[181] Freudenthal 1995, 135.   [182] Nussbaum 1978, 356.
[183] Cf. *HA* III 5 passim, in particular 515[b]10 sqq.
[184] Corcilius/Gregoric 2013, 70–1, and Gregoric/Kuhar 2014, 99.

alterations combined with desire or whether they are, more properly, the effects of the operation of the connate *pneuma*.[185]

10. The Practical Syllogism

Aristotle several times compares the psychological and cognitive antecedents of action to the role and structure of a syllogism in theoretical thinking. This equivalent of the syllogism in the realm of action has been dubbed the 'practical syllogism', although Aristotle himself never uses this expression. One remarkable fact about the practical syllogism is that this model was eagerly taken up by important representatives of action theory in the twentieth century, in particular in the 1950s–60s. Elizabeth Anscombe, Georg Henrik von Wright, and Donald Davidson, just to mention the most prominent ones, commented on Aristotle's practical syllogisms and, to some extent, incorporated them into their own systems. This philosophical interest again had an echo in scholarly work:[186] (some) interpreters started to interpret the practical syllogism with a view towards innovations in action theory, and the changing preferences of leading action theorists (e.g. from anti-causal to causal accounts) surreptitiously crept into paradigmatic interpretations of Aristotle's famous theorem and also allowed for a clearer specification of the interpretative options.

(i) The Textual Evidence

Above all there are two passages in which Aristotle explicitly describes the source or explanation of action in terms that derive from his syllogistic theory, e.g. by distinguishing, most notably, the major premise, the minor premise—one of them as general, one as particular—, and the conclusion; one of these passages is *EN* VII 3, 1147ᵃ24–ᵇ3, the other is *MA* 7, 701ᵃ7–36. Several other passages also seem to allude to this model of the practical syllogism, e.g. by contrasting general or particular knowledge or by mentioning premises or the middle term, without, however, elaborating on these points;[187] it is controversial to what extent these other

---

[185] Corcilius/Gregoric 2013, 70–1, conjecture that the alteration within the flesh around the joints is a second effect of the thermic alteration connected with desire (in addition to the *pneuma*'s pushing and pulling), but not mediated by the connate *pneuma*. They hence speak of a 'bifurcation' of the effect of the initial thermic alterations. Gregoric/Kuhar 2014, 99, suggest that the thermic alteration responsible for the solidification and softening of the flesh around the joint is transmitted by blood through the vascular system—as opposed to the pushing and pulling that uses the system of *neura*.

[186] Cf., e.g., Charles 1984.

[187] Cf., e.g., *De An.* III 11, 434ᵃ16–21: 'Since the one premise and judgment (ὑπόληψις καὶ λόγος) is universal, and the other is of what is particular (for the former says that such a kind of man should do such a kind of thing, and the latter that this here is a thing of such a kind and that I am a person of such

passages actually contribute to the model of the practical syllogism.[188] The two main passages, in *EN* VII 3 and *MA* 7, by contrast, explicitly refer to similarities and differences between the syllogism in theoretical thinking on the one hand and the practical syllogism on the other—the most pertinent difference being that in the theoretical case the acceptance of the premises lead to a conclusion, whereas in the practical case the premises or what corresponds to the premises are said to lead to action. In both passages one of the main upshots of the use of this model is that the distinction between two sorts of premise—the major general premise and the minor particular premise—helps to explain why it is that, although a sort of knowledge or thought about what is good or needs to be done is given, no corresponding action results.

It seems that Aristotle regards at least the following examples as genuine instantiations of 'practical syllogisms':

Every man should go walking; he is a man. Immediately, he goes walking. (*MA* 7, 701ª13–14)

No man should go walking; he is a man. Immediately he refrains from walking. (*MA* 7, 701ª14–15)

Something good should be made by me; a house is a good thing. Immediately, he makes a house. (*MA* 7, 701ª16–18)

If there is to be a cloak, there must necessarily be this first, and if this, this. And this he does immediately. (*MA* 7, 701ª21–2)

I have to drink; this is a drink. Immediately he drinks. (*MA* 7, 701ª32–3)

If everything sweet ought to be tasted, and if this is sweet, it is necessary that one acts accordingly. (*EN* VII 3, 1147ª29–31)

Aristotle emphasizes several times that the action follows immediately—provided that there is no external hindrance. The major premises usually include a gerundive form (ending with *-teon*) or a form of 'must' or 'should', which in the early days sometimes misled commentators into thinking that Aristotle wishes to express moral obligations or ethical principles by these premises. In fact, he remains entirely neutral with respect to the question of why these things should be done; the examples given at any rate show no preference for moral obligations, so that it seems justified to see Aristotle's model as relatively independent from questions of normative ethics.

---

a kind), it is either this latter opinion that imparts motion, not the universal one, or both do, but the former does so rather being at rest, while the latter is not.'

[188] For a list of other passages that have been associated with the practical syllogism, see Corcilius 2008d, 103, n.6. In general, the following survey on the practical syllogism is indebted to this very useful article.

(ii) Rule—Case vs. Means—End Examples

It is also noteworthy that many examples seem to instantiate what has been labelled 'rule–case' reasoning, in which a particular item is subsumed under a general proposition, while some examples deviate from this pattern and instead instantiate 'means–end' reasoning (broadly conceived).[189] For example: health is good or is to be the case; for health to come about X is necessary; for X to come about Y is necessary (and Y is something one can do); one does Y immediately.[190] Hence scholars came to distinguish two types of practical syllogism, depending on whether the major premise expresses a rule or an end.[191] Scholars have discussed whether Aristotle's additional distinction, in *MA* 7, between two sorts of premises—one through the good and one through the possible (701^a24–5)— refers to the two types of practical syllogism[192] or whether it applies to the several premises of one and the same syllogism.[193] Strategies have been conceived to translate the two types of practical syllogism into one another or to reduce one type to the other.[194] With regard to the means–end type of practical syllogism, many authors emphasize that this must not be taken in a narrow, i.e. purely instrumental sense, since Aristotle uses the 'means' language also to include: (a) constituents of ends (putting, to take up John Ackrill's example, is a part of playing golf, but putting is not a means in a purely instrumental sense, i.e. one that we use to reach an independent end, namely golfing, but rather a constitutive part of playing golf); and (b) parts of the definition of ends (if health is the end, and 'balance' part of the definition of health, we try to bring about balance, though not in a purely instrumental sense).[195] Occasioned by the occurrence of rule–case syllogisms several modern commentators (a) underline Aristotle's own scepticism about general rules in practical thought and (b) highlight that the rule–case deductions cannot be meant to establish a hierarchically structured ethical system.[196]

---

[189] For an overview of these two types of cases see Charles, 1984, 262.

[190] For this example, see *Metaph.* Z 7, 1032^b6–9.   [191] Cf. for example Allan 1955, 336.

[192] Cf. Allan 1955, 330–1, who wants to associate the premise through the good with the rule–case syllogism and the premise through the possible with the means–end syllogism; this attempt was rightly rejected, e.g., by Hardie 1968, 247–8, Wiggins 1975, and Nussbaum 1978, 189.

[193] So, correctly, Wiggins 1975 and others.

[194] Hardie 1968, 246–8, takes the rule–case syllogism to be the standard form, while Santas 1969, 168 sqq., tends by contrast to reduce all practical syllogisms to rule–case syllogisms.

[195] (a) is emphasized, e.g., by Allan 1955, 337–9, Cooper 1975, 22, and Nussbaum 1978, 176–7; (b), e.g., by Cooper 1975, 22, and Wiggins 1975; the latter also protests against an instrumental interpretation by offering a peculiar reading of the minor premise, whose function, he says, is to identify the most salient features through an act of perception.

[196] (a) is prominent, e.g., in Wiggins 1975 and Nussbaum 1978, 165–75, 184, 198–201, 210–19, (b), e.g., in Hardie 1968, 254 sq., and Nussbaum 1978, 165–75, 184, 198–201, 210–19.

(iii) Exegetical Difficulties

There are a number of notorious exegetical disputes about the practical syllo-gism, some of which have not been settled to the present day.[197] The general problem is how to flesh out the analogy to the theoretical syllogism. If we regard the theoretical syllogism as a sequence of propositions in which the conclusion follows by (logical) necessity from the premises, it is not easy to see how this is applicable to the practical case. For the relation between an action and its psychological antecedents does not seem to be a logical one. Faced with this fundamental difficulty one can either picture the practical syllogism as a stretch of reasoning, so that the relation in question would hold between propositions, or one accepts a causal relation between, say, psychic states that are not identical with, but only expressed or verbalized by, propositions and the resulting action. This fundamental difficulty relates to various more particular controversies. For example, since Aristotle repeatedly says that the conclusion of the practical syllogism is an action, there seems to remain little room for doubting that, according to Aristotle, the conclusion is indeed identical with or nothing but the action. However, on second thoughts, it does not seem possible then to establish a genuinely logical relation between the action as such and the prem-ises from which the action is said to follow. Also, one could wonder why, if Aristotle is serious about the conclusion being an action, such conclusions can be put in a form like 'I ought to make a cloak' (*MA* 7, 701ª20).[198] And whether or not the conclusion of the practical syllogism is an action or just a proposition that specifies an action makes all the difference, for example, because a propositionally conceived conclusion cannot rule out the possibility that the corresponding action will never take place. The logical space between the drawing of a conclu-sion and the performance of the corresponding action might be useful in accounting for (certain) cases of akratic behaviour,[199] but, by the same token, might threaten the sufficiency of the premises or antecedents in explaining why a particular action takes place.

Obviously, these debates are inseparably connected with the question of what function the model of the practical syllogism is ultimately meant to fulfil. Is it meant to model an agent's practical *reasoning* (or deliberation or what corresponds in animals to practical reasoning) in the light of which a certain course of action appears to be rational or consequent? Or is it meant to tell us

---

[197] For more recent contributions on this topic, see, for example, the contributions by Crubellier and Gourinat in Laks/Rashed 2004 or the contributions (by Corcilius, Gottlieb, Gourinat, Morel, Müller, and Price) in Rapp/Brüllmann 2008, Corcilius 2008c, and Fernandez 2014.

[198] The example mentioned, though, is used in *MA* 7 to exemplify just an interim conclusion. For a discussion of passages that seem ambiguous with respect to the status of the conclusion, see Charles 1984, 91–5.

[199] Cf., e.g., Charles 2009b.

that certain psychic states (say thoughts, episodes of imagination, perceptions, desires) are, in the appropriate circumstances, causally productive of or even causally sufficient for, an episode of animal locomotion? Or can it be somehow meant to do both?[200] If, in formulating this last alternative, one emphasizes the notion of deliberation and if deliberation is thought to be a distinctively human activity, the issue boils down to whether the practical syllogism is meant to apply to non-human animals. Now, given that the *MA* clearly concerns both human and non-human animals, the very appearance of this model in the centre of the treatise at first glance seems to rule out that it is intimately connected with exclusively human deliberation. However, a closer look into the text of *MA* 7 reveals that matters are more complicated[201] in that most of Aristotle's examples of practical syllogisms there are of markedly human thoughts and activities. Nevertheless, the entire passage dealing with practical syllogisms culminates in a general conclusion about all animals (701ᵃ34: τὰ ζῶια) alike. It is likely, hence, that although many instances of the practical syllogism exclusively concern human deliberation, *some* are also suitable for illustrating the locomotion of non-human animals.[202]

(iv) Making Sense of the Practical Syllogism

Most interpretations of the practical syllogism address the above-mentioned difficulties in one way or the other; the basic options are well represented by the following accounts.

In his monograph from 1975 Cooper keeps deliberation and the practical syllogism apart, on the grounds that deliberation 'takes the form of working out [...] what to do in order to achieve given ends'[203] and, hence, cannot be expected to take a syllogistic form.[204] The syllogistic structure is suggested by Aristotle only for a very limited part of practical thinking, namely 'the final step which actually issues in the performance of an action'.[205] The practical syllogism thus provides the link between a course of deliberation or the decision it yields and the actual action, for the deliberation culminates in the decision 'to perform an act of some suitable specific type'[206] and such decisions are taken up by the major premise of a practical syllogism that 'specifies a type of action to be done';[207] it remains for the minor premise to 'record by means of demonstratives and personal pronouns the fact that persons or objects of types specified in the

---

[200] Corcilius 2008b draws attention to the 'two jobs' of the practical syllogism and argues against the 'two-job' view (based on a slightly different understanding of what these two jobs consist in).

[201] As Cooper 2020 has pointed out.

[202] See also Fernandez 2014 on this topic.   [203] Cooper 1975, 22.

[204] Cooper 1975, 46; see also 24: 'Deliberation as Aristotle represents it does not take a form that remotely resembles an Aristotelian syllogism, and Aristotle never says or implies that it does.'

[205] Cooper 1975, 24.   [206] Cooper 1975, 23.   [207] Cooper 1975, 25.

major are present; and the performance of the action follows immediately, as the syllogism's outcome'.[208] Owing to the role of the minor premise it follows that 'the practical syllogism is not for the most part conceived of as a form of reasoning at all, but is only a way of expressing the content of the intuitive perceptual act by which the agent recognizes the presence and availability of the ultimate means previously decided upon'.[209]

For her interpretation of the practical syllogism, Nussbaum (1978) draws on von Wright's 'anankastic' model of practical thought:

> G is to be done (or desired).
> If G is to be realized it is necessary for me to do A.

If the agent does not do A and was not prevented from doing it, he or she either did not want A or did not believe that it is necessary to do A in order to achieve G.[210] Nussbaum interprets the necessity involved in this anankastic model in terms of Aristotle's 'hypothetical necessity'; drawing on von Wright, Nussbaum sees the practical examples as not reducible to deductive validity, but as 'logically conclusive in their own way'.[211] The 'so-called conclusion' is not a proposition, but an action.[212] Admittedly this is, she says, a 'very odd way of talking about the conclusion to a syllogism'; however the practical syllogism is 'only a piece of formal apparatus that we invoke to explain what is supposed to be going on psychologically'.[213] It serves a 'dual function' in that it provides 'a model of explanation generally, and, in the case of human rational agents, [...] a scheme for the justification of action, often also for conscious deliberation'.[214] The psychological states the practical syllogism refers to are sometimes conscious, corresponding to an agent's 'actual deliberation', but even in the non-conscious case—apparently including the case of non-human animals— the psychological states have 'reality' and are sufficient conditions for the occurrence of action.[215]

Because of her predilection for the anankastic model of practical reasoning and her case against 'deductive rationalism'[216] Nussbaum's interpretation of the practical syllogism tends to treat the rule–case deductions as problematic within Aristotle's account,[217] and focuses instead on means–end examples. Indeed, she

---

[208] Cooper 1975, 25–6.   [209] Cooper 1975, 46–7.

[210] Nussbaum 1978, 176.

[211] Nussbaum 1978, 180; she quotes von Wright who says that practical syllogisms are 'logically valid pieces of argumentation in their own right'.

[212] Nussbaum 1978, 186.   [213] Nussbaum 1978, 187.

[214] Nussbaum 1978, 207.   [215] Nussbaum 1978, 174.   [216] Nussbaum 1978, 184.

[217] Nussbaum 1978, 195 sqq. Martha Nussbaum pointed out to me though that she used to think of von Wright's anankastic model as deriving from a sensible exegesis of Aristotle's texts, so that her use of this model was not meant as a modernist move.

describes the premises of Aristotle's practical syllogism in terms of the anankastic scheme: the major premise mentions the object as desirable, the minor one expresses 'a belief to the effect that if the goal is to be realized such-and-such must be done'.[218] This description does not seem to fit many of the Aristotelian examples as they stand. Accordingly, Nussbaum complains that Aristotle misleadingly subsumes two different functions under the rubric of the 'minor premise', namely 'the belief about what must be done if the goal is to be realized' and 'the perception that one can do that act now'.[219]

As opposed to both Cooper and Nussbaum, Charles (1984) takes the conclusion of a practical syllogism to be a proposition. This follows from his adoption of a straightforward desire–belief model, in which belief is the acceptance of a proposition as true, and desire a mode of accepting a proposition in such a way that it leads to action (in appropriate conditions).[220] For the practical syllogism this means that an agent has a desire which accepts the major premise and a belief which asserts the minor premise. 'These propositions support a further proposition, which is the conclusion of the syllogism. If the agent appropriately accepts this conclusion, he desires to do the action which is the subject matter of the conclusion and acts accordingly.'[221] Desire thus conceived is 'open to cognitive factors (via the content of the propositions it accepts)',[222] but might also be influenced by non-cognitive factors, which can determine the strength of the desire. It follows that, although desire implies that the agent sees a good-making characteristic in a given object, it is not required that the agent desires the object as strongly as he or she judges it to be good.[223] The action, at any rate, is thus explained, not by the conclusion of the practical syllogism as such, but by the activity of desire which accepts it.[224] Within this framework, the practical syllogism primarily articulates Aristotle's conception of practical reasoning,[225] while in non-rational animals that lack the capacity to reason and to make inferences, desire may lead to intentional (or 'voluntary') action 'without the agent's reasoning practically'.[226]

Cooper 2020 chooses a quite different approach. As in his 1975 monograph he holds the view that the practical syllogism is 'a final step of thought, in which that deliberation (or rather the decision to which it leads) is carried into effect, into immediate action'.[227] In his new text, Cooper emphasizes the role of thought in *MA* 6–7: given that Aristotle calls the desired object the first mover, it is thought's function to provide the needed connection between desire and the objective for action. '[A]lthough the objective for action is indeed the causal

---

[218] Nussbaum 1978, 190.   [219] Nussbaum 1978, 191.   [220] Charles 1984, 87.
[221] Charles 1984, 89.   [222] Charles 1984, 88.   [223] Charles 1984, 88.
[224] Charles 1984, 90.   [225] Charles, 1984, 94.   [226] Charles, 1984, 96.
[227] Cooper 2020, 364.

origin of the changes and movements within the animal that generate or consti-
tute the action of self-locomotion, it is thought that is the immediate cause of
this objective's being capable of moving the animal.'[228] At least this holds, he says,
of fully reasoned human actions. In *MA* 7 it is only in 701ª31–3, when Aristotle
turns to the final example of the practical syllogism (I need a drink, this can be
drunk—he drinks immediately), that the discussion shifts to actions and movements brought about by non-rational desires. Only in this latter case (non-
rational) desire (e.g. for a drink) takes the place that, in reasoned actions, is held
by a decision, i.e. the result of deliberation.

11. The Role of *Phantasia*

The notion of *phantasia* ('imagination', 'appearance', or the like) occurs frequently (twelve times) in *MA* 6–8 and 11. For the most part, it is mentioned
together with perception and thought,[229] as these three—perception, *phantasia*,
thought—represent the cognitive–discerning (*kritika*) capacities,[230] one of
which is always needed in combination with desire to initiate motion. While
thought is distinctive of human animals, perception and *phantasia* are shared by
human and non-human animals alike;[231] they can 'hold the same place'
(700ᵇ19–20) as thought in that they also involve discernment—though, of
course, in a different way. According to common Aristotelian doctrine, it is by
virtue of *phantasia* that animals are able to apprehend objects that are not currently present to their senses,[232] which seems to justify the mention of *phantasia*
alongside perception—for, obviously, not everything that animals pursue or try
to avoid is immediately present. On this basis, it is natural to assume that in the
generation of animal motion *phantasia* is perfectly on a par with sense-perception
or thought,[233] the only differences being that *phantasia*, as opposed to perception, can be of envisaged objects that are not present and that *phantasia* is also in

---

[228]   Cooper 2020, 349.

[229]   Perception, *phantasia*, thought: 700ᵇ17, ᵇ19, 701ª30, ª33, ª36, 701ᵇ16; *phantasia* and thought: 701ᵇ18,
ᵇ35, 703ᵇ18; *phantasia* and perception: 701ª5; without perception and thought: 703ᵇ10; in 702ª19 *phantasia*
seems to stand on its own, but in the next line it gets associated with perception and thought.

[230]   Drawing on the evidence of *De An.*, Corcilius 2020, 317–20, raises difficulties for the idea that
phantasia is suited to make veridical discriminations (in this respect not dissimilar to Wedin 1988, ch. 2);
however, he ends up with the conciliatory claim that *phantasia* is important for cognition and discriminations as a source of information. Schofield 2011, 123, by contrast, takes this claim to be in line
with *De An.* III 3.

[231]   However, Aristotle famously holds that some animals have no *phantasia*; according to *De An.* III 3,
428ª8–11, at least worms or grubs lack this capacity.

[232]   Cf. *De An.* II 5, 417ᵇ20, III 3, 417ᵇ28–9.

[233]   In *MA* 7, 701ª30, ª33, ª36, e.g., the role of perception, *phantasia*, and thought seems to be perfectly
parallel.

use when thought is not available—be it, in the case of non-human animals, human children, or adult human beings whose thought, or their ability to access it, is temporarily impaired.[234]

(i) A Privileged or Even Necessary Role for *Phantasia*?

This first impression notwithstanding, the last decades have seen a scholarly debate focused on the questions of whether, and if so how, *phantasia* is meant to play a *privileged* and even *necessary* role either in the generation of animal locomotion ('*weaker thesis*') or also in the generation of desire ('*stronger thesis*'), and whether such a necessary role can be accounted for on the basis of the minimal conception of *phantasia* found at *De An*. III 3, 428ᵇ10–17,[235] or whether the role of *phantasia* in locomotion requires a somehow extended account,[236] as for example Furley 1978 and Nussbaum 1978 have famously suggested.[237]

---

[234] Cf. *De An*. III 3, 429ª4–8 (trans. Shields): 'Because instances of imagination persist and are similar to perceptions, animals do many things in accordance with them, some because they lack reason, e.g. beasts, and others because their reason is sometimes shrouded by passion, or sickness, or sleep, e.g. humans.'

[235] According to this minimal conception, *phantasia* is a movement (*kinēsis*) deriving from the actuality of a previous sense-perception and is thus similar to this sense-perception, which means that it inherits its perceptual content (modified or weakened to one or another degree) and its causal powers (see, e.g., Caston 1996).

[236] 'Extended' in the sense that it goes beyond the account of *De An*. III 3. This mentioned alternative has been posed by Moss 2012, ch. 3, who takes Nussbaum 1978 and Lorenz 2006 as representatives of the camp that goes beyond the basic account of *phantasia*, while Moss herself attempts to show that a necessary role of *phantasia* can be derived without assigning interpretative tasks to it.

[237] Nussbaum develops her interpretative theory of *phantasia* in Nussbaum 1978, 'interpretive essay 5'. To be precise, Nussbaum's reading of *phantasia* includes two independent claims that should be assessed on their own. The first claim is that *phantasia* is a necessary condition for desire (see Nussbaum 1978, 221 and 334); the second is that, while ordinary sense-perception is affected only by proper sensibles, i.e. things that have colour, taste, sound, etc., it is through *phantasia* that the animal 'becomes aware of the object as a thing of a certain sort' (257) or as 'something *qua* what-it-is-called' (259), i.e. 'as a unitary object under some description, not just as an assortment of various perceptible characteristics' (259). The second claim concerns the notorious scholarly question of which capacity is responsible for the animal perceiving the common and the accidental sensibles and combining scattered perceptions from various senses (for a discussion of this second claim, see Everson 1997, 159 sqq.). Even though the connection between these two claims is not entirely clear to me (do we have to subsume objects under substance terms in order to find them desirable? Counterexamples could easily be provided), I take it that this second claim is meant to provide the background for the first claim, because Nussbaum also says that it is in order 'to be moved to action' (259) that an animal has to become aware of something *qua* what-it-is-called. Similarly, she says that *phantasia* 'somehow presents the object of desire to the animal in such a way that it can be moved to action' (240) or that *phantasia* is the capacity 'in virtue of which an animal becomes aware of its object of desire' (241). These last two formulations are slightly ambiguous between saying that *phantasia* presents an object as being of a general sort which is considered to be desirable and saying that it presents the object as desirable or as an object to be pursued; the latter alternative would come close to saying that it presents the object as good in some way. Both alternatives however suggest that it is an immediate consequence of the interpretative function of *phantasia* that an animal sees an object as desirable.

(a) Dealing with the strong thesis. A quick rejoinder to the strong thesis that even the generation of *desire* requires *phantasia* is provided by passages that, as already mentioned, directly combine desire with basic sense-perception[238] or deny *phantasia* to certain lower animals, without at the same time questioning their capacity to desire.[239]

(b) Dealing with the weak thesis. A quick rejoinder to the weaker thesis that *phantasia* plays a necessary role in the initiation of episodes of animal loco- motion could, among other things, draw on several passages in the *MA* in which sense-perception proper is presented as an independent cognitive– discerning capacity, which, together with desire, is sufficient for initiating animal locomotion. At the end of *MA* 6, 701ᵃ4–5, for example, Aristotle says: 'For the animal is moved and progresses forward by desire or deci- sion, with something having been altered on the basis of sense-perception or *phantasia*.' Clearly, it is *either* perception *or phantasia* that is alone sufficient to set this process into motion. Similarly, the important general remark that concludes the long discussion of the practical syllogism in *MA* 7, 701ᵃ33–6, makes no attempt to privilege *phantasia* or to present the proper contribution of sense-perception as insufficient: 'In this way then animals have impulses to move and act, with desire being the last cause of their movement, and coming about either through perception or through *phantasia* and thought.' In this account *phantasia* is coupled with thought ('and' instead of 'or')—probably for the reason that the effects of thought are always mediated by *phantasia* or *phantasmata*—, but again perception is presented as an autonomous source of the desire that ultimately leads to the impulse to move. This is also confirmed by a passage in *MA* 9 (702ᵇ21–5): '...when the area around the origin is altered because of sense-perception, and changes, the neighbouring parts change along with it, and get both stretched out and compressed, so that by necessity motion comes about in animals because of these things.' Again, there is no reason for doubting that the chain of alterations is triggered by sense- perception alone.

At 701ᵇ18, 701ᵇ35, and 703ᵇ18 *phantasia* and thought are mentioned without perception, which might suggest, at first glance, that perception is being sup- pressed, being insufficient for the generation of action, while perceptual con- tents presented by *phantasia* are. However, the latter two passages are dependent

---

[238] Most famously, *De An.* III 3, 414ᵇ1–6.
[239] Lorenz 2006, ch. 10, offers an elaborate refutation of this strong thesis by offering a new reading of *De An.* III 10, 433ᵇ27–9, which, on a traditional reading, could be taken to claim that there is no desire without *phantasia*. A similar strategy has already been adopted by Labarrière 2004, 136.

on the first, 701^{b}17–19, according to which the required alterations are brought about by perception immediately, while *phantasia* and thought have (only) 'the power' of the objects being imagined or thought of. Read prosaically, this amounts to nothing more than saying that in the case of *phantasia* and thought, the lack of the direct causal impulse deriving from a perceived object, is made up for by *phantasia*'s peculiar capacity to retain and reproduce the causal powers of the originally perceived object. But since these powers are ultimately inherited from previous sense-perceptions, these passages do not support the alleged indispensability of *phantasia*; on the contrary, the peculiar relation between perception and *phantasia* suggests that, if the merely *inherited* powers of *phantasia* are sufficient for initiating motion, the original impulse of sense-perception must be even more so.[240]

(ii) The Alleged Star Witnesses for a Necessary Role of *Phantasia*

The best case for a privileged or necessary role of *phantasia* from within the text of the *MA* must draw on 702^{a}17–21 and 703^{b}9–11,[241] where *phantasia* is mentioned alone, without reference to sense-perception and thought. The first of these two passages[242] summarizes the famous chain of alterations: *phantasia* 'prepares' desire, desire the affections, affections again bring the instrumental parts into a suitable condition.[243] Aristotle completes this chain by adding, in the next sentence, that *phantasia* comes about through perception or thought. Clearly, this passage deviates from the standard account we have encountered so far, as *phantasia* is no longer on a par with perception and thought, but represents a further step in the bringing about of animal motions. This is indeed a natural reading of this passage in isolation; the only drawback is that it would involve a blatant contradiction with the earlier statements, which treated *phantasia* as on a par, at least with sense-perception. Commentators have tried to avoid such a contradiction by presenting the passage in question here as the principal witness for Aristotle's considered view, which revises the position expressed in the

---

[240] For a similar argument, see Schofield 2011, 125.

[241] There might be passages outside the *MA* that are suitable for justifying a necessary role of *phantasia* for goal-directed locomotion the discussion of which, however, would go beyond the limits of this survey. For example, *De An*. III 10, 433^{b}27–9, seems to be a strong candidate; *De An*. III 9, 432^{b}15–16, is sometimes mentioned, but it belongs to a pretty explorative part of the discussion.

[242] The passage is used, e.g., by Nussbaum 1978, 233 and Moss 2012, 49—their readings of the role of *phantasia* are different, although they converge in claiming that the *MA* takes *phantasia* to be necessary for animal locomotion.

[243] For a seminal discussion of this section, cf. Labarrière 2004, 232–40.

earlier, allegedly provisional statements.[244] However, the context of this passage includes no hints whatsoever of such a revisionist scenario.[245]

It seems more promising, hence, to explain the exposed role of *phantasia* in 702ᵃ17–21 by constraints of the immediate context, for the lines in question are part of the justification for the claim made in the previous line, that whenever someone *thinks* that he should walk, he will almost simultaneously walk. By showing how the sequential steps (from *phantasia* via desire and affections down to the instrumental parts) are interlocked, Aristotle introduces an important premise for the statement that all pertinent factors within this sequence are by nature related as active and passive and can thus bring about a motion 'almost simultaneously'. The presence of *phantasia* alone at the head of this sequence is simply a reflection of the particular example at hand, in which an act of *thinking* triggers the motion; for in such cases it is, strictly speaking, the thought-accompanying *phantasia* that directly brings about the alterations involved in an episode of desire. After the sequence has been established, the next line (702ᵃ19: 'But appearance comes about either through thought or through perception') is needed to remind the reader that the *phantasia* at the head of the sequence comes about through thinking—here through the thought that one should walk—since, in general, *phantasia* accompanies thinking. But Aristotle also mentions 'through perception' because, in general, *phantasia* can also result from perception (though in another way as from thought), not because perception cannot initiate locomotion except via *phantasia*.

The remaining star witness, *MA* 11, 703ᵇ9–11, is part of the concluding chapter on involuntary and non-voluntary motions. Of these motions (either both kinds or only the latter)[246] Aristotle says: 'For none of these is straightforwardly controlled by *phantasia* or desire.' One could be tempted to conclude that 'these two'—*phantasia* and desire—are meant to be 'necessary conditions of voluntary movement'.[247] The problem with this conclusion, again, is that Aristotle says nothing between the programmatic statements in *MA* 7–9 and *MA* 11 that indicates a change of mind on the issue of *phantasia*. Also, it would be surprising if such an essential part of the account of voluntary motion were revealed only in a random remark about involuntary and non-voluntary motions, which are, recall, at the very least not central topics. So, this passage just does not have the makings of a star witness. The choice of '*phantasia*' in this context may have several reasons; perhaps episodes of *phantasia* are (often or

---

[244] This is the strategy of Nussbaum 1978, 233 ('a more careful and schematic account'), as noticed by Schofield 2011, 132–3.

[245] As, again, observed by Schofield 2011, 213–14, though the following depiction of the context, as I see it, deviates from Schofield's.

[246] Cf. Morel 2020, 455 sqq.   [247] Cf. Moss 2012, 49.

typically) in the background of the uncontrollable motions (e.g. leaps of the heart, erections) that are the topic of this chapter, so that it would (often or typically) be up to *phantasia*—if to any of the three cognitive capacities—to 'control' them.

(iii) Other Considerations in Favour of a Necessary Role for *Phantasia*

It has been argued that it must be possible for animals to form desires for objects that are not currently present to their senses. Aristotle shows at least indirect awareness of situations like these, when he highlights the fact that *phantasia* and thought have the power of objects (i.e. even of not present objects) and are capable of providing, as it were, the forms of these things (i.e. regardless of whether they are around or not).[248] Nothing speaks against concluding, then, that—because of its anticipatory power—*phantasia* is necessarily involved whenever an animal purposefully moves towards remote objects that are not currently in view or otherwise perceived. This is the simple picture; in real life, the simple picture probably applies to a significant share of cases.[249] We do not yet perceive, e.g., the beer in the fridge, but by imagining beer, or by thinking that there must be one beer left in the fridge, we form a locomotion-inducing desire for it.

Is the anticipatory power of *phantasia* also required, as long as the desired object is actually perceived? One might think that it is not. Imagine a hungry rabbit that actually perceives a carrot with at least one of its distance senses. Why should this perception be considered insufficient for triggering the rabbit's locomotion-inducing desire?[250] After all, the carrot is not concealed by brambles or the like, so that there is no need to imagine a perceptually non-accessible object. To this scenario it has been objected that the rabbit—though seeing, hearing, or smelling the carrot—might need *phantasia* and its anticipatory machinery to anticipate that the carrot is actually *tasty*, i.e. that the carrot meal will be enjoyable or good. Lorenz developed an account along these latter lines. What motivates the rabbit to engage in locomotion is not the look of the carrot, but 'the prospect of making a meal of it'.[251] This is, according to Lorenz, why the formation of the rabbit's purpose of eating a carrot 'involves accomplishing

---

[248] Cf. *MA* 7, 701^{b}18–22; 11, 703^{b}18–20.

[249] And the statistical prevalence of cases like these might even explain why Aristotle sometimes speaks as if all cases were like this.

[250] Pearson 2012, 52–3, sees a difference between a capacity triggering a desire and that capacity envisaging an object of desire; he assigns the former capacity to perception (since it only requires that this capacity provides a sort of information), but not the latter (since it requires to present something as valuable). Pearson 2012, 55, n. 29, also considers the possibility that perception is sometimes used in an extended sense including both perception proper and perceptual *phantasia*.

[251] Lorenz 2006, 132 (Lorenz uses lions and stags though).

the cognitive task of envisaging a prospective situation, one that does not currently obtain and that may, as a matter of fact, never come to obtain'.[252]

Basically, the often-quoted and regularly criticized[253] 'interpretative' interpretation of *phantasia*—though resulting in a quite different account—originally derives from a similar worry. It cannot be the carrot as such, i.e. taken as an external physical object, that motivates the rabbit to locomote, but only the carrot insofar as it is somehow related to the rabbit's preferences or attitudes. Hence the supporters of the 'interpretative' camp would say that it is the carrot 'under certain descriptions'[254] or the carrot seen 'as an object of a certain sort'[255]—in our example under the description of 'tasty meal' or selectively interpreted 'as a tasty meal-providing object'—that is apt to elicit the rabbit's locomotion. Again, this is a sensible challenge to raise for Aristotle's account of animal motion, but whereas the anticipatory function of *phantasia* (or versions of it) has a strong basis in Aristotle's texts, it is much more difficult to see why *phantasia* in particular should do the job of *interpreting* objects *as* good or choiceworthy—apart from the fact that of the two competing cognitive capacities, sense-perception seems too simple to do this demanding job and the gift of thought is not widespread enough in the animal kingdom.

(iv) Conclusions and Suggestions

There is an observable tendency among commentators to use *phantasia* as the wild card that can do a job within Aristotle's conceptual framework that no other capacity is qualified to do. With regard to the *MA* in particular one might wonder whether one should expect this treatise to provide evidence for how animals come to consider some objects *as* desirable and others not. The second part of the treatise focuses, as we have seen, on the narrow question of how locomotion is initiated within the animals' bodies through certain capacities of the soul. For this particular purpose, it may just be presupposed that animals come with certain desiderative dispositions. Whether these dispositions are innate or, if not innate, how animals came to acquire them in the first place, is part of a different story. In the formation of some of these desiderative dispositions *phantasia* may play an important role, for example if they derive from an individual's past experience or from an individual's peculiar way of envisaging future challenges, while other desiderative dispositions, by contrast, might just

---

[252] Lorenz 2006, 131. Lorenz admits (131) that there is no *direct* evidence in the text of the *MA* or elsewhere for the existence of these 'envisaging prospects' or for the claim that animals in general are able to envisage prospects in virtue of having *phantasia*; he suggests, though, that this may go without saying. For a critique of Lorenz' claim, cf. Moss 2012, 56, n. 23, and Pearson 2012, 44 sqq.

[253] For a list of friends and critics of the interpretative theory, see Corcilius 2020, n. 52.

[254] Furley 1978, 175 (= Furley 1994, 12).   [255] Nussbaum 1978, 255. See also n. 237 above.

be given as part of the nature of the species; the sponge's natural desire, e.g., not to be detached from its reef (if Aristotle's report is right), does not take much imagination. Some of the problems that encumber the discussion about the role of *phantasia* may, hence, derive from the failure to distinguish two distinct questions concerning the formation of desire.[256] On the one hand, there is the question of how an animal comes to have certain desiderative dispositions or, as it were, certain 'general desires', say 'the general desire for *F* ', e.g. for sweet things in general. *This* question is probably not within the scope of our brief treatise *MA*. On the other hand, there is the question of how a particular episode of desire is initiated, say an episode of desiring this particular *F*. This *latter* question is indeed discussed in the *MA* and it is, within the framework of the *MA*, the only way of making sense of the formulas of 'forming' or 'shaping the desire'. Provided that a given animal has the general desire (or the desiderative disposition) for *F* (which thus need not be formed or generated in the course of the initiation of a particular action or locomotion), the explanatory apparatus of the *MA* is well suited to explain how, through perception, *phantasia, or* thought, the animal comes to actually desire a particular *F* (or, to put it in means–end language, to desire a particular *G* that is a means towards the desired objective *F*) and to move towards it. Seen from this perspective, there is no longer any need for one of the involved discerning capacities to *interpret* or *evaluate* the particular *F* as good or pleasant;[257] nor is there a need for *anticipating* a situation of joyful engagement with the particular *F*.

12. Desire and Affections

Desire plays a crucial role in the *MA*'s account of animal motion. From the second part of *MA* 7 on, the discussion emphasizes the bodily alterations that are connected with desire, perhaps thus giving an example of what it means to treat desire as a function that is 'common to body and soul'. The fundamental assumption, presented at the beginning of *MA* 8, is that desire is accompanied by thermic alterations: the desire to pursue an object is accompanied by warming, that to avoid an object is accompanied by cooling. This assumption about desire provides

---

[256] A similar view has been put forward by Schofield 2011, 127, as an interpretation of the drink example in *MA* 7: 'In other words, sense-perception or *phantasia* or thought shapes a desire that is on that account now determinate, ready to function at once as the *immediate* cause of movement [...] that, then, seems to be the sense in which desire "comes about...through" sense-perception or through *phantasia* and thinking.'

[257] It might also be helpful in this context to distinguish, as David Charles kindly suggested to me, between 'seeing that A is pleasant' and 'seeing A in a pleasure involving way'. For what it's worth, I take this as a convenient way of reconciling the two Aristotelian claims: (i) that sensual perception is connected with the feeling of pleasure and pain; and (ii) that, in the non-accidental case, sensual perception is of the proper and common sensibles, and of nothing else.

a link to a different, though related, phenomenon, namely affections, since affections, such as feeling timid or confident, or sexual arousal, are similarly directed at painful or pleasant objects and are known to be similarly connected with thermic alterations. The bodily alterations that are notoriously and vividly connected with affections of the soul thus illustrate the kind of bodily alteration that Aristotle takes to be involved in each and every episode of desiring—though they occur on a smaller scale and are sometimes unnoticed.

(i) Emotions and Other Affections

In *MA* 7–8 and 11 Aristotle refers several times to *pathē* or *pathēmata*—terms that he often uses to single out emotions such as anger, shame, fear, etc. And, indeed, the *MA* also refers to such emotions by mentioning confidence (702ª2) and fear (701ᵇ20, ᵇ22, 702ª3), frightening things (701ᵇ20–2), things that make us shiver and shudder (701ᵇ32), or things that cause blushing and becoming pale (701ᵇ31).[258] In all these instances Aristotle emphasizes the bodily alterations that emotions are known to involve,[259] e.g. shivering, shuddering, blushing, becoming pale, and the underlying effects of cooling and warming. He also seems to assume a continuity between phenomena like (i) confidence and fear, (ii) non-rational desires such as sexual appetites (702ª3), and (iii) 'the other painful and pleasant bodily things' (702ª3–4). Compared to passages in other works, where Aristotle introduces affections or emotions as *pathē tēs psychēs*, i.e. as affections *of the soul*, and where he adds extensive lists of exemplary emotions,[260] the *MA* seems to involve a certain shift in emphasis. While it is not at all unusual that Aristotle uses the terms *pathos* and *pathēma* for a wide range of psychic and bodily phenomena,[261] it is significant, first, that the *MA* seems mostly interested in the bodily alterations and, second, that it easily shifts back and forth between a narrower use of *pathē* and *pathēmata* for emotions or their typical bodily manifestations (e.g. the often-quoted boiling of the blood in the case of anger) and a broader use that embraces all kinds of bodily alterations that are involved in the initiation of locomotion (e.g. expansion and contraction of the *pneuma*, softening and solidification of the flesh around the joints).[262]

A broad notion of *pathē* might also be at issue in the context of Aristotle's assumption that there are inner parts of the body that are by their nature *pathētika*, i.e. capable of being acted upon.[263] It is owing to these parts together

---

[258] On the use of affections in *MA*, see also Morel 2016.

[259] In *EN* IV 9, 1128ᵇ13–15, Aristotle refers to the bodily effects of shame, in order to show that shame is rather a *pathos* than a virtue.

[260] Cf. *EN* II 5, 1105ᵇ21–3, *EE* II 2, 1220ᵇ12–14, *De An.* I 1, 403ª16–18, and *Rh.* II 1, 1378ª20–3.

[261] Cf. Bonitz 1867.   [262] See, e.g., 701ᵇ23 and ᵇ29.

[263] *MA* 8, 702ª11, ª14, ª20.

with their active counterparts *(poiētika)* that impulses are transmitted through the body swiftly or almost simultaneously (702ᵃ10–21). Now, whenever a bodily part that is capable of being acted upon is actually acted upon by an active agent, it follows that there is a *pathos* or *pathēma* of this particular *pathētikon*-part.[264] This background might be relevant also for the discussion of the often-quoted lines 702ᵃ17–19, according to which *phantasia* prepares desire, desire the *pathē*, and the *pathē* the instrumental parts,[265] since these lines are sandwiched by remarks about the active and the passive parts—*poiētika* and *pathētika*—and are themselves part of an explanation that is occasioned by a claim about alterations taking place in the tissue around the joints of the instrumental parts (702ᵃ7–10). Because of the repeated allusions to emotions throughout *MA* 7–8 one might be tempted to understand *pathē* here in the specific sense of emotions or feelings.[266] However, it would be a disturbing consequence of this reading that all instances of intentional locomotion would thus depend on the animal being in an emotional state. This would be a quite implausible claim, unless one takes the emotions or feelings here in a sense that is broad enough to include all sorts of desires; however, then, it would not make sense anymore to say that these *pathē* (being or including desires) are prepared by desires. In this particular context *pathē* should therefore be taken as referring to physiological affections taking place in the region around an animal's joints.[267]

(ii) Desire (*Orexis*)

The *MA* contributes to the understanding of *orexis* mostly by elucidating the physiological alterations connected with episodes of desiring and by embedding *orexis* into a sequence of alterations that leads from sense-perception, *phantasia*, or thought to the actual locomotion of animals. It also unfolds the idea already stated at the end of *De Anima* III 10, that *orexis* as a moved mover is intermediate between the desired object as the unmoved mover on the input side, and the moved animal on the output side (*MA* 6, 700ᵇ35–701ᵃ2, *MA* 10, 703ᵃ4–5). Other important claims and assumptions about *orexis* are rather presupposed than explicitly defended. Most notably, it is taken for granted that *orexis* plays an indispensable role in animal locomotion. Also, Aristotle does not enter anymore into the discussion of whether desire should be treated as a distinct part of the soul, which was one of the main concerns in *De An.* III

---

[264] For this use, see, e.g., *Ph.* III 3, 202ᵃ22–4.

[265] On these lines, see also section 11 (ii).

[266] This is how, e.g., Furley 1967, 217–18, seems to read the passage. More recently Moss 2012, 91, quotes the passage as evidence for the claim that Aristotle unequivocally characterizes *phantasia* 'as able to cause action, by inducing *emotions* and desires' (my emphasis).

[267] See also Hankinson 2020, 399.

9–11.[268] Relying on the discussions in *De Anima* and in the ethical writings he just repeats in *MA* 6 that desire comes in three different forms—appetite (*epithumia*), 'spirit' (*thumos*), and wish (*boulēsis*)—and that choice (*prohairesis*) also includes desire as one of its components. The specification of these three forms of desiring raises a couple of serious questions: are they, e.g., individuated in terms of their specific objects or in accordance with the cognitive efforts involved in each of them? In the former case, what are the specific objects of each kind of desire? These questions have been the subject of recent scholarly studies;[269] however the *MA* itself does not answer them directly.

What does come to the fore within the *MA* is the contrast between rational and non-rational desires or, correspondingly, between broad and narrow notions of *orexis*,[270] the first of which is a genus-term and includes all three abovementioned species of desire, while the second is restricted to the species of non-rational desire.[271] In *MA* 7, 701ᵃ35–ᵇ1, Aristotle clearly contrasts cases of acting on non-rational desire with cases of acting on rational desire. The occurrence of the transmitted words *dia orexin ē boulēsin*—'because of desire or wish'—in this context (701ᵇ1) would only make sense if *orexis* was used in the narrow sense of non-rational desire. According to the new textual evidence, there seems to be a better way of reading this line, so that there would be no need to postulate the inconsistency between the generic and the specific use of *orexis*.[272] Still, and irrespective of line 701ᵇ1, one can argue that there are passages that require a narrow reading of *orexis*; for example, when towards the end of the practical syllogism passage Aristotle speaks of desires that 'replace' thought (701a31–2), it seems that '*orexis*' must refer to non-rational desires as opposed to rational ones. In addition to the debate about broad and narrow senses of *orexis*, the discussion of the practical syllogism (see above, section 10) gives rise to the question of whether Aristotle presupposes a distinction between general and specific desires. If the major premise articulates the suitable *type* of action to be done, it seems to go with a general desire for actions of this type, while the minor premise channels this general desire into a desire for some specific available thing. Alternatively, if the major premise articulates a general good-making

---

[268] On this question, see Whiting 2002, Corcilius/Gregoric 2010, Johansen 2012, 47–72 (for the individuation of parts of the soul in general) and 246–51 (for the locomotive capacity in particular).

[269] See most notably Corcilius 2008a, ch. 4, and Pearson 2012, part II—the latter author opts for an individuation of species of *orexis* by the type of desired object, the former emphasizes the different kinds and amounts of cognitive effort characteristic of the different species.

[270] For the philosophical impact of the difference between a broad and a narrow notion of desire, see Pearson 2012, ch. 8.

[271] This claim goes back to Loening 1903, 36, n. 4, who, however, identifies the narrow sense of *orexis* with sensual desiring, i.e. *epithumia*.

[272] The β-branch reads διὰ προαίρεσιν ἢ βούλησιν, thus referring consistently to two ways of rational desiring. This reading is defended in Part II of the introduction to this volume, section 11 (iii). Cooper 2020, n. 34, sticks to the reading of the α-branch.

characteristic, the desire that corresponds to the acceptance of this major premise is on a different level of generality as the desire corresponding to the acceptance of the conclusion, that a particular thing is to be done.

(iii) The Somatic Implementation of Desire

Since in the default case the activity of desire results (not just in a mental state, but) in the motion of bodily limbs and subsequently in the movement of the animal as a whole, the common explanation of animal locomotion must at some point explain how the activity of a psychic capacity is translated into visible bodily movements. And, indeed, the physiological part of *MA* (from chapter 7, 701^{b}2 to chapter 10) seems to tackle this very task. As we have seen (cf. section 5 above), there is room for scholarly disagreement about how to understand the formulation that the soul moves the body or uses the body as an instrument. If we assume, for the time being, that the *MA*'s account of desire has to be read against the background of a hylomorphic theory of the soul and also that, by the same token, all psychic states (with the sole exception of thought), involve certain bodily organs, one can expect that the activation of the psychic capacity to desire similarly involves a certain part or organ of the body. In this context commentators regularly refer to the programmatic claims in *De An.* I 1, where Aristotle points out that affections such as anger, courage, or appetite, though referred to as 'affections *of the soul*', do not belong to the soul exclusively, but rather necessarily involve the body (403^{a}6–8, 16–19).[273] The corresponding definitions of such affections of the soul must thus include a reference to 'a certain mode of movement of such-and-such a body or part of it' (403^{a}27–8)—in the case of anger, e.g., a reference to the boiling of the blood or the warm stuff around the heart (403^{b}1). Does the physiological part of *MA* aim at the formulation of a corresponding definition of the somatic aspect of desire? That certain bodily parts must become involved, at some point, is clear. That the connate *pneuma* plays a crucial role within this story is similarly clear. However, several points remain controversial. For example, is the expanding and contracting *pneuma* mentioned in *MA* 10 meant to play the same role in relation to desire that the boiling blood mentioned in *De An.* I 1 plays in relation to anger, namely materially realizing it? This view stands to reason,[274] most notably because it seems to be implied by the beginning of *MA* 10, where Aristotle says that desire is a moved mover and that in the case of living bodies there must be a body of this sort (703^{a}4–6). Indeed, one could take this to mean that the body functionally corresponding to the role of desire is the same body in which

---

[273] Charles 2009b and 2011 takes this parallel to be crucial for the interpretation of desire.
[274] This is, by and large, already Nussbaum's view (1978, 156–7).

desire is materially realized. If, however, the connate *pneuma* is the bodily instrument of desire that was announced in *De An.* III 10 (and mentioned in the summary of *MA* 10 at 703ᵃ28–9) one might wonder whether we can be sure that the bodily instrument *by which* the animal's movement is accomplished is meant to be the same bodily item *in which* desire is 'materially realized' or to which it stands in a genuinely hylomorphic relation. For, alternatively, one might think that the part of the body in which desire is realized will be warmed or cooled (depending on whether the animal pursues an object or tries to avoid it) and will confer this thermic effect on the connate *pneuma*, which must therefore be distinct from it.²⁷⁵ In this sense one could say that the psycho-physical acts of desiring are not hylomorphically realized in the *pneuma*, but use it as an instrument for transmitting the alterations already given by episodes of, first, perceiving and, then, desiring, to the motion-enabling parts of the animal's body.

Whether or not desire is directly associated with the connate *pneuma*, it seems clear that the discussion of *MA* 7–10 is not at all confined to the identification of the one particular part in which desire is materially realized. The main upshot of these chapters is rather that there is a neatly interlocking *series* of alterations that, starting from sense-perception, *phantasia*, or thought, leads to the movement of the extremities and that this series of alterations again requires an analogous anatomic structure in animals of all kinds. So, even if the connate *pneuma* is the centrepiece of the account of how the soul moves the body through a bodily instrument, it is the integration of the connate *pneuma* into a suitable anatomic structure enabling the described series of alterations, not its identification alone, that provides the sought-after explanation.

13. Self-Movers and Unmoved Movers

(i) Self-Movers

Throughout the *MA* animals are treated as self-movers. In *MA* 1, Aristotle finds it so natural to associate animal locomotion with the general category of things which move themselves by themselves (1, 698ᵃ8) that he feels no need to justify or even comment on his doing so. Animals move themselves by themselves in

---

²⁷⁵ This is considered as a possibility by Charles 2011, 90; he also conjectures that desire should be associated with the blood or the hot stuff mentioned in *De An.* I 1. Corcilius 2008a, 334 sq., denies a direct hylomorphic relation between desire and the connate *pneuma* and emphasizes that the thermic alterations are the direct antecedents of the *pneuma*'s movements; a similar view is expressed in Corcilius/ Gregoric 2013, 65, where desires seem to be *identified* with the *kinēseis* of heating and cooling. For a full discussion, see also Laks 2020, section 4.

respect to place (4, 700ᵃ8; 5, 700ᵃ26). There are things that move themselves by themselves, and animals belong to them (4, 700ᵃ17–18). There is no indication within the *MA* that this claim needs to be restricted or qualified. In accordance with *Phys.* VIII and *Cael.*, Aristotle assumes in the *MA* that the phenomenon of self-movement is not restricted to sublunary animals, but also occurs in the movement of the universe as a whole. This is why, right from the beginning, the treatise of the *MA* appeals to general principles that can be applied to the case of cosmic motion and animal motion alike. Obviously, Aristotle is happy to say that the movement of self-movers depends on certain principles or origins (1, 698ᵃ7–9); more specifically, saying that something is a self-mover is not seen as incompatible with saying that it is moved by an unmoved mover: 'it is the object of desire and the object of discursive thought that primarily cause movement' (6, 700ᵇ23–4). It therefore seems that Aristotle is quite unconcerned that the role of the desired object—say, a carrot that is recognized and desired by a rabbit—could threaten the rabbit's status as a self-mover. After all, or so he might have thought, being moved by a desired object is categorically different from being pushed or kicked away by another external mover. As a rationale for this assumption one might adduce that even if it is the carrot that primarily moves the rabbit, it is not without the rabbit's contribution that the locomotion comes about—on the contrary, the carrot in the role of the unmoved mover requires a specific activity on the animal's side, namely an activity that involves the animal's soul—i.e. that the animal *discerns* and *desires* this particular carrot.

Even if so much is agreed upon, one might wonder what exactly it is that makes the relation between an animal and a desired object so distinctive and what grounds the status of a self-mover as opposed to things that are moved by other kinds of external movers as the result of being pushed, kicked, thrown, etc. Scholars have assumed that this task becomes particularly urgent because of arguments in *Ph.* VIII, where, they thought, Aristotle restricts the animals' status as self-movers on the grounds that they are dependent on certain external factors or stimuli. An intense scholarly debate on this family of questions has been triggered by a seminal article by David Furley deriving from 1978. Furley himself points to the fact that a desired object (*orekton*) cannot be identified as such independently of the psychic capacity to desire, which is not external, but 'inside' the agent.[276] The external object is only a mover, he adds, in that it 'is seen as such' by a faculty of the soul.[277] A collection from the year 1994 puts the questions raised by Furley into a broader context; the contributions highlight, among other things, the role of active capacities, of intentional objects, or of

---

[276] Cf. Furley 1978, 175 (= 1994, 12).
[277] Cf. Furley 1978, 177 (= 1994, 13); on the 'interpretative' reading that seems to result from this rendering, see above section 11 (iii).

goal-directedness.[278] Berryman adds to this discussion the idea that animals are self-movers 'inasmuch as they can initiate local motion in response to other kinds of change'.[279]

(a) Animal self-movers as a threat to eternal motion? The notion of self-motion seems to be a constant challenge to Aristotle, especially since Plato used to characterize the soul as self-mover and made a self-mover the ultimate cause for the movement of the cosmos. In *Ph.* VIII 2 and VIII 6—in particular in the two passages VIII 2, 253^{a}7–12, and VIII 6, 259^{b}1–22—Aristotle faces the question of whether the phenomenon of animal self-movers provide a threat to some of his core tenets, most notably that motion exists eternally and that the first mover of the universe is by necessity unmoved. For, if animals are at rest in one moment and set themselves into motion in the next, even if nothing external made them move, what hinders then that the same happens in the universe as a whole (VIII 2, 252^{b}24–6), i.e. what hinders that from a state of total rest the motion of the universe comes into being spontaneously? A closer analysis of the animal's case quickly reveals that they only *seem* to alternate between total rest and motion, since, among other things, some connatural part within the animal is changing, even if the animal does not locomote, and these changes are not brought about by the animal's own agency, but may be due to the animal's environment. Animals, hence, are self-movers only with respect to locomotion, but not with respect to any kind of change. They do not exemplify, and not surprisingly so, the idea of causally fully autonomous beings and their spatial motions are not instances of change that comes about in a thing without having been in existence at all before.

(b) Restricting the sense of animal self-motion? With this, the threat to Aristotle's cosmological tenets seems to be neutralized, but doesn't the argument leave us with a restricted sense of animal self-motion? After all, in defence of the pre-suppositions of his big cosmological picture, Aristotle had to admit that animal self-movers are in some sense dependent on external factors. Indeed, Aristotle says in the course of his argument that one has to acknowledge that animals move themselves with one kind of motion only and that they do this *ou kuriōs*—i.e. not in the full or proper sense (VIII 6, 259^{b}6–7). One could object that the arguments given only imply that animals as living beings are not causally independent and detached from the environment, but that these arguments are not meant to restrict the sense in which animals spatially move themselves

---

[278] Cf. Gill/Lennox 1994. The contributions to this volume are discussed in Berryman 2002 and in Hankinson 2020, sections 5–7.

[279] Cf. Berryman 2002, 91.

through themselves. Again, it can be argued that the desired object involved in the initiation of locomotion provides an example of an external moving factor, because of which the animal does not qualify as a self-mover in the fullest sense.[280] Against this type of worry, Morison argues convincingly that Aristotle in *Ph.* VIII 2 and 6 does not intend to show that when an animal moves itself the principle of this motion comes from its environment and that hence the self-motion of animals does not become improper because the moving principle derives from outside the animal.[281] But what to make then of Aristotle's claim that animals are self-movers '*ou kuriōs*'? According to Morison the sense in which animals are self-movers is not 'straightforward', because self-movers in general are, according to a theorem from *Ph.* VIII 5, internally divided into a moving and a moved part;[282] this is why the moving part is strictly speaking no self-mover, as it is not itself moved—except accidentally, while the moved part is no self-mover too, because it is no mover at all. This theorem, to be sure, is an important move in Aristotle's argument against the Platonic attempt to make self-movers the ultimate cause of cosmic motion.[283] However, this is also the reason why it is not specific to animal self-movers, while we were looking for possible motives for restricting the sense in which animals are self-movers. Also, what Aristotle actually argues against in *Ph.* VIII 2 and 6 is the idea that animals through being self-movers are causally fully autonomous beings. This latter idea is probably not yet implied by the ordinary (though unrestricted) notion of being a self-mover (in the sense of self-locomotion); thus, what Aristotle rejects is just the fallacious step from calling something a 'self-mover' to thinking that it is a self-reliant being throughout. Maybe, the formulation '*ou kuriōs*' is just meant to deny that animals are self-movers *throughout*, i.e. causally fully autonomous self-movers in the sense that they can bring about motion from within themselves without any pre-existing change.[284]

---

[280] This is what, e.g., Furley 1978, 177 (= 1994, 13), almost literally says (in spite of his notable insights into the difference between other external movers and desired objects, see n. 276 above): 'However, there must be an external object, and hence the movement of an animal does not provide an example of a totally autonomous motion.' A similar claim can be found in Nussbaum 1978, 119.

[281] Cf. Morison 2004.

[282] Cf. Morison 2004, 67–8; indeed, Aristotle appeals to this internal subdivision in the course of the relevant *Ph.* VIII 6 passage (cf. 259^{b}16–20).

[283] For the role of this theorem within the argument of *Ph.* VIII 5–6, see Coope 2015. Coope also points out that this subdivision could turn self-motion into other-motion, unless one comes up with an argument for the unity of the whole consisting of a moving-imparting and a moved part. In the case of animals, she argues, this can be accomplished by the idea that the mover within a self-mover is the form of the self-mover. The account of the *MA* clearly seems to be faithful both to the requirement of an internal subdivision and to the unity requirement, for Aristotle cautiously distinguishes moved and unmoved items within the animal and accommodates the soul as the ultimate unmoved mover.

[284] For an interpretation of the '*ou kuriōs*'-phrase along these lines, see Ferro 2021, ch. 2.

(ii) Unmoved Prerequisites and Unmoved Movers

Within the *MA* the notion of self-movers is inextricably connected with the notion of unmoved movers. The envisaged common cause of self-propelled animal locomotion will have to refer to such unmoved movers. However, in the course of the *MA* Aristotle identifies more than one unmoved factor involved in animal motion.

(a) Joints and platforms as unmoved factors. At the beginning of *MA* 1 the reader is told that self-movers are dependent on an unmoved principle/origin and that the first mover is unmoved.[285] These general statements are immediately applied to the particular case of animals, for it seems to follow that it is impossible for living beings to move, if nothing is at rest.[286] This latter claim is in turn substantiated by the introduction of both internal and external resting points for animals in *MA* 1 and 2. The following chapters *MA* 3 to 5 first explore the implications of this interim result for the movement of the universe as a whole and then try to apply the initial general statements about self-movers and unmoved movers to inanimate beings and to the several types of movement/change (*kinēsis*). Thus, the first step towards formulating the common cause of animal motion seems to be fully governed by the requirement that we identify the unmoved element in each case of self-propelled locomotion. We have good reasons to expect, then, that these unmoved elements are meant to be an important part of the envisaged common cause of animal motion.

(b) The desired object enters the stage. However, from *MA* 6 onwards the pair of the internal joint and the external platform or springboard—which represented the unmoved elements in the first chapters of the treatise—no longer seem to play a crucial role. By contrast, *MA* 6 mentions an altogether different player, namely the *orekton*, the object of desire, as the unmoved mover;[287] the same result is directly confirmed in *MA* 8[288] and indirectly in *MA* 10.[289] We might have reasons, hence, to correct our initial expectation and to take the object of desire—not joints and platforms—to represent the unmoved element within the common account of animal motion.

This weaker emphasis on joints and platforms in the second half of the treatise might be due to the discovery that, although joints and stable platforms belong to the unmoved prerequisites of animal motion and hence provide genuine examples of the general rule that motion requires something that remains at rest, they do not yet qualify as unmoved *movers*.[290] This being said, it should be noted that among the two unmoved prerequisites of *MA* 1–5 the internal resting points receive much more recognition than the external

---

[285] *MA* 1, 698ᵃ7–9.   [286] *MA* 1, 698ᵃ14–15; see Rapp 2020a.   [287] *MA* 6, 700ᵇ24 sqq.
[288] *MA* 8, 701ᵇ33–4.   [289] *MA* 10, 703ᵃ4–5.
[290] This is part of the thesis of Coope and Morison; see n. 13 above.

ones. After all, they are called 'origins' (*archē*) of motion[291] and one part within the joint is acknowledged as a mover of a kind.[292] Also and more importantly, joints are invoked throughout *MA* 8, 9, and 10[293]—not as flesh-and-blood joints (e.g. elbows, knees, hips, shoulders), but as providing a model for a unity that is internally divided, can accommodate moved and unmoved parts, and can be potentially one, while actually two, and vice versa. In this decisive part of the treatise the psychic origin of motion within the animal's body is described in accordance with the model of a joint—the main difference being that the psychic origin is not the endpoint of something else as in the case of ordinary, peripheral joints.[294] This is a respect in which the contribution of *MA* 1–5 to the common cause of animal motion clearly goes beyond the identification of certain necessary prerequisites and also beyond the negative result that these prerequisites (i.e. joints and stable platforms) are not movers in the required sense.

(c) *The soul as unmoved mover.* Still, apart from the observation that *MA* 6–10 offers quite different candidates for the role of the required unmoved element than *MA* 1–5, there is the problem that *MA* 6–10 nominates not only the *orekton*, the desired object, as unmoved mover, but also the soul. This follows from the end of *MA* 9, where Aristotle argues that in the middle of the body there must be something else over and above the origins of the right-hand and left-hand sides of the body, something that imparts movement, while itself being unmoved.[295] This postulated unmoved but motion-imparting entity is then identified with the soul, which is said to reside in the middle of the body, but is different from the extended middle region.[296] It follows that not only the *orekton*, the desired object, but also the soul qualifies as an unmoved mover—though an unmoved mover of an entirely different type. At first glance, this seems to be an unwelcome result, for shouldn't Aristotle (or his interpreters) settle for only one type of unmoved mover? And doesn't the triple scheme of unmoved mover–moved mover–moved object allow for only one item to play the role of the unmoved mover?

Moreover, the claims of both (α) the desired object and (β) the soul to be unmoved movers are well-grounded. (α) That the desired object is an unmoved mover is unequivocally stated in *De An.* III 10, 433[b]15–16, and repeated in *MA* 6 and 8. Also, the analogy to the cosmic case and the unmoved mover of *Physics* VIII

---

[291] *MA* 1, 698[b]1–4.   [292] *MA* 8, 702[a]28–9.

[293] *MA* 8, 702[b]21 sqq., *MA* 9, 702[b]25 sqq., *MA* 10, 703[a]11–14.

[294] *MA* 8, 702[b]6–7. This is, to my mind, also the best explanation of the pervasiveness of the joint *motif* in *De An.* III 10's announcement of the project of the *MA*.

[295] *MA* 9, 702[b]34–5.

[296] *MA* 9, 703[a]1–3. Note that the claim that the soul is unmoved does not at all depend on Jaeger's conjecture (see n. 34 above). The same result is indirectly confirmed by *MA* 10, 703[a]11–14.

and *Metaphysics Λ* requires that the desired object plays a role for the self-moving animal that is analogous to that of the divine eternal mover for the first heaven (and this analogy does matter for the *MA*). Moreover, desire is constantly characterized as the moved mover, and desire can only be said to be moved if it is set into actuality by a desired object. (β) That the soul is a mover in a sense is presupposed by the leading question of *MA* 6–10, namely the question of how the soul moves the body. Also, if the discerning and the desiring capacities are said to move the animal (*MA* 6, 700^{b}17) and if we think of the soul as a structured set of capacities, it follows that the soul that consists of such capacities is a mover too. And that the soul is an *unmoved* mover can be derived from the categorical claim of *De An.* I 4 that the soul cannot be moved except in an accidental sense. Again, a bit more speculatively, one might see an analogy to the cosmic case, for it seems to follow from the *aporiai* in *MA* 3–4 that the movement of the cosmos needs a mover that is by its nature and not just relatively or incidentally unmoved; and in a vaguely similar vein *MA* 9 seems to argue for an origin of movement in the animal that is not relatively or incidentally unmoved in one or the other situation, but is essentially unextended and unmoved—and this is how the soul as a central internal resting point enters the picture. Also, *Ph.* VIII 5 requires that self-movers are internally divided into a moving and a moved part. And for the animal as a whole the role of the internal (unmoved) moving principle can only be played by the soul.

Since both claims—(α) and (β)—make sense and since both (α) and (β) are actually defended by Aristotle in close vicinity, we cannot so easily get rid of one of the two candidates. At this point at least two interpretative moves seem to be available:

(d) *One unmoved mover or two of them?* One move is to say that ultimately there is only one unmoved mover because there is a particularly intimate relation between the desired object and the desiring soul. This strategy could be motivated by the observation that it is not the external object as such—say, the carrot—that is the mover, but the object only insofar as it is desired—e.g. the carrot insofar as it is desired by a rabbit—or even the rabbit's prospect of eating the carrot.[297] Indeed, in a memorable formulation of *De An.* III 10 Aristotle says that the desired object is the first that moves as unmoved 'through being thought of or imagined'.[298] The object, insofar as it is thought of or imagined (or perceived), one could argue, is somehow in the soul or is represented by the soul and is, thus, no longer external and not clearly distinct from the soul. On this account, saying that the desired object is a mover boils down to saying that it is the soul in a certain state that moves—namely the soul that perceives, imagines, or thinks of such an object. One problem of this approach might be

---

[297] For this latter option (with lions and lambs though), see also Meyer 1994, 69.
[298] *De An.* III 10, 433^{b}13–14.

the following. The soul construed as capacity is certainly unmoved, but in the state of mere capacity it is not yet directed at a desirable object (with which the soul, according to this strategy, is supposed to form a unified mover). For the desiring soul to be directed at a particular desirable object certainly means that the capacity to desire gets activated. Now, although the soul as such is unmoved, the activated capacity to desire is certainly not—on the contrary, this is what Aristotle classifies as moved mover.

A variant of this strategy has been defended by Corcilius and Gregoric, who claim that 'the unextended and unmoved internal supporting point of animal motion is the inner representation of the goal of the animal's motion, what the animal "has in mind", as it were, when moving towards a pleasant object it craves for'.[299] However, they do not refer to the soul as an organized set of capacities and not to desire, but—more specifically—to 'the activity of perceiving [...] a pleasant or painful object'. Since for the soul to perceive is not for the soul to undergo motion (even if there is alteration involved), one might say, the perceiving soul is certainly not 'moved' and qualifies thus as an unmoved mover. But does this render the perceiving soul the real unmoved mover (provided that the desiring soul is already moved)? And wouldn't we prefer to say that it is the soul's capacity to desire that moves the body?

The alternative interpretative move consists in just granting that there is more than one unmoved mover.[300] The plurality of unmoved movers is only worrying, one might say, if the several movers are in competition. However, if the several unmoved movers are meant to play complementary roles or if they are supposed to give answers to different questions, the plurality of movers as such is no longer disturbing. For example, claim (*a*) that the desired object is the unmoved mover[301] derives from the kind of discussion that we know from *De An.* III 9–10 and which is repeated in *MA* 6, while claim (*β*), i.e. the characterization of the soul as unmoved origin of movement within the body, essentially belongs to the kind of enquiry that is peculiar to *MA* 7–10 and is part of the answer to the (more specific) question of how the soul moves the body. This is the reason why the thesis that motion within the animal's body originates from an unmoved factor in the middle of the body does not really compete with the claim that the capacity to desire is moved or activated by a desired object that, as an end or goal, imparts movement without being moved. It is also striking that the characterization of the soul's role borrows heavily

---

[299] See Corcilius/Gregoric 2013, 76; indeed, this claim is pivotal for what they call the CIOM ('centralized incoming and outgoing motions') model.

[300] This option is also explored by Hankinson 2020, section 4.

[301] The object of desire and thought is introduced in *MA* 6, 700ᵇ23–4, by the remark that it imparts movement *first*, thus leaving open the possibility that there are other movers, even unmoved ones, that also impart movement though not first.

from the discussion of the joints as internal supporting points and thus assigns to the soul a function within the middle region of the body (which again, by being the origin of movements coming from or going to the two sides of the body, plays the role of a central, ultimate joint)—that is, a function at least analogous to the resting point within a joint. By characterizing the soul as a distinctively internal supporting point, Aristotle even seems to invite the interpretation that, just as on the level of joints and platforms there is a complementary pair of internal and external resting points, there must be an external unmoved mover corresponding to the internal unmoved soul.

Introduction Part II

The Text of De Motu Animalium

OLIVER PRIMAVESI

Recentiores, non deteriores

According to the Philosopher, the bodily instrument by means of which desire produces animal self-motion—a subject central to *MA*—is to be examined within the treatment of the 'activities common to body and soul',[1] i.e. in the first group of his so-called '*Parva Naturalia*' (= *PN1*).[2] Similarly, at the end of *MA* Aristotle combines this treatise with those on Sensation, Sleep, Memory, i.e. with *PN1*,[3] into one set.[4] This authorial assignment of *MA* sheds some light on its position within our Corpus as edited in the first century BC by Andronicus of Rhodes,[5] and as catalogued in later antiquity by Ptolemy-el-Garib in the

---

[1] Aristotle, *De An*. III 10, 433ᵇ13–21: ἐπειδὴ δ' ἐστὶ τρία, ἓν μὲν τὸ κινοῦν, δεύτερον δ' ὧι κινεῖ, τρίτον τὸ κινούμενον, τὸ δὲ κινοῦν διττόν, τὸ μὲν ἀκίνητον, τὸ δὲ κινοῦν καὶ κινούμενον—ἔστι δὲ τὸ μὲν ἀκίνητον τὸ πρακτὸν ἀγαθόν, τὸ δὲ κινοῦν καὶ κινούμενον τὸ ὀρεκτικόν (...), τὸ δὲ κινούμενον τὸ ζῷον· ὧι δὲ κινεῖ ὀργάνωι ἡ ὄρεξις, ἤδη τοῦτο σωματικόν ἐστιν· διὸ ἐν τοῖς κοινοῖς σώματος καὶ ψυχῆς ἔργοις θεωρητέον περὶ αὐτοῦ.

[2] For the bipartition of the *Parva Naturalia* see Rashed 2004, 191: '...on commençera par distinguer dans les *PN* deux sous-ensembles *PN1* et *PN2*, le premier regroupant les traités *Sens.*, *Mem.*, *Somn. Vig.*, *Insomn.*, *Div. Somn.*, et le second les traités *Long.* + *Iuv*.'. The abbreviation '*Iuv*.' here refers to the combination *Iuv.* + *VM* (*De Vita et Morte*) + *Resp.* which is to be regarded as one single treatise, as Ross 1955, 2–3, has shown.

[3] Cf. Aristotle's characterization of the subject matter of this group of writings in *Sens.* 1, 436a6–8: φαίνεται δὲ τὰ μέγιστα, καὶ τὰ κοινὰ καὶ τὰ ἴδια τῶν ζῴων, κοινὰ τῆς τε ψυχῆς ὄντα καὶ τοῦ σώματος. It is hard to believe that the authenticity of *MA* was once denied on the ground that its place in the Corpus is *unclear*; cf. Rose 1854, 163: 'Propterea unus hic liber est cui inter Aristotelis physicos locum suum assignare plane desperes.' For further details, see Part I of this introduction.

[4] *MA* 11, 704ᵇ1–2: ἔτι δὲ καὶ περὶ αἰσθήσεως καὶ ὕπνου καὶ μνήμης καὶ τῆς κοινῆς κινήσεως εἰρήκαμεν τὰς αἰτίας.

[5] Andronicus' edition of a corpus of hitherto partly unknown writings of Aristotle which L. Cornelius Sulla had brought from Athens to Rome in 86 BC is attested by Plu., *Sull.* 26.1–3. For the transmission of the Corpus up to Andronicus' edition, see Primavesi 2007 and Rashed 2021.

third section of his list of Aristotelian works.[6] This section contains, *inter alia*, a group of three books: *On Sense Perception and the Perceived—On Memory and Sleep—On the Movement of Animals*.[7] The first and the third of these books clearly correspond to our *Sens.* and *MA* respectively, whereas the second is likely to be the result of Andronicus' editorial combination of our *Mem./Somn. Vig./Insomn./Div.Somn.* into one book, since none of the four treatises is mentioned elsewhere in this catalogue.[8] So Andronicus' three work titles, when taken together, represent a little corpus mainly consisting of *PN1* but rounded off by *MA*. This corpus has survived into the Byzantine transmission, where *MA* forms part of a series—*Sens./Mem./Somn.Vig./Insomn./Div.Somn./MA*—almost throughout.[9] With regard to textual history, then, *MA* is part and parcel of *PN1*. Furthermore, there is no evidence for there having been a text of *MA* in Hellenistic times other than the one contained in the first-century BC edition of Andronicus (as catalogued by Ptolemy). In particular, *MA* does not belong to those Aristotelian works which had remained accessible after the death of Theophrastus and were already catalogued in the Hellenistic work list preserved by Diogenes Laertius and by Hesychius.[10] Therefore, it seems probable that our transmission goes back to Andronicus' edition alone. Yet inquiring into the relationship that obtains between Andronicus' edition and the Aristotelian materials on which it was based is normally beyond our reach.[11] It follows that the ultimate aim of an edition of *MA* can only be to reconstruct, as far as possible, the text as edited by Andronicus. In order to do so, the editor must acquaint himself not only with the direct tradition—i.e. with the extant

---

[6] On Ptolemy's list of Aristotle's works, which is extant in an Arabic translation only, see Moraux 1951, 287–309, and Goulet 1989; it is translated in Düring 1957, 221–31 (with notes on pp. 241–6), and edited by Hein 1985, 415–39; on the indirect tradition, see further Gutas 1986. For the section corresponding to our Corpus Aristotelicum, see Düring 1957, 224–6, nos 29–56, and Hein 1985, 424–9, nos 29–54. The extent to which the order of writings in Ptolemy's list corresponds to Andronicus' bibliographical introduction to Aristotle's works (to which Ptolemy explicitly refers) or to his edition of Aristotle is a matter of some controversy: for an optimistic assessment, see Moraux 1973, 60–6, for a pessimistic one, 85–94.

[7] Düring 1957, 225, nos 45–7; Hein 1985, 426–7, nos 44–6.

[8] Moraux 1951, 296: 'La dénomination περὶ μνήμης καὶ ὕπνου...résulte de la fusion de plusieurs petits traités, les pièces 2 à 5, des *Parva naturalia*.' This assumption squares well with Porphyry's fundamental account of Andronicus' editorial method; cf. Porph., *Plot.* 24, lines 9–11 Henry/Schwyzer: ὁ δὲ (scil. Ἀνδρόνικος) τὰ Ἀριστοτέλους καὶ Θεοφράστου εἰς πραγματείας διεῖλε, τὰς οἰκείας ὑποθέσεις εἰς ταὐτὸν συναγαγών.

[9] Rashed 2004, 192 : 'Il est au contraire hors de doute que toute la tradition conservée remonte à un exemplaire où *DMA* suivait immédiatement *Div. Somn.*' For further details, see below, section 9.

[10] On the Hellenistic catalogue preserved by Diogenes Laertius and Hesychius, see Moraux 1951, 15–193, 195–209, and 211–47; Düring 1957, 13–79 and 80–93; and Goulet 1989.

[11] Exceptions to this rule are very rare, but the transmitted title of *MA*, Περὶ ζῴων κινήσεως, seems to be an editorial addition of an *incipit* since it is by far too general and clearly derived from the first sentence of the text.

Byzantine copies of the Greek text—but also with the indirect tradition. The latter begins with T. Aurelius Alexander of Aphrodisias (*c.* AD 200):[12] Within the corpus consisting of *PN1* + *MA*, the only treatise on which there is a full commentary by Alexander is *Sens.*,[13] but his own *De Anima* features an extensive treatment of *MA* 7–8 (701ᵇ13–702ᵃ10).[14] In the middle ages, *MA* did not reach the Arabic world as Ibn Rušd tells us,[15] but there are Byzantine commentaries and paraphrases,[16] a Latin paraphrase by Albert the Great,[17] and a Latin translation by William of Moerbeke.[18]

The direct tradition consists of forty-seven Greek manuscripts which transmit either the complete text of *MA* or parts of it[19] and which go back to two late-antique ancestors, **α** and **β**.[20] Neither of them is extant, but both can be reconstructed on the basis of their respective progeny, i.e. of the **α**-branch and of the **β**-branch of our manuscript tradition. The two ancestors, in turn, are shown, by shared significant errors[21]—one of which was still absent from the text used by Alexander (*c.* AD 200)—to go back to two copies made from one

---

[12] The full name of the commentator is transmitted by an inscription from Aphrodisias (Chaniotis 2004) which also shows that the public chair of Aristotelian Philosophy entrusted to him by the Emperor Septimius Severus and his son Caracalla at some point between AD 198 and 209 (Alex. Aphr. *Fat.* 164,3–15 Bruns) was indeed the Athenian one founded in AD 176 by Marcus Aurelius (Philostr. *VS* II 2; II 73,28–31 Kayser).

[13] The commentary was edited by Wendland 1901. On Alexander as a textual witness to *Sens.*, see Bloch 2003.

[14] Identified by Accattino/Donini 1996, 262 (on Alex. Aphr. *De An.* 76,18–78,2 Bruns).

[15] Averroes, *Comm. Magn. in De An.*, 524,59–62 Crawford (= Nicolaus Damascenus, *Compendium*, Test. 11 Drossaart Lulofs): 'Et ipse locutus fuit de hoc in tractatu quem fecit de Motu Animalium, sed iste tractatus non venit ad nos, sed quod transferebatur ad nos fuit modicum de abbreviatione Nicolai.'

[16] Michael of Ephesus (ed. Hayduck 1904), Theodoros Metochites (our knowledge of his paraphrase, which has remained unedited, rests on a collation of ms. Vat. gr. 303), Georgios Pachymeres (*Philosophia*, Cod. Hamilton 512 [= Berol. gr. 408]; autograph), and Gennadios Scholarios (Cod. Vat. gr. 115; autograph).

[17] *De principiis motus processivi*, edited from the Cologne autograph—Köln, Historisches Archiv, Bestand 7010 (Handschriften (Wallraf)), 258A, f. 339v–350v—by Stadler 1909 and by Geyer 1955.

[18] Edited by Geyer 1955 (in an *apparatus specialis* to his text of Albert's paraphrase), Torraca 1958a, and De Leemans 2011a.

[19] Apart from the forty-five manuscripts transmitting the complete text (as correctly listed for the first time by De Leemans 2011a, CLXXIX–CLXXXIV), there is Par. Coisl. 166 which has preserved the original last part (mᴵᴵ.¹) of the *MA* text of Parisinus gr. 1921 (mᴵ + mᴵᴵ.²), and Scor. *Φ*. III. 11 (ff. 177r–179v: Sᶜ) which features *excerpts* from *MA*. All forty-seven *MA* manuscripts are listed in Appendix I to the present introduction.

[20] For the *stemma codicum* of the independent tradition, see below, section 15.

[21] Cf. Trovato 2017, 55: 'The only ones [i.e. the only errors] that really count are those that do not have an intrinsically high probability of occurring independently of the exemplar—that is, errors that are not polygenetic'; 56: 'Only errors of this kind—errors that copyists can reproduce, but that as a rule cannot be made independently by several scribes (monogenetic errors)—should be used for the classification of witnesses.'

and the same model. Therefore, this model is, for us, the 'archetype', i.e. the latest common ancestor of all *extant* manuscripts,[22] whereas the ancestors of the *α*-branch and of the *β*-branch respectively, are our 'hyparchetypes', i.e. the lost manuscripts which were the product of the first ramification of *our* manuscript tradition. Yet the archetype of our direct tradition was just one among the several descendants of Andronicus' text which must have been circulating in antiquity. So in order to reconstruct the text of Andronicus' edition as far as possible, we will have (i) to reconstruct the text of our archetype on the basis of the two hyparchetypes *α* and *β*, and (ii) to identify the small number of obvious errors by which already the text of the archetype was marred and to correct them, as far as possible. Hitherto, however, not even our step (i), i.e. the reconstruction of the archetype of our direct tradition, could be taken, since the *β*-branch had remained unknown to all previous editors of the Greek text of *MA* from Aldo Manuzio's *editio princeps* (AD 1497) onwards, so that their editions were based exclusively on manuscripts transmitting the *α*-text. Werner Jaeger in his 1913 edition correctly divided up the limited number of manuscripts at his disposal among two manuscript families, but he was mistaken in thinking that *these* two families represent the primary ramification of the extant direct tradition as a whole.[23] Rather, the text of *both* of Jaeger's families goes back to our hyparchetype *α*,[24] and the same is true for the more recent edition by Martha Nussbaum (1978), which is to say that until now the serious *α*-errors which are common to both of Jaeger's families[25] could not be corrected by drawing on the *β*-text.

In the present volume, we will submit the first edition of *MA* which is based on a full collation of all extant Greek manuscripts[26] and which accordingly takes into account both branches of the manuscript tradition, *α* and *β*, the latter being preserved in uncontaminated form by two mss. now kept in Berlin and

[22] On the concept of 'archetype', see Emonds 1941, 6, and Trovato 2017, 67, who defines it as a 'lost copy marred at least by one error of the conjunctive type, from which the whole *surviving* tradition derives'. We suggest modifying the definition as follows: 'the *latest* lost copy marred at least by one error of the conjunctive type from which the whole surviving *direct* tradition derives'. On conjunctive errors, see Maas/Flower 1958, 43 (= Maas 1937, 290): 'It can be proved that two witnesses (B and C) belong together as against a third (A) by showing an error common to B and C of such a nature that it is highly improbable that B and C committed it independently of each other. Such errors may be called "conjunctive errors" (*errores coniunctivi*).'

[23] Hence the labelling of the two families as *α* and *β* (Jaeger, Torraca) or as *a* and *b* (Nussbaum), which can no longer be justified.

[24] Except a few *β*-readings which entered the *α*-branch by way of 'contamination'.

[25] For an examination of the four most problematic cases, see below, section 11.

[26] The full collation of all *MA* manuscripts was made possible by the 'Gottfried Wilhelm Leibniz-Programm' of the *Deutsche Forschungsgemeinschaft* and was mainly conducted by Dr Christina Prapa, partly on the basis of the microfilms kept at the *Aristoteles-Archiv* in Berlin, partly on the basis of digital copies, partly *in situ* (especially in Florence). The Codex Parisinus gr. 1853 (E), in particular, was thoroughly examined by Dr Lutz Koch and again by Dr Pantelis Golitsis. We intend to publish an *apparatus lectionum omnium* in a forthcoming *editio maior* of *MA*.

Erlangen respectively, which were both written shortly before the fall of Constantinople in AD 1453.[27] Furthermore, our edition is the first to take into account Alexander's extensive quotations from chapters 7-8 and the two *different* Greek models, both lost, to which De Leemans 2011a has convincingly traced back William's Latin translation. Our new text differs from Martha Nussbaum's 1978 edition in 120 cases,[28] i.e. on average ten times per column of Bekker's 1831 edition; yet this is not due to methodological drawbacks of Nussbaum's editorial choices but rather to the limitations of the evidence at her disposal. Our radical revision of the text has been made both possible and inevitable by the improved picture of the transmission which was gradually achieved by scholars from Jaeger 1913b to Isépy 2016, the decisive turning point being marked by the ground-breaking work of Pieter De Leemans (2011a).

We will now outline this development by taking as our starting point one passage from *MA* 6 which is of key importance for the *stemma codicum* of *MA*. In this passage, Aristotle takes up a theorem from *Metaph.* Λ 7 according to which the first causes of self-motion are the object of desire (*orekton*) and the object of cognition (*noeton*):[29] this theorem is adapted to a general theory of animal self-motion in *MA* 6, 700^b17–25. Now the transmission of this passage features a *significant error*, i.e. an error which yields stemmatic conclusions,[30] since in forty out of forty-five complete *MA* manuscripts the passage is unintelligible due to the omission of four words,[31] whereas the five remaining manuscripts have preserved them. This error is the main piece of evidence for the true division of the *MA* transmission into two branches. First, it is a monogenetic error, not a polygenetic one, which is to say that it is clearly unlikely to have been independently committed more than once;[32] by consequence, it must count as a *conjunctive error*: the forty manuscripts marred by it must go back to a common ancestor which featured it in the first place. Second, it is a *separative error* in that it is altogether unlikely to have been corrected by a Byzantine emendation, so that the five remaining manuscripts must—at least in this passage—be *independent* of all faulty ones.[33]

---

[27] Cod. Berolinensis Phillippicus 1507, 1ˢᵗ part (B^c), and Cod. Erlangensis UB A 4 (E^r). The present writer meticulously sifted through both manuscripts *in situ*.

[28] The 120 divergences are listed in Appendix III to the present introduction.

[29] Cf. *Metaph.* Λ 7, 1072ᵃ26-7: κινεῖ δὲ ὧδε τὸ ὀρεκτὸν καὶ τὸ νοητόν· κινεῖ οὐ κινούμενα.

[30] Cf. Maas/Flower 1958, 42 (= Maas 1937, 289): 'Errors arising in the course of transcription are of decisive significance in the study of the interrelationships of manuscripts…In geology those fossils which are characteristic of certain epochs of the earth's history are denoted in German by the technical term *Leitfossilien* (index fossils); I have similarly employed the term *Leitfehler* (indicative errors, *errores significativi*) for errors which can be utilized to make stemmatic inferences.'

[31] The importance of this omission for the text history of *MA* is similar to the importance of the omission which has impaired the Π branch of Arist., *Po.* in chapter 16, 1455ᵃ14; see further Kassel 1965,VII and 26.

[32] Cf. Trovato 2017, 55-6.

[33] Cf. Maas/Flower 1958, 42 (= Maas 1937, 289): 'We can prove that a witness (B) is independent of another witness (A) by finding in A as against B an error so constituted that our knowledge of the state

1. The Key Passage: *MA* 6, 700ᵇ17–25

Immanuel Bekker, when editing *MA* in 1831,[34] made use of four Greek manuscripts, i.e. the *codex vetustissimus* Parisinus gr. 1853 (E), from the mid-tenth
century,[35] and three manuscripts which postdate the liberation of Constantinople
from Frankish occupation in AD 1261: Vaticanus gr. 1339 (P), Laurentianus Plut.
81.1 (S), and Vaticanus gr. 261 (Y).[36] Generally speaking, Bekker valued the
authority of Parisinus E very highly, but in a few passages he preferred readings
solely transmitted by Vaticanus P.[37] One case in point is an argument from
chapter 6 (700ᵇ17–25). Here Vaticanus P is the only one out of Bekker's four
manuscripts in which the final conclusion (ᵇ23–4) is a syntactically complete
clause, whereas the version offered by the three remaining ones is deficient
with regard both to syntax and meaning:

|17|ὁρῶμεν δὲ τὰ κινοῦντα τὸ ζῷον διάνοιαν καὶ φαντασίαν καὶ|18|προαίρεσιν καὶ βούλησιν καὶ ἐπιθυμίαν·	[1ˢᵗ PREMISS] We see that the things which move animals are discursive thought and imagination and decision and wish and appetite;
ταῦτα δὲ πάντα|19|ἀνάγεται εἰς νοῦν καὶ ὄρεξιν...·	[2ⁿᵈ PREMISS] yet all of these are reduced to thought and desire...;
ὥστε κινεῖ πρῶ-|24|τον τὸ ὀρεκτὸν καὶ τὸ διανοητόν·	[CONCLUSION] from whence it follows that what first imparts movement is the *object* of desire (*orekton*) and the *object* of discursive thought (*dianoeton*);
οὐ πᾶν δὲ διανοητόν,|25|ἀλλὰ τὸ τῶν πρακτῶν τέλος.	[QUALIFICATION] though not just any object of discursive thought, but the goal of what is achievable through action.

ᵇ23–4 ὥστε κινεῖ πρῶτον τὸ ὀρεκτὸν καὶ P Bekker : ὥστε καὶ ESY || ᵇ24 οὐ πᾶν δὲ P : οὐ πᾶν δὲ τὸ
ESY Bekker

of conjectural criticism in the period between A and B enables us to feel confident that it cannot have
been removed by conjecture during that period. Errors of this kind may be called "separative errors"
(*errores separativi*).'

[34] Bekker 1831, col. 698ᵃ1–704ᵇ3.

[35] This manuscript was described in detail by Moraux 1967.

[36] Vaticanus Y was shown to have been copied from Parisinus E by Luna/Segonds 2007, CCXLIV, and
by Isépy 2016, 57–9; therefore, it will not be included in our stemma of the independent transmission
(see below, section 15). Y's superior readings are due to the fact that it was copied (i) by an accomplished
scholar, Georgios Pachymeres, and (ii) after the Parisinus had already been revised by a second hand (E²).

[37] Cf. 698ᵃ26: κινεῖται τῶν μαθηματικῶν οὐδέν P : κινεῖσθαι τῶν μαθηματικῶν οὐδέν ESY.– 700ᵇ35:
εἶναι πρὸς ἕτερον P : εἶναι πρότερον ESY.– 702ᵃ3: τὰ ἄλλα τὰ σωματικὰ λυπηρὰ P : τὰ ἄλλα σωματικὰ
λυπηρὰ ESY.– 702ᵇ29–30: εἰ μέλλει τὸ μὲν κινεῖσθαι τὸ δὲ κινεῖν P : εἰ μέλλει (μέλλοι SY) τὸ μὲν
κινήσεσθαι τὸ δὲ κινεῖν ESY.

According to the P version of 700^{b}23–4, the conclusion would introduce the theorem that animal self-motion is first caused by the *orekton* ('object of desire') and by the *dianoeton* (the object of a cognitive activity apparently identified here with discursive thought—*dianoia*).[38] The authenticity of a theorem of this kind is indeed supported, in substance, by a famous parallel passage from *Metaph. Λ* 7, where Aristotle illustrates the causal role he ascribes to the first unmoved mover of the universe with the general fact that we are moved by the object of desire (*orekton*) and by the object of cognition (*noeton*).[39] It is all the more striking that, according to manuscripts E, Y, and S, Aristotle's conclusion in 700^{b}23–4 would only consist of the four words ὥστε καὶ τὸ διανοητόν ('so that... the object of discursive thought, too'): in this truncated sequence of words both the causation of animal self-motion and the object of desire are missing. No attempt at making sense of this version[40] is likely to yield anything near a satisfactory substitute for the important point made by the P version of our passage. Small wonder, then, that the P version has been admitted to the text not only by Bekker 1831 but also by all subsequent *MA* editors. By contrast, the syntactical ruin transmitted by E, Y, and S goes back, in all probability, to an omission committed by the scribe of a common ancestor of these manuscripts. So it seems that Vaticanus P had access to a source preserving the four indispensable words κινεῖ πρῶτον τὸ ὀρεκτόν, which are missing in E S Y.

2. P's Reading of 700^{b}23–4: A Byzantine Conjecture?

Can we rule out the possibility that the absence of κινεῖ πρῶτον τὸ ὀρεκτόν in E S Y falls short of qualifying as a separative error, after all? Could the presence of these words in the P version of 700^{b}23–4 not be the result of a brilliant emendation by which the scribe of P or of a previous manuscript tried to

---

[38] The position of the *dianoeton* ('object of *discursive* thought') in the present argument remains problematic even on the P-reading; cf. below, section 12.

[39] *Metaph. Λ* 7, 1072^{a}26: κινεῖ δὲ ὧδε τὸ ὀρεκτὸν καὶ τὸ νοητόν (quoted as a parallel already by Farquharson 1912 *ad loc.* n. 2).

[40] The missing predicate would presumably have to be supplied from the preceding sentence ('whereas decision belongs to both discursive thought and desire') in the following way: 'so that the object of discursive thought, too (viz., belongs to both discursive thought and desire)'. But the assumption that *decision* belongs to both discursive thought and desire does not imply that the *object of discursive thought* also belongs to both discursive thought and desire. It seems even unclear what that could mean.

remedy the lacunose version of the passage as it is known to us from E S Y?[41] A problem with this scenario is that the short version lacks the notion both of the first mover and of the object of desire, neither of which would have been suggested as a supplement by the immediate context. It is true that the presence of the *dianoeton* ('object of discursive thought') indicates a transition from faculties of the soul to their objects, but this by itself does not imply that these objects are characterized as the first movers here. And the notion of an 'object of desire' (*orekton*)—for all its undeniable importance—is not explicitly mentioned in any other passage of *MA*. It follows that in order to compose the P version by way of conjecture one would have had to draw on the parallel passage from *Metaph. Λ* 7, already quoted. This use of the *Metaph.* passage *for the purpose of emendation*, however, can be shown to have been beyond the capacities even of the two leading Byzantine interpreters of *MA*, i.e. Michael of Ephesus and Georgios Pachymeres.

Michael of Ephesus wrote his commentary on *MA* soon after AD 1118 for Anna Comnena, the daughter of emperor Alexius Comnenus.[42] In the *MA* manuscript on which he worked the two lines 700^{b}23-4 were obviously as lacunose as in our manuscripts E, Y, and S. Michael assumed that the grammatical subject of the truncated sentence should be just *ti dianoeton* ('some object of discursive thought')—so he replaced *to dianoeton* by the indefinite *ti dianoeton*—and that we should supply *prohaireton* ('object of decision') as a grammatical predicate:

Lacunose version of *MA* 6, 700^{b}23–5	Michael *In MA* 113, 22–6 Hayduck
|23|ἡ δὲ προαίρεσις κοινὸν διανοίας καὶ ὀρέξεως· ὥστε...|24|... καὶ τὸ διανοητόν.	καὶ ἐπεὶ ἡ προαίρεσις κίνησις διανοίας καὶ ὀρέξεως, ἔσται καί τι διανοητὸν προαιρετόν·
οὐ πᾶν δὲ διανοητόν,	οὐ γὰρ πᾶν διανοητόν (τὰ γὰρ μαθήματα διανοητὰ μέν, οὐ προαιρετὰ δέ),
|25|ἀλλὰ τὸ τῶν πρακτῶν τέλος	ἀλλ' ὅσων διανοητῶν ἐστι τὸ τέλος πρακτόν (ὡς ἐπὶ τῶν τεχναστῶν καὶ ἄλλων τινῶν), τούτων καὶ τὸ τέλος προαιρετόν.

---

[41] This question was raised but too quickly dismissed by Nussbaum 1975a, 104–5 (= 1976, 130; cf. 1978, 16): 'The reading of P could not, it seems, be the result of a correction of those mutilated readings; such ingenuity would be astounding.'

[42] Edited by Hayduck 1904, 101–31. Michael's activity as a commentator is put into its historical context by Georgios Tornikes, *Funeral Speech for Anna Comnena*, f. 29v, l. 4–12 (= ed. Darrouzès 1970, 283), as was pointed out by Browning 1962.

Decision is common to both discursive thought and desire, so that . . . the object of discursive thought, too.

Since decision is a movement of discursive thought and desire, *some* object of discursive thought will also be an object of decision.

But not just every object of discursive thought,

For this would not be true of *every* object of discursive thought (for mathematical objects are objects of discursive thought, but not of decision),

but the goal of what is achievable through action.

but for all objects of discursive thought the end of which is an object of a feasible action (as with artefacts and the like), the end is also an object of decision.

Michael has filled the lacuna in 700ᵇ23–4 by anticipating the point which will be made, albeit in a slightly different way, in the following line anyway: '<*some*> object of discursive thought will also be <an object of decision>, for *not every* object of discursive thought will be an object of decision'. Measured against the important point transmitted by the P version of 700ᵇ23–4 this makeshift supplement is altogether unsatisfactory. And yet it has remained the only original attempt at supplementing the truncated version of 700ᵇ23–4: Whenever later scribes and scholars try to rewrite the passage, they make use of Michael's *prohaireton*.[43]

This observation holds good even for the learned Georgios Pachymeres (1242–*c*.1310) who copied and paraphrased the text of *MA*. The *MA* manuscript written by him is Cod. Vaticanus gr. 261 (Y), which is one of the three manuscripts so far considered that have transmitted the truncated version of 700ᵇ23-4. Now in copying several other passages Pachymeres so competently corrected the text offered by his model, Cod. Parisinus E, that scholars have

---

[43] This point was overlooked in a recent treatment of Michael's commentary (Koch 2017, on which see below, section 14).Yet cf. the readings of manuscripts NXHᵃLVᵍ (ἡ δὲ προαίρεσις κοινὸν διανοίας καὶ ὀρέξεως· ὥστε καὶ τὸ προαιρετόν. οὐ πᾶν δὲ τὸ διανοητὸν προαιρετόν), and of ZᵃBᴾMᵒ (ἡ δὲ προαίρεσις κοινὸν διανοίας καὶ ὀρέξεως· ὥστε καὶ τὸ διανοητὸν οὐ πᾶν προαιρετόν). See also Theodoros Metochites, *Paraphrase* (here quoted from the Codex Vaticanus gr. 303, f. 327r, l. 12–15): ὥστε καλῶς εἴρηται τὴν προαίρεσιν κοινὸν εἶναί τι διανοίας καὶ ὀρέξεως ἅ τε μηδετέρου μόνου γε ὄν. καὶ δῆλον γε ἐντεῦθέν φησιν ὡς οὐ πᾶν τὸ διανοητὸν προαιρετὸν ἀλλ' ἐν τούτοις εἴρηται τὸ προαιρετὸν ἐν οἷς ἔστι μόνοις τὸ πρακτόν, and Gennadios Scholarios, *Epitome* (here quoted from the autograph, Codex Vaticanus gr. 115, f. 226r, l. 9–13), who also took over Michael's parenthetical remark on mathematics: ἡ μὲν προαίρεσις κοινόν τι διανοίας καὶ ὀρέξεως· οὐ γὰρ τὸ διανοεῖσθαι ἁπλῶς προαιρεῖσθαί ἐστιν· διανοητὰ γὰρ τὰ μαθηματικὰ

even been tempted to believe, wrongly, that Vaticanus Y does not depend on Parisinus E after all, but on a common ancestor.[44] When it came to copying 700[b]23-4, by contrast, Pachymeres did not conceive of any conjectural emendation, which is all the more significant. In his paraphrase of *MA*,[45] Pachymeres depends on *Michael* in his dealings with the truncated passage.[46] Having quoted verbatim Aristotle's last complete sentence ('Decision is common to both discursive thought and desire')[47] before the textual problems begin, he prefers not to paraphrase the deficient sentence which comes next in his text of Aristotle, but rather Michael's version of it, according to which '*some* object of discursive thought will also be an object of decision'.[48] This seems to be the reason for which, in Pachymeres' next sentence, the causation of movement is said to begin with thought and decision alone,[49] quite unlike the description given by Aristotle himself in *De Anima Γ* 10.[50] Pachymeres might have in mind here that desire in its most specific form is activated only when deliberation has already taken place (*orexis bouleutike*).[51] In order to elucidate the notion of desire in itself, Pachymeres passes on immediately to 700[b]35-701[a]2, where Aristotle describes the middle position of desire between the object of desire and the moved body:

Aristotle, *MA* 6, 700[b]35–701[a]2	Pachymeres, *Philosophia* 8, f. 165v, l. 25–7
|35| τὸ μὲν οὖν πρῶτον οὐ κινούμενον κινεῖ, ἡ δὲ |701[a]1| ὄρεξις καὶ τὸ ὀρεκτικὸν κινούμενον κινεῖ. τὸ δὲ τελευταῖον τῶν |2| κινουμένων οὐκ ἀνάγκη κινεῖν οὐθέν.	ἡ γοῦν ὄρεξις, |26| ἐνεργείᾳ γενομένη ὀρεκτική, ὑπὸ τοῦ ὀρεκτοῦ κινουμένη κινεῖ τὸ |27| ζῷον. τὸ δὲ τελευταῖον τῶν κινουμένων τὸ ζῷον οὐκ ἀνάγκη κινεῖ οὐδέν.

ἀλλ' οὐ προαιρετά. τὰ δὲ πρακτὰ μόνα προαιρετά, τοῦ ὀρεγομένου καὶ κρίσει τινὶ προαιρουμένου· ὥστε καλῶς εἴρηται κοινόν τι εἶναι τὴν προαίρεσιν διανοίας τε καὶ ὀρέξεως, καὶ μηδετέρου μόνου.

[44] Jaeger 1913b, VI: 'Y Vaticanus graecus 261 ... quamvis E codici affinis tamen sui iuris apographon eiusdem stirpis habendus est, a qua E deducitur.' This claim was accepted by Nussbaum 1975a but refuted by Luna/Segonds 2007, CCXLIV; and in greater detail by Isépy 2016, 57–9.

[45] The paraphrase of *MA* by Pachymeres forms part of the eighth book of his summary of the whole of Aristotelian philosophy ('Φιλοσοφία'), the autograph of which has been preserved (Codex Hamilton 512 [= Berolinensis gr. 408]).

[46] Since the eighth book of Pachymeres' *Philosophia* remains unedited, we quote from the Codex Hamilton f. 165v.

[47] *MA* 6, 700[b]23: ἡ δὲ προαίρεσις κοινὸν διανοίας καὶ ὀρέξεως, quoted by Pachymeres, *Philosophia* 8, Codex Hamilton 512, f. 165v, l. 23–4.

[48] Michael 113,23 Hayduck: ἔσται καί τι διανοητὸν προαιρετόν.

[49] Pachymeres, *Philosophia* 8, Codex Hamilton 512 f. 165v, l. 24–5: προηγεῖται γὰρ ἡ περί του συζήτησις καὶ γνῶσις, ἵνα τις ἢ φύγῃ ὡς βλαβερὸν ἢ προέλοιτο ὡς ὠφέλιμον.

[50] *De An.* III 10, 433[a]18–20: τὸ ὀρεκτὸν γὰρ κινεῖ, καὶ διὰ τοῦτο ἡ διάνοια κινεῖ, ὅτι ἀρχὴ αὐτῆς ἐστι τὸ ὀρεκτόν.

[51] Cf. *EE* II 10, 1226[b]19–20: λέγω δὲ βουλευτικὴν (scil. ὄρεξιν) ἧς ἀρχὴ καὶ αἰτία βούλευσίς ἐστι, καὶ ὀρέγεται διὰ τὸ βουλεύσασθαι.

So then the first thing causes movement without itself being moved, but
desire and the faculty of desire cause
movement while being moved.

Desire, i.e. the faculty of desire having
been actualized, is moved by the
object of desire and in turn moves
the animal.

But it is not necessary for the last of
the moved things itself to cause
anything to move.

But it is not necessary for the last of
the moved things itself to cause
anything to move.

Pachymeres correctly spells out Aristotle's abstract reference to the unmoved
mover (700ᵇ35 *to prōton*, 'the first thing') by means of the notion of the *orekton*
'object of desire'. In all probability, he is thinking here of our parallel passage in
Metaph. Λ 7 where the object of desire and the object of cognition are similarly
characterized as unmoved movers.[52] So it seems that thanks to his knowledge
of this passage[53] Pachymeres was able to introduce, in his rendering of 700ᵇ35,
precisely the notion of the object of desire (*orekton*) which his *MA* text was
lacking in 700ᵇ23–4. But as his paraphrase clearly shows, it did not occur to him
to make use of this knowledge in order to *emend* 700ᵇ23–4.

So it seems that even the most competent Byzantine Aristotelians were
unable to restore the original wording of 700ᵇ23–4 or anything near to it by
means of a conjecture. We conclude that the presence of κινεῖ πρῶτον τὸ
ὀρεκτόν in the P version of 700ᵇ23–4 does not go back to a Byzantine emendation, but to a branch of transmission which is independent of manuscripts E S
Y. This result would be quite harmless if the distribution of readings in our
passage were in correspondence with the family division of Bekker's four
manuscripts in general, i.e. if manuscripts E S Y were representing one branch
of the transmission, and P the other. But this is not so, as became clear in 1913
when the next edition of *MA* came out.

3. Jaeger 1913: Two Manuscript Families and One Open Question

Having just obtained his Berlin doctorate (1911), Werner W. Jaeger went off to
Italy in search of manuscripts of Gregory of Nyssa;[54] and during his stay in Italy
he prepared, as a parergon, his Teubner text of *MA*, *IA*, and *Spir.* As far as *MA*

---

[52] Cf. *Metaph.* Λ 7, 1072ᵃ26–7: κινεῖ δὲ ὧδε τὸ ὀρεκτὸν καὶ τὸ νοητόν· κινεῖ οὐ κινούμενα.

[53] See Pachymeres, *Philosophia* 10; 80,3–81,4 Pappa: τόδ' ἐστὶ τὸ ἄριστον καὶ καλὸν καὶ ἐφετόν, πρὸς ὃ
πᾶσα ἔφεσις ἵσταται, ὃ δὴ καὶ κινεῖ τὸν νοῦν ὡς ὀρεκτῶν τὸ ἀκρότατον, ὥσπερ δῆτα τὴν αἴσθησιν τὸ
φαινόμενον ὀρεκτόν, καὶ μὴ μόνον κινεῖ, ἀλλὰ καὶ τελειοῖ.

[54] Jaeger 1913b, III.

was concerned, Jaeger could build on the work of two predecessors who had prepared but not achieved a new edition:[55] Franz Littig (Munich) had re-collated Bekker's four manuscripts and two additional ones,[56] and Ernst Neustadt (Berlin) had checked Bekker's *apparatus criticus* against the original collations by Bekker himself and by Christian August Brandis.[57] Even so, Jaeger based his text of *MA* just on the same four manuscripts as Immanuel Bekker. He soon discovered, however, that these manuscripts are to be divided into two families and that Michael's commentary presupposes a text belonging with the second of those families:[58]

1st family	*2nd family*
Parisinus E	Michael of Ephesus
Vaticanus Y	Laurentianus S
	Vaticanus P

Jaeger assigned Vaticanus P to the second family which is to say that he regarded a number of readings shared by P and S (and Michael) as conjunctive errors;[59] and this is quite plausible as far as it goes. Yet we have already seen that only P among Bekker's four manuscripts has preserved the four words κινεῖ πρῶτον τὸ ὀρεκτὸν in 700^{b}23–4, whereas these words are absent both in the remaining three manuscripts E, Y, and S, and in the lost manuscript used by Michael, and we have also seen that the four words in question are rather unlikely to have been found by way of conjecture. On the other hand, the omission of text will certainly not have occurred twice, i.e. both in the remaining members of the second family and, independently, in the first family. It follows that the transmission of 700^{b}23–4 cannot be reconciled with P's assignment to Jaeger's second family except under the following condition: In copying 700^{b}23–4 the scribe of P must have had recourse to an additional source which offered the four words missing in his first model. This would have to be classified as a case of 'extra-archetypal' contamination,[60] since the ultimate source of all manuscripts

---

[55] Jaeger 1913b, III with n. 1.   [56] Vat. gr. 253 (L) and Vat. Pal. gr. 163 (V^q).

[57] On these sources, see further Torstrik 1857 and 1858.

[58] Jaeger 1913b, IV: 'Libelli codices vel obiter examinanti duo classes librorum mss. occurrunt, quarum una α codicibus E et Y, altera β P et S continetur'; V: '. . . eadem huic [scil. Michaeli Ephesio] est condicio textus atque memoriae quae classi β.' See for example: 699^{a}13 θέλει PS Mich.^{l} 107,8 (Jaeger) : τε δεῖ EY.– 699^{b}19 ἀδύνατον φαμὲν εἶναι EY (Jaeger) : εἶναι om. PS.– 700^{b}28–9 ἀγαθοῦ – ἀγαθόν PS (Jaeger) : om. EY.– 701^{b}4 ὅπερ EY Mich.^{c} (Jaeger) : ὥσπερ PS.– 701^{b}15 πάλιν συστελλομένων διὰ PS Mich.^{p} : πνεῦμα καὶ EY.

[59] See for example: 699^{b}2–3 οὐδὲν μᾶλλον ἀντερείδειν δεῖ EY (Jaeger) : οὐδὲν μᾶλλον ἀντερείδειν PS.– 699^{b}19 ἀδύνατον φαμὲν εἶναι EY (Jaeger) : εἶναι om. PS.– 701^{b}4 ὅπερ EY Mich.^{c} (Jaeger) : ὥσπερ PS.– 703^{b}15–16 καὶ αἱ ἐντὸς EY (Jaeger) : καὶ ἐντὸς PS.

[60] Cf. Trovato 2017, 134: 'If . . . a ms. that descends to some extent from a known exemplar contains high-quality variants not found in any known ms. or subfamily, we shall need to assume that "extra-stemmatic" (Timpanaro) or rather "extra-archetypal" contamination has occurred.'

known to Jaeger—i.e. his archetype—had, of course, to be reconstructed on the basis of his two families, and the archetype so reconstructed *did* feature the omission of text in 700^b23–4. Jaeger, however, did not reconsider the peculiar distribution of variants in 700^b23–4 in light of his family division, or else he would have used *this* passage as evidence for the particular importance of Vaticanus P, rather than the supposed twelfth-century date of this manuscript or the similarity between P and Michael's text.[61] Thus, Jaeger failed to see that his own family division, when taken in conjunction with the transmission of 700^b23–4, clearly implies that P must have had access to an independent source. A possible reason for this oversight seems to be the fact that both Bekker and Jaeger himself employed the 'negative' form of the *apparatus criticus*, in which only the readings *rejected* by the editor and their manuscript sources are indicated, and not also, as is customary in a 'positive' apparatus, the manuscript source or sources of the readings which the editor has accepted. In his apparatus to lines 700^b23–4, for instance, Bekker states that a truncated version of these lines (*ὥστε καὶ τὸ διανοητόν*) is transmitted by E, S, and Y, but he does not spell out the implication that the full version which he has printed in his text (*ὥστε κινεῖ πρῶτον τὸ ὀρεκτὸν καὶ τὸ διανοητόν*) is transmitted by the only remaining one among his four manuscripts, i.e. by Vaticanus P: this fact has to be deduced by the reader himself and may thus be overlooked.[62] It is true that Jaeger inspected further *MA* manuscripts in Rome—and perhaps also in Venice and Florence—in search of independent evidence, but in hindsight these inquiries were doomed to failure since all twenty-six *MA* manuscripts kept in Italy[63] are now known to go back to the first hyparchetype, i.e. to the one that omitted the four words in 700^b23-4. Furthermore, Vaticanus P is the only manuscript in which this omission has been corrected from a second source. Quite understandably, Jaeger formed the erroneous opinion that Bekker's four manuscripts provide a sufficient basis for constituting the text.[64] Jaeger would probably have assessed

[61] Jaeger 1913b, VII: 'P Vaticanus graecus 1339 . . . pro sua cum M necessitudine et aetate pluris quam apud Dittmeyerum aestimabitur.'

[62] The same is true of Jaeger's apparatus *ad loc.* (Jaeger 1913b, 10): '23 *ὥστε* - 24 *οὐ*: *ὥστε καὶ τὸ διανοητόν* ESY.'

[63] *Florence*: Laurentiani Plut. 81.1 (S), Plut. 87.4 (C^a), Plut. 87.11 (F^d), Plut. 87.21 (Z^a). Riccardiani 14 (F^s), 81 (F^r).- *Milan*: Ambrosiani A 174 sup. (M^i), H 50 sup. (X).- *Modena*: Estensis gr. 76 (M^d).- *Naples*: BN III D 2 (gr. 286 bis) (N^e).- *Rome*: Vaticani gr. 253 (L), 258 (N), 259 (G^r), 261 (Y), 266 (V), 1339 (P), 1950 (V^g). Vaticani Palatini gr. 97 (V^p), 163 (V^q). Vaticanus Urbinas gr. 41 (V^u).- *Udine*: B. arcivesc. 1 (olim VI. I) 254 (U^t).- *Venice*: Marciani gr. 200 (Q), 206 (f), 209 (O^d), 212 (G^a), 214 (H^a). We have adopted the sigla employed by Bekker 1831 and by De Leemans 2011a respectively.

[64] Jaeger 1913b, III-IV: 'relegi Romanos codices omnes librorum *περὶ κινήσεως ζῴων*; *περὶ πνεύματος* et *περὶ πορείας ζῴων* de integro contuli, item codices Marcianos et Laurentianos, quorum post mentio erit. etiam alios codices non paucos adhibui partim ipse quos inspicere potui partim photographice depictos, quorum te vexare numeris nolo, postquam abiciendam esse totam turbam et in Bekkeri libris acquiescendum cognovi.' Jaeger's Latin is not at its best here (it is tempting to delete the plural 'librorum'

the transmission of *MA* more adequately if he had not prepared his Teubner text in Italy but rather stayed in Berlin. For in this case, he would almost certainly have had a look at Cod. Berolinensis Phillippicus 1507, a manuscript forming part of the famous *Bibliotheca Meermaniana* which had been acquired, thanks to the good offices of Theodor Mommsen, by the Royal Library of Berlin in 1889.[65] The manuscript in question is the only Berlin manuscript to contain the Greek text of *MA*, and it contains it even twice, as Studemund and Cohn had emphasized in their 1890 catalogue of the Greek *Codices Meermaniani*.[66] Now the first of these two Berlin *MA* copies (= B^e) shares with Vaticanus P the authentic wording of lines 700^b23-4.[67] What is more: B^e is, unlike P, independent of Jaeger's two families throughout, as we will see in due course. Jaeger, however, restricted his efforts to Italian libraries.

4. Torraca 1958: William of Moerbeke and Cod. Vaticanus P

The next editor of *MA* who did independent work on the textual tradition was Luigi Torraca. In his 1958 edition of *MA* he made known the variants of a Milan manuscript (Ambrosianus H 55 sup. = X) which represented a new subgroup of Jaeger's second family[68] the ancestor of which had tried to remedy the lacuna shared by Jaeger's two families in 700^b23-4 on the basis of Michael's paraphrase.[69] A far more interesting observation, however, was made by Torraca when he studied the mediaeval Latin translation of *MA* by William of Moerbeke (c. AD 1261)[70] which Arthur Farquharson had drawn attention to in 1912.[71] In

---

before '*περὶ κινήσεως ζῴων·*' and to insert it before '*περὶ πνεύματος* et *περὶ πορείας ζῴων*'), but even so the expression 'Romanos codices omnes' clearly includes the Vatican manuscripts of *MA*, whereas the following remarks on manuscripts kept elsewhere seem to be restricted to *IA* and *Spir*.

[65] Cf. Rebenich/Franke 2012, 252, n. 663 to letter 146; and 258 (letter 152 with note 689). See also Rose 1893, Preface: 'da erfolgte (im Sommer 1887) aus Sir Thomas Phillipps Schätzen (ursprünglich in Middlehill, jetzt in Cheltenham) die Erwerbung des einzigen gleichmässig wertvollen ihrer geschlossenen grösseren Teile, der Bibliotheca Meermanniana, für Berlin—621 Hss. Zunächst vorläufig in der Kgl. Bibliothek aufbewahrt, wurde sie der Handschriften-Sammlung endgiltig einverleibt Ostern 1889.'

[66] Studemund/Cohn 1890, 44 (No. 103).

[67] This important fact was first noted by De Leemans 2011a, CLXXXIX. For further details, see below, section 8.

[68] Nussbaum 1975a: b_2; our stemma: θ.

[69] This sub-group is characterized by the fact that in 700^b23-4 the defective expression *ὥστε καὶ τὸ διανοητόν* has been replaced by *ὥστε καὶ τὸ προαιρετόν* under the influence of Michael's paraphrase.

[70] On the ascription of the translation to William, see De Leemans 2011a, XXV.

[71] Farquharson 1912, v: 'I have noted some readings from an *antiqua uersio*...(Ball. Coll. MS CCL) of the late XIIIth century. I refer to it as *Γ*.' His Balliol manuscript is listed by De Leemans 2011a, p. XXXV as No. 81a (*Ob*).

the meantime, William's translation had been edited by Bernhard Geyer in 1955,[72] but since this edition had remained unknown to Torraca, he provided yet another one as an appendix to his text of *MA*.[73] Adding the Ambrosianus X and William's translation (or rather its Greek model Γ) to Jaeger's second family,[74] Torraca arrived at the following enlarged picture of the tradition:

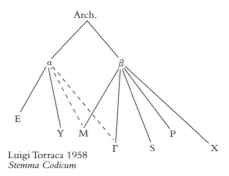

Luigi Torraca 1958
Stemma Codicum

Generally speaking, the assignment of William's translation (or rather of its Greek model) to Jaeger's second family was supported by significant conjunctive errors, but it did not account for a fundamental fact first observed by Torraca himself. In 700ᵇ23-24 William translates:[75]

> Quare *movet primum quod appetibile* et quod intellectuale,

which obviously corresponds to the full version transmitted by Vaticanus P:

> ὥστε κινεῖ πρῶτον τὸ ὀρεκτὸν καὶ τὸ διανοητόν
> ('so that the first mover is the object of desire and the object of discursive thought').[76]

---

[72] Geyer 1955 equipped his edition of the *MA* paraphrase by Albert the Great with an *apparatus specialis* containing the text of William's translation; see Geyer 1955, XXV and 48–55, 57–8, 60, 62–70. His text of William's translation is based on four manuscripts: *Erlangen*: Universitätsbibliothek 199 (= De Leemans 2011a, XXXIII No. 43).– *Mainz*: Stadtbibliothek II, 194 (= De Leemans 2011a, XXXIV No. 68).– *Munich*: Staatsbibliothek Clm. 162 (= De Leemans 2011a, XXXIV No. 69 [*Je*]).– *Schaffhausen*: Eisenbibliothek AG 20 (= De Leemans 2011a, XXXVII No. 123 [*Xe*]).

[73] Torraca 1958a, 51–63; cf. De Leemans 2011a, XXI–XXII. Torraca used two manuscripts: *Oxford*: Balliol 250 (= De Leemans 2011a, XXXV No. 81a [*Ob*]).– *Rome*: Vat. lat. 2083 (= De Leemans 2011a, XXXIX No. 148 [*Uv*]).

[74] Torraca 1958a, 8: 'Le lezioni di Guglielmo di Moerbeke si accordano quasi sempre con quelle dei testimoni di β.'

[75] Geyer 1955, 57, 66–7, Torraca 1958a, 58, 8–9.

[76] This correspondence was duly registered by Torraca 1958a, 8, whereas it had not been noticed by Farquharson 1912. In his note to 700ᵇ35, however, Farquharson had pointed out a similar correspondence between a P reading accepted by Bekker (πρὸς ἕτερον P : πρότερον ESY) and William's translation (*ad alterum*).

But Torraca did not put his observation to adequate use. Having overlooked that in 700^{b}23-4 Vaticanus P is independent of Jaeger's two families in the first place, Torraca also failed to see the impact of the agreement between P and William in that passage, although he accepts readings known to him only from P and William in two further significant passages.[77] Thus, he presented the agreement as part of his evidence for affiliating William to Jaeger's second family,[78] whereas in fact this piece of evidence clearly shows that in 700^{b}23-4 William of Moerbeke joins Vaticanus P in having recourse to an independent additional source.[79]

The failure of scholars to see the special position of Vaticanus P in 700^{b}23-4 soon led to a disturbing consequence. Elpidio Mioni observed, correctly, that a Venice manuscript of *MA* (Marc. gr. 214 = H^a) sides with Jaeger's second family against the first one[80] and that it is older than Vaticanus P. He claimed, wrongly, that P *depends* on H^a, and accordingly suggested replacing P with H^a in future editions of *MA*:[81] Mioni did not realize that this bold step would eliminate the only Greek witness then known to offer the correct version of 700^{b}23-4. It is very much to Torraca's credit that he immediately refuted Mioni's suggestion in his second thoughts about the text of *MA*:[82] On the basis of a collation of

---

[77] 701^{b}35 πρὸς ἕτερον P Γ (Bekker Torraca) : πρότερον EY SX.– 702^{a}29 κινεῖ καὶ κινεῖται Γ (Torraca) vel κινεῖται καὶ κινεῖ P : κινεῖται EY SX Mich.

[78] Torraca 1958a, 8.

[79] In 698^{b}25, Torraca replaced the reading Τιτυός (τητυὸς E) of our Greek manuscripts, i.e. the name of a giant, by Κίρκιος, i.e. a distinctively *Latin* name of a wind, and he did so only on the basis of William's *Circius*. This change is obviously very unconvincing (see further Isépy 2016, 100–5). In 703^{a}22–3, by contrast, William's *tractiva* may well go back to a sensible conjecture made in William's Greek model, and a case could be made for accepting, with Torraca, Farquharson's suggestion to emend the βιαστικὴ transmitted by the Greek manuscripts to ἑλκτικὴ on the basis of William's translation. This emendation, however, leaves still unexplained how the reading of the Greek manuscripts came to be in the first place. Both for this reason and with regard to the context we will rather suggest emending βιαστικὴ to βίαι <ἑλκ>τικὴ.

[80] Cf. 699^{a}13 τε δεῖ EY (Bekker) : θέλει H^a PS Mich.^{i} 107,8 (Jaeger).– 699^{a}30 συμβαίνοι EY (Bekker) : συμβαίνῃ H^a PS (Jaeger).– 701^{b}15 πνεῦμα καὶ EY : πάλιν συστελλομένων διὰ H^a PS Mich.^{p} (Bekker, Jaeger).

[81] Mioni 1958, 59: '3. Codex H^a apographon eiusdem stirpis codicis P primo attutu videtur; sed si aetatem et lectiones et lacunas aliquot accurate perspexerimus, statim P, mendis multis et coniecturis deformatum, ab ipso H^a exaratum esse persuasum nobis erit... Igitur in editione critica, P eiecto, H^a constituendus est.'

[82] Torraca 1959 tried to defend himself against the merciless review of his 1958 edition by Franceschini 1958, who criticized, in particular, that Torraca had based his text of William's translation on only two manuscripts—Oxon. Balliol 250 (= De Leemans No. 81a [*Ob*]) and Vat. lat. 2083 (= De Leemans No. 148 [*Uv*]). So Torraca 1959, 15–26, provided a collation of eight further manuscripts: *Bologna*: coll. Hispan. 162 (Z, = De Leemans No. 12).- *Cesena*: Malatestani VII sin. 1 (T, = De Leemans No. 17 [*Mh*]), VII sin. 4 (M, = De Leemans No. 19 [*Ce*]), XXII dextr. 1 (A, = De Leemans No. 20 [*Ug*]), XXIV sin. 4 (L, = De Leemans No. 21 [*De*]).- *Florence*: Laur. Ashburnham 1674 (H, = De Leemans No. 46 [*Xa*]).- *Naples*: Bibl. nat. VIII E 24 (N, = De Leemans No. 75 [*Nm*]).- *Rome*: Vat. Borgh. 134 (G, = De Leemans No. 138 [*Bv*]).

Marcianus H^a,[83] he was able to show that this manuscript, while belonging to the same sub-group of Jaeger's second family as Ambrosianus X,[84] is inferior to X because of its additional errors,[85] and that it was certainly not used as a model by the scribe of Vaticanus P.[86] Part of the evidence used by Torraca to prove that Vaticanus P does not depend on Marcianus H^a is our passage 700^{b}23-4: The four words preserved by P ($\kappa\iota\nu\epsilon\hat{\iota}$ $\pi\rho\hat{\omega}\tau o\nu$ $\tau\grave{o}$ $\grave{o}\rho\epsilon\kappa\tau\grave{o}\nu$) are missing in H^a, too.[87]

Torraca's work—for all its notorious shortcomings—has contributed to the research on the transmission of *MA* in important ways. He was the first to attach the name of Vaticanus P explicitly to the restoration of $\kappa\iota\nu\epsilon\hat{\iota}$ $\pi\rho\hat{\omega}\tau o\nu$ $\tau\grave{o}$ $\grave{o}\rho\epsilon\kappa\tau\grave{o}\nu$ in 700^{b}23-4[88] and to point out that William's translation agrees with that reading; and he has enriched Jaeger's second family by adding a sub-group (Ambrosianus X and, eventually, Marcianus H^a) which features an emendation of the lacuna in 700^{b}23-4 based on Michael's paraphrase. The general result was that the difference which obtains in 700^{b}23-4 between Vaticanus P and William on the one hand and the remaining Greek manuscripts on the other had become much more obvious. Unfortunately, Torraca did not inquire into the *source* of P's and William's version of 700^{b}23-4.

5. Wartelle 1963: The First List of *MA* Manuscripts

A new basis for such inquiries became available in 1963 when André Wartelle published his *Inventaire des manuscrits grecs d'Aristote et de ses Commentateurs*.[89] This inventory is based on all *catalogues* of manuscript collections accessible in Paris, and it is equipped with an 'Index Aristotelis operum' which indicates for every treatise of the Corpus Aristotelicum the manuscripts containing it.[90]

---

[83] Torraca 1959, 8–11.

[84] Torraca 1959, 12: 'Con H^a è strettamente imparentato X.' Torraca does not actually argue for this proximity between X and H^a, but it is best illustrated by the fact that in both manuscripts the incomplete version of 700^{b}23-4 ($\H{\omega}\sigma\tau\epsilon$ $\kappa\alpha\grave{\iota}$ $\tau\grave{o}$ $\delta\iota\alpha\nu o\eta\tau\acute{o}\nu$) has been changed to $\H{\omega}\sigma\tau\epsilon$ $\kappa\alpha\grave{\iota}$ $\tau\grave{o}$ $\pi\rho o\alpha\iota\rho\epsilon\tau\acute{o}\nu$ under the influence of Michael's paraphrase.

[85] Torraca 1959, 12: 'X, quindi, discende da un esemplare perduto della stessa stirpe di H^a ed ha conservato la tradizione più fedelmente di H^a.'

[86] Torraca 1959, 11–12.

[87] Torraca 1959, 12: '700 b 23 sq. (29) $\H{\omega}\sigma\tau\epsilon$ $\kappa\alpha\grave{\iota}$ $\tau\grave{o}$ $\pi\rho o\alpha\iota\rho\epsilon\tau\grave{o}\nu$ $o\mathring{\upsilon}$ H^a : $\H{\omega}\sigma\tau\epsilon$ $\kappa\iota\nu\epsilon\hat{\iota}$ $\pi\rho\hat{\omega}\tau o\nu$ $\tau\grave{o}$ $\grave{o}\rho\epsilon\kappa\tau\grave{o}\nu$ $\kappa\alpha\grave{\iota}$ $\tau\grave{o}$ $\delta\iota\alpha\nu o\eta\tau\acute{o}\nu$. $o\mathring{\upsilon}$ P.'

[88] See Torraca 1958a, 8 (on the agreement of William with P), 18 (apparatus to line 29); Torraca 1959, 12 (on P's being independent of H^a).

[89] Wartelle 1963. For corrections and additions, see Harlfinger/Wiesner 1964 and Argyropoulos/Caras 1980.

[90] Wartelle 1963, 173–82.

Wartelle's pioneering compilation must still be the starting point for every Aristotelian editor, since the far more ambitious *Aristoteles Graecus*—being based not on catalogues of manuscripts but on autopsy of the manuscripts themselves and/or of microfilms thereof—has remained incomplete.[91] For the *MA*, Wartelle's 'Index' yields the following forty-seven items:[92]

2 (Alexandrinus B. Patr. 87), **306** (Berolinensis Phillippicus 1507),[93] **441** (Scorialensis B. T. *II*. 13), **537** (Laurentianus Plut. 81.1), **581** (Laurentianus Plut. 87. 2), **583** (Laurentianus Plut. 87.4), **589** (Laurentianus Plut. 87.11), **599** (Laurentianus Plut. 87.21), **631** (Riccardianus 14), **643** (Riccardianus 81), **862** (Matritensis BN N 26 (4563)), **905** (Ambrosianus A 174 sup.), **946** (Ambrosianus H 50 sup.), **1038** (Mutinensis B. Estense 76), **1089** (Mosquensis GIM Sinod. 240 (Vlad. 453)), **1169** (Neapolitanus BN III D 2 (gr. 286 bis)), **1208** (Yalensis Beinecke MS 234), **1264** (Bodleianus Canonicianus 107), **1289** (Oxoniensis N.C. 226), **1338** (Parisinus gr. 1853), **1344** (Parisinus gr. 1859), **1346** (Parisinus gr. 1861), **1407** (Parisinus gr. 1921), **1458** (Parisinus gr. 2027), **1466** (Parisinus gr. 2035), **1558** (Parisinus Coislinianus 166), **1589** (Parisinus Suppl. gr. 333), **1700** (Vaticanus gr. 253), **1705** (Vaticanus gr. 258), **1706** (Vaticanus gr. 259), **1708** (Vaticanus gr. 261), **1713** (Vaticanus gr. 266), **1782** (Vaticanus gr. 1339), **1931** (Vaticanus Palatinus gr. 97), **1940** (Vaticanus Palatinus gr. 163), **1970** (Vaticanus Reginensis gr. 118), **1989** (Vaticanus Urbinas gr. 39), **1991** (Vaticanus Urbinas gr. 41), **2094** (Utinensis B. arcivescov. 1, 254), **2101** (Marcianus gr. 200), **2107** (Marcianus gr. 206), **2110** (Marcianus gr. 209), **2113** (Marcianus gr. 212), **2115** (Marcianus gr. 214), **2187** (Vindobonensis phil. gr. 64), **2200** (Vindobonensis phil. gr. 134), **2207** (Vindobonensis phil. gr. 157).

Since 1963, four items of Wartelle's list had to be removed since they are either printed books[94] or do not contain *MA*;[95] three items, in turn, could be added

---

[91] Only the first volume of the *Aristoteles Graecus*, which covers the libraries from Alexandria to London, has been published (Moraux et al. 1976).

[92] Wartelle 1963, 178. Wartelle gives only the relevant numbers of his 'inventaire'; we have added (in brackets) the relevant ms.-signatures which we have taken over (with modifications) from the main part of the 'inventaire'.

[93] No. **306** = Berolinensis Phillippicus 1507 contains *two* copies of *MA*, as was correctly noted by Studemund/Cohn 1890, 44 (no. 103), and Wartelle 1963, 19–20.

[94] Wartelle no. **581** = Laur. 87. 2 (the relevant volume of the Aldine edition [AD 1497] which Wartelle 1963, 40, had himself already classified as a printed book; cf. Harlfinger 1971, 102).

[95] No. **1208** = Yalensis Beinecke MS 234 (contains *IA* instead of *MA*; see Shailor 1984, 338–41).– No. **1970** = Vat. Regin. gr. 118 (does not contain the text of *MA*, but only the relevant ὑπομνήματα of Metochites; see Stevenson 1888, 85).– No. **1989** = Vat. Urb. 39 (contains *IA* instead of *MA*; see Harlfinger 1971, 240–2).

which Wartelle did not recognize as *MA* manuscripts[96] or which are not listed in his *Inventaire* at all.[97] Among the items overlooked by Wartelle there is one *MA* manuscript of key importance for the history of the transmission and for the constitution of the text: the Erlangensis UB A 4.[98]

6. Louis 1973: An Intuition—but No Evidence

The first editor of *MA* who had Wartelle's *Inventaire* at his disposal was Pierre Louis, whose *Budé* text of *IA* and *MA* came out in 1973. In his introduction to *MA,* Louis prints a slightly revised version of Wartelle's list of *MA* manuscripts;[99] in doing so, he repeats Wartelle's errors except the obvious one[100] and adds a new one.[101] A more serious drawback is that Louis does not make any *use* of his manuscript list at all, neither in respect of the history of the transmission nor with regard to the constitution of the text.[102] It is true that Louis stands in defence of Vaticanus P against Mioni's preposterous suggestion to eliminate it; and in doing so he makes an observation of fundamental importance, although he presents it as 'just an impression': *the scribe of Vaticanus P did not just copy his*

---

[96] Wartelle No. **426** = Erlangen UB A 4 (contains *MA* instead of *IA*; see Harlfinger/Wiesner 1964, 252).– No. **457** = Scor. Φ. III. 11 (ff. 177r–179v contain excerpts from *MA*; see Moraux et al. 1976, 169).

[97] One manuscript containing *MA*, the Vat. gr. 1950, is missing from Wartelle's inventaire altogether (see Argyropoulos/Caras 1980, 44, No. *344).

[98] Cf. Irmischer 1852, 16, No. 89/7; Harlfinger/Wiesner 1964, 252; Moraux et al. 1976, 136–9; Thurn 1980, 24–8. For an up-to-date list of the forty-seven *MA* manuscripts, see Appendix I to the present introduction.

[99] Louis 1973, 46-8. The fact that his list depends entirely on Wartelle 1963, 178 is not immediately obvious since Louis replaced Wartelle's geographical arrangement of the manuscripts by a chronological one.

[100] Louis 1973 justly removed Wartelle's no. 581, i.e. the Aldine edition, but he kept in his list all three manuscripts listed by Wartelle which in fact do not contain *MA*: Yalensis Beinecke MS 234 (Louis no. 15); Vat. Urb. gr. 39 (Louis no. 37); Vat. Regin. gr. 118 (Louis no. 42). On the other hand, Louis failed to add any of the three items missing in Wartelle 1963, not even the important cod. Erlangensis UB A 4 the omission of which by Wartelle had already been pointed out by Harlfinger/Wiesner 1964, 252.

[101] Louis 1973, 46 n. 1, removed Par. Coisl. 166 (Wartelle No. 1558) on the ground that it contains just 'les dernières lignes du traité'. But in fact Coisl. 166 contains the last part of *MA* from chapter 9, 702b27 (θατέρου ἠρεμοῦντος), to the end, and this considerable *MA* fragment originally formed part of the *MA* text of Parisinus gr. 1921 (Bekker: m) as was pointed out by Wiesner 1981, 235: The scribe of m, Malachias, first copied the complete text of *MA*, but then replaced the *final part* of his copy—(our siglum: m[II.1])—by a revised copy of it (our siglum: m[II.2]), whereas he left untouched the preceding *main part* of his copy (our siglum: m[I]). Now his original copy of the final part—i.e. m[II.1]—was not discarded but made its way into Coisl. 166, which should, accordingly, be treated as part and parcel of Par. 1921.

[102] Cf. the apposite quotation in Kassel 1971, 102, n. 11: 'Übrigens hat noch im Jahre 1956 ein Aristoteleseditor folgenden Programmsatz zu Papier gebracht: "*J'ai gardé le texte de la vulgate, sauf lorsque l'autorité des manuscrits s'y opposait absolument*" (Aristote, Les parties des animaux, texte établi et traduit par Pierre Louis, Paris, les Belles Lettres, 1956, XL[1]).'

main model, but had recourse to another manuscript, too.[103] But neither does Louis tell his readers on which evidence this impression is based nor does he consider the possibility that the additional manuscript or a descendant of it might be *preserved* among the forty-five manuscripts of his list. Yet even by checking just those manuscripts in his list which are being kept in the Bibliothèque Nationale de France[104] he would have hit on a *MA* manuscript that in 700^{b}23-4 shares the four words κινεῖ πρῶτον τὸ ὀρεκτὸν with Vaticanus P and William's translation, the Parisinus graecus 1859 (b). But Louis shut himself off from this possible discovery by claiming that all manuscripts of his list (*tous ces manuscrits*) belong to one of Jaeger's two manuscript families.[105] This statement amounts to *allocating a stemmatic position to uncollated manuscripts*, for neither is it based on an inspection of all manuscripts by Wartelle himself,[106] nor had E. Mioni, to whom Louis misleadingly refers his reader, been in the position to conduct such an inspection.[107] Thus, Louis failed to identify the evidence which would have confirmed his intuition concerning the additional model of Vaticanus P.

7. Nussbaum 1975: The Lost 'Majuscule MS'

The next *MA* edition was presented, in May 1975, by Martha L. Craven Nussbaum as a PhD thesis to the Department of the Classics of Harvard University. Important parts of this thesis have been published, either in Nussbaum's 1976 article on

---

[103] Louis 1973, 48: 'Après bien des hésitations j'ai cependant pris le parti de conserver le manuscrit P, *car il me semble que son copiste a eu à sa disposition un autre manuscrit que celui qu'il était chargé de recopier. Ce n'est là qu'une impression.* Mais elle m'a paru suffire pour justifier le maintien de P dans l'apparat critique' (our italics).

[104] Parisini graeci 1853 (E), 1859 (b), 1861 (c), 1921 (our sigla: m^I + m$^{II.2}$), 2027 (P^f), 2035 (P^g), Suppl. gr. 333 (P^h). With the exception of Par. gr. 1921 we have once more adopted the sigla employed by Bekker 1831 and by De Leemans 2011a respectively.

[105] Louis 1973, 48: 'Tous ces manuscrits se répartissent en deux familles nettement distinctes, dont les meilleurs témoins sont pour la première le Parisinus gr. 1853 (E) et le Vaticanus gr. 261 (Y); pour la seconde le Laurentianus LXXXI-1 (S), le Marcianus gr. Z 214 (H^a), l'Ambrosianus 435 (X) et le Vaticanus gr. 1339 (P). Tous les autres ou bien ont été copiés directement sur l'un de ces manuscrits anciens, ou bien ont la même source qu'eux.'

[106] That Louis did not examine the manuscripts himself is proved beyond doubt by the fact that he took over from Wartelle three manuscripts which do not contain *MA* at all: nos 15 (Yalensis Beinecke MS 234), 37 (Vat. Urb. gr. 39), and 42 (Vat. Regin. gr. 118) of his list.

[107] In order to support his claim according to which each and every *MA* manuscript goes back to one of Jaeger's two families, Louis 1973, 48 n. 1, refers to Mioni 1958: 'Cf. E. Mioni, *op. cit.*, 58.' Yet writing in 1958, Mioni could not possibly have had Wartelle's *Inventaire* (1963) at his disposal. In fact, he had just observed that *all of the six manuscripts from Udine and Venice which he had inspected* belong to either of Jaeger's two families; cf. Mioni 1958, 57–8: 'Codices Veneti: Utin. I (A^u); Marc. 200 (= Q), 206 (= f), 209 (= E^m), 212 (= G^a), 214 (= H^a). Codices *De Motu Animalium*, ut fere singulae lectiones ostendunt, duas in familias dividuntur, quarum prioris sunt E (= Par. 1853), Y (= Vat. 261), alterius P (= Vat. 1339), S (Laur. 81.1).'

'The Text of Aristotle's *De Motu Animalium*' or in her 1978 edition of *MA*;[108] other parts, however, which are equally important from a textual point of view, have remained unpublished and must accordingly be studied in the 1975 thesis.[109] Her list of manuscripts[110] depends almost entirely on Louis 1973: she took over his errors[111] and added a new one.[112] But with regard to one manuscript she corrected a conspicuous blunder committed by Wartelle and overlooked by Louis.[113] And quite unlike Louis, Nussbaum by no means shied away from studying Greek manuscripts: She collated all ten manuscripts which are quoted in her apparatus as permanent or occasional witnesses,[114] and she read through an eleventh manuscript, Laurentianus Plut. 87.21 (Z^a), although she came to classify it as useless.[115] Her collations fall into two groups: On the one hand, she *re-collated* six manuscripts—Bekker's four manuscripts[116] and the two collated by Torraca 1958a[117] and Torraca 1959[118] respectively—, on the other hand, she provided *first collations* of four manuscripts all kept by Italian libraries.[119]

---

[108] In Nussbaum 1978, 384, however, the comments on 703^b22–3 and 703^b26–36 seem to have been missed by the typesetter, so that the lemma introducing 703^b22–3 is immediately followed by the comment on 703^b32. The missing section of the commentary can be found in Nussbaum 1975a, 602–4; the comment on 703^b22–3 was also reproduced in Nussbaum 1976, 157–8 (textual problem no. 14).

[109] On the text and transmission the 1975 thesis is fuller than the 1976 article, which in turn is fuller on those matters than the 1978 edition. Suffice it here to say that not only Nussbaum's list of Greek *MA* manuscripts (1975a, 71–2), but also her notes on the thirty-four manuscripts which she did *not* use for her edition (1975a, 110–18), and her collations of major manuscripts (1975a, 128–38), are accessible only in the PhD thesis.

[110] Nussbaum 1975a, 71–2.

[111] Nussbaum's list, too, contains three manuscripts (Yale 234, Vat. Urb. 39, Vat. Regin. 118) which in fact do not contain *MA*, and it lacks four manuscripts which in fact do contain *MA* (Erlangen UB A 4, Scor. Φ. III. 11, Par. Coisl. 166, Vat. gr. 1950).

[112] Nussbaum 1975a, 122 n. 1, eliminates Bodl. Canon. 107 (Wartelle No. 1264 = Louis No. 40), since she assumes that this item is not a manuscript but a printed book. This assumption was corrected by Escobar 1990, 55: only the first text contained in Bodl. Canon. 107 (*Sens*) is a print, whereas all remaining texts, including *MA*, belong to the manuscript part; see further Coxe 1854, col. 98.

[113] In describing Cod. Par. Suppl. 333 (Wartelle No. 1589 = Louis No. 41) Wartelle 1963, 118, had mixed up *PA* and *MA*, thereby ascribing to that manuscript a *MA* in four books and a *PA* in one book. Nussbaum 1975a, 118, correctly observes: 'It seems likely that the designations *PA* and *MA* should be reversed here.' So it is a mere oversight that she omitted precisely this manuscript in her manuscript list (Nussbaum 1975a, 71–2): That is why she announces forty-four manuscripts, but actually lists only forty-three.

[114] These ten manuscripts are described and evaluated in Nussbaum 1975a, 72–108. The collations are accessible only in Nussbaum 1975a, 128–38 ('Appendix').

[115] Nussbaum 1976, 132–3 ('the sloppiest manuscript of Aristotle I have ever examined').

[116] Parisinus gr. 1853 (E), Vaticanus gr. 261 (Y), Laurentianus Plut. 81.1 (S), Vaticanus gr. 1339 (P).

[117] Ambrosianus 435 (H 50 sup.) (X).

[118] Marcianus gr. Z 214 (H^a). Since Nussbaum had not taken notice of Torraca 1959, she was unaware of his collation of H^a. That is why she believes herself to have collated H^a for the first time and why she claims to have provided first collations of *five MA* manuscripts (Nussbaum 1975a, 4 = 1976, 111: 'I have collated five new manuscripts, three of which—L, O^d, and H^a—are of particular interest'), whereas in fact this was true only of four manuscripts.

[119] Vaticanus gr. 266 (V), Marcianus gr. Z 209 (O^d), Vaticanus gr. 253 (L), Vaticanus gr. 258 (N).

Nussbaum's re-collations yielded several corrections of previous collations. Yet her collation of the *codex vetustissimus* Parisinus gr. 1853 (E), which she did not study *in situ*,[120] can still not be considered as definitive, since in a number of passages it is impossible to read the first-hand readings or to distinguish the second-hand readings from those of the first hand, unless one uses the original or else a digital copy—a device not available when Nussbaum wrote her thesis. The four Italian manuscripts which she collated for the first time belong, without exception, in one or the other of Jaeger's two families, and they are even closely related to certain individual members of these families. To Jaeger's first family Nussbaum added Vaticanus gr. 266 (V)—to little avail, since that manuscript shares with Vat. gr. 261 (Y) the feature of having been *copied* from Par. gr. 1853 (E) after the latter had been revised by the second hand (E²). Within Jaeger's second family, the sub-group identified by Torraca 1959, on the basis of Ambrosianus X and Marcianus Hᵃ (Nussbaum: b_2), was enriched both by a third member, Vat. gr. 253 (L), and by a slightly more distant relative, Vat. gr. 258 (N). Furthermore, Nussbaum correctly observed that Laur. 87.21 (Zᵃ), the manuscript which she had read but rejected, shows a certain proximity to Vat. gr. 1339 (P);[121] she did not, however, include Zᵃ in her *stemma codicum*. Last but not least, Laur. 81.1 (S), which had been used since Bekker 1831, was joined by its close relative Marcianus gr. 209 (Oᵈ) in order to form Nussbaum's sub-group b_1.

Nussbaum's threefold distinction between b_2(XHᵃL)+N,[122] ZᵃP,[123] and b_1(SOᵈ)[124] made the internal structure of what she and Jaeger conceived of as *the* second family (Nussbaum: b) much clearer. The one indispensable item still missing in her picture of that part of the transmission was Laurentianus Plut. 87.4 (Cᵃ), written in the scriptorium of Ioannikios.[125] She was unaware of the fact that this is by far the oldest manuscript of her second family: it was only in 1983 that Nigel Wilson dated the activity of Ioannikios to the twelfth century, his evidence being the relationship between the scriptorium of Ioannikios and the twelfth-century translator Burgundio of Pisa.[126] Nussbaum's most important

---

[120] Nussbaum 1975a, 73 (= 1976, 115–16): 'I have collated Hᵃ, Oᵈ, S, Y, V, L, N, P, and, for selected passages, Zᵃ *in situ*, E and X from microfilm and photographic reproduction.'

[121] Nussbaum 1975a, 110–11 (= 1976, 132): 'But it…may very well be a copy of some immediate ancestor of P, many of whose characteristic errors it incorporates.'

[122] Common errors of this group include 700ᵃ8 αὐτοῦ τὸ] αὐτῶν τὸ NXHᵃL.– 700ᵇ24 διανοητόν²] προαιρετόν NXHᵃL.– 701ᵇ30 καὶ ἐν ταύτηι] εἰ καὶ ἐν ταύτηι NXHᵃL.– 702ᵃ20 διὰ τὸ] διὰ τὸ τὸ NXHᵃL.

[123] Common errors of this group include 698ᵃ26 κινεῖσθαι] κινεῖται ZᵃP.– 699ᵃ26–7 διαπορήσειεν] ἀπορήσειε(ν) ZᵃP.– 700ᵃ8 αὐτοῦ τὸ] αὐτοῖς τοῦτο ZᵃP.– 701ᵃ31 ποιεῖ] ποιεῖται ZᵃP.

[124] Common errors of this group include 698ᵇ1 ἡ πρὸς ὅ] ἡ πρώτη OᵈS.– 699ᵃ10 ὠθῶν ἢ ἕλκων] ἕλκων ἢ ὠθῶν OᵈS.– 701ᵇ4 ὀχούμενον αὐτὸ] ὀχούμενος αὐτὸ OᵈS.– 703ᵃ25–6 κρατεῖ ἀλλήλων] κρατεῖται ἀλλήλων OᵈS.

[125] Nussbaum 1975a, 112.

[126] See Wilson 1983 who lists our manuscript on p. 165. In a more recent contribution, Vuillemin-Diem/Rashed 1997, 175–9 ('Aperçu historique') have restricted the date further to AD 1135–40; cf. Rashed 2001, 132–4.

contribution to our overall picture of the transmission, however, rests on the link she made between Louis' vague hint at a second source used by P and Torraca's observation that P and William preserve, in 700^{b}23-4, the four words lacking in all other manuscripts known to him. *Nussbaum is the first scholar to have stated in so many words that for their text of 700^{b}23–4 both P and William had recourse to an independent source.*[127] Nussbaum termed this presumable source 'Majuscule MS' and entered it on her stemma exactly at the same level as her archetype:[128]

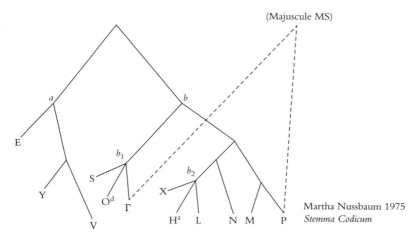

Martha Nussbaum 1975
Stemma Codicum

Nussbaum's stemma clearly shows that she thought herself to be dealing with a case of 'extra-archetypal' contamination.[129] But given that descendants of an independent late-antique majuscule manuscript were still accessible to the scribe of Vaticanus P and to William of Moerbeke—*why not consider the possibility that these or other descendants of the 'Majuscule MS' are still extant?* Although Nussbaum was acquainted with just eleven manuscripts (including Z^a) out of a total of forty-four (according to her own list), and although she had discovered that besides her two families there were traces of an independent tradition,[130]

---

[127] Nussbaum 1975a, 104–5 (= 1976, 130; cf. 1978, 16): 'There can, however, be no doubt that P has access to an independent source, probably also used by Γ...There are two passages where PΓ have, alone, the correct reading'; with regard to the first and foremost of these two passages, 700^{b}23–4, Nussbaum writes: 'In other manuscripts, the passage is hopelessly corrupt... The reading of P could not, it seems, be the result of a correction of those mutilated readings; such ingenuity would be astounding. The reading is surely correct; no editor has even questioned this.'

[128] Nussbaum 1975a, 121 (= 1976, 134 = 1978, 17): 'Stemma'.

[129] The simple fact that Nussbaum was perfectly able to depict the position of the 'Majuscule MS' in her stemma shows why Trovato's term 'extra-archetypal contamination' is more adequate than Timpanaro's 'extra-stemmatic contamination'; see further Trovato 2017, 134 (already quoted).

[130] Nussbaum 1975a, 74 (= 1976, 116 = 1978, 14): 'There is, in addition, a tradition independent of both major families, represented occasionally in P and Γ, though both of these belong for the most part in the *b* family.'

she nevertheless claimed that the thirty-three manuscripts which had remained uncollated 'are usually late, and almost certain to contain nothing of real value'.[131] It is true that Nussbaum was acutely aware of, and had drawn attention to, the shortcomings of Louis' editorial method,[132] but her own expedient of judging uncollated manuscripts on the basis of their *age* is also problematic: The 'exterior age' of a manuscript must be sharply distinguished from its 'interior age', as Johann Salomo Semler once put it,[133] since even a very late copy may, under certain circumstances, have been copied immediately from a ninth-century exemplar now lost.

If Nussbaum had overcome the prejudice according to which 'late' manuscripts can be assumed *a priori* to be copies of extant models ('*codices descripti*') and hence be safely ignored, she could have checked quite easily whether direct progeny of her 'Majuscule MS' is extant or not. Since she had observed that the strongest evidence for P's and William's occasional access to an independent source consists in their unique version of 700^b23-4, she could have checked *just these two lines 700^b23-4* in all uncollated *MA* manuscripts, for instance by means of the microfilm collection of the Berlin Aristotle Archive.[134] And in fact, she would have scored a hit already by checking the two very first items in her list of manuscripts,[135] since both Alexandria Bibl. Patr. 87 and Berolinensis Phill. gr. 1507 (I) share the correct reading of 700^b23-4 with Vaticanus P and William's translation.[136] She could then have examined whether the manuscript in question is linked by significant common errors with one of her families *a* and *b*. If so, she would have been faced once more with 'extra-archetypal contamination' as in the case of Vaticanus P; but if not, she would have identified a direct descendant of a second hyparchetype and thereby have downgraded the common source of her two families, which she had thought of as the archetype, to

---

[131] Nussbaum 1975a, 72, on her list of manuscripts: 'Many of these are late, and of no importance in constituting the text'; 110, introducing her brief description of the uncollated manuscripts: 'The manuscripts to be described are usually late, and almost certain to contain nothing of real value.'

[132] Nussbaum 1975b, 207 (on Louis 1973): 'Previous collation errors remain uncorrected; no new MSS are consulted. The discussion of the MS families is seriously misleading.'

[133] Semler 1765, 88: 'Ich setze es hier nemlich voraus, daß das innere Alter viel mehr muß beobachtet werden als das äusserliche, so nur auf dem Alter des Pergament und der gebrauchten Schriftzüge beruhet; wonach freylich ein *Codex* äusserlich älter seyn (das heißt eher der Zeit nach geschrieben worden seyn) kan, als ein und mehr andere, die erst drey–vier Jahrhunderte nachher abgeschrieben worden; aber das innere Alter ist oft bey diesem letzten viel grösser als bey jenen.'

[134] The priceless help to be gained by editors of Aristotle from this important tool had been emphasized already by Rudolf Kassel in the *Prolegomena* to his edition of *Rh.*; cf. Kassel 1971, V–VI: 'Ein unschätzbarer Vorteil für die Arbeit war, daß die Mikrofilme des von meinem Kollegen Paul Moraux geleiteten Aristotelesarchivs an Ort und Stelle zur Verfügung standen.'

[135] Nussbaum 1975a, 71.

[136] In Italy, by contrast, where Nussbaum looked for manuscripts to be collated for the first time, there are no further witnesses to the correct reading of 700^b23-4 at all.

the status of one out of two hyparchetypes; so that instead of 'extra-archetypal' contamination she would have been dealing with the innocent feature of 'intra-archetypal' contamination.[137]

8. De Leemans 2011: William's Two Models and a New Group of Greek Mss.

The decisive identification of Greek manuscripts which are much closer to the independent additional source than Vaticanus P was made by Pieter De Leemans in 2011, in his exemplary edition of the mediaeval Latin translations of *IA* and *MA* by William of Moerbeke.[138] For William's translation of *MA*, De Leemans took into account 168 Latin manuscripts[139] which he divided up into three groups according to their textual variants. The *first* group consists of the manuscripts of family x,[140] the *second* group consists of the manuscripts of family y; the *third* consists of both the manuscripts of family z[141] and the very considerable number of manuscripts which go back to the exemplar of the copies circulating in mediaeval Paris (P).[142] Reliable evidence for the relative chronology of these three groups seems to be provided by William's translation of the three Homeric lines which Aristotle quotes in *MA* 4.[143] To judge by the translation as transmitted by family x[144] those Homeric lines were clearly beyond William's capacities, whereas the version transmitted by family y and the P/z group is by

---

[137] Trovato 2017, 134: 'if all the sources of a contaminated ms. or of a subfamily of contaminated mss. are preserved, there is no need to use the contaminated ms. or subfamily, which can be eliminated as *codices descripti…*, or rather *inutiles*.'

[138] De Leemans 2011a (= *Aristoteles Latinus* XVII 2.II–III).

[139] See De Leemans 2011a, XXX–XL, for a catalogue of these manuscripts. In order to do justice to this considerable achievement, one should keep in mind that Geyer 1955 had based his text of William's *MA* translation on four Latin manuscripts; Torraca 1958a had used just two; and Torraca 1959 had added collations of another eight.

[140] Family x in turn consists of sub-groups x_1 and x_2.

[141] Family z in turn consists of sub-groups z_1, z_2, and z_3.

[142] From the mid-thirteenth to the mid-fourteenth century, Paris booksellers divided each of the major works (or group of works) of the Corpus Aristotelicum up into quires ('peciae') which were then given on loan to scribes as models for producing copies. Within this system, *MA* was accessible both as part of the zoological works (P^1 = exemplar '*Item de historiis animalium*') and as part of the *Parva Naturalia* (P^2 = exemplar '*Item de motibus animalium, et aliorum parvorum*'). See De Leemans 2011a, XLI–XLVII, and Trovato 2017, 131-2, with further references.

[143] *MA* 4, 700ᵇ37-701ᵃ2 (after Nussbaum) ≈ Hom., *Il.* VIII, 21-2 + 20: ἀλλ' οὐκ ἂν ἐρύσαιτ' ἐξ οὐρανόθεν πεδίονδε / Ζῆν' ὕπατον πάντων, οὐδ' εἰ μάλα πολλὰ κάμοιτε· / πάντες δ' ἐξάπτεσθε θεοὶ πᾶσαί τε θέαιναι.

[144] *Sed non utique effluet celitus campum autem / vivere infimum omnium neque si multo magis laborent / extrudere omnes dii omnesque theanee.*

far superior.[145] De Leemans concluded that the manuscripts of family x transmit the original stage of William's translation (*Editio pristina* = G1),[146] whereas both family y and the P/z group represent the later revisions to which William subjected his original manuscript over time (y: *Recensio prima* = GR'; P/z: *Recensio altera* = GR"):[147]

The Principal Manuscript Families		Development of W.'s Manuscript
x_1 } x_2 }	x	**G1**: *W.'s original translation* ↓
	y	**GR'**: *W.'s 1st Revision*
P¹ (Exemplar "*De historiis animalium*") } **P²** (Exemplar "*De motibus animalium,* *et aliorum parvorum*") } P (source of the Parisian Exemplaria)	↓	
z_1 } z_2 } z_3 } z		**GR"**: *W.'s 2nd Revision*

De Leemans also observed that in more than one case William's original translation (G1) and the later revisions (GR' and GR") differ from each other also with regard to the presupposed *Greek text*. In William's original translation (G1), our paradigm passage (700^b23-4), for instance,[148] was rendered as follows:

> *Quare et intellectuale,*[149]

a reading which previous editors of William[150] had not documented at all and which clearly presupposes the truncated version of our passage as transmitted by all manuscripts of Nussbaum's families *a* and *b* except Vaticanus P:

---

[145] *Sed non utique amovebunt e celo in terram / Iovem suppremum omnium neque si valde multum laborent / apprehendere omnes dii omnesque dee.*

[146] De Leemans 2011a, CXCIX: 'I believe, therefore, that the x-manuscripts represent an older (first) stage of the translation.'

[147] For a more detailed overview of De Leemans' analysis of the Latin tradition, see Appendix II to the present introduction.

[148] De Leemans 2011a, CLXXXVIII (passage [9]).

[149] Whereas this reading *is* attested by one of the four Latin manuscripts used by Geyer 1955—*Schaffhausen*: Eisenbibliothek AG 20 (= De Leemans 2011a, XXXVII No. 123 [*Xe*])—Geyer edited the text of his three other manuscripts, which represent the Paris text—i.e. William's second revision (GR") —and he did not provide an *apparatus criticus* for his text of William. All ten Latin manuscripts collated by Torraca equally belong to the Paris group (P)—except *Rome*: Vat. Borgh. 134 (G, = De Leemans No. 138 [*Bv*]), but this manuscript also represents William's second revision (GR"). Accordingly, De Leemans 2011a was the first scholar to make known the important fact that William had first translated the truncated version of our passage.

[150] Geyer 1955, 57.66–7, Torraca 1958a, 58.8–9.

ὥστε καὶ τὸ διανοητόν ('so that...the object of discursive thought, too').

William's later revisions (GR' and GR"), by contrast, offered the version already edited by Geyer 1955 and Torraca 1958a:

Quare movet primum quod appetibile et quod intellectuale,

a reading which presupposes the full version of 700ᵇ23-4 as transmitted by Vaticanus P:

ὥστε κινεῖ πρῶτον τὸ ὀρεκτὸν καὶ τὸ διανοητόν

('so that the first mover is the object of desire and the object of discursive thought')

De Leemans concluded that William had at his disposal two Greek *MA* manuscripts: his primary model *Γ*1 and an additional model *Γ*2. In our passage (700ᵇ23-4), William's original translation (G1) is based on his primary Greek model *Γ*1 which contained the truncated version, whereas the later revisions (GR' and GR") are based on his additional Greek model *Γ*2, which transmitted the complete version of our passage *and hence had access to, or even formed part of, an independent branch of the Greek transmission.*[151]

In order to get a clear picture of the relationship between William's two Greek models on the one hand and the extant Greek manuscripts on the other De Leemans drew up both a list of forty-five Greek *MA* manuscripts[152]— which is clearly superior to the lists of Wartelle, Louis, and Nussbaum[153]—and a list of passages in which William made significant changes when revising his

---

[151] De Leemans 2011a, CCVII: 'Moerbeke's main model (*Γ*1) was thus not contaminated with the same independent source as *P*. Rather, the manuscript that he used for revising his text had access to this independent tradition.'

[152] De Leemans 2011a, CLXXIX, claims that the total of extant Greek *MA* manuscripts is forty-four ('*De motu animalium* is extant in many more, *in concreto* forty-four manuscripts'), but actually his list comprises forty-five items, not forty-four: the five manuscripts collated up to and including Torraca 1958a (De Leemans 2011a, CLXXIX), another five manuscripts first collated by Torraca 1959 (Hᵃ), and Nussbaum 1975a respectively (De Leemans 2011a, CLXXX), and finally the thirty-five manuscripts first collated by De Leemans himself either fully or in part (De Leemans 2011a, CLXXXIII-CLXXXIV). This discrepancy is due to the fact that De Leemans counted Berol. Phill. gr. 1507 (which consists of four initially independent parts) just once when calculating his total, whereas he treated either of the two parts which contain *MA* as a separate entity when drawing up his list (p. CLXXXIII). The latter approach seems preferable also from a codicological point of view; see now Isépy/Prapa 2018.

[153] All forty-five manuscripts listed by De Leemans do in fact contain *MA*: He removed the three wrong items introduced by Wartelle 1963 and taken over by Louis 1973 and Nussbaum 1975a (Yale 234, Vat. Urb. 39, Vat. Regin. 118); he corrected the misguided elimination of Bodl. Canon. 107 by Nussbaum 1975a, 122 n. 1; and he supplied two out of four items missing both in Louis 1973 and in Nussbaum 1975a: Erlangensis UB A 4 and Vat. gr. 1950. The two items of our list *not* listed by De Leemans offer only parts of the text: Par. Coisl. 166, wrongly eliminated by Louis 1973, has preserved the original

Latin translation.[154] Then he checked these passages in all forty-five Greek manuscripts of his list, and the result of that survey was striking: Four Greek *MA* manuscripts never before collated offer a number of readings which *do not* correspond to the text of Nussbaum's two families *a* and *b*, whereas they *do* correspond to William's 'second readings', i.e. to Latin readings introduced by William only on second thought, at the first or the second stage of his revision (GR' and GR" respectively). The four new Greek manuscripts in question are the following:

- B^e: Berlin, Staatsbibliothek Preußischer Kulturbesitz, Cod. Phillippicus 1507 (part I)
- E^r: Erlangen, Universitätsbibliothek A 4
- b: Paris, Bibliothèque nationale de France, Par. gr. 1859
- T^p: Alexandria, Βιβλιοθήκη τοῦ Πατριαρχείου 87

We will focus on the gist of De Leemans' just mentioned survey[155] by selecting just those of De Leemans' examples in which the new Greek manuscripts— either the first two (B^eE^r) or all four of them (B^eE^rbT^p)—are joined by P only or are even alone in offering readings which clearly correspond to William's 'second readings'. In our selection, we will in each case first quote William's original translation (accompanied by the underlying Greek equivalent and by the sigla of the Greek manuscripts which have preserved it) and then William's revised translation (again together with the Greek equivalent and its manuscript attestation).[156] We will begin with a handful of passages, once more including our paradigm passage 700^b23-24, in which the Greek equivalent of William's second reading is not only attested by the new manuscripts but also by Vaticanus P:

> **[9]** 700^b23-24 *quare et intellectuale* G1 (ὥστε καὶ τὸ διανοητόν EYV Z^a C^aO^dS) → *Quare movet primum quod appetibile et quod intellectuale* GR'GR" (ὥστε κινεῖ πρῶτον τὸ ὀρεκτὸν καὶ τὸ διανοητόν B^eE^rbT^p P).- **[11a]** 700^b34-35 *quam ut sit* G1GR' (ἢ ὥστ(ε) εἶναι EYV NXH^aL Z^a C^aO^dS bT^p) → *aliqualiter esse* GR" (πως εἶναι B^eE^r P).- **[11b]** 700^b35 *prius* G1 (πρότερον EYV NXH^aL Z^a C^aO^dS bT^p) → *ad alterum* GR'GR" (πρὸς ἕτερον B^eE^r P).- **[14]** 702^a29 *movetur* G1GR' (κινεῖται EYV NXH^aL C^aO^dS) → *movet*

---

last part of the *MA* text contained in Parisinus gr. 1921, and Scor. *Φ*. III. 11 (ff. 177r–179v), already left out by Wartelle, contains *excerpts* from *MA*. So while our total of *MA* manuscripts is forty-seven, as opposed to De Leemans' forty-five, De Leemans is still to be credited with having first listed all forty-five *complete* copies of *MA*.

[154]   De Leemans 2011a, CLXXXII, with n. 123.

[155]   De Leemans 2011a, CLXXXV–CXCVI: '4.1. Survey'.

[156]   Bold numbers in square brackets will refer to the entries in De Leemans' survey. We have modified the selection of manuscripts and checked all readings on the basis of the *apparatus lectionum omnium* supplied by Christina Prapa.

et movetur GR" (κινεῖ καὶ κινεῖται BᶜEʳbTᴾ; cf. κινεῖται καὶ κινεῖ P).- **[23]** 703ᵇ36 *hec* GɪGR' (ταῦτα EYV NXHᵃL Zᵃ CᵃOᵈS) → *eadem* GR" (τὰ αὐτὰ BᶜEʳbTᴾ P).

In the greater part of De Leemans' examples, however, the Greek equivalent of William's second reading as transmitted by BᶜEʳ(bTᴾ) is *not* shared by Vaticanus P:[157]

> **[3]** 698ᵇ1 *divisibile* GɪGR' (διαιρετά EYV NXHᵃL ZᵃP CᵃOᵈS) → *dividitur* GR"
> (διαιρεῖται BᶜEʳbTᴾ).- **[4]** 699ᵇ2-3 *nichil magis contratendere* GɪGR' (οὐδὲν μᾶλλον
> ἀντερείδειν NXHᵃL ZᵃP CᵃOᵈS bTᴾ) → *non oportet magis contratendere* GR" (οὐ δεῖ
> μᾶλλον ἀντερείδειν BᶜEʳ).- **[5]** 700ᵃ1 *multo magis* Gɪ (μάλα πολλά EYV NXHᵃL
> P CᵃOᵈ [μάλλα πολλά S] bTᴾ) → *valde multum* GR'GR" (πάνυ πολλά BᶜEʳ).- **[6]**
> 700ᵃ17 *omnium* GɪGR'GR"(P) (πάντων EYV NXHᵃL ZᵃP CᵃOᵈS) → *omnium simi-*
> *liter* GR"(z) (πάντων ὁμοίως BᶜEʳbTᴾ).- **[10]** 700ᵇ32 *hec quidem* GɪGR' (τὰ μὲν
> EYV NXHᵃL P CᵃOᵈS) → *hoc quidem* GR" (τὸ μὲν BᶜEʳbTᴾ Zᵃ).- **[15]** 702ᵇ14 *et*
> *rursus* Gɪ (μηδ' αὖ EYV NXHᵃL ZᵃP CᵃOᵈS) → *neque* GR'GR" (μὴ δὲ BᶜEʳbTᴾ).-
> **[19]** 703ᵃ17 *sit* Gɪ GR' (ἔστω EYV XHᵃL ZᵃP CᵃOᵈS)[158] → om. GR" (BᶜEʳbTᴾ).

On the other hand, De Leemans also singled out a small number of passages in which he had found a hitherto isolated reading of P (or P and Zᵃ) to be shared by BᶜEʳbTᴾ *without* being reflected by William's translation:[159]

> 698ᵇ8 αὐτῶι EYV NXHᵃL CᵃOᵈS : αὐτοῖς PZᵃ BᶜEʳbTᴾ.- 699ᵃ26–27 διαπορήσειεν
> EYV NXHᵃL CᵃOᵈS : ἀπορήσειε(ν) PZᵃ BᶜEʳbTᴾ.- 700ᵃ14 ταῦτα EYV NXHᵃL Zᵃ
> CᵃOᵈS : πάντα ταῦτα BᶜEʳbTᴾ : πάντα post ταῦτα inseruit P.

Finally, De Leemans pointed out that some BᶜEʳ(bTᴾ) readings which are independent of Nussbaum's two families *a* and *b* are neither shared by Vaticanus P nor translated by William:[160]

> 698ᵃ16–17 δεῖ...ἠρεμεῖν EYV NXHᵃL PZᵃ CᵃOᵈS : ἀεί...ἠρεμεῖ BᶜEʳbTᴾ || 698ᵇ5
> ἕκαστόν τι δεῖ EYV NXHᵃL PZᵃ CᵃOᵈS : ἕκαστον δεῖ τι BᶜEʳbTᴾ || 698ᵇ26 πνέων

---

[157] It is noteworthy that in one of the following passages (**[4]**: 699ᵇ2-3) the Greek equivalent of William's *first* reading is only attested by manuscripts belonging with Jaeger's second family, thereby confirming Torraca's and Nussbaum's observation according to which William's original translation (Gɪ) was based on a manuscript belonging to that family. In another passage (**[10]**: 700ᵇ32), William's second reading is transmitted also by Laurentianus Plut. 87.21 (Zᵃ), which suggests that Zᵃ or its group was to some extent contaminated with readings from the BᶜEʳbTᴾ-branch of the tradition.

[158] Due to what must be an oversight, De Leemans 2011a, CXCIV ascribes the secondary error ἔσται (for ἔστω) to Nussbaum's group *a* (= EYV) and to a manuscript Mᵃ, which does not form part of his own list (pp. CLXXIX-CLXXX and CLXXXIII-CLXXXIV) at all. In fact, ἔσται is transmitted by Parisinus gr. 2027 (Pᶠ: ἔσται ἄλλος λόγος) and Matritensis N 26 (Mⁿ: ἔσται ἄλλης λόγος), whereas Parisinus gr. 1853 E offers ἔστω ἄλλος λόγος, which is provided with an initial smooth breathing (ἔστω ἄλλος λόγος) in E², Y, and V.

[159] De Leemans 2011a, CCXIV, n. 215.　　　[160] De Leemans 2011a, CCXIV, n. 216.

EYV NXHᵃL PZᵃ CᵃOᵈ : πλέων BᶜEʳbTᴾ S || 699ᵃ13 εἶναί τε δεῖ EYV (unde εἶναι θέλει NXHᵃL PZᵃ CᵃOᵈS) : εἶναί τε τι δεῖ Bᶜ vel εἶναί τι δεῖ Eʳ vel εἶναι δεῖ τι bTᴾ.

De Leemans correctly concluded that manuscripts BᶜEʳbTᴾ

> appear to make an original contribution to the text history of *de Motu Animalium* and provide information about the Greek manuscript that Moerbeke used to revise his translation.[161]

He also observed that the new group is in this respect superior to Vaticanus P:

> The survey of passages that were revised by Moerbeke has now shown that P appears to be less interesting for explaining Moerbeke's revision than four other manuscripts [i.e. BᶜbEʳTᴾ].[162]

De Leemans did not, however, illustrate the impact of his discovery for the *Greek text* of *MA,* and, in particular, he decided not to locate, for the time being, the new group BᶜEʳbTᴾ in the *stemma codicum* of the Greek transmission:[163]

> In the present context, it is not my intention to determine the place of these manuscripts in the *stemma codicum.*

9. On the Eve of the 2011 Symposium

When De Leemans' ground-breaking edition of William of Moerbeke came out in spring 2011, the present writer was already preparing an up-to-date account of the transmission and the text of *MA* for the Symposium Aristotelicum which was to be held in July. A first recent discovery to be taken into account was due to Paolo Accattino and Pierluigi Donini: In 1996 they had found out that Alex. Aphr. *De An.* not only refers to *MA* 9, as was already emphasized by Nussbaum 1975a,[164] but also provides a detailed paraphrase of *MA* 7–8, 701ᵇ13–702ᵃ2 which is packed with verbal quotations:[165] These quotations represent the earliest accessible state of the text.

---

[161] De Leemans 2011a, CLXXXII.   [162] De Leemans 2011a, CCXIV.

[163] De Leemans 2011a, CCXIV, n. 214.

[164] Cf. Nussbaum 1975a, 23–4, on Alexander *De Anima* 97,26ff. Bruns, where Alexander clearly refers to *MA* 9, 702ᵇ12–20.

[165] Cf. Accattino/Donini 1996, 262 (on Alexander *De Anima* 76,18–78,2 Bruns): 'Tutto questo passo è ispirato, con coincidenze verbali anche fortissime, ad Aristotele *M.A.* 7 e 8, spec. 701a 13–702a 2,' where '701a 13' should be corrected to '701b 13'.

With regard to the direct tradition, the present writer disposed of collations of all forty-seven known *MA* manuscripts[166] which were mainly prepared by Dr Christina Prapa.[167] On the basis of these collations, thirty manuscripts were identified as *codices descripti*—i.e. as copies of other extant manuscripts—and could be eliminated. The remaining seventeen independent *MA* manuscripts are the following:

> *Berlin*: Phillippicus 1507, ms. I (**B^e**) and ms. II (**B^p**).- *Erlangen*: Univ. Library A 4 (**E^r**).- *Florence*: Laurentiani Plut. 81.1 (**S**), 87.4 (**C^a**), and Plut. 87.21 (**Z^a**).- *Milan*: Ambrosianus H 50 sup. (**X**).- *Moscow*: Synodal library 240 (**M^o**).- *Paris*: Parisini graeci 1853 (**E**) and 1859 (**b**).- *Rome*: Vaticani graeci 253 (**L**), 258 (**N**), 1339 (**P**), and 1950 (**V^g**); Vat. Palatinus gr. 97 (**V^p**).- *Venice*: Marciani graeci 209 (**O^d**) and 214 (**H^a**).

In all but one of these independent *MA* manuscripts our treatise is combined either with both groups of the *Parva Naturalia* (*PN1* and *PN2*) as defined at the outset of the present introduction,[168] or with one of these groups.[169] In eight independent *MA* manuscripts, *MA* comes in between the two groups of the *Parva Naturalia*.[170] In six further independent *MA* manuscripts that do *not* contain *PN2*, *MA* is still combined with *PN1*,[171] whereas there are just two

---

[166] For a complete list of *MA* manuscripts, see Appendix I to the present introduction.

[167] For more detailed acknowledgements, see above, section 1. Dr Prapa's full collations of the seventeen independent manuscripts were checked in a workshop which took place in Munich in early June 2012 and was directed by Dr Pantelis Golitsis. A further result of this workshop was a draft of a *stemma codicum*, in which Golitsis ascribed to the *MA* text used by Michael of Ephesus a much higher stemmatic position than had been assumed by Nussbaum: Golitsis suggested that Michael's *MA* text is a direct descendant of Nussbaum's second hyparchetype (**b**). The collations of all *codices descripti* were later completed by Dr Prapa so that since spring 2013 we have been working with a full *apparatus lectionum omnium* which we intend to publish in a forthcoming *editio maior* of *MA*.

[168] *PN1*: Sens. / Mem. / Somn. Vig. / Insomn. / Div. Somn.—*PN2*: Long. / Iuv. + VM + Resp.

[169] The one exception is Vaticanus V^g, a manuscript that does not contain any further Aristotelian treatise at all: Xenophon/Marcus Aurelius/Epictetus/Maximus of Tyrus/Albinus/*MA*.

[170] Five manuscripts (Ambrosianus X, Vaticanus L, Marcianus H^a; Mosquensis M^o, and Vaticanus P) feature the sequence *PN1*—*MA*—*PN2*; in two manuscripts (Berolinensis B^e, Laurentianus S), as well as in the Aldine and Juntine editions, this sequence has been internally expanded by inserting, after *PN1* + *MA*, the *de Generatione Animalium*: *PN1*—*MA*—*GA*—*PN2*, the insertion being motivated by the fact that at the very end of *MA*, *GA* is announced as coming next (*MA* 11, 704^b2–3: λοιπὸν δὲ περὶ γενέσεως εἰπεῖν). By contrast, there is only one independent *MA* manuscript, Vaticanus N, in which more treatises on natural philosophy have been inserted between *PN1* + *MA* on the one hand and *GA* + *PN2* on the other: *PN1* + *MA*—*GC*/*Mete.*/*PA*/*IA*—*GA* + *PN2*.

[171] In three of these manuscripts (Par. E, Laur. Z^a, and Vat. Pal. V^p), *MA* immediately follows the complete set of *PN1*, in one further manuscript, Marc. O^d, it is immediately followed by *PN1*, and in the two remaining manuscripts (Par. b and Berol. B^p) *MA* rounds off a slightly defective version of *PN1*: Par. b has *Mem.* / *Somn. Vig.* / *Insomn.* / *Div. Somn.* / *MA*, whereas Berol. B^p offers *Somn. Vig.* / *Insomn.* / *Div. Somn.* / *MA*.

independent *MA* manuscripts which lack *PN1* or the greater part of it and in which *MA* is combined with *PN2*.[172] The most important general result of this brief survey is that in fourteen out of a total of seventeen independent manuscripts, *MA* is combined with or, rather forms part of *PN1*. What is more: These fourteen manuscripts cover all branches of the *MA* tradition, not only Nussbaum's two families,[173] but also De Leemans' new group.[174] It follows that the arrangement *Sens./Mem./Somn.Vig./Insomn./Div.Somn./MA* goes back to the archetype of our tradition.[175]

The seventeen independent manuscripts were subject to a preliminary classification by Lutz Koch at the Aristoteles-Archiv, Berlin. The conclusion to which the present writer felt entitled by Koch's observations was that Nussbaum's stemma has to be supplemented and modified in various ways,[176] but that its overall structure need not be corrected—apart from the urgent task of accounting for the new group identified by De Leemans 2011a (B^eE^rb)—, since all remaining fourteen independent manuscripts could be located in Nussbaum's bipartite world of two manuscript families *a* and *b*. Here are the details:

Nussbaum's family *a* (EYV) was reduced to its oldest member, Par. gr. 1853 (E) alone (as written by the first hand), since the remaining two members of this family, Vat. gr. 261 (Y) and Vat. gr. 266 (V), were found to be *codices descripti* and had thus to be eliminated: They were copied from Par. E *after* this manuscript had been revised by a second hand (E^2).[177] – Nussbaum's family *b* ($NXH^aL/PZ^a/C^aO^d$), by contrast, could be augmented by new, independent members. To Nussbaum's sub-group b_2(XH^aL) + N we had to add Vat. gr. 1950 (V^g), the one manuscript altogether omitted in the lists of Wartelle 1963, Louis 1973, and Nussbaum 1975a. – The group Z^aP as identified by Nussbaum 1975a[178] was increased in two ways. On the one hand, Vat. gr. 1339 (P) was joined by a pair of two late (mid-fifteenth-century) but independent relatives, namely by Mosqu. Sinod. 240 (M^o)[179] and by the second part of Berol.

---

[172] In Erlang. E^r, *MA* comes immediately after *PN2*: *Long./Iuv.* [+ *VM* + *Resp.*]/*MA*), whereas in Laur. C^a, *MA* is preceded by *Sens.* (i.e. by the first treatise of *PN1*) and followed by *PN2*: *Sens./MA/Long./Iuv.* [+ *VM* + *Resp.*].

[173] Nussbaum's family *a*: Par. E. – Nussbaum's sub-group b_2+N: Vat. N, Ambr. X, Marc. H^a, Vat. L. – Nussbaum's sub-group Z^aP (enlarged): Laur. Z^a, Mosqu. M^o, Berol. B^p, Vat. P. – Nussbaum's sub-group b_1 (enlarged): Laur. S, Vat. Pal. V^p, Marc. O^d.

[174] Parisinus b, Berolinensis B^e.   [175] Cf. Rashed 2004, 192–3.

[176] This applies, in particular, to William's translation which goes back to two different Greek models, as De Leemans 2011a had shown, and to the stemmatic position of the text commented upon by Michael of Ephesus, for which, see above, n. 167, and below, section 14.

[177] Luna/Segonds 2007, CCXLIV; Isépy 2016, 57–9 (both already quoted). In this context, Dr Pantelis Golitsis was able to prove that E^2 used Laurentianus Plut. 81.1 (S) as a source.

[178] Nussbaum 1975a, 110–11 (= 1976, 132).

[179] Mosquensis M^o is no. 240 among the Greek manuscripts from the Moscow Synodal Library now held in the State Historical Museum (GIM); in the 'systematic description' of these manuscripts published by the Archimandrite Vladimir in 1894 (Part I, Greek manuscripts) it bears the number 453.

Phill. 1507 (B^p).[180] As to Laur. Plut. 87.21 (Z^a), Pieter De Leemans had been able to show in yet another important contribution to the *Aristoteles Latinus* that this manuscript is closely related to the lost Greek model (**A**) of the equally lost Latin *translatio anonyma* paraphrased by Albert the Great in his *De principiis motus processivi*.[181] Nussbaum's sub-group *b*₁ (Laur. Plut. 81.1 = S, and Marc. gr. 209 = O^d) was not only augmented by a younger brother of Laur. S—i.e. Vat. Pal. gr. 97 (V^p)[182]—, but had been shown by Friederike Berger[183] to be closely related to Laur. Plut. 87.4 (C^a). The latter manuscript, which in view of its twelfth-century date made evident by Wilson 1983 must count as the second oldest *MA* manuscript extant, is even the most authoritative witness of what Nussbaum had called sub-group *b*₁. As to the new group of manuscripts singled out by De Leemans 2011a (B^cE^rbT^p), Alexandrinus T^p was identified as a copy of Par. b,[184] whereas Par. b itself turned out to be independent but 'contaminated' with readings from the group NXH^aLV^g, i.e. by the augmented version of what used to be Nussbaum's sub-group *b*₂.[185] So the new group identified by De Leemans comprises *three* independent manuscripts, after all, one of which (Par. b) is once in a while contaminated with readings from Nussbaum's sub-group *b*₂, whereas the remaining two (Berol. B^c and Erlang. E^r) are not. More recently, Peter Isépy and Christina Prapa have shown[186] that the Codex Berol. Phill. 1507 not only contains two copies of *MA* (B^c and B^p respectively), as was already pointed out by Studemund/Cohn 1890, but that this surprising duplication is due to the fact that the two copies belong with two different manuscripts now bound together within the Cod. Berol., the first of which (B^c, written some years before AD 1453) was originally quite independent from the second (B^p, written soon after AD 1453), not only with regard to its stemmatic position, but also codicologically; this fact had been overlooked

---

[180] Cf. Escobar 1990, 171–9.

[181] De Leemans 2011b, LXXXI. De Leemans' reconstruction of a lost mediaeval Latin translation of *MA* on the basis of its paraphrase by Albert the Great, and his convincing demonstration that the lost Greek model (**A**) of this lost Latin translation shows striking resemblances with one and only one extant Greek manuscript, i.e. the Laurentianus Plut. 87.21 (Z^a), stand out as an altogether remarkable achievement.

[182] Cf. Escobar 1990, 161–6.   [183] Berger 2005, 73, n. 291.

[184] That much had already been suggested by De Leemans 2011a, CCXV: 'In turn, T^p might well be a copy of *b*, as is the case in *De insomniis*.' This impression is confirmed, for instance, by the following individual errors of Parisinus b shared by Alexandrinus T^p: 701^a15–16 ταῦτα ἄμφω] τοῦτ' εὐθὺς bT^p.- 702^a7 εὐλόγως] ἀλλόγως bT^p.- 702^b9 τούτου] τὸν τοῦ b, T^p ante correcturam.- 703^b35 ὡς ἐπ' ἀρχήν] ὥσπερ ἀρχὴν b, T^p ante correcturam. An additional model of Alexandrinus T^p seems to have been Mosquensis M°.

[185] For a passage where Parisinus b has adopted a characteristic reading of Nussbaum's sub-group *b*₂ see 700^b24: post οὐ πᾶν δὲ διανοητόν supra lineam προαιρετόν add. b : οὐ πᾶν δὲ τὸ διανοητὸν προαιρετόν NXH^aLV^g : οὐ πᾶν δὲ τὸ διανοητόν E C^aO^dSV^p. It is plausible, then, to trace back to the same source both the *b*-reading adopted by Parisinus b in 702^b31: ἔστιν B^cE^r : ἔσται NXH^aLV^g C^aO^dSV^p Z^aPB^pM° b : ἔστε E^1 and the readings shared by Parisinus b with Nussbaum's two families against B^cE^r: 699^a10 ἕλκων καὶ ὠθῶν B^cE^r : ὠθῶν ἢ ἕλκων E NXH^aLV^g C^a PB^pM° b.- 699^a13 οὐρανοῦ B^cE^r : οὐρανοῦ μόριον b cett.- 701^b4 ὀχούμενος αὐτὸς B^cE^r : ὀχούμενον αὐτὸς b : ὀχούμενον αὐτὸ E NXH^aLV^g C^a PB^pM° : ὀχούμενος αὐτὸ O^dSV^p.- 702^a29 ἠρεμεῖν E NXH^aLV^g C^aO^dSV^p Z^aPM° b : ἠρεμοῦν B^c, unde εἶναι ἠρεμοῦν E^r.- 703^a18 δ' εὐφυῶς b E NXH^aLV^g Z^aB^pM° C^a : δὲ ὑφ' ὧ ὡς B^cE^r : δὲ εὐφυῶς O^dSV^p P.- 703^b16 ὑπάρχουσιν αἱ φυσικαί B^cE^r : ὑπάρχουσαι αἱ φυσικαί b : ὑπάρχουσαι φυσικαί cett.

[186] Isépy/Prapa 2018.

because two quires which had fallen out in B^e were later supplied by the team responsible for the production of B^p. And to Luigi Orlandi we owe the important information that Erlang. E^r was written when its scribe, Andronikos Kallistos, still lived in Constantinople, i.e. before the fall of the capital to the Turks in AD 1453.[187]

The stemmatic position of the new group B^{e}E^{r}b as a whole, by contrast, had still to be determined, since this decisive question had been expressly left open by De Leemans, as we have seen.[188] Now thanks to De Leemans' findings, it seemed reasonably clear that the readings which B^{e}E^{r}b share with William's additional model Γ2 and/or Vaticanus P (in 700^{b}23-4 as well as in a number of other passages) ultimately go back to the independent source ('Majuscule MS') that had been postulated already by Nussbaum 1975a. Given that there are no clear separative errors shared by B^{e}E^{r}b with one of Nussbaum's two families against the other one, the obvious way of accounting for this state of affairs seemed to consist in assuming that B^{e}E^{r}b have transmitted the complete text of Nussbaum's 'Majuscule MS'. And as soon as this 'Majuscule MS' would thus be provided with extant direct progeny (while remaining independent from Nussbaum's two families), it would have to be classified as a *second hyparchetype*, thereby downgrading Nussbaum's archetype, i.e. the common source of her two families, to the status of one out of two hyparchetypes. On the other hand, however, this radical modification of the stemma of *MA* seemed to be obstructed by recent work on the transmission of *other parts* of the little corpus (*Parva Naturalia 1 + MA*) to which *MA* belongs, as we will now see.

10. A Final Challenge: Escobar 1990 on *De Insomniis*

Among the three independent members of De Leemans' new group (B^{e}E^{r}b), the Erlangensis E^r does not contain any treatise from *Parva Naturalia 1* at all, and the stemmatic position of Parisinus b in its (incomplete) text of *PN1* has, as far as our present knowledge goes, nothing in common with b's affiliation in the transmission of *MA*.[189] By contrast, Berolinensis B^e contains the whole set (*Sens./Mem./Somn.Vig./Insomn./Div.Somn./MA*), and it is—at least in the

---

[187] This observation is one of the results of Orlandi's Hamburg PhD thesis ('ANDRONIKOS KALLISTOS: Manuscripts, Activities, Texts') about which he kindly informed us in October 2017.

[188] De Leemans 2011a, CCXIV, n. 214: 'In the present context, it is not my intention to determine the place of these manuscripts in the *stemma codicum*.'

[189] Parisinus b, which does not contain *Sens.*, is a copy of Vaticanus Y in *Mem.* according to Bloch 2008, 8–10, and in *Insomn.* according to Escobar 1990, 110–11.

transmission of *De Insomniis*—related to Vaticanus P in a way which is strongly reminiscent of the relationship between De Leemans' new group (B^{e}E^{r}b) and Vaticanus P in the transmission of *MA*: Angel Escobar, in his Berlin PhD thesis (1990) on the transmission of *Insomn.*, had pointed out that Berolinensis B^e and Vaticanus P share a number of readings which are either not attested elsewhere at all or only by the remaining members of the group to which P belongs (Z^{a}B^{p}M^{o}P) and which he labelled **ε**, whereas on the other hand in an even greater number of cases B^e does *not* share the idiosyncratic readings of P or of its group.[190] So it seemed likely that the stemmatic position of Berolinensis B^e in the transmission of *Insomn.* is similar to that of B^{e}E^{r}b in *MA*.

Now Escobar assumed two main families of *Insomn.* manuscripts, **α** and **β**, which correspond, by and large, to Nussbaum's two families **a** and **b**. But unlike Nussbaum, Escobar did not assign the group which contains Vaticanus P (**ε**: Z^{a}PB^{p}M^o) to his **β**-family; instead, he derived it from a third, intermediate prototype **γ** the text of which would have been based, in each case where **α** and **β** disagree with each other, on a choice between these divergent **α**- and **β**-readings. Therefore, Escobar placed the **γ**-family (and its descendant **ε**) in a middle position beneath both **α** and **β**. Yet the most striking feature of Escobar's stemma was, from our point of view, that he regarded Berolinensis Phill. 1507/I (B^e) as a descendant of **γ**, and in particular of **ε**. Here is Escobar's stemma in a strongly simplified form:[191]

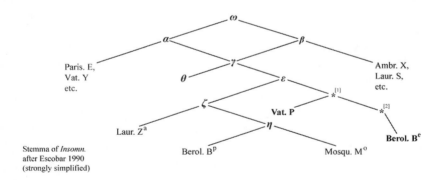

Stemma of *Insomn.*
after Escobar 1990
(strongly simplified)

---

[190] By contrast, David Bloch's study of the transmission of *Sens.* and *Mem.*, i.e. of the two first treatises of the corpus *PN1* + *MA*, did not yield any insights on Berolinensis B^e since he did not examine this or any other manuscript written after AD 1400; cf. Bloch 2008, 1: 'The mss. written later than the 14th century were never likely to provide interesting material and though I often disagree with Siwek's stemmatic conclusions, his investigations seem to justify ignoring them.' Bloch's reference to Siwek 1963, however, does not apply to the Berolinensis B^e, since this manuscript had been omitted without further notice already in the list of manuscripts offered by Siwek 1963, XVII–XVIII.

[191] For the complete stemma, see Escobar 1990, 205.

Such a marginal position of Berolinensis B^e would be incompatible, in the case of MA, with De Leemans' important discovery according to which manuscripts B^eE^rb (and William's second Greek model $\Gamma2$) *appear to make an original contribution to the text history of MA.*[192] This incompatibility was brought home to us in June 2011: A few weeks before the Symposium was to take place, Lutz Koch kindly sent us his draft of a stemma of MA, in which he stuck to the model of Escobar's stemma of *Insomn.* as closely as possible; according to that stemma, the three independent MA manuscripts of De Leeman's new group (B^eE^rb) would belong to the same unexciting sub-group as manuscripts $Z^aPB^pM^o$. It follows that accepting Koch's stemma would have ruled out the possibility of admitting superior readings transmitted only by B^eE^rb to the text of MA. Facing this dilemma we thought it advisable to examine the implicit presupposition of Koch's suggestion, i.e. the plausibility of the place Escobar had assigned to Berolinensis B^e in the stemma of *Insomn.*

The upshot of this examination was that Escobar's contention according to which B^e is a descendant of ϵ and γ is simply not borne out by his evidence.[193] For out of the total of fifty-four readings by which either the whole γ-family or its ϵ-group diverge from the two main families a and β, forty readings are *not* shared by B^e whereas only fourteen are; and out of the total of thirty-nine readings which while being rejected by Bekker are shared by γ either with a or with β, twelve are again absent from B^e. By consequence, Escobar had to postulate two hypothetical ancestors of B^e: The first one ($\star^{[1]}$), a common ancestor of Vaticanus P and B^e, would have introduced the twelve idiosyncratic readings transmitted only by P and B^e, whereas the second one ($\star^{[2]}$), a model of B^e alone, would have removed (by 'counter-contamination', as it were) the $40 + 12 = 52$ peculiar readings which B^e, according to Escobar's stemma, *should* have inherited from ϵ but in fact has not.

It seemed far more plausible to assume that besides the common ancestor (ω) of Escobar's a and β there was a second hyparchetype ψ of which B^e is a direct descendant, whereas P and his ancestors ϵ and γ go back mainly to ω and were only *contaminated* with ψ-readings to varying degrees: Vaticanus P with twelve such readings, ϵ with eleven, and γ with three. This assumption is strongly supported by the fact that a similar contamination of P and its group with readings from an independent source had already been observed in MA by Nussbaum 1975a. So it seems that the twenty-six readings shared by B^e with P,

---

[192]   De Leemans 2011a, CLXXXII.

[193]   The following remarks offer just a very brief summary of the detailed exposition of the evidence which the reader will find in Appendix IV to the present introduction. We are indebted to Christina Prapa for checking a considerable number of readings in the relevant *Insomn.* manuscripts.

ϵ, or γ against $\alpha\beta$ do not indicate any *direct* stemmatic relationship of B^e with P, ϵ, or γ at all. Furthermore, the readings rejected by Bekker while being shared by γ and B^e either with α or with β turned out to be, in general, as good as or even superior to Bekker's readings, so that these readings cannot be regarded as conjunctive errors on the basis of which one could prove B^e's dependence on γ.[194] Rather, the fact that those $\alpha\gamma$- or $\beta\gamma$-readings despised by Bekker are transmitted also by B^e is to be explained by the assumption that they go back to the archetype and were shared by both hyparchetypes ω and ψ from whence they could reach γ and B^e by two completely different routes: In these cases, Bekker failed to reconstruct the reading of ω.

As far as Berolinensis B^e is concerned, then, it seemed inevitable to modify the results of Escobar's otherwise quite useful study: His own hypothesis on the position of B^e is clearly less suitable to account for his evidence than the assumption according to which B^e is a direct descendant of a second hyparchetype (ψ) from which P and its ancestors ϵ and γ were contaminated. With this result at hand, the case of *Insomn.* had ceased to be an external obstacle against adopting an analogous hypothesis in the case of *MA*, where this solution was so strongly suggested by De Leemans' discovery.

11. Primavesi 2011: A New Hyparchetype

On 21 July 2011, at the nineteenth Symposium Aristotelicum, the present writer read a paper on 'The Text of *MA*' in which he made two points.

First, he claimed that the results both of previous research up to De Leemans 2011a and of his own analysis of manuscripts B^e, E^r, and b can be summed up in a line of argument which leads to the conclusion, not drawn by De Leemans 2011a, that these three manuscripts are direct independent descendants of Nussbaum's 'Majuscule MS', so that this source has henceforth to be regarded as a *second hyparchetype*:

1) The first model of William's translation (Γ1), as reconstructed by De Leemans 2011a, and the main model of Vaticanus P both belong to Jaeger's second family, i.e. to Nussbaum's family **b**.

2) The transmission, by Vaticanus P, of the four words $\kappa\iota\nu\epsilon\hat{\iota}\ \pi\rho\hat{\omega}\tau\sigma\nu\ \tau\grave{\sigma}\ \grave{\sigma}\rho\epsilon\kappa\tau\grave{\sigma}\nu$ in 700^{b}23-4 (which had fallen out in Jaeger's and Nussbaum's archetype) does not go back to Byzantine conjecture but to a source independent of

---

[194] The fact that Escobar used Bekker's edition as a basis for his collations (which is a quite reasonable thing to do) did not entitle him to treat deviations from Bekker's edition, without further ado, as 'errors'. In his treatment of the $\alpha\gamma$- or $\beta\gamma$-readings rejected by Bekker, Escobar seems to have lost sight of this point.

Nussbaum's archetype (i.e. to Nussbaum's 'Majuscule MS') a descendant of which served as an additional model for P.

3) The literal translation of 700^{b}23-4 κινεῖ πρῶτον τὸ ὀρεκτὸν offered by William's revised versions GR' and GR" (*movet primum quod appetibile*) also goes back to the independent source, so that William's additional Greek model *Γ*2 was (or had access to) a descendant of the independent source.

4) Inasmuch as other readings both presupposed in William's revisions and diverging from the text of Nussbaum's two families are shared by Vaticanus P, they also go back to the independent source used by William and P as an additional source.

5) William and Vaticanus P have now been joined by the new B^{e}E^{r}b-group in preserving the correct reading of 700^{b}23-4.

6) Further readings of this new B^{e}E^{r}b-group which diverge from the text of Nussbaum's two families *and* are either presupposed in William's revisions, or shared by Vaticanus P, or both, also go back to the independent source.

7) The new B^{e}E^{r}b-group, or its two uncontaminated members B^e and E^r, offer *more* readings demonstrably going back to the independent source than do either William alone or Vaticanus P alone.

8) The text offered by the new B^{e}E^{r}b-group does not share any clear *separative error* with one of Nussbaum's two families against the other one.

9) The new group goes back to a separate transliteration from majuscule into minuscule script, as the following shared errors of its two uncontaminated members (B^e and E^r) show: 698^{b}8 ἡ ἐν] μὲν B^{e}E^r.– 700^{b}34 ἢ ὥστ'] πως B^{e}E^r.– 703^{a}18 δ' εὐφυῶς] δὲ ὑφ' ὧ ὥς B^e vel δὲ ὑφ' ὧ ὡς E^r.

10) *Hence*: The new B^{e}E^{r}b-group goes back directly to the independent source, i.e. to Nussbaum's 'Majuscule MS', so that the latter has to be regarded as a second hyparchetype (henceforth: *β*), thereby downgrading Jaeger's and Nussbaum's archetype to the status of one out of two hyparchetypes (henceforth: *α*).

Second, the present writer had formed the opinion that the new hyparchetype does not just 'make an original contribution to the text history of *De Motu Animalium*'[195] but also to the *text itself*. In order to illustrate this point, he examined, in the paper he read at the Symposium, the most notorious *textual corruptions* in *MA*: four passages in which the reading of Jaeger's and Nussbaum's archetype had been shown, in the previous scholarly literature, to be seriously corrupt and in which neither Vaticanus P nor William's translation had provided a suitable

---

[195] That much had been claimed by De Leemans 2011a, CLXXXII, for his new B^{e}E^{r}b-group.

alternative reading. In all four passages, the new hyparchetype made a decisive contribution to the solution to the problem in question, and it did so in a surprising variety of ways. For in the *first* case it brought to light a superior reading which was afterwards discovered to have been also the original reading of the *codex vetustissimus* (Parisinus E) before erasure; in the *second* case it confirmed a very convincing emendation published only in 1989; in the *third* case it offered an impeccable reading transmitted nowhere else and never considered before; and in the *fourth* case it disentangled a complex textual corruption by showing that the corruption is *partly* due to an error of the first hyparchetype—from which it is free so that this error could be removed immediately—, and *partly* due to an error of the archetype—which it shares but for the conjectural solution to which the removal of the first error cleared the way.

(i) MA 2, 698ᵇ12–17: Mice in Pitch

This passage was edited by Bekker 1831 in the following form:

|698ᵇ12| ὥσπερ γὰρ καὶ ἐν|13| αὐτῶι δεῖ τι ἀκίνητον εἶναι, εἰ μέλλει κινεῖσθαι, οὕτως ἔτι|14| μᾶλλον ἔξω δεῖ τι εἶναι τοῦ ζώιου ἀκίνητον, πρὸς ὃ ἀπερει-|15| δόμενον κινεῖται τὸ κινούμενον.

For just as there must also be something unmoving within it, if it is to move, so even more so must there be something unmoving external to the animal, by pressing against which the moving thing moves.

εἰ γὰρ ὑποδώσει ἀεί, οἷον τοῖς|16| μυσὶ τοῖς ἐν τῆι γῆι, ἢ τοῖς ἐν τῆι ἄμμωι πορευομένοις, οὐ|17| πρόεισιν·

For if it always gives way—as it does with the mice on earth, or with people trying to walk on sand—then the thing will not advance:

698ᵇ16 μυσὶ YPS : ποσὶ E

Aristotle wants to show that an external resting point is a necessary condition of animal locomotion. By way of illustration, he offers two examples the second of which is fairly straightforward: People trying to walk on sand (presumably very loose sand) will not advance. But the first example, by contrast, is incomprehensible: Why should mice on earth be unable to move forward, although earth is 'a resistant medium *par excellence*'?[196] This obvious difficulty provoked an impressive array of conjectures:

[196] Barnes 1980, 224. It is true that Renehan 1994 tried to defend the reading τοῖς μυσὶ τοῖς ἐν τῆι γῆι by classifying the example as *hypothetical*. Cf. p. 252: 'The next thing to grasp, crucial for an understanding of

Farquharson 1912 n. 2: τοῖς μυσὶ ('mice') ἐν τῇ ζειᾷ ('grain').– Diels ap. Jaeger 1913b: τοῖς ἐμύσι ('tortoises') τοῖς ἐν τῇ γῇ ('earth').– Nussbaum 1975a and 1976: τοῖς μυσὶ ('shellfish', G. W. Owen's translation) τοῖς ἐν πηλῷ ('mud').– Nussbaum 1978: τοῖς ἐμύσι ('tortoises') τοῖς ἐν πηλῷ ('mud').– In the following conjectures, the two examples ('mice' and 'walking on sand') were run together: Platt 1913, 295: τοῖς ποσὶ ('feet', following Parisinus E) τοῖς ἐν τῇ ἄμμῳ ('sand').– Barnes 1980, 224: τοῖς μυσὶ ('mice') τοῖς ἐν τῇ ἅλῳ ('threshing floor').

Now both Berolinensis B^e and Erlangensis E^r offer 'in pitch' (ἐν τῆι πίττηι), instead of 'on earth' (ἐν τῇ γῆι). On the new reading, the first example would refer to a kind of *mouse trap* well known to us from a popular proverb which is attested from the fourth century BC onwards:[197] In a speech held around 360 BC the orator Apollodorus, son of Pasion, compared the opponent with the proverbial mouse that—having been lured, by its own greed, into a pitch trap—cannot move on and understands, by tasting the pitch, the cause of its imminent disaster. In our passage, adopting the B^eE^r variant ἐν τῆι πίττηι (but keeping the second τοῖς immediately before ἐν, which B^eE^r lack) yields the following text:

| |698^b15|εἰ γὰρ ὑποδώσει ἀεὶ οἷον τοῖς|16|μυσὶ τοῖς ἐν τῆι πίττηι, ἢ τοῖς ἐν τῆι ἄμμωι πορευομένοις, οὐ|17|πρόεισιν· | For if it always gives way—as it does with the proverbial 'mice in pitch' or with people trying to walk on sand—then the thing will not advance. |

698^b15–16 τοῖς μυσὶ τοῖς NXH^aLV^g Z^aPB^pM° : τοῖς ποσὶ τοῖς E : τοῖς μυσὶν B^eE^r : τοῖς b : sententiam a *b* (Nussbaum) traditam (τοῖς μυσὶ τοῖς ἐν τῇ γῇ ἢ τοῖς ἐν τῆι ἄμμωι πορευομένοις) in τοῖς ἐν τῇ γῇ πορευομένοις μυσὶν contraxit Mich.^P 105,25, unde verbis a *b* (Nussbaum) traditis novum ordinem τοῖς ἐν τῇ γῇ πορευομένοις μυσὶν ἢ τοῖς ἐν τῇ ἄμμω imposuerunt C^aO^dSV^p | ἐν τῇ(ι) πίττη(ι) B^eE^r, E ante rasuram : ἐν τῇ γῇ ΓΙΝ Z^aPB^pM° E^2, unde ἐν τῇ ἐν τῇ γῇ b : ἐν γῇ XH^aLV^g

---

the passage, is that *the entire sentence, including the οἷον clause, is hypothetical.* Mice *can* scamper over earth or sand, but here the οἷον is part of a "what if", not a real situation: what if earth or sand were not mediums of resistance, and absolutely so? Then mice, for example, could not move over them.' But that attempt does not carry conviction: Why should Aristotle have illustrated his point with a counterfactual example, when suitable examples are provided by empirical observation?

[197] Ps.-Demosthenes 50 (i.e. Apollodorus Pasionis filius, *Contra Polyclem*), 26: ἄρτι μῦς πίττης γεύεται· ἐβούλετο γὰρ Ἀθηναῖος εἶναι.– Cf. also Theocritus 14, 50–1: κεἰ μὲν ἀποστέρξαιμι, τὰ πάντα κεν ἐς δέον ἕρποι. / νῦν δὲ πόθεν; μῦς, φαντί, Θυώνιχε, γεύμεθα πίσσας.– Hero(n)das 2, 62–4: πέπονθα πρὸς Θάλητος ὅσσα κἠν πίσσῃ / μῦς· πὺξ ἐπλήγην, ἡ θύρη κατήρακται / τῆς οἰκίης μευ.– Zenobius restitutus e cod. Par. Suppl. 676 (S), Cohn 1887, 69 (= Lucillus Tarrhaeus. fr. IV Linnenkugel): οἱ δέ φασι τὸ ζῷον ἐμπεσὸν εἰς πίσσαν δεινὰ πάσχειν, καὶ τέλος ἀποθνήσκειν ἀνελθεῖν μὴ δυνάμενον.– Suetonius Περὶ βλασφημιῶν VIII 222; Taillardat 1967, 61: Ἁρμόζει δὲ εἰς γέροντας φειδωλοὺς ...καὶ ὁ 'μυσάλμης', γενόμενος ἐκ τοῦ μυστιλᾶσθαι ἅλμην, ἤγουν ἐκ τῶν εὐτελεστάτων ζῆν· ἦν γὰρ σκεύασμά τι εὐτελές, ὃ θαλασσίαν ἅλμην ἐκάλουν. Αὐτὸ δὲ δύναται δηλοῦν καὶ τὸ ἐπιπόνως βιοῦν· παροιμίαν γὰρ τὴν 'μῦς ἐν πίσσῃι' ἔνιοι 'μῦς ἐν ἅλμῃι' μεταγράφουσι.– Libanius ep. 192, 6 (Vol. X 177.9 Foerster): ἀλλ᾽ ἄρτι δὴ μῦς πίττης.– Nicetas Eugenianus, *Drosilla et Charicles* IV,

The whole point of a pitch trap is precisely to deprive, as it were, the mouse of an external point of rest: First, the little feet of the mouse sink downwards into the pitch; the pitch, in turn, will not release the feet but stick to them and even follow, as it were, their feeble efforts to move upwards. So the reading transmitted by B^c and E^r clearly suits the argument and it is backed by a well-attested contemporary proverb:[198] It seems highly probable, therefore, that this is what Aristotle wrote and Andronicus edited.

Prudent readers will perhaps feel a moment's doubt as to whether the introduction of so well-known a proverb could not also be due to a later scholar who wanted to emend an evidently corrupt passage. But such doubts were dispelled by an astounding discovery made by Lutz Koch in the *codex vetustissimus*, Parisinus gr. 1853 (E). Whereas it had been thought since Bekker 1831 that Parisinus E shares the common reading ἐν τῇ γῇι, Koch observed that this reading was introduced by the second hand (E²) over an erasure, and that the *scriptio inferior*, i.e. the original reading before erasure, is still partly visible: the letters ιττηι being preceded by faint traces of π. In other words: The reading 'in pitch' (ἐν τῆι πίττηι) as attested by our mid-fifteenth-century manuscripts B^cE^r has been confirmed by the oldest representative of the first hyparchetype, Parisinus E, in which this reading was, however, concealed in the thirteenth century. On the other hand, it is obvious that the B^cE^r reading and the original reading of Parisinus E are mutually independent: In Parisinus E the phrase τοῖς μυσὶ τοῖς ἐν τῆι πίττηι is marred by the erroneous replacement of μυσὶ ('mice') by ποσὶ ('feet'), from which B^cE^r are free,[199] whereas in B^cE^r the phrase has been impaired by the loss of the second τοῖς (immediately before ἐν) which is indispensable—lest ἐν τῆι πίττηι be an adverbial phrase in danger of being linked with πορευομένοις—and which has been preserved in Parisinus E. So it seems clear that both the B^cE^r reading and the original reading of Parisinus E (ante rasuram) go back, independently, to the reading of the archetype, against the reading ἐν τῇ γῇι introduced by *b* (Nussbaum)—presumably out of ignorance of the proverb—and preserved by all other Greek *MA* manuscripts.

(ii) *MA* 3, 699ª12–14: An External Point of Rest for the Universe?

This passage was edited by Bekker 1831 in the following form:

408–10 (pp. 119–20 Conca): Οὕτως ἐρῶν πᾶς—ὡς ἄφυκτόν τι πόθος—/ ἁλίσκεται γὰρ τοῖς Ἔρωτος δικτύοις, / ὡς μῦς πρὸς ὑγρᾶς ἐμπεσὼν πίσσης χύτραν. See further Romero 2001, 241–5.

[198] For Aristotle's general predilection for proverbs, cf. Bonitz 1870, 569ª60–570^b57 ('proverbia ab Ar usurpata vel explicata').

[199] τοῖς μυσὶν ἐν τῆι πίττηι B^cE^r : τοῖς ποσὶ τοῖς ἐν τῆι πίττηι E ante rasuram.

|699ᵃ12| Ἀπορήσειε δ' ἄν τις,	Someone might pose this problem:
ἆρ' εἴ τι κινεῖ τὸν ὅλον οὐρανόν,	if something moves the whole heavens,
|13| εἶναί τε δεῖ ἀκίνητον	must it be both unmoving
καὶ τοῦτο μηθὲν εἶναι τοῦ οὐρανοῦ	and must this be no part of the heavens,
μόριον |14| μηδ' ἐν τῶι οὐρανῶι.	nor in the heavens?

699ᵃ13 εἶναί τε δεῖ EY : εἶναι θέλει PS

The text is unsatisfactory with regard to both the Greek (a) and the argument (b).

(a) The syntactical subject of the conditional clause 'if something moves the whole heavens' (εἴ τι κινεῖ τὸν ὅλον οὐρανόν) is the indefinite pronoun 'something' (τι). The conditional clause is followed by a main clause in the form of a question which consists of two parts, the first part being 'must it be both unmoving' (εἶναί τε δεῖ ἀκίνητον), and the second 'and (must) this be no part of the heavens, nor in the heavens' (καὶ τοῦτο μηθὲν εἶναι τοῦ οὐρανοῦ μόριον μηδ' ἐν τῶι οὐρανῶι). The subject of this double main clause can, in principle, either be identical with the subject of the preceding conditional clause, or not. If it is, the identity can either be emphasized by means of a demonstrative pronoun 'this' (τοῦτο) referring back to the subject of the conditional clause, or the identity of subject can be just implied by the lack of any new subject coming up in the main clause. *If* one were to emphasize, however, that the subject of the double main clause is the same as the subject of the preceding conditional clause, it would be decidedly strange to place the demonstrative 'this' (τοῦτο) in the *second* part of the main clause alone, as is attested by Jaeger's and Nussbaum's two families, i.e. by the progeny of the first hyparchetype, and accepted by Bekker. For if such a demonstrative is needed at all, it is needed already in the first part of the main clause, and if it is omitted there, it should not be inserted in the second part either.[200] The same observation applies if we prefer, with Jaeger, the curious εἶναι θέλει (Nussbaum's family *b*)[201] over Bekker's εἶναί τε δεῖ (Nussbaums's family **a**). In order to remove this oddity, both Farquharson 1912 and Forster 1937 suggested shifting the boundary between the two parts of the main clause in such a way that the demonstrative (τοῦτο) still belongs to the first part—either by inserting

---

[200] Manuwald 1989, 117: 'Wenn das τι das gemeinsame Subjekt des Bedingungs- und des Fragesatzes darstellt, dann sollte es mit τοῦτο gleich im ersten Teil des Fragesatzes aufgenommen werden und nicht erst im zweiten...'.

[201] One might compare Plato's remake of Parmenides B 8, line 38, Diels/Kranz in *Theaetetus* 180d–e (according to the Berlin Papyrus *P. Berol.* 9782, col. 70, lines 41–3): οἶον ἀκίνητόν τε θέλει τῶι παντ(ὶ) ὄνομ(α) εἶναι. See further Primavesi 2008, 363–7.

a further (connective) καὶ after τοῦτο (Farquharson), or by having τοῦτο and καὶ swap places (Forster):

|699ᵃ12| Ἀπορήσειε δ' ἄν τις,	Someone might pose this problem:
ἆρ' εἴ τι κινεῖ τὸν ὅλον οὐρανόν,	If something moves the whole heavens,
|13| εἶναί τε δεῖ ἀκίνητον καὶ τοῦτο,	must *this*, too, be unmoving,
<καὶ> μηθὲν εἶναι τοῦ οὐρανοῦ μόριον	and be no part of the heavens, nor
|14| μηδ' ἐν τῶι οὐρανῶι.	in the heavens?

699ᵃ13 εἶναί τε δεῖ *a* Bekker : εἶναι θέλει *b* Jaeger | καὶ τοῦτο, <καὶ> Farquharson Nussbaum : τοῦτο, καὶ Forster : καὶ τοῦτο *a b*

(b) Apart from the linguistic problem addressed by the aforementioned conjectures, there is also a problem with the argument. In chapter 2, Aristotle has established that (i) animal self-motion requires an external resting point, and (ii) that moving an *object*, in particular, requires an external resting point which is also external to the moved object. So at the beginning of chapter 3, Aristotle could reasonably proceed to the question as to whether the mover of the universe, too, stands in need of such an external resting point.[202] This initial question would then be plausibly motivated, in 699ᵃ14–17, by introducing a case distinction and by showing that in both cases an unmoved item is involved: The mover of the universe may be either a *moved* mover—in which case it would probably need a point of rest external both to itself and to the universe—or an *unmoved* mover—in which case the mover itself could be the external point of rest, on condition that it be neither a part of nor located within the object moved by it:

|699ᵃ14| εἴτε γὰρ αὐτὸ κινούμενον	For if it moves the universe while itself
κινεῖ αὐτόν, ἀ-|15| νάγκη τινὸς	moving, it must move it while itself
ἀκινήτου θιγγάνον κινεῖν καὶ	touching something unmoving and this
τοῦτο μηθὲν εἶναι |16| μόριον τοῦ	must be no part of the thing moving
κινοῦντος·	the universe.
εἴτ' εὐθὺς ἀκίνητόν ἐστιν τὸ κινοῦν,	And if that which moves the universe is
ὁμοίως |17| οὐθὲν ἔσται τοῦ	immediately unmoving, similarly it will
κινουμένου μόριον.	be no part of the moving thing.

---

[202] Nussbaum 1978, 292. Cf. Manuwald 1989, 118: 'Das Problem, das man nach dem Zusammenhang erwartet, ist doch, ob ein ruhender Stützpunkt, wie für die (irdischen) Lebewesen, so auch für das All anzunehmen sei.' See also Coope 2020.

But why should Aristotle already at the beginning of chapter 3, instead of applying the problem of the external resting point to the mover of the universe, immediately shift his attention to the *unmovedness* of the mover of the universe (which has not been prepared by chapter 2 at all)?[203] And how could this initial move, once admitted, then be *supported* ($\gamma\acute{\alpha}\rho$) by opening up again the alternative 'moved mover vs. unmoved mover' in the following sentence (699^{a}14–17)?[204] And yet this unmotivated initial shift to the unmovedness of the mover of the universe is the common feature of the text as transmitted by the progeny of the first hyparchetype, be it with or without the emendations suggested by Farquharson (Nussbaum) or Forster.

For this reason, Manuwald 1989 suggested inserting, in the first part of the main clause, an additional $\tau\iota$ ('something'). This emendation solves both problems (a) and (b) at once, since the additional $\tau\iota$ could serve as point of reference for the demonstrative 'this' ($\tau o\hat{v}\tau o$), and would refer to *any* external point of rest, be it the mover himself or not:[205]

|699^{a}12\|$\mathit{A}\pi o\rho\acute{\eta}\sigma\epsilon\iota\epsilon$ δ' ἄν τις,	Someone might pose this problem:
ἆρ' εἴ τι κινεῖ τὸν ὅλον οὐρανόν,	If something moves the whole universe,
|13|εἶναί τι δεῖ ἀκίνητον,	must there indeed be **something** unmoving,
καὶ τοῦτο μηθὲν εἶναι τοῦ οὐρανοῦ	where this must be nothing of the
μόριον|14|μηδ' ἐν τῶι οὐρανῶι.	universe, and not in the universe?

699^{a}13 εἶναί τι δεῖ Manuwald : εἶναί τε δεῖ E

Seen against the background of this convincing emendation[206] it is altogether remarkable that in 699^{a}13 the common feature of the B^{c}E^{r}b readings in that passage is precisely the presence of the additional indefinite $\tau\iota$ which is absent

---

[203] Manuwald 1989, 118: 'Es geht doch um das Problem des äußeren, ruhenden Stützpunktes, unabhängig von der Art der Bewegungsverursachung (etwa Selbstbewegung oder Bewegung durch eine äußere Ursache). Da überrascht die Frage schon, ob beim All der Beweger unbewegt sein müsse.'

[204] Manuwald 1989, 118: 'Außerdem würde, wenn es im Einleitungssatz um einen unbewegten Beweger ginge, die Alternative des folgenden Satzes unverständlich.'

[205] Manuwald 1989, 118. Already Barnes 1980, 244, had not only presupposed the $\tau\iota$ in his *interpretation* of the passage, as it were, but he had also mentioned the possibility of restoring it to the text by way of conjecture. Yet he deemed this conjecture unnecessary because he made the assumption that ἀκίνητον on its own can also mean $\tau\iota\ldots$ ἀκίνητον. This assumption, however, was an over-generous one, since ἀκίνητον is neither predicate nor object here, nor does it occur within a negative clause: See Kühner/Gerth 1898–1904, I, 58–60 (§ 360 with n. 1).

[206] Seeck 1992, Col. 192: 'eine überzeugende Konjektur, die dem umstrittenen Satz in sich und im Kontext einen befriedigenden Sinn gibt'.

from all manuscripts of Nussbaum's two families *a* (εἶναί τε δεῖ EYV) and *b* (εἶναι θέλει cett.):

εἶναί τε τι δεῖ B^c : εἶναί τι δεῖ E^r : εἶναι δεῖ τι b

The reading of the common *source* of B^cE^rb seems to be preserved by the Berlin manuscript (B^c), since this manuscript alone features also the τε attested by Parisinus E and its descendants VY. So we assume that the remaining independent members of the new group (i.e. E^rb) lost the τε, whereas the omission of τι is a conjunctive error of all manuscripts going back to the first hyparchetype (τε δεῖ then being further corrupted—via τέλει—to θέλει in Nussbaum's family *b*). We conclude that Manuwald's conjecture has been confirmed, in substance, by the new B^cE^rb-group, and that Berolinensis B^c, in particular, has preserved exactly the wording of the archetype: εἶναί τέ τι δεῖ. This passage is one of De Leeman's four examples of B^cE^rb readings which are independent of Nussbaum's two families *a* and *b* and are neither shared by Vaticanus P nor translated by William.[207]

(iii) *MA* 7, 701ª36–ᵇ1: Prohairesis

This passage was edited by Bekker 1831 in the following form:

τῶν|37|δ' ὀρεγομένων πράττειν	With animals that desire to act,
τὰ μὲν δι' ἐπιθυμίαν ἢ θυμὸν	it is partly from appetite or spirit,
τὰ δὲ|701ᵇ1|δι' ὄρεξιν ἢ βούλησιν	partly from desire or wish
τὰ μὲν ποιοῦσιν, τὰ δὲ πράττουσιν.	that some of them produce, some of them act.

This form of the text goes back to the first hyparchetype: It corresponds to what the manuscripts belonging to Jaeger's and Nussbaum's two families have transmitted without any major variant reading. But Nussbaum 1975a correctly identified a problem here: In the present passage, the psychic causes of acting or producing are subdivided into appetite (*epithumia*), spirit (*thumos*), desire (*orexis*), and wish (*boulesis*). And yet, in the preceding chapter 6 Aristotle has characterized appetite, spirit, and wish as the three *kinds* of

---

[207] De Leemans 2011a, CCXIV, n. 216. De Leemans, however, did not alert his readers to the striking fact that in this case, the essential feature of the new reading had already been postulated before B^cE^rb came to light.

desire,[208] a doctrine upheld by him in other works, too.[209] Even at the beginning of our passage, the idea that desire is to be regarded as the superordinate genus seems, in a way, to be suggested by the partitive genitive 'with animals that *desire* to act' ($\tau\hat{\omega}\nu$ δ' $\dot{o}\rho\epsilon\gamma o\mu\acute{e}\nu\omega\nu$ $\pi\rho\acute{a}\tau\tau\epsilon\iota\nu$) which defines the set that all animals which produce or act belong to. Seen against this background, it is decidedly strange that desire itself should be listed in our passage on the same level with its three kinds appetite, spirit, and wish. That is why Nussbaum suggested deleting $\ddot{o}\rho\epsilon\xi\iota\nu$ $\ddot{\eta}$:[210]

$\tau\hat{\omega}\nu\|37\|\delta$' $\dot{o}\rho\epsilon\gamma o\mu\acute{e}\nu\omega\nu$ $\pi\rho\acute{a}\tau\tau\epsilon\iota\nu$	With creatures that desire to act,
$\tau\grave{a}$ $\mu\grave{e}\nu$ $\delta\iota$' $\dot{e}\pi\iota\theta\upsilon\mu\acute{i}a\nu$ $\ddot{\eta}$ $\theta\upsilon\mu\grave{o}\nu$	it is sometimes from appetite or spiritedness
$\tau\grave{a}$ $\delta\grave{e}\|701^b\iota\|\delta\iota<\grave{a}>$ $\{\ddot{o}\rho\epsilon\xi\iota\nu$ $\ddot{\eta}\}$ $\beta o\acute{\upsilon}\lambda\eta\sigma\iota\nu$	and sometimes from wish
$\tau\grave{a}$ $\mu\grave{e}\nu$ $\pi o\iota o\hat{\upsilon}\sigma\iota\nu,$ $\tau\grave{a}$ $\delta\grave{e}$ $\pi\rho\acute{a}\tau\tau o\upsilon\sigma\iota\nu.$	that they make or act.

Klaus Corcilius quite understandably tried to defend the reading of the manuscripts then known against the admittedly severe deletion proposed by Nussbaum. He proceeded from the theory, advanced by Richard Loening in 1903, according to which the word *orexis* has a double meaning ('Doppelbedeutung') in Aristotle, 'desire' and 'irrational desire'.[211] On the strength of this theory, Corcilius maintained that Aristotle uses *orexis* in the restricted meaning 'irrational desire' whenever he is thinking of a contrast between desire and intellect (*nous*).[212] Our passage could then be read as follows: Aristotle would introduce the two irrational kinds of desire, i.e. appetite and spirit, exclusively with regard to non-human animals in the

---

[208] *MA* 6, 700^{b}22: $\beta o\acute{\upsilon}\lambda\eta\sigma\iota\varsigma$ $\delta\grave{e}$ $\kappa a\grave{\iota}$ $\theta\upsilon\mu\grave{o}\varsigma$ $\kappa a\grave{\iota}$ $\dot{e}\pi\iota\theta\upsilon\mu\acute{i}a$ $\pi\acute{a}\nu\tau a$ $\dot{o}\rho\acute{e}\xi\epsilon\iota\varsigma.$

[209] *De An.* II 3, 414^{b}2: $\ddot{o}\rho\epsilon\xi\iota\varsigma$ $\mu\grave{e}\nu$ $\gamma\grave{a}\rho$ $\dot{e}\pi\iota\theta\upsilon\mu\acute{i}a$ $\kappa a\grave{\iota}$ $\theta\upsilon\mu\grave{o}\varsigma$ $\kappa a\grave{\iota}$ $\beta o\acute{\upsilon}\lambda\eta\sigma\iota\varsigma.-$ *EE* B 7, 1223^{a}26–7: $\dot{a}\lambda\lambda\grave{a}$ $\mu\grave{\eta}\nu$ $\dot{\eta}$ $\ddot{o}\rho\epsilon\xi\iota\varsigma$ $\epsilon\dot{\iota}\varsigma$ $\tau\rho\acute{\iota}a$ $\delta\iota a\iota\rho\epsilon\hat{\iota}\tau a\iota,$ $\epsilon\dot{\iota}\varsigma$ $\beta o\acute{\upsilon}\lambda\eta\sigma\iota\nu$ $\kappa a\grave{\iota}$ $\theta\upsilon\mu\grave{o}\nu$ $\kappa a\grave{\iota}$ $\dot{e}\pi\iota\theta\upsilon\mu\acute{i}a\nu.$

[210] Nussbaum 1975a, 541 (= 1976, 146; cf. 1978, 346–7 *ad loc.*): 'The use of $\ddot{o}\rho\epsilon\xi\iota\varsigma$ as a species is unparalleled, and inexplicable here, especially in view of $\tau\hat{\omega}\nu$ δ' $\dot{o}\rho\epsilon\gamma o\mu\acute{e}\nu\omega\nu$ $\pi\rho\acute{a}\tau\tau\epsilon\iota\nu$ above. It is better to bracket it and see the $\tau\grave{a}$ $\mu\acute{e}\nu$...$\tau\grave{a}$ $\delta\acute{e}$ as contrasting the actions involving rational wanting with those involving the two irrational species. The corruption may have come about because of the interest of some literary scribe in having two alternatives in each group.'

[211] Loening 1903, 36 n. 4: 'Wenn in Psych. III 10 $\nu o\hat{\upsilon}\varsigma$ und $\ddot{o}\rho\epsilon\xi\iota\varsigma$ bald alternativ, bald kumulativ als Ursachen der Bewegung genannt werden, so hängt das mit der Doppelbedeutung des Wortes $\ddot{o}\rho\epsilon\xi\iota\varsigma$ zusammen, welches bei Aristoteles bald das Begehren schlechthin, bald das sinnliche Begehren, gleichbedeutend mit $\dot{e}\pi\iota\theta\upsilon\mu\acute{i}a$, bezeichnet; vgl. Psych. III 9 a. E.'

[212] Corcilius 2008a, 324: '‹Strebung› (*orexis*) ist hier wieder im Sinne von arationalen Strebungen zu verstehen, da sie mit der rationalen Strebung ‹Wunsch› kontrastiert wird'; and n. 63: 'Nussbaums Tilgung von [Strebung oder] in 701b1 (von Kollesch übernommen) scheint mir nicht erforderlich.'

first place. Only then would he shift to rational animals, which are characterized by a coexistence of irrational and rational desires. In referring to them, he would take up again the two irrational kinds of desire just mentioned and subsume them under the genus 'irrational desire' (here called *orexis*, according to the theory) in order to contrast the irrational desire of rational animals with their rational desire, i.e. with wish.

Both Loening's theory and Corcilius' attempt at defending Bekker's text of our passage on the basis of that theory have failed to convince the present writer. It goes without saying that specific episodes of desire which are in conflict with the intellect will belong to one of the irrational kinds of desire. But this truism does by no means imply that—over and above the distinction of three *kinds* of desire—there are also two different meanings of 'desire' as the theory of the double meaning assumes. This becomes immediately clear when we look at the passage once quoted by Loening from Aristotle *De An.* III 9 as evidence for his theory:[213]

> | 433ᵃ6 | Yet not even desire (*orexis*) is in complete control of | 7 | this kind of movement (i.e. locomotion). For continent people when they are having an appetitive desire (*oregomenoi kai epithumountes*), do not | 8 | do the things for which they have this desire (*orexis*), but they follow reason.

It is clear that *orexis*, on its first occurrence in 433ᵃ6, refers to the genus 'desire', whereas on its second occurrence in 433ᵃ8, it refers to a specific episode of desire, i.e. to an appetitive desire suppressed by reason. But Loening was simply wrong in claiming that we are dealing here with a double 'meaning' of *orexis*. For just in between the two occurrences of *orexis*, i.e. in line 433ᵃ7, Aristotle makes it clear that he is now shifting from the genus 'desire' to an episode of appetitive desire, by means of the hendiadys *oregomenoi kai epithumountes* ('having a desire in the sense of having an appetite' = 'having an appetitive desire'). The second occurrence of *orexis* refers back, by means of the definite article (*ten* orexin = 'the aforementioned desire'), to the specific episode of appetitive desire introduced by the two participles. Therefore, the appropriate translation of that second occurrence is 'this desire', certainly not 'the appetitive desire'—just as in the preceding hendiadys *oregomenoi kai epithumountes* the first participle on its own means 'having a desire', certainly not 'having an appetitive desire'. No double meaning of *orexis* is involved here.

---

[213] *De An.* III 9, 433ᵃ6–8, cited by Loening 1903, 36 n. 4: 'vgl. Psych. III 9 a. E.'

In our *MA* passage, by contrast, no shift of reference is hinted at between the initial introduction of 'animals that *desire* to act' (τῶν δ' ὀρεγομένων πράττειν) and line 701ᵇ1 where the progeny of the first hyparchetype read 'from desire' (*di'orexin*): In order to make sense of *di'orexin* here, we would indeed need the double meaning of *orexis* which Loening's reference to *De An.* III 9, 433ᵃ6–8, failed to justify. So the text of the first hyparchetype seems to leave us with an uncomfortable alternative: Resuscitating the dubious double-meaning theory just in order to save the text of the first hyparchetype in our passage would seem to be special pleading, but Nussbaum's deletion of ὄρεξιν ἢ must count as a fairly drastic intervention. With this dilemma in mind, we were delighted to find out that in 701ᵇ1 the new BᶜEʳb-group has transmitted the reading διὰ προαίρεσιν ('from decision') instead of the problematic reading δι' ὄρεξιν ('from desire'):

τῶν|37| δ' ὀρεγομένων πράττειν	With animals that desire to act,
τὰ μὲν δι' ἐπιθυμίαν ἢ θυμὸν	it is partly from appetite or spirit,
τὰ δὲ|701ᵃ1| διὰ προαίρεσιν ἢ βούλησιν	partly from decision or wish
τὰ μὲν ποιοῦσιν, τὰ δὲ πράττουσιν.	that some of them produce, some
	of them act.

701ᵇ1 διὰ προαίρεσιν ἢ βούλησιν BᶜEʳb : δι' ὄρεξιν ἢ βούλησιν cett. : διὰ βούλησιν Nussbaum

This new BᶜEʳb-reading evidently sets us free from the dilemma created by the reading of the first hyparchetype, *di'orexin*. What is more: A list of the psychic causes which prompt living beings to act would be seriously incomplete without *prohairesis*. Aristotle has already provided, in *MA* 6, a list of psychic causes of animal movement in which 'decision' is mentioned alongside with 'wish':[214]

> For all animals both cause movement and are moved for the sake of some end, so that this is the limit of every one of their motions, the end. But we see that the things which move animals are discursive thought (*dianoia*) and appearance (*phantasia*) and decision (*prohairesis*) and wish (*boulesis*) and appetite (*epithumia*).

And a little further down, he has also emphasized the difference between the three standard kinds of desire—appetite, spirit, and wish—and 'decision':[215]

> But wish (*boulesis*) and spirit (*thumos*) and appetite (*epithumia*) are all desires (*orexeis*), whereas decision (*prohairesis*) belongs to both discursive thought (*dianoia*) and desire (*orexis*).

---

[214] *MA* 6, 700ᵇ15–18.   [215] *MA* 6, 700ᵇ22–3.

An application of the distinction of wish and decision to the theory of animal self-motion as expounded in *MA* seems to be provided by the following description of a complex practical syllogism from *MA* 7:[216]

> 'I need a covering, but a cloak is a covering. I need a cloak.—That which I need should be made. But I need a cloak.' He makes a cloak. And the conclusion that a cloak should be made is an action.

> But his action starts somewhere: 'If there is to be a cloak, necessarily this must happen first; but if this is to happen, this.' And he does that immediately.

Given that the *ends* of rational actions fall within the province of *boulesis*, whereas the *means* fall within the province of *prohairesis*,[217] the covering (*skepasma*), and perhaps also the cloak (*himation*), would count as objects of wish, whereas the steps necessary for the making of a cloak would count as objects of decision. And since the movement is explicitly said to begin with the first step towards making a cloak, the immediate causation of movement would have to be brought about by *prohairesis*. Hence, no list of psychic causes of action could be complete without mentioning *prohairesis*. We conclude that in our passage (*MA* 7, 701ª36–ᵇ1) the list of psychic causes of acting or producing in the soul must, by any means, include the *dia prohairesin* transmitted by BᶜEʳb. Its replacement by *di' orexin* seems to be a conjunctive error of all manuscripts going back to Nussbaum's archetype (our hyparchetype **α**).

But one might ask whether the difficult reading *di' orexin* is not more likely to have been emended, by a competent scribe, to the easy reading *dia prohairesin* than the other way round: Why should anybody have replaced *dia prohairesin* by *di' orexin*?[218] We think that *di' orexin* originated as a marginal summary. Aristotle himself does not simply introduce his list of kinds of action as a dihaeresis of actions *di'orexin*, but rather as an overview of actions by 'animals that desire to act' (τῶν δ' ὀρεγομένων πράττειν). The point of this circumstantial expression seems to be that Aristotle's list (in its original form, as preserved by BᶜEʳb) includes actions *dia prohairesin*, i.e. actions not just caused by *orexis* alone but by a *combination* of *orexis* and *dianoia*,[219] so that, strictly speaking, not all of the causes mentioned are just species of the genus *orexis*. Now a more simple-minded reader may of course feel that what Aristotle is talking about, after all, is kinds of action caused 'by desire', *di'orexin*, since all four kinds of causation

---

[216] *MA* 7, 701ª17–22.

[217] Cf., e.g., *EN* III 3, 1111ᵇ26–7 (ἔτι δ' ἡ μὲν βούλησις τοῦ τέλους ἐστὶ μᾶλλον, ἡ δὲ προαίρεσις τῶν πρὸς τὸ τέλος) and *EE* II 10, 1226ª7–8 (οὐθεὶς γὰρ τέλος οὐδὲν προαιρεῖται, ἀλλὰ τὰ πρὸς τὸ τέλος) and ibid., 1226ª16–17 (βούλεσθαι μὲν καὶ δόξα μάλιστα τοῦ τέλους, προαίρεσις δ' οὐκ ἔστιν).

[218] Cf. Cooper 2020.

[219] *MA* 6, 700ᵇ22–3: βούλησις δὲ καὶ θυμὸς καὶ ἐπιθυμία πάντα ὀρέξεις, ἡ δὲ προαίρεσις κοινὸν διανοίας καὶ ὀρέξεως.

(τὰ μὲν δι' ἐπιθυμίαν ἢ θυμὸν τὰ δὲ διὰ προαίρεσιν ἢ βούλησιν) do in fact, *in one way or another*, involve desire. So it is quite easy to imagine that such a reader would supply, in a marginal note, precisely what Aristotle had carefully avoided: a reference to the 'genus', i.e. the general phrase δι' ὄρεξιν. Such a note, when put close to διὰ προαίρεσιν, could then easily be misunderstood as a correction of it, and accordingly replace it in the text.

(iv) *MA* 7, 701ᵇ1–7: The automatic theatres

This passage was edited by Bekker 1831 in the following form:

ὥσ-|2|περ δὲ τὰ αὐτόματα κινεῖται μικρᾶς κινήσεως γινομένης	Just as the *automata* are set moving when a small motion occurs—
− |3| λυομένων τῶν στρεβλῶν καὶ κρουόντων ἀλλήλας τὰς στρέβλας −	The cables are released and they (*masc./neutr.*) strike each other (*fem.*), the cables—
|4| καὶ τὸ ἁμάξιον...	and as the little wagon...
|7| οὕτω καὶ τὰ ζῷα κινεῖται.	so too are animals moved.

γινομένης P : γενομένης ESY

The general structure of the passage is clear: Animal self-motion (ᵇ7 οὕτω καὶ τὰ ζῷα κινεῖται) is compared to the way *automata* (ᵇ1–3) and a little wagon (ᵇ4–6) are set moving. In the present context, we will be concerned mainly with the first comparison, i.e. with the *automata*. The point of this comparison seems to be the surprising difference in kind between input and output: In an animal, the mere perception of an object of desire may swiftly cause a movement of the limbs, just as in an *automaton*, as soon as a small initial movement (ᵇ2 μικρᾶς κινήσεως) has been carried out by an external agent, a movement of a very different kind results.[220] The details of this comparison are indicated in line 701ᵇ3 by means of two absolute genitives, λυομένων τῶν στρεβλῶν ('the cables being released') and κρουόντων ἀλλήλας τὰς στρέβλας ('striking/each other/the cables'). Yet the second genitive construction, as it stood in Nussbaum's archetype (our hyparchetype **a**), is obscured by textual corruption.[221] There are two problems:

(a) *The syntactical impossibility of* κρουόντων ἀλλήλας: This expression must be corrupt, since the reciprocal pronoun ἀλλήλας ('each other', feminine plural) would have to refer not only to the object of the striking but also to

---

[220] Berryman 2003, 358: 'According to Aristotle, the definitive feature of a self-mover is to be so constituted as to react to nonlocal change stemming from the environment by moving locally. Animals—unlike stones or artifacts—can instigate local motion when there are changes in their environment, but nothing pushing or pulling them. The automata he describes do not precisely do this, but they share with self-movers the capacity to transform one kind of input into motion of a different kind.'

[221] Nussbaum 1975a, 548: 'hopelessly corrupt'.

the subject, implying that both subject and object are feminine. The participle κρουόντων, however, implies that the subject of the striking is masculine or neuter. Therefore, ἀλλήλας cannot refer back to the subject, and if it cannot do that, it cannot refer to the object either.

(b) *The dubious role of the 'cables' (στρέβλαι) in the second genitive construction*: The first genitive construction (λυομένων τῶν στρεβλῶν) is impeccable as far it goes, but its genitive τῶν στρεβλῶν cannot also serve as the implicit subject of the second genitive construction (κρουόντων), since τῶν στρεβλῶν is feminine, whereas κρουόντων is not. And the final accusative τὰς στρέβλας must be corrupt, since it does not suit either syntax or content. As to the syntax: τὰς στρέβλας could not serve as a direct object of the preceding participle (κρουόντων) even if this participle were a feminine one (κρουουσῶν). When a reciprocal pronoun is used as a direct object, only the syntactical subject can be expressed on its own (if it is not to be supplied from the context), whereas the syntactical object is determined exclusively by the reciprocal pronoun that marks it as identical to the subject. It follows that a separate expression for the syntactical object is strictly inadmissible here. As to the content: The idea that the initial release of the cables yields the result that these very cables are striking each other is not only bizarre in itself, but also quite ill-suited to illustrate the surprising *transformation* of an initial input.

Whereas Bekker, Jaeger,[222] and Louis[223] printed the transmitted version without further ado, the corruption of our passage was diagnosed by Farquharson 1912 and by Forster 1937. Both scholars suggested emendations, and Torraca 1958a and Nussbaum 1975 tried to improve on their suggestions:

λυομένων τῶν στρεβλῶν καὶ	κρουόντων	ἀλλήλας	τὰς στρέβλας	Nussbaum's archetype
λυομένων τῶν <u>ξύλων</u> καὶ	κρουόντων	ἀλλήλα<u>ις</u>	τὰς στρέβλας	Farquharson
λυομένων τῶν στρεβλῶν καὶ	κρου<u>ουσῶν</u>	ἀλλήλας	{τὰς στρέβλας}	Forster (and Kollesch)
λυομένων τῶν στρεβλῶν καὶ	κρουόντων	ἄλληλ<u>α</u>	{τὰς στρέβλας}	Torraca
λυομένων τῶν στρεβλῶν καὶ	κρουόντων	ἄλληλ<u>α</u>	<u>τῶν ξύλων</u>	Nussbaum

These emendations contributed to our two problems (a) and (b) in the following way. (a) *The syntactical impossibility of* κρουόντων ἀλλήλας: It was suggested to change either the case of ἀλλήλας (Farquharson: ἀλλήλαις 'against one another'),

[222] Jaeger 1913b, 12.　　[223] Louis 1973, 62.

or the gender of the participle (Forster: κρουουσῶν), or the gender of ἀλλήλας (Torraca and Nussbaum: ἄλληλα). Interestingly, Kollesch 1960 envisaged the possibility of inserting a *preposition* between κρουόντων and ἀλλήλας, but she did not pursue this idea further: As soon as the reciprocal pronoun ceases to be the direct object, one has to supply another one, and it did not occur to Kollesch that instead of merely deleting τὰς στρέβλας (with Forster), one could also replace it with a more suitable object.[224] (b) *The dubious role of the 'cables' (στρέβλαι) in the second genitive construction*: In order to supply κρουόντων with a suitable subject, Farquharson and Nussbaum replaced either the preceding genitive τῶν στρεβλῶν or the final accusative τὰς στρέβλας with τῶν ξύλων.[225] As far as the final accusative τὰς στρέβλας is concerned, there has been a general consensus since Forster 1937 that it must be either deleted or replaced.

The manuscripts of the new BᶜEʳb-group, however, have now suggested precisely the solution to problem (a) that was envisaged but not pursued by Kollesch 1960, since they have preserved the prepositional phrase πρὸς ἀλλήλας instead of the direct object ἀλλήλας:

κρουόντων πρὸς ἀλλήλας τὰς στρέβλας[226]

If the preposition πρός goes back to Andronicus' text, ἀλλήλας does not serve as a direct object of κρουόντων but forms part of the prepositional phrase πρὸς ἀλλήλας, so that the gender difference between κρουόντων and ἀλλήλας is, in fact, no problem at all: Two or more items A', A", ... (masculine or neuter) strike two or more items B', B"... (feminine) *against one another* (κρουόντων πρὸς ἀλλήλας).

And yet, only problem (a) is solved by restoring the preposition πρός as transmitted by the BᶜEʳb-group, whereas problem (b) seems in any case to go back to the archetype of all extant manuscripts. It is true that the new reading κρουόντων πρὸς ἀλλήλας τὰς στρέβλας is syntactically less objectionable than κρουόντων ἀλλήλας τὰς στρέβλας (Nussbaum's archetype), but even on the new reading the preceding genitive τῶν στρεβλῶν cannot supply the syntactical *subject* of κρουόντων, so that this subject is still missing. And as an object of κρουόντων, the final τὰς στρέβλας remains altogether unsatisfactory with regard

---

[224] Kollesch 1960, 143: 'Die Einfügung einer Präposition vor ἀλλήλας würde dagegen κρούειν unzulässigerweise zu einem intransitiven Verbum machen.'

[225] Torraca 1958a, 33, by contrast, suggested that κρουόντων goes with a subject nowhere expressed at all. He translated 'quando le funicelle sono sciolte' (λυομένων τῶν στρεβλῶν) and 'e un *pezzo* trasmette l'impulso all'altro' (καὶ κρουόντων ἄλληλα). This is unconvincing.

[226] κρουόντων πρὸς ἀλλήλας τὰς στρέβλας Eʳb : πρὸς ἀλλήλας κρουόντων τὰς στρέβλας Bᶜ. The former reading must be the original one since the sequence κρουόντων...ἀλλήλας is confirmed by the reading κρουόντων ἀλλήλας of the first hyparchetype.

to the sense. In order to produce a convincing emendation on the basis of the B^{c}E^{r}b-reading, then, one would have to assume that *a line containing both the subject and the direct object of κρουόντων had already fallen out in our archetype*, and that τὰς στρέβλας was nothing but an unoriginal attempt to fill the gap at least partially, an attempt that was suggested by the preceding τῶν στρεβλῶν.

Before embarking on emendation, however, we will do well to ask ourselves whether we can at all *trust* the B^{c}E^{r}b-reading here or whether it might not have been inserted by a scribe who understood, and wanted to solve, our problem (a), i.e. *the syntactical impossibility of κρουόντων ἀλλήλας*. Now it seems fairly obvious that τὰς στρέβλας is meant to function as the syntactical object of κρουόντων, and since τὰς στρέβλας is clearly corrupt, as we have seen, its presence in the whole manuscript tradition must goes back to a secondary insertion which was meant to supply the missing object of κρουόντων. But the syntactical object of κρουόντων could only be felt to be missing if the reciprocal pronoun ἀλλήλας was clearly not itself serving as that object. This condition, in turn, would have been fulfilled if ἀλλήλας formed part of the prepositional phrase πρὸς ἀλλήλας, whereas it would certainly *not* have been fullfilled if ἀλλήλας stood alone, immediately after κρουόντων. In other words: The insertion of τὰς στρέβλας presupposes the presence of πρὸς ἀλλήλας in the first place. We conclude that it is much easier to account for the presence of τὰς στρέβλας in the archetype of all extant manuscripts by assuming that the prepositional phrase πρὸς ἀλλήλας, too, goes back to that archetype. Therefore, we will base our attempt to solve problem (b) on the assumption that the new B^{c}E^{r}b-reading πρὸς ἀλλήλας is authentic and that the solution to problem (a) that it offers is the correct one.

Any attempt to make further progress must be based on the only extant ancient Greek monograph on *automata*, the *Automatopoetica* (Περὶ αὐτοματοποιητικῆς) by Hero of Alexandria, who probably wrote in the second half of the first century AD.[227] His *automata* are automatic puppet shows—Schmidt 1899: 'Automatentheater', hence our rendering: 'automatic theatre'—of which there are two kinds, one mobile (αὐτόματα ὑπάγοντα) and one stationary (αὐτόματα στατά).[228] Hero describes the technology of the *automata hupagonta* as still immature and as less reliable than that of the *automata stata*.[229] For his treatment of

---

[227] Moraux 1959, 364–5: 'Le passage sur les automates et le chariot (701 b 1 ss.) reste difficile et obscur, malgré les essais d'émendation proposés. Il y aurait lieu, sans doute, d'exploiter les αὐτοματοποιικά d'Héron pour tenter de l'éclairer.'

[228] Freely 2012, 122: 'The first of these, which moved among the audience under its own power, showed Dionysus pouring out a libation while bacchantes danced around him to the sound of trumpets and drums. The other represented a naval battle in which Athena destroyed the ships of Ajax with thunder and lightning.'

[229] Hero, *Aut.* § I; Schmidt 1899, 340/2: ἔστι δὲ ἡ τῶν στατῶν αὐτομάτων ἐνέργεια ἀσφαλεστέρα τε καὶ ἀκινδυνοτέρα καὶ <μᾶλλον> πᾶσαν ἐπιδεχομένη διάθεσιν τῶν ὑπαγόντων.

the latter, by contrast, he can almost entirely rely on the αὐτοματοποιητικά by Philo of Byzantium (third century BC).[230] For historical reasons, then, it seems most likely that the *automata* Aristotle is referring to in our passage as well as elsewhere[231] are more or less closely related to Philo's early Hellenistic *automata stata*.

In a description of an *automaton*, however, we must distinguish two possible subjects: (i) the inner mechanics; (ii) what the spectators can see on stage. Accordingly, the first step in emending our lacunose passage is to grasp which of those two subjects is at stake here, or, more technically speaking, to find out whether the phrase κρουόντων πρὸς ἀλλήλας refers to an *intermediate stage* of the transmission of power or rather to its *visible end point*. Our evidence comprises Hero's description of the transmission of power in Philo's hellenistic *automaton staton*[232] and his description of *what can be seen on the stage* of this *automaton*.[233] As to Hero's description of the visible effect, the first scene of Philo's *automaton staton* will suffice for our purposes: As soon as the *automaton* has been set moving and the stage has been opened, painted figures (ζῴδια γεγραμμένα) become visible which are equipped with one movable arm and which represent the Greeks before Troy after the end of the war. They are repairing their ships in order to lower them into water again: They are sawing, and hewing with axes.[234]

Hero's description of the transmission of power within the *automaton* has been conveniently summarized by Aage Gerhardt Drachmann in the following terms:[235]

> ...the moving force is a heavy weight fitting into a container full of millet or mustard seeds; the seeds run out through a narrow hole, the weight comes down at a determined rate, and it turns an axle from which it is suspended by a cord. All the movements are taken from this axle by means of strings.... If a thing has to happen only once, as a back cloth being dropped, it may be worked by a separate weight which is released by a string pulling out a pin....A movement of the arm of a puppet, e.g. hammering, is produced by pins on a wheel acting on the short end of a lever.

It seems fairly evident that within the transmission of power here described there is no room for an *intermediate stage* at which two or more items A',

---

[230] Hero, *Aut.* § XX; Schmidt 1899, 404: καὶ βέλτιον τῶν πρὸ ἡμῶν ἅμα καὶ πρὸς διδασκαλίαν μᾶλλον ἁρμόζον οὐδὲν εὕρομεν τῶν ὑπὸ Φίλωνος τοῦ Βυζαντίου ἀναγεγραμμένων.

[231] GA II 1, 734[b]10–14, 5, 741[b]7–9; *Metaph.* A 2, 983[a]12–15.

[232] Hero, *Aut.* §§ XXIII–XXX; Schmidt 1899, 416–53.

[233] Hero, *Aut.* § XXII; Schmidt 1899, 412–14.

[234] Hero, *Aut.* § XXII; Schmidt 1899, 412–14: ἀνοιχθέντος ἐν ἀρχῇ τοῦ πίνακος ἐφαίνετο ζῴδια γεγραμμένα δώδεκα· ταῦτα δὲ ἦν εἰς τρεῖς στίχους διῃρημένα· ἦσαν δὲ οὗτοι πεποιημένοι τῶν Δαναῶν τινες ἐπισκευάζοντες τὰς ναῦς καὶ γινόμενοι περὶ καθολκήν. ἐκινεῖτο δὲ ταῦτα τὰ ζῴδια τὰ μὲν πρίζοντα, τὰ δὲ πελέκεσιν ἐργαζόμενα.

[235] Drachmann 1963, 197, based on Hero, *Aut.* §§ XXIII–XXX; Schmidt 1899, 416–53.

A", ... (masculine or neuter) strike two or more items B', B"... (feminine) *against one another* (κρουόντων πρὸς ἀλλήλας). Apart from the fact that this scenario would introduce a kind of complication which is quite alien to Philo's straightforward mechanics, it seems also difficult to imagine how the transmission of power could at all continue after A', A", ... would have managed to strike B', B"... *against one another.* The description of *what can be seen on stage*, by contrast, is much more hospitable to such a constellation: Since according to Hero the movable arms of several painted figures could be shown to be sawing, and hewing with axes, it must have been equally possible to represent couples of figures opposed to each other either of which holds an instrument in its movable arm and which strike these instruments against one another. Furthermore, in Attic prose κρούειν πρός + acc. typically refers to striking *pieces of armour* or *weapons* against one another.[236] So we deem it highly probable that the figures of Aristotle's automatic theatre are striking cutting weapons against one another with their movable arm. If this is correct, the missing syntactical *object* of the striking was a *feminine* noun designating a cutting weapon (preferably a noun used by Aristotle elsewhere, e.g. μάχαιρα),[237] whereas the missing syntactical *subject* of the striking is likely to be ζώιδια, the technical term for the painted and partly movable figures of an *automaton staton*. So we suggest the following *exempli gratia* reconstruction of our passage, which is based on the new BᵉEʳb variant πρὸς ἀλλήλας, and which aims at restoring at least the *structure* of the phrase, even though we cannot, of course, be sure of the exact wording:[238]

ὥσ-|2|περ δὲ τὰ αὐτόματα κινεῖται	Just as the automatic theatres are set in
μικρᾶς κινήσεως γενομένης —|3|	motion when only a small movement has
λυομένων τῶν στρεβλῶν καὶ	happened—when the cables are released
κρουόντων πρὸς ἀλλήλας <εὐθὺς	and the <figures immediately> strike
τῶν ζωιδίων τὰς μαχαίρας> ...	their <sabres> against one another...

701ᵇ3 πρὸς ἀλλήλας BᵉEʳb : ἀλλήλας cett. | <εὐθὺς τῶν ζωιδίων τὰς μαχαίρας> exempli gratia dedi : τὰς στρέβλας ω : secl. Forster

★ ★ ★

---

[236] Cf. Thuc. III, 22, 2: ὅπως τὰ ὅπλα μὴ κρουόμενα πρὸς ἄλληλα αἴσθησιν παρέχοι; Xen. *Anabasis* 4, 5, 18: τὰς ἀσπίδας πρὸς τὰ δόρατα ἔκρουσαν.

[237] *Pol.* I, 2, 1252ᵇ2.

[238] *MA* 7, 701ᵇ1–3, with our supplements. Thanks to Christopher Shields for the suggestion to mark the temporal relation between the initial release and its result visible on stage by means of the adverb εὐθύς: In the same chapter of *MA*, εὐθύς and εὐθέως were used repeatedly (701ᵃ14, 15, 17, 22, 30, 33) in order to introduce the outcome of a practical syllogism.

On the basis of these four passages, the present writer claimed in his contribution to the Symposium that the three manuscripts B^{e}E^{r}b are not only direct descendants of what Nussbaum had called the 'Majuscule MS', i.e. of our second hyparchetype (β), but that they make an outstanding contribution to the text of *MA*. Furthermore, it seemed that Berolinensis B^e and Erlangensis E^r are *uncontaminated* descendants of β, whereas Parisinus b, while going back to the second hyparchetype, too, was contaminated from Nussbaum's second family (our γ). Finally, the *common error* remaining in passage (iv)—i.e. the omission of both the syntactical subject and the syntactical object of the striking—confirms that our two hyparchetypes α and β go back to one post-Aristotelian archetype.

12. Back to Andronicus: Second Thoughts on 700^{b}17–25

In the contribution just summarized, the present writer had focused on the improvements of the Greek text of *MA* that were made possible by the reconstruction of the true archetype on the basis of both Nussbaum's archetype (i.e. our hyparchetype α) and the new hyparchetype β. Yet as we pointed out at the beginning of the present introduction, even our archetype, i.e. the latest common ancestor of *all* extant manuscripts known to us, was just one among the several descendants of Andronicus' text which must have been circulating in antiquity, and there is no reason to believe that any one of these descendants was *entirely* free from scribal errors. As far as our direct transmission is concerned, all extant *MA* manuscripts share a few clear cases of corruption that are quite unlikely to have marred already the text of Andronicus' edition. It is precisely this set of universally shared errors which yields the conclusion that our whole direct transmission goes back to an archetype deriving from Andronicus' text but not identical to it. In order to come as close as possible to Andronicus' text, we have attempted to correct these archetypal errors, as far as possible. We have already submitted one case in point when discussing, towards the end of the preceding chapter, the passage on automatic theatres (*MA* 7, 701^{b}1–3). We will now single out one further example which is philosophically more rewarding. It is again supplied by our key passage *MA* 6, 700^{b}17–25 the text of which was disfigured, already in our archetype, by a well-meant interpolation which renders Aristotle's argument invalid:

|17| ὁρῶμεν δὲ τὰ κινοῦντα τὸ
ζῷον διάνοιαν καὶ φαντασίαν
καὶ |18| προαίρεσιν καὶ βούλησιν
καὶ ἐπιθυμίαν·

[1st PREMISS] We see that the things which
move animals are discursive thought
(*dianoia*) and imagination and decision
and wish and appetite;

ταῦτα δὲ πάντα |19| ἀνάγεται
εἰς νοῦν καὶ ὄρεξιν—καὶ γὰρ ἡ
φαντασία καὶ ἡ |20| αἴσθησις τὴν
αὐτὴν τῶι νῶι χώραν ἔχουσιν
(κριτικὰ γὰρ |21| πάντα,
διαφέρουσιν δὲ κατὰ τὰς εἰρημένας
ἐν ἄλλοις δια-|22| φοράς), βούλησις
δὲ καὶ θυμὸς καὶ ἐπιθυμία πάντα
ὀρέξεις, |23| ἡ δὲ προαίρεσις κοινὸν
διανοίας καὶ ὀρέξεως—·

[2nd PREMISS] yet all of these are reduced
to thought (*nous*) and desire—for (i) both
imagination and sense-perception hold
the same place as thought (*nous*), since
they are all apt for making discriminations
(but differ in the ways described in other
works), and (ii) wish and spirit and
appetite are all desires, and (iii) decision is
common to both discursive thought
(*dianoia*) and desire—;

ὥστε κινεῖ πρῶ-|24| τον τὸ ὀρεκτὸν
καὶ τὸ διανοητόν·

[CONCLUSION] from whence it follows
that what first imparts movement is the
object of desire (*orekton*) and the *object* of
discursive thought (*dianoeton*);

οὐ πᾶν δὲ διανοητόν, |25| ἀλλὰ τὸ
τῶν πρακτῶν τέλος.

[QUALIFICATION] though not just any
object of discursive thought, but the goal
(*telos*) of what is achievable through action.

---

b23–4 ὥστε κινεῖ πρῶτον τὸ ὀρεκτὸν καὶ β : ὥστε καὶ α || b24 διανοητόν...διανοητόν ω, sed cf. supra
700b18–19 ταῦτα δὲ πάντα ἀνάγεται εἰς νοῦν καὶ ὄρεξιν et *Metaph.* Λ 7, 1072a26 κινεῖ δὲ ὧδε τὸ
ὀρεκτὸν καὶ τὸ νοητόν

On the β-reading, to be sure, the conclusion (700b23–4) is a syntactically complete consecutive clause, but, unfortunately, this consecutive clause still does not
follow from its premisses. In the *first premiss* (700b17–18), Aristotle enumerates
several activities of the soul which can play a role in causing animal self-motion
(discursive thought, imagination, decision, wish, and appetite), a list which,
in the course of the argument, will be further augmented by the addition of
sense-perception (*aisthesis*) and spirit (*thumos*). In the *second premiss* (700b18–23),
he reduces all of these activities to two basic types of psychic activity, *orexis*
(desire) and *nous* (thought). While subsection (ii) of the second premiss, i.e. the
subsumption of wish (*boulesis*), spirit (*thumos*), and appetite (*epithumia*) under
the genus *orexis*, does not pose any problem,[239] subsections (i) and (iii) need

---

[239] Cf. *De An.* II 3, 414b2: ὄρεξις μὲν γὰρ ἐπιθυμία καὶ θυμὸς καὶ βούλησις; *EE* B 7, 1223a26–7: ἀλλὰ
μὴν ἡ ὄρεξις εἰς τρία διαιρεῖται, εἰς βούλησιν καὶ θυμὸν καὶ ἐπιθυμίαν.

some extra justification. As to (i),[240] Aristotle assumes that '*phantasia* and perception play the role of *nous*, or hold the place of *nous*, because they too enable creatures to make distinctions (*krinein*)', and that 'they can be conveniently put under the heading "*nous*" for the purposes of this argument (rather than definitively)'.[241] So we may note but need not overemphasize the tension between the present passage and Aristotle's official account of the psychic faculties,[242] according to which all other animals except humans do *not* have a share in '*nous*'.[243] As to (iii), decision (*prohairesis*) is characterized as a hybrid combining *orexis* and *dianoia* ('discursive thought'), and in order to get the point of that characterization, the reader has to supply one further step: Given that *dianoia* obviously falls within the province of *nous*, the description of *prohairesis* as a combination of *orexis* and *dianoia* is meant to support the claim that all psychic causes of self-motion can be reduced to *orexis* and *nous*, even if *prohairesis* is the only one to be reduced to both.

Now the *conclusion* (700[b]23–4) as transmitted by our archetype states that animal self-motion is *first* caused by the object of desire (*orekton*) and by the object of discursive thought (*dianoeton*). This claim, however, does not follow from the premisses: According to them, not only *dianoia* ('discursive thought'), but also non-discursive forms of *nous* (according to the flexible use just introduced), i.e. *aisthesis* and *phantasia*, can serve as the 'noetic' cause of self-motion. Therefore, the transmitted conclusion blatantly fails to provide a sufficiently large set of *first* causes of animal self-motion: Since the psychic causes of self-motion as listed in the first premiss have been reduced to *orexis* and *nous* in the second premiss, the only satisfactory conclusion would consist, rather, in identifying the first causes of self-motion with the *orekton* and with the *noeton* ('object of thought'). And why should Aristotle have introduced the flexible use of *nous* in the second premiss, if the *noeton* was not to be mentioned in the conclusion anyway?

In order to defend the transmitted wording of the conclusion one would have to claim that *dianoeton* is simply used as an equivalent of *noeton*. But this claim would be rather unconvincing. While it is true that the difference between *nous* and *dianoia* may at times be a rather subtle one (for instance, if they refer to subsequent phases of one and the same cognitive episode),[244] it is

---

[240] Our thanks go to Benjamin Morison for sending us a helpful exposition of Aristotle's rather flexible use of '*nous*' in subsection (i) from which the two following quotations are taken.

[241] Cf. *De An.* III 10, 433[a]9–10: φαίνεται δέ γε δύο ταῦτα κινοῦντα, ἢ ὄρεξις ἢ νοῦς, εἴ τις τὴν φαντασίαν τιθείη ὡς νόησίν τινα.

[242] See, e.g., the list in *De An.* II 3, 414[a]31–32: δυνάμεις δ' εἴπομεν θρεπτικόν, ὀρεκτικόν, αἰσθητικόν, κινητικὸν κατὰ τόπον, διανοητικόν.

[243] Cf., e.g., *De An.* II 3, 414[b]18–19: ἑτέροις δὲ (scil. ὑπάρχει) καὶ τὸ διανοητικόν τε καὶ νοῦς, οἷον ἀνθρώποις καὶ εἴ τι τοιοῦτον ἕτερόν ἐστιν ἢ καὶ τιμιώτερον; ibid. III 3, 429[a]4–9: καὶ διὰ τὸ ἐμμένειν (scil. τὰς φαντασίας) καὶ ὁμοίως εἶναι ταῖς αἰσθήσεσι, πολλὰ κατ' αὐτὰς πράττει τὰ ζῷα, τὰ μὲν διὰ τὸ μὴ ἔχειν νοῦν, οἷον τὰ θηρία, τὰ δὲ διὰ τὸ ἐπικαλύπτεσθαι τὸν νοῦν πάθει ἢ νόσοις ἢ ὕπνωι, οἷον οἱ ἄνθρωποι; III 10, 433[a]11–12: καὶ ἐν τοῖς ἄλλοις ζῴοις οὐ νόησις οὐδὲ λογισμός ἐστιν, ἀλλὰ φαντασία.

[244] Cf. *Metaph.* Γ 7, 1012[a]2–3 (ἔτι πᾶν τὸ διανοητὸν καὶ νοητὸν ἡ διάνοια κατάφησιν ἢ ἀπόφησιν) and the reading of that passage proposed by Oehler 1962, 247: 'Aber abgesehen von der historischen Genesis

also true that *in the present argument* both *nous* and *dianoia* have been embedded in specific contexts in a way which precludes the possibility of treating them as equivalent: In 700ᵇ18–22, a flexible use of '*nous*' has been introduced in order to cover also animals' *aisthesis* and *phantasia*, whereas in 700ᵇ23, '*dianoia*' has been introduced as the noetic component of the specifically human, discursive activity of *prohairesis*. It follows that *dianoeton* cannot possibly serve as an equivalent of *noeton* in 700ᵇ24.

This observation is confirmed by the fact that with *noeton*, the conclusion would correspond precisely to the theorem introduced in *Metaph.* Λ 7[245]—a chapter which Aristotle has just referred his reader back to.[246] Why should Aristotle have replaced the *noeton* of that theorem with the specifically discursive *dianoeton* precisely when taking the theorem over into a *general theory of animal self-motion?*

So it seems unavoidable to admit that in 700ᵇ23–5, Aristotle wrote in fact twice νοητόν, not διανοητόν:

ὥστε κινεῖ πρῶτον τὸ ὀρεκτὸν καὶ τὸ νοητόν. οὐ πᾶν δὲ νοητόν, ἀλλὰ τὸ τῶν πρακτῶν τέλος.

Much later, an additional δια- was added to both original occurrences of νοητόν by a scribe who probably thought, rather short-sightedly, that the antecedent to the ὥστε-clause in 700ᵇ23–4 does not consist of the two premises as unfolded in 700ᵇ17–23 but merely of the description of *prohairesis* in 700ᵇ23. So he produced the version of 700ᵇ23–5 as transmitted by our archetype, which, on first glance, may indeed be mistaken as a conclusive, self-contained argument exclusively concerned with *prohairesis*:

... |23| ἡ δὲ προαίρεσις κοινὸν διανοίας καὶ ὀρέξεως, ὥστε κινεῖ πρῶ-|24|τον τὸ ὀρεκτὸν καὶ τὸ <δια>νοητόν, οὐ πᾶν δὲ <δια>νοητόν, |25| ἀλλὰ τὸ τῶν πρακτῶν τέλος.

...decision (*prohairesis*) is common to both discursive thought (*dianoia*) and desire, so that what first imparts movement is the *object* of desire and the *object* of discursive thought (*dianoeton*), though not just any object of discursive thought, but the goal of what is achievable through action.

dieses Problembestandes ist es ja sachlich so, daß das Denken nicht bei der einheitlichen noetischen Erfassung des Gegenstandes stehenbleibt, sondern das noetisch Gegebene im Urteil expliziert und damit in den Bereich möglicher Falschheit transponiert. Das bedeutet: das νοητόν wird zum Gegenstand der διάνοια, wird bejaht und verneint und wird dadurch ein διανοητόν.'

[245] Cf. *Metaph.* Λ 7, 1072ª26–27: κινεῖ δὲ ὧδε τὸ ὀρεκτὸν καὶ τὸ νοητόν· κινεῖ οὐ κινούμενα.

[246] Cf. *MA* 6, 700ᵇ7–9: περὶ δὲ τοῦ πρώτου κινουμένου καὶ ἀεὶ κινουμένου, τίνα τρόπον κινεῖται καὶ πῶς κινεῖ τὸ πρῶτον κινοῦν, διώρισται πρότερον ἐν τοῖς περὶ τῆς πρώτης φιλοσοφίας.

Yet restricting the scope of the conclusion to *prohairesis* in this way would not only leave the non-discursive 'noetic' causes of self-motion (i.e. *aisthesis* and *phantasia*) out of account and thereby ruin the overall argument of the present passage,[247] it would also, on a more general level, deprive *MA* of *any* comprehensive account of the first causes of animal self-motion. According to the restored wording, by contrast, Aristotle would present a conclusive argument the result of which is absolutely central to his theory:

1ˢᵗ premiss (700ᵇ17–18):	Animal self-motion is brought about by discursive thought, imagination, decision, wish, or appetite;
2ⁿᵈ premiss (700ᵇ18–23):	yet these psychic causes can all be reduced to *orexis* (desire) and to *nous* (thought);
Conclusion (700ᵇ23–4):	from whence it follows that animal self-motion is *first* caused by the *object* of desire (*orekton*) and by the *object* of thought (*noeton*);
Qualification (700ᵇ24–5):	not any object of thought (*noeton*), though, can play a role in bringing about animal self-motion, but the goal of what is achievable through action.

We conclude that in 700ᵇ23–4 already our archetype was characterized by the erroneous replacement of νοητόν by διανοητόν. And we submit that this misguided intervention is much more likely to have occurred at some point during the centuries between Andronicus' first-century BC edition and our (probably late-antique) archetype than to have been committed by Andronicus himself. Therefore, we have ventured to credit Andronicus' text with the emended version of the argument.

13. Isépy 2013 on the Greek Models of the Two Mediaeval Translations

In the present writer's contribution to the 2011 Symposium, only the general outlines of a new stemma of the independent tradition were established: Taking

---

[247] This restriction would not even square with the qualification added in 700ᵇ24–5: On the transmitted reading, this qualification would identify the object of *dianoia*, i.e. of the discursive component of *prohairesis*, with the *goal* (*telos*) of feasible actions, whereas according to Aristotle, *prohairesis* is not about the ends, but about the means towards the ends; cf. *EN* III 3, 1111ᵇ26–7: ἔτι δ' ἡ μὲν βούλησις τοῦ τέλους ἐστὶ μᾶλλον, ἡ δὲ προαίρεσις τῶν πρὸς τὸ τέλος. See also *EE* II 10, 1226ᵃ7–8: οὐθεὶς γὰρ τέλος οὐδὲν προαιρεῖται, ἀλλὰ τὰ πρὸς τὸ τέλος, and 1226ᵃ16–17: βούλεσθαι μὲν καὶ δόξα μάλιστα τοῦ τέλους, προαίρεσις δ' οὐκ ἔστιν.

Nussbaum's stemma as a starting point, we must—apart from the modifications already mentioned above in section 9 of the present introduction—downgrade Nussbaum's archetype to the status of one out of two hyparchetypes (α) and upgrade her 'Majuscule MS' to the status of a new hyparchetype (β) since it has now been seen to be equipped with extant direct progeny, i.e. with De Leemans' new group B^{c}E^{r}b(T^p). By consequence, the true archetype has to be reconstructed on the basis of both hyparchetypes α and β, and what Nussbaum presented as evidence for an extra-archetypal contamination (of Vaticanus P and of William's translation) can now be regarded as innocent cases of intra-archetypal contamination.

Many questions of detail, however, were still unanswered. This was true, in particular, with regard to the three lost Greek models to which De Leemans had traced back the mediaeval Latin tradition, i.e. the two Greek models of William's translation and the Greek model of the Latin translation paraphrased by Albert the Great. The position of these venerable if lost models within the new stemma remained to be determined, and this was the task of Peter Isépy's Munich PhD thesis which he defended in 2013 and which came out as a book in 2016. First, Isépy showed that William's main Greek model (Γ1) was, in all likelihood, the lost second part of the famous Codex Vindobonensis phil. gr. 100, from the ninth century AD, which is known to have contained the biological works and which was used by William for his translation of *HA*, as Friederike Berger had demonstrated in 2005 on the basis of an extant fragment (Par. suppl. gr. 1156 = W).[248] That is to say that William's Latin translation provides access to the earliest tangible version of the text of Nussbaum's *b* family, i.e. of our γ-branch, and, in particular, of its δ-group. Second, he showed that the lost Latin translation (De Leemans' 'translatio anonyma') on which Albert based his paraphrase of *MA* and which De Leemans had already demonstrated to be most closely related to the Greek manuscript Laurentianus Z^a, was in fact translated from the same lost Greek manuscript (**A**) of which Z^a is a copy. This result has further improved our picture of the group Z^{a}M^{o}B^{p}P (in our stemma: ι) which we have already mentioned.

The most important results of Isépy concern the new β-branch. He was able to show that the common source η of Marcianus gr. 209 (O^d), Laurentianus Plut. 81.1 (S), and Vaticanus Palatinus gr. 97 (V^p)—i.e. of the group which corresponds to Nussbaum's *b*$_1$—was originally a β-text that had been heavily annotated throughout with readings from the γ-branch (more precisely, from the lost manuscript ϵ from which Laurentianus C^a was copied); accordingly, in the extant progeny of η almost all β-readings of note were replaced by those

---

[248] Berger 2005, 182–6.

ε-readings from the margins. Even if the contribution of O^d and SV^p to the reconstruction of the hyparchetype β is very limited, these manuscripts show that the progeny of β is far less detached from the mainstream of the direct transmission than it had at first seemed: In a way, some characteristics of the β-text had been known all the time, not only via the important β-readings adopted by William and by Vaticanus P, but also via the inconspicuous β-readings which had escaped the notice of the annotator of η.[249] Last but not least, Isépy found evidence that except for the Berolinensis B^e the remaining part of the new β-branch—including not only Erlangensis E^r and Parisinus b, but also η in its original form—goes back to William's additional Greek model ($\Gamma\mathbf{2}$). It follows that William had at his disposal two Greek manuscripts of paramount importance: As far as our limited knowledge goes, the stemmatic position of $\Gamma\mathbf{2}$ is as close to the archetype as that of the Berolinensis B^e and that of the *codex vetustissimus*, Parisinus E, whereas the position of $\Gamma\mathbf{1}$ is as close to the archetype as the position of our second eldest manuscript Laurentianus Plut. 87.4 (C^a), from the scriptorium of Ioannikios. In other words: The importance of William's translation as edited by De Leemans 2011a for the reconstruction of the Greek archetype of *MA* is much greater than, for instance, in the case of the various mediaeval Latin translations of *Metaphysica*.

14. Koch 2015 on Michael of Ephesus

Michael's commentary on *MA* is earlier than all extant *MA* manuscripts except Parisinus gr. 1853 (E). The commentary was studied by Lutz Koch in his Hamburg PhD thesis which he defended in February 2015 and which was published online in August 2017.[250] Hayduck's text is reprinted (with small modifications) and provided with a facing-page German translation.[251] As to the textual transmission of Michael's commentary, Hayduck had distinguished two branches of the tradition, one being represented by Parisinus gr. 1925 (S: dated back by Koch to the twelfth century)[252] and the Aldine edition (a: AD 1527), the other by Vaticanus Columnensis gr. 2199 (C: twelfth century), Parisinus gr. 1923 (R: twelfth-thirteenth century), and Parisinus gr. 1921 (P: fourteenth century).[253] Koch added one further independent manuscript to each branch respectively: The first branch (Sa) was enlarged by Marcianus gr. 237 (M^a: dated back by

---

[249] Isépy 2016, 76–82.   [250] Koch 2017.   [251] See Koch 2017, 24-95.
[252] Koch 2017, 99-101.
[253] Hayduck 1904,VI: 'Horum librorum ea ratio est, ut *Sa* et rursus *CPR* affinitatis vinculo artissimo inter se coniunctos esse appareat.'

Koch to the twelfth century),[254] the second branch (CRP) by Laurentianus Plut. 85.1 'Oceanus' (L: mid-thirteenth century).[255] The fact that both branches of the tradition are now known to be represented by one or two extant twelfth-century manuscripts indicates that Michael's commentary must have been widely disseminated right from the start.[256] A quite interesting feature of Koch's thesis is an edition of the *MA* scholia that are contained in the *MA* manuscripts Ambrosianus H 50 sup. (X: approx. AD 1200, seventy-six scholia) and Par. gr. 1859 (b: approx. AD 1300, twelve scholia):[257] In a number of cases these scholia are closely related to Michael's commentary on the passage in question.[258] Koch suggested that these scholia may partly depend on Michael's commentary, partly go back to an earlier annotation on which Michael himself had been drawing.[259] From our present point of view, however, the two most important results of Koch's thesis are (i) that he abandoned his initial 'Escobarian' approach to the stemma of *MA* and accepted our claim according to which De Leemans' new group of *MA* manuscripts goes back to a second hyparchetype,[260] and (ii) that he demonstrated in detail what Pantelis Golitsis had surmised already in the 2012 workshop mentioned earlier: The *MA* text used by Michael goes back immediately to Nussbaum's second hyparchetype (i.e. to the reconstructed ms. γ of our stemma).[261]

15. A New Stemma of the Independent Tradition

The result of our analysis of the textual history is depicted in our new stemma as displayed at the end of the present section 15.[262] Extant Greek manuscripts

---

[254] Koch 2017, 102–5. In this context, Koch 2017, 106–8, pointed out that a copy of the text of Marcianus gr. 237 (M^a) is transmitted by Marcianus gr. 238, and that a copy of the text of Marcianus gr. 238, in turn, is transmitted by Parisinus gr. 2066 (P^k: written between 1466 and 1474 by Andronikos Kallistos), which anticipates in many respects the text of the Aldine edition (**a**).

[255] Koch 2017, 101–2.

[256] Koch 2017, 105: 'Für die Kommentare M.s sind also mehrere Handschriften erhalten, die der Zeit ihrer Entstehung nahe kommen. Dies spricht... für ihre frühe Verbreitung.'

[257] Koch 2017, 152–71.

[258] Furthermore, Koch 2017, 178–83, also shows that the contents of some of the X- or b-scholia as well as of passages from Michael's commentary turn up again in the scholia of Par. 1921 (approx. AD 1360).

[259] Cf. Koch 2017, 245.

[260] Cf. Koch 2017, 118 with n. 2. The basic structure of our new stemma was accessible to Koch via the PhD thesis of Peter Isépy.

[261] Cf. Koch 2017, 119: 'Die Sondierung der Lemmata, Zitationen und Paraphrasen zeigt, dass der in M.s Kommentar zugrundeliegende Text der γ-Tradition angehört... Auch δ und ϵ zeigen Trennfehler gegen M., so dass M. am ehesten auf der Höhe dieser beiden rekonstruierten Textstufen anzusiedeln ist, also aus dem Kontext von γ als der Wurzel der "byzantinischen Vulgata" hervorgehend.'

[262] We intend to set out the readings and the stemmatic position of the *codices descripti* in an *editio maior* of *MA*.

are designated by Latin upper-case letters: Here, we have kept the letters introduced by Bekker 1831 and by De Leemans 2011a throughout. Reconstructed Greek manuscripts, by contrast, are designated by Greek lower-case letters, except William's two lost models (Γ1 and Γ2) and the lost Greek model (**A**) of the Latin translation used by Albert: These three sigla have again been taken over from De Leemans 2011a and 2011b. Nussbaum's archetype corresponds to our hyparchetype **α**, the role of her first family (**a**) has been taken over by Parisinus gr. 1853 (E), her second family (**b**) corresponds to our **γ**-branch, whereas her 'Majuscule MS' has become the new hyparchetype **β**. The following remarks offer a quick first glance at the evidence which underlies the main ramifications of our stemma. For a full presentation of the relevant variants the reader is referred to the *apparatus plenior* which has been appended to our Greek–English edition.

The earliest accessible state of the text is represented by Alexander's paraphrase of and verbal quotations from *MA* 7–8, 701^{b}13–702^{a}2,[263] which are contained in his *De Anima*[264] and extensively quoted by Michael of Ephesus.[265]

The evidence for our first hyparchetype (**α**) consists of Parisinus E and the **γ**-branch which go back to two different *transliterations* of one and the same majuscule text into minuscule script. There are two separative errors of our whole **α**-branch that are obviously due to majuscule confusion: 698^{a}16–17 ἀεί...ἠρεμεῖ **β** : δεῖ...ἠρεμεῖν **α**, and 699^{a}4 αὐτὸν **β** : αὐτὸ ἢ **α**,[266] which is to say that the **α**-branch goes back to a majuscule text of its own. But there is also a separative error of **γ** which was caused by an attempt to make sense of a further majuscule confusion: 699^{a}13 εἶναί τέ τι δεῖ **β** : εἶναί τε δεῖ E : εἶναι θέλει **γ** (< ΕΙΝΑΙΤΕΛΕΙ).

As far as the new **β**-branch is concerned, we have already mentioned, in section 11, the common errors of its two uncontaminated mss. B^e and E^r which show that the **β**-branch goes back to a majuscule ms. on its own.[267] Berolinensis B^e, in particular, is an extremely faithful copy of an old exemplar

---

[263] Cf. Accattino/Donini 1996, 262.   [264] Alexander, *De Anima* 76,18–78,2 Bruns.

[265] Michael *in MA* 114,27–115,22, 115,23–5, 119,16–20, 119,22–5, and 120,3–7 Hayduck.

[266] We may perhaps add 698^{b}26 πλέων **β** : πνέων **α** (as was kindly suggested to the present writer by Tiziano Dorandi), although in this case the error might also go back to the occurrence of πνέων in the preceding line 698^{b}25.

[267] 698^{b}8 ἤ ἐν] μὲν B^{e}E^r.– 700^{b}34 ἤ ὥστ'] πως B^{e}E^r. A third error common to B^e and E^r testifies to the difficulty caused by the absence of accents and word-division in a majuscule ms.: 703^{a}18 δ' εὐφυῶς] δὲ ὑφ' ὦ ὡς B^e vel δὲ ὑφ' ὦ ὡς E^r.

which was the uncorrected product of a transliteration, as a number of additional B^e-errors shows.[268] So it seems that from a stemmatical point of view, Berolinensis B^e is as close to the archetype as the *codex vetustissimus* Parisinus E, although the Berolinensis is 500 years younger than the Parisinus. It follows that our direct tradition as a whole goes back to *three* transliterations, an observation which squares with what has been observed in the case of Plato:[269] The comparatively high number of transliterations in both cases is probably due to the scholarly activity which must have accompanied the foundation of a philosophical faculty in Constantinople, the school of the *Magnaura*, around AD 855.[270]

Within our γ-branch, a first ramification appears in 701^a19, where in all manuscripts of the δ-group[271] the correct 'conclusion' of a practical syllogism (ἱμάτιον ποιεῖ βEε) is replaced by ἱμάτιον ποιητέον. The further subdivisions of the γ-branch betray already the influence of Michael's commentary which yields the year AD 1118 as a *terminus post quem* for the lost models in question (ε and ζ). In ε, the text of which is best represented for us by the Laurentianus Plut. 87.4 (C^a), the corrupt γ-wording of the passage on mice[272] was revised[273] under the influence of Michael's abridged version.[274] Similarly, the way in which Michael has glossed over the lacuna in our paradigm passage 700^b23–4[275] has left its mark in ζ, since both descendants of ζ, i.e. θ and ι, made use of the new element introduced by Michael (προαιρετόν), although they did so in two different ways.[276]

---

[268] 699^b37 οὐρανόθεν] οὐ ῥανόθεν B^e.- 701^a32 ποτέον μοι] ποτὲ ὄν μοι B^e.- 701^b10 αὐτομάτοις] αὐτὸ μάτοις B^e.- 702^b13 τἀναντία] τὰ ναντία B^e.- 702^b35 ἀπερείδοιντο] ἀπερείδον τό B^e.- 704^a1 τοσαύτην] τὸ σαύτην B^e.

[269] Cf. Carlini 1972, 137: 'I tre rami in cui si scinde la tradizione platonica delle prime sei tetralogie sono il frutto di tre diverse traslitterazioni.'

[270] Cf. Lemerle 1971, 158–65. Rashed 2002, 713–17 (= 2007, 533–7) suggested a connection between the foundation of the school of the *Magnaura* and the production of the manuscripts belonging to the so-called *collection philosophique*.

[271] Including William's first Greek model Γι which was probably contained in the second part, now lost, of the ninth-century ms. Vindobonensis gr. 100 (see above, section 13).

[272] 698^b15–^b16 (γ): τοῖς μυσὶ τοῖς ἐν τῆι γῆι ἢ τοῖς ἐν τῆι ἄμμωι πορευομένοις.

[273] ε(C^aO^dSV^p): τοῖς ἐν τῇ γῇ πορευομένοις μυσὶν ἢ τοῖς ἐν τῇ ἄμμω.

[274] Michael 105,25 Hayduck: τοῖς ἐν τῇ γῇ πορευομένοις μυσίν.

[275] Michael 113,22–4 Hayduck: ἐπεὶ ἡ προαίρεσις κίνησις διανοίας καὶ ὀρέξεως, ἔσται καί τι διανοητὸν προαιρετόν· οὐ γὰρ πᾶν διανοητόν.

[276] θ(NXH^aLV^e): ἡ δὲ προαίρεσις κοινὸν διανοίας καὶ ὀρέξεως, ὥστε καὶ τὸ προαιρετόν. οὐ πᾶν δὲ τὸ διανοητὸν προαιρετόν.- ι(A[Z^aAnon.]B^pM^o): ἡ δὲ προαίρεσις κοινὸν διανοίας καὶ ὀρέξεως, ὥστε καὶ τὸ διανοητὸν οὐ πᾶν προαιρετόν.

The binary internal structure of the new β-branch is best illustrated by 704^{b}1, where the uncontaminated Erlangensis E^r, the three contaminated η-manuscripts (O^{d}SV^p), and William's second source Γ2 share the formula ἔτι δὲ καὶ περὶ (the authenticity of which is strongly supported by *HA* III 15, 519^{b}22–3), whereas Berolinensis B^e and the α-manuscripts lack the καί.[277] This is, of course, not a conjunctive error (the καὶ may be omitted independently by more than one scribe), but it is surely a separative one: No scribe with ἔτι δὲ περὶ in front of him would feel the need to insert an additional καί. A further distinctive feature of Berolinensis B^e is the considerable number of antediluvian errors of word-division which we have already mentioned. In almost all other aspects, however, the two uncontaminated β-manuscripts B^e and E^r are extremely close to each other. In order to account for this close relationship, we assume that an early, perhaps even ninth-century manuscript produced by transliteration was copied twice: One very late but still uncorrected copy is the extant Berolinensis B^e, whereas a carefully edited copy of the same exemplar was prepared much earlier and then used by William as his additional model Γ2, to which also the remaining Greek β-manuscripts—both uncontaminated (E^r) and contaminated (b and O^{d}SV^p)— go back.

If we look at the stemma from a comparative point of view, our γ-branch corresponds to the whole manuscript tradition of *HA* as analysed by Berger 2005, in that according to Isépy 2016 our γ-branch is related to the lost part of Vindobonensis 100 (J = William's first Greek model Γ1) in the same way as the total of the *HA*-manuscripts. Our first hyparchetype α, in turn, is equivalent to the whole manuscript tradition of *GC* as analysed by Rashed 2001, where our α is represented by the equivalent of our γ-branch on the one hand and by Parisinus E on the other. Our new β-branch, by contrast, goes completely beyond the tradition available in those other treatises.

---

[277] *MA* 11, 704^{a}3–^{b}2: περὶ μὲν οὖν τῶν μορίων ἑκάστου τῶν ζώιων, καὶ περὶ ψυχῆς, <u>ἔτι δὲ καὶ περὶ</u> (καὶ om. B^e, a) αἰσθήσεως καὶ ὕπνου καὶ μνήμης καὶ τῆς κοινῆς κινήσεως, εἰρήκαμεν τὰς αἰτίας.

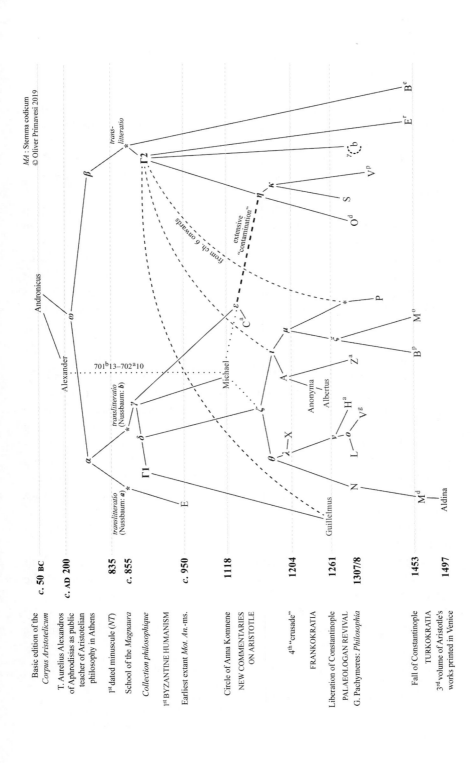

MA : Stemma codicum
© Oliver Primavesi 2019

16. The New Text, Its Three Apparatus, and the English Translation

The first and most important aim of the present edition has been to reconstruct the text of the archetype (**ω**) of all extant manuscripts known to us: The overwhelming majority of the 120 readings by the adoption of which our new edition of the Greek text differs from Martha Nussbaum's 1978 edition[278] are due to identification of the second hyparchetype (**β**). In cases were a **β**-reading is also attested by one half of the progeny of hyparchetype **a**, i.e. either by Parisinus E or by the **γ**-branch, we have adopted the reading in question without further ado—except in the few cases where we were dealing with potentially polygenetic errors, i.e. with errors that may very well have been committed twice independently: Among the features likely to provoke a misguided scribal intervention more than once are the apodotic use of δέ,[279] and Aristotle's peculiar and highly significant use of the binary reflexive pronoun (αὐτὸ αὐτό) according to which the first αὐτό comes in the nominative irrespective of the syntactical context.[280] In cases, however, where a **β**-reading stands against an **a**-reading, our choice was based on the individual merits of the readings in question, not on a prejudice in favour of one of the two hyparchetypes, let alone on a general enthusiasm for hitherto unknown readings: Either hyparchetype is, by definition, free from the specific errors of the other hyparchetype, but it is equally true that either is entitled, as it were, to its own errors. In chapters 1, 9, and 11, we have restored to the Greek text the three *diagrams* the survival of which in some important manuscripts was not mentioned by any previous editor. We have followed the *codex vetustissimus*, Parisinus gr. 1853 (E), in printing *iota adscriptum* throughout. Last but not least, in chapters 1 and 8 we could restore, on the joined authority of Parisinus E, the new **β**-group, and the two leading **γ**-manuscripts Laurentianus Cᵃ and Vaticanus N, the true Attic spelling of the Greek word for 'elbow' (ὀλέκρανον) instead of the inveterate misspelling (ὠλέκρανον) admitted by all previous editors.[281]

We did not content ourselves, however, with reconstructing the text of our archetype **ω**: Our professed ultimate aim was, rather, the reconstruction of the text of Andronicus. Some improvements which go beyond our archetype were suggested by the indirect tradition, i.e. by Alexander's paraphrase of *MA* 7–8, or by the hitherto unknown diagram transmitted in *MA* 11, which clearly presupposes

---

[278] Cf. Appendix III to the present introduction.

[279] Cf. 700ᵇ9 λοιπὸν δ' ἐστὶν EbΓ2 : λοιπόν ἐστιν BᶜEʳγ.

[280] Cf. 700ᵃ27 ἐν τῶι ἀλλοιουμένωι αὐτὸ ὑφ' αὐτοῦ Eι : ἐν τῶι ἀλλοιουμένωι αὐτῶι ὑφ' αὐτοῦ **βθ**.

[281] Cf. 698ᵇ3, 702ᵃ28, 702ᵇ4, 702ʳ11; the reference to Helladius by which LSJ (s.v. ὠλέκρανον) create the impression that the spelling ὠλέκρανον is mentioned by an ancient grammarian is altogether unfounded, as Isépy/Primavesi 2014 have shown.

a text different from our archetype. All in all, we have adopted *twenty-one* corrections of archetypal error;[282] and in the first of these cases we have even taken a step beyond Andronicus: The transmitted title of *MA*, Περὶ ζώιων κινήσεως, is both far too general and clearly derived from the first sentence of the text; accordingly, we have printed it in braces, as a secondary editorial addition of an *incipit*.

At the bottom of each page of the Greek text there are two apparatus: (i) The first apparatus offers passages that are referred to by Aristotle in the text of *MA* or that are otherwise immediately relevant for the establishment of that text. (ii) The second apparatus is a short *apparatus vere criticus* which is, in general, limited to cases where our text differs from the archetype ω, or where the two hyparchetypes α and β or the two halves of α's progeny (i.e. Parisinus E and γ) differ from each other. In this apparatus, the sigla α, β, and γ, do not indicate that the reading in question is shared by each and every manuscript belonging to the respective group, but that this reading was displayed by the common ancestor of the respective group as we have reconstructed it. (iii) As an appendix to our edition, we offer an *apparatus plenior*, in which we have set out the manuscript evidence for the readings mentioned in the *apparatus criticus*, and documented a few additional *variae lectiones* which, while not posing a problem of textual criticism, illustrate the relationship between the manuscripts. In the *apparatus plenior*, sigla like α, β, and γ stand for *all* independent manuscripts belonging to the group in question unless stated otherwise. In particular, the contaminated manuscripts b and O^dSV^p have been assigned either to β or to γ, according to their respective adherence in the passage in question.

In his English translation Benjamin Morison has brought out the impact of the new text as clearly as possible; in order to facilitate comparison, we have inserted references at the beginning of each English sentence which indicate the Bekker-line in which the beginning of the corresponding Greek sentence is to be found.[283]

---

[282] 1) Titulum operis delevi.- 2) 699ᵃ17 ἔσται dedi cum Thomæo : ἔσεσθαι ω.- 3) 699ᵇ22 εἶναι (ω), quod iam Bonitz delevit, post ᵇ23 ἐξ ἀνάγκης transposui.- 4) 700ᵃ8–9 δεῖ γὰρ—κινεῖσθαι (ω) post ᵃ10 κινήσεται transposui cum Renehan.- 5) 700ᵃ15 ἀλλ᾽, <ἀλλ᾽> dedi : ἀλλ᾽ ω.- 6) 700ᵇ24 νοητόν...νοητόν dedi : διανοητόν...διανοητόν ω.- 7) 700ᵇ33 καλὸν καὶ dedi : καλὸν καὶ τὸ ω.- 8) 701ᵃ24 δυεῖν ὁδῶν feci ex δύ᾽ εἰ ποδῶν Bᵉ (et Ea.c.?) : δύο εἰδῶν Ep.c. cett.- 9) 701ᵇ3 <εὐθὺς τῶν ζωιδίων τὰς μαχαίρας> exempli gratia restitui : τὰς στρέβλας ω, quod iam Forster seclusit.- 10) 701ᵇ4 <ὅ> inserui : om. ω.- 11) 701ᵇ4–5 <πάλιν> καὶ πάλιν dedi : καὶ πάλιν ω.- 12) 701ᵇ14–15 αὐξανομένων <καὶ συστελλομένων> dedi : αὐξανομένων ω.- 13) 701ᵇ30 κατὰ μέγεθος (ω) cum Alexandro omisi.- 14) 701ᵇ34 διωκτόν τε dedi cum Alexandro : διωκτὸν ω.- 15) 702ᵃ29 δ<ἢ> εἶναι dedi : δ᾽ εἶναι ω.- 16) 702ᵃ30 εἶναι (ω) delevi.- 17) 702ᵇ19 καὶ τὰς dedi cum θ : πρὸς τὰς ω.- 18) 703ᵃ2 <ἐν> inserui cum Γι A : om. ω.- 19) 703ᵃ22 συστελλομένη <τε καὶ ἐκτεινομένη> dedi cum Farquharson : συστελλομένη ω.- 20) Ibidem βίαι <ἑλκ>τικὴ dedi : βιαστικὴ ω : tractiva iam G, unde ἑλκτικὴ Farquharson.- 21) 703ᵇ34 ἀπὸ δὲ τοῦ E...ἀπὸ μὲν τοῦ E dedi secundum diagramma : ἀπὸ δὲ τοῦ B...ἀπὸ μὲν τοῦ B ω.

[283] Thanks are due to Anna Kathrin Bleuler for reading and commenting upon a draft, to Nigel Wilson for valuable bibliographical hints, to Luigi Orlandi and Rudolf Stefec for more accurate dates of some mss., and to Francesco Ademollo, Christian Brockmann, David Charles, Paolo Crivelli, Gabriel Richardson Lear, Gyburg Uhlmann, Christopher Shields, and Kurt Sier for organizing workshops on the text and transmission of *MA* from which we have drawn much profit.

Appendix I: The Forty-Seven Known
Greek Manuscripts of *MA*

Alexandria, *Patriarchal Library* (Βιβλιοθήκη τοῦ Πατριαρχείου)

1) 87 (ff. 283r–292r): **T**ᴾ	AD 1484–85: Förstel 1999, 252.

Berlin, *Staatsbibliothek Preußischer Kulturbesitz*

2) Phill. 1507/I (ff. 105r–113r): **B**ᵉ	*c.* AD 1440–53: Isépy/Prapa 2018, 23.[284]
3) Phill. 1507/II (ff. 214r–219r): **B**ᴾ	*c.* AD 1455: Moraux et al. 1976, 40–2 (Harlfinger).

Erlangen, *Universitätsbibliothek Erlangen-Nürnberg*

4) Erl. Univ. Bibl. A 4 (ff. 94r–99v): **E**ʳ	*c.* AD 1440–53: Luigi Orlandi (by letter).[285]

Escorial, *Real Biblioteca del Monasterio de San Lorenzo de El Escorial*

5) Scor. *T*. II. 13 (ff. 91v–98r): **E**ˢ	4th quarter of the 15th cent.: Moraux et al. 1976, 161–2 (Harlfinger).
6) Scor. *Φ*. III. 11 (ff. 177r–179v): **S**ᶜ	middle to 2nd half of the 14th cent.: Moraux et al. 1976, 169 (Harlfinger).

Florence, *Biblioteca Medicea Laurenziana*

7) Laur. Plut. 81.1 (ff. 127v–130r): **S**	*c.* AD 1280–1320: Rudolf Stefec (by letter): 'archaisierende Minuskel der frühen Palaiologenzeit'.
8) Laur. Plut. 87.4 (210r–215r):[286] **C**ᵃ	*c.* AD 1135–40: Vuillemin-Diem/ Rashed 1997, 178: 'le travail de Ioannikios remonte probablement aux alentours des années 1135-1140.'

---

[284] For a codicological description of the manuscript and its dating, see now the thorough article of Isépy/Prapa 2018: While Bᵉ is nowadays the first part of codex Berol. Phill. 1507, it was originally a manuscript on its own, written before AD 1453 by Ioannes Arnes. Only after AD 1453 was it combined with three further sets of Aristotelica—among them a second copy of *MA* (= Bᴾ)—that were written by other hands after the fall of the capital.

[285] Orlandi's dating of the Erlangensis to the period before AD 1453 is based on his Hamburg PhD thesis, defended on 13 November 2017: 'ANDRONIKOS KALLISTOS: Manuscripts, Activities, Texts'.

[286] According to Wilson 1983, 165, the ms. was copied in the scriptorium of Ioannikios in Constantinople.

9) Laur. Plut. 87.11 (311r-317v): $\mathbf{F^d}$ *c.* AD 1450–78: according to Moraux et al. 1976, 301 (Wiesner: '15. Jh. 2. H.') and R. Stefec (by letter) 'vor 1478: Tod des Michael Apostoles, von dem eine Notiz im Codex stammt'.

10) Laur. Plut. 87.21 (42v-52r): $\mathbf{Z^a}$ late 13th cent.: Isépy 2016, 163; cf. Harlfinger 1971, 149.

Florence, *Biblioteca Riccardiana*

11) Ricc. 14 (170r-176v): $\mathbf{F^s}$ *c.* AD 1475–8: Speranzi 2012/17.

12) Ricc. 81/II (12r-30r): $\mathbf{F^r}$ 16th–17th cent.: Moraux et al. 1976, 362–3 (Harlfinger).

Madrid, *Biblioteca Nacional de España*

13) N 26 (4563) (107r-111v): $\mathbf{M^n}$ AD 1470 according to the subscription on f. 339v; cf. De Andrés 1987, 39.

Milan, *Veneranda Biblioteca Ambrosiana*

14) Ambr. A 174 sup. (204r-208v): $\mathbf{M^i}$ *c.* AD 1470: Harlfinger 1971, 271–3.

15) Ambr. H 50 sup. (99v-110r): $\mathbf{X}$ 12th cent.: Cavallo 2000, 232: 'al XII vanno riferiti …i testi aristotelici Vat. gr. 244, Ambr. H 50 sup.'.

Modena, *Biblioteca Estense*

16) Mut. gr. 76 (41v-50r): $\mathbf{M^d}$ last quarter of the 15th cent.: Rashed 2001, 306–9. The *terminus ante quem* is AD 1497 when the Aldine was printed from the Mutinensis (or from a copy of it).

Moscow, *State Historical Museum* (Государственный Исторический музей)

17) Sinod. 240/Vlad. 453 (51v-56v): $\mathbf{M^o}$ mid-15th cent. or shortly after: Harlfinger 1971, 247–51.

Naples, *Biblioteca Nazionale di Napoli 'Vittorio Emanuele III'*

18) III D 2 (250v-273v): $\mathbf{N^e}$ AD 1493: Formentin 2008, 79.

Oxford, *Bibliotheca Bodleiana*

19) Bodl. Canon. 107 (53r-66r): $\mathbf{B^o}$ 2nd half of the 16th cent.: Escobar 1990, 55.

Oxford, *New College*

20) 226 (38v–47r): **N^c** 2nd half of the 15th cent.: Escobar 1990, 56.

Paris, *Bibliothèque Nationale de France*

21) Par. gr. 1853 (221r–225v): **E** (scribe E III) mid-10th cent.: Hecquet-Devienne 2000, 132: 'milieu du Xe siècle'.

22) Par. gr. 1859 (245r–252v): **b** early 14th cent.: Rashed 2001, 110.

23) Par. gr. 1861 (81r–83v): **c** last quarter of the 15th cent.: Rashed 2001, 309.

24) Par. gr. 1921 (182v–185v):[287] **m^I** + (186r–187r): **m^{II.2}**

25) Par. Coisl. 166 (485r–485v): **m^{II.1}** both no. 24 and no. 25 were written *c.* AD 1360 according to Wiesner 1981, 234 ('nach den zahlreichen Wasserzeichen').[288]

26) Par. gr. 2027 (180v–190r): **P^f** AD 1439: on f. 50r, the date is given both as </a>νμθ· (AD 1449) and as ἰνδ. β′ (2nd indiction).[289] Since the two dates are incompatible with each other, Peter Isépy emended the year to </a>νλθ· (AD 1439).[290]

27) Par. gr. 2035 (50r–62r): **P^g** 3rd quarter of the 15th cent. according to R. Stefec (by letter): '*terminus ante quem* ist 1478 (Tod des Kopisten)', i.e. Michael Apostoles.

28) Par. Suppl. gr. 333 (216v–222v): **P^h** before AD 1511 (death of the scribe, Demetrios Chalkondyles).[291]

---

[287] As Wiesner 1981, 235, has pointed out, our no. 25 (Coisl. 166) preserves the final part (m^{II.1}) of *MA*—chapter 9, 702^b27 (θατέρου ἠρεμοῦντος) to end—that originally belonged to no. 24 (Par. gr. 1921) until it was there replaced by a revised copy (m^{II.2}), written by the same scribe. The copyist in question, previously known as 'Anonymus Aristotelicus', was identified by Mondrain 2005, 25, with 'Malachias Papas' on the strength of a codex (Laur. Plut. 74.10) by the same hand, where the name of that scribe is twice indicated (foll. 207r and 215r).

[288] Cf. Harlfinger 1971, 55: 'im dritten Viertel des 14. Jhs. angelegt'.

[289] The *indiction* indicates the position of a given year within the fifteen-year cycle of taxation; the year AD 312/13 counted as the first indiction of the first cycle; cf. Bagnall/Worp 2004, 7–11.

[290] Omont 1892, 15 (followed, e.g., by Mondrain 2011, 93), tried to remove the incompatibility by emending the indiction to ἰνδ. <ι>β′ (12th indiction) which would square with the transmitted year AD 1449. According to Canart 1980, 97, however, Byzantine scribes err in indicating the *Annus Domini* rather than the indiction: 'più di una volta succede che i vari elementi di datazione si contraddicano. Si tenta di risolvere il problema tenendo conto degli elementi più sicuri: generalmente sono la cifra dell'indizione ed il giorno della settimana ...'.

[291] This *terminus ante quem* yields a more exact date than the one given by Escobar 1990, 63 ('Vor 1515').

Rome (Vatican City State), *Biblioteca Apostolica Vaticana*

29) Vat. gr. 253 (203v–211v): **L**
30) Vat. gr. 258 (57v–68r): **N**

both written *c.* AD 1300 (Rashed 2001, 59), since one of the scribes of no. 30, Ioannes Bardales, was killed AD 1300,[292] whereas no. 29 was copied by Leon Bardales, also a member of the team responsible for no. 30.[293]

31) Vat. gr. 259 (156v–162v): **G^r**

after AD 1464/5: According to Vendruscolo 2008, 293, Michael Lygizos (identified by Gamillscheg 1997, 172, no. 465) copied no. 31 for Ioannes Argyropulos after he had arrived in Florence.

32) Vat. gr. 261 (131r–138v): **Y**

c. AD 1300: (Harlfinger 1971, 252: 'anhand der Wasserzeichen') by Georgios Pachymeres (AD 1242–*c.*1310) and his collaborators (Gamillscheg 1997, 60, no. 115).[294]

33) Vat. gr. 266 (60v–66r): **V**

1st quarter of the 14th cent.: (Harlfinger 1971, 131: 'aufgrund der Wasserzeichen').

34) Vat. gr. 1339 (245r–252v): **P**

written in the 2nd half of the 14th cent. by Ioasaph (Harlfinger 1971, 251–5).

35) Vat. gr. 1950 (542r–545v): **V^g**

early 14th cent., since part of the ms. was written by Leon Bardales, who copied also no. 29 (Vat. gr. 253) and part of no. 30 (Vat. gr. 253, scribe A).[295]

36) Palat. gr. 97 (38r–43v): **V^P**

14th cent.: Escobar 1990, 70.

---

[292] Scribe C of no. 30 (Vat. gr. 258) was Ioannes Bardales according to the subscription on f. 325v (see Harlfinger 1971, 132).

[293] Harlfinger 1971, 165–6, identified the man who wrote no. 29 (Vat. gr. 253) with scribe A of no. 30 (Vat. gr. 258)—i.e., according to Canart 2008, 54, with Leon Bardales. On the basis of the watermarks, Harlfinger 1971, 131, had suggested dating no. 30 to the first quarter of the fourteenth-century.

[294] See further Golitsis 2011, 168, and Isépy 2016, 57, n. 283.

[295] Cf. Canart 2008, 54.

37) Palat. gr. 163 (37v-43r): **V**^q

c. AD 1442: according to Rashed 2001, 118 the ms. forms part of the same collection of *Aristotelica* (copied by J. Skutariotes for G. Manetti) as cod. Palat. gr. 159 which was written AD 1442.

38) Urb. gr. 41 (17r-27v): **V**^u

AD 1613: according to the subscription of the scribe (i.e. *Ἰωσὴφ ὁ Κρής*) on f. 17r (Stefec 2012, 99, n. 27)

Udine, *Biblioteca arcivescovile*

39) Utinensis 254 (393v-401v): **U**^t

c. AD 1480: cf.Vendruscolo 2008, 292–4.

Venice, *Biblioteca Nazionale Marciana*

40) Marc. gr. 200 (234v-237v): **Q**

AD 1457: according to the subscription on f. 594r (Mioni 1981, 312).

41) Marc. gr. 206 (329v-333v): **f**

AD 1467: according to the subscriptions on ff. 67r and 165v (Mioni 1981, 320).

42) Marc. gr. 209 (65r-73v): **O**^d

early 14th cent.: the scribe was identified by Harlfinger with the copyist of a dated document (see Escobar 1990, 164).

43) Marc. gr. 212 (439r-442r): **G**^a

c. AD 1430: the date of the main part of the codex to which also *MA* belongs (Harlfinger 1971, 175).

44) Marc. gr. 214 (184r-187v): **H**^a

AD 1290–1300: Rashed 2001, 250.

Vienna, *Österreichische Nationalbibliothek*

45) Vind. phil. gr. 64 (186v-192v): **W**^g

AD 1457: according to the subscription on f. 447v (Hunger 1961, 182).

46) Vind. phil. gr. 134 (205r-225r): **W**^w

15th cent.: Hunger 1961, 241.

47) Vind. phil. gr. 157 (81v-89v): **W**^x

15th cent.: Hunger 1961, 260.

Appendix II: The Principal Manuscripts of William's Translation and Their Affiliation According to De Leemans 2011a

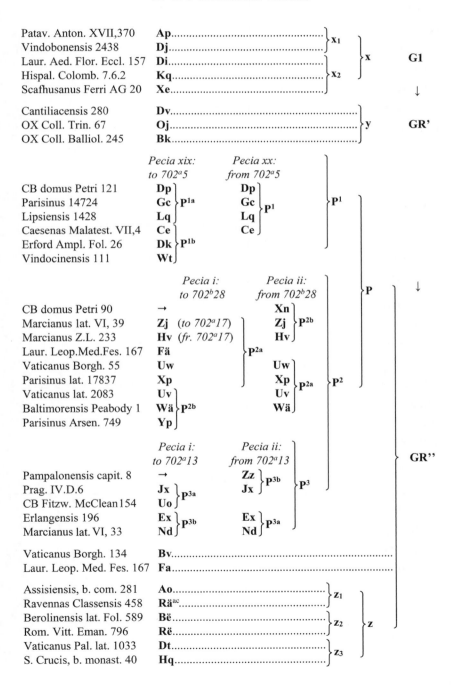

Patav. Anton. XVII,370	**Ap**		
Vindobonensis 2438	**Dj**	x_1	
Laur. Aed. Flor. Eccl. 157	**Di**		x **G1**
Hispal. Colomb. 7.6.2	**Kq**	x_2	
Scafhusanus Ferri AG 20	**Xe**		↓

Cantiliacensis 280	**Dv**		
OX Coll. Trin. 67	**Oj**	y	**GR'**
OX Coll. Balliol. 245	**Bk**		

	Pecia xix: to 702ª5	*Pecia xx:* from 702ª5	
CB domus Petri 121	**Dp**	**Dp**	
Parisinus 14724	**Gc** P^{1a}	**Gc** P^1	P^1
Lipsiensis 1428	**Lq**	**Lq**	
Caesenas Malatest. VII,4	**Ce**	**Ce**	
Erford Ampl. Fol. 26	**Dk** P^{1b}		
Vindocinensis 111	**Wt**		

	Pecia i: to 702ᵇ28	*Pecia ii:* from 702ᵇ28		
CB domus Petri 90	→	**Xn**		P ↓
Marcianus lat. VI, 39	**Zj** (*to 702ª17*)	**Zj** P^{2b}		
Marcianus Z.L. 233	**Hv** (*fr. 702ª17*)	**Hv**		
Laur. Leop.Med.Fes. 167	**Fä** P^{2a}			
Vaticanus Borgh. 55	**Uw**	**Uw**		
Parisinus lat. 17837	**Xp**	**Xp** P^{2a}	P^2	
Vaticanus lat. 2083	**Uv**	**Uv**		
Baltimorensis Peabody 1	**Wä** P^{2b}	**Wä**		
Parisinus Arsen. 749	**Yp**			

	Pecia i: to 702ª13	*Pecia ii:* from 702ª13		
Pampalonensis capit. 8	→	**Zz** P^{3b}		**GR''**
Prag. IV.D.6	**Jx** P^{3a}	**Jx** P^3		
CB Fitzw. McClean154	**Uo**			
Erlangensis 196	**Ex** P^{3b}	**Ex** P^{3a}		
Marcianus lat. VI, 33	**Nd**	**Nd**		

Vaticanus Borgh. 134	**Bv**
Laur. Leop. Med. Fes. 167	**Fa**

Assisiensis, b. com. 281	**Ao**	z_1	
Ravennas Classensis 458	**Rä**ᵃᶜ		
Berolinensis lat. Fol. 589	**Bë**	z_2	z
Rom. Vitt. Eman. 796	**Rë**		
Vaticanus Pal. lat. 1033	**Dt**	z_3	
S. Crucis, b. monast. 40	**Hq**		

Appendix III: 120 Divergences
(Primavesi 2023 | Nussbaum 1978)

Chapter 1

(1): Titulus   delevi | περὶ ζῴων κινήσεως (**ω**)

(2): 698ª1   τῆς τῶν ζῴων κινήσεως **β** | κινήσεως τῆς τῶν ζῴων (**α**)

(3): 698ª8   αὐτὸ αὐτὸ **β**E | αὐτὸ ἑαυτὸ (**γ**)

(4): 698ª15–16   πρῶτον μὲν **βγ** | πρῶτον μὲν οὖν (E)

(5): 698ª16–17   ἀεὶ γάρ … ἠρεμεῖ τι **β** | δεῖ γάρ … ἠρεμεῖν τι (**α**)

(6): 698ª22–4   Diagramma *ΑΒΓΔ* **α** | non habet Nussbaum

(7): 698ª23   ἡ μὲν *Α* καὶ ἡ *Δ* **βε** | ἡ μὲν *ΑΔ* coniecit Nussbaum

(8): 698ª26   κινεῖσθαι **β**EθCª | κινεῖται (**ι**)

(9): 698ᵇ1   διαιρεῖται **β** | διαιρετά (**α**)

(10): 698ᵇ1   ἡ ἀρχή γε **β** | ἡ ἀρχὴ (**α**)

(11): 698ᵇ3   ὀλέκρανον **β**ENCª (item infra 702ª28, ᵇ4, ᵇ11) | ὠλέκρανον (**ληι**)

(12): 698ᵇ5   ἕκαστον δεῖ τι **β** | ἕκαστόν τι δεῖ (**α**)

(13): 698ᵇ6   ἐστίν **β**E | ἔσται (**γ**)

Chapter 2

(14): 698ᵇ8   αὐτοῖς **βι** | αὐτῷ (E**Γ**ı**θε**)

(15): 698ᵇ9   ἔξω **β**E | ἔξωθεν (**γ**)

(16): 698ᵇ16   μυσὶ τοῖς **α** | ἐμύσι τοῖς (coniecit Diels)

(17): 698ᵇ16   τῆι πίττηι **β**, E ante rasuram | πηλῷ coniecit Nussbaum

(18): 698ᵇ23   ἐπ᾽ αὐτῶι **β** | ἐν αὐτῷ (**α**)

(19): 698ᵇ24–5   οὐδ᾽ … οὐδ᾽ **β** | οὐδ᾽ ἂν … οὔθ᾽ (coniecit Jaeger)

(20): 698ᵇ26   πλέων **β** | πνέων (**α**)

(21): 699ª4   αὐτὸν **β**(Bᵉ) | αὐτὸ ἢ (**α**)

(22): 699ª10   ἕλκων καὶ ὠθῶν **β** | ὠθῶν ἢ ἕλκων (**α**)

Chapter 3

(23): 699ª13   τέ τι δεῖ **β**(Bᵉ) | τε δεῖ (E)

(24): 699ª13   καὶ τοῦτο **ω** | καὶ τοῦτο, <καὶ> (coniecit Farquharson)

(25): 699ª13   οὐρανοῦ **β** | οὐρανοῦ μόριον (**α**)

(26): 699ª17   ἔσται coniecit Thomæus | ἔσεσθαι (**ω**)

(27): 699ᵃ26   τὰ κινούμενα δι' αὐτῶν **β** PBᵖMᵒ | καὶ τὰ κινούμενα δι' αὐτῶν (**α**)

(28): 699ᵇ2   τοιοῦτον ἕτερόν ἐστιν **β** P | τοιοῦτόν ἐστιν ἕτερον (**α**)

(29): 699ᵇ2   οὐ δεῖ...**β** | οὐδὲν...(**α**)

(30): 699ᵇ2–3   ἀντερείδειν **βγ** | ἀντερείδειν δεῖ (E)

(31): 699ᵇ7   καὶ τοῦ **β** | καὶ τῆς τοῦ **γ**(HᵃLVᵍιε)

Chapter 4

(32): 699ᵇ14   ὑπερβάληι L Cᵃ Bᵉ et al. | ὑπερβάλλῃ (E N Eʳ et al.)

(33): 699ᵇ19   ἀδύνατον εἶναί φαμεν **β** | ἀδύνατόν φαμεν εἶναι EN

(34): 699ᵇ23   ἐξ ἀνάγκης <εἶναι> e ᵇ22 transposui | ἐξ ἀνάγκης (**ω**)

(35): 699ᵇ25   εἰσιν αἱ **βE θ** | εἰσιν (Michael ι Cᵃ)

(36): 699ᵇ30   εἴπερ **β** | εἰ (**α**)

(37): 700ᵃ1   μήστωρ' **β** | πάντων (EΓιε)

(38): 700ᵃ8–9   δεῖ γὰρ—κινεῖσθαι post ᵃ10 κινήσεται transposui cum Renehan | δεῖ γὰρ—κινεῖσθαι (**ω**)

(39): 700ᵃ8   αὐτοῦ τὸ **β**ECᵃ | αὐτῶν τὸ (**θ**)

(40): 700ᵃ12   αὐτοῖς **β**ιCᵃ | ἑαυτοῖς (E**θ**)

(41): 700ᵃ13   καὶ τὸ κινούμενον **β** | καὶ τὸ κινοῦν (**α**)

(42): 700ᵃ13   πρὸς τῶν ἔξωθέν **β** | πρὸς τῶν ἔξω (**α**)

(43): 700ᵃ13   ἠρεμοῦν **β** | ἠρεμούντων (**α**)

(44): 700ᵃ14   πάντα ταῦτα **β** | ταῦτα (**α**)

(45): 700ᵃ15   τι ἄλλ', <ἀλλ'> dedi | τι, ἀλλ' (**ω**)

(46): 700ᵃ17   πάντων ὁμοίως **β** | πάντων (**α**)

(47): 700ᵃ20   πρῶτον κινοῦν **βθ**Cᵃ | πρώτως κινοῦν (Eι)

(48): 700ᵃ25   καὶ οἱ ἐκπνέοντες **β**Cᵃ | καὶ ἐκπνέοντες (E**ζ**)

Chapter 5

(49): 700ᵃ26   αὐτὸ αὐτὸ **β**E NPMᵒCᵃ | αὐτῷ αὐτὸ (**λ**)

(50): 700ᵃ27   αὐτὸ ὑφ' αὐτοῦ Eι | αὐτῷ ὑφ' αὐτοῦ (**βθ**)

(51): 700ᵃ27–28 καὶ ἐν τῶι αὐξανομένωι **β** | καὶ αὐξανομένῳ (**α**)

(52): 700ᵃ29   ἥνπερ **ω** | ἥπερ Nussbaum (*perperam?*)

(53): 700ᵃ29–30 γενέσεως μὲν καὶ φθορᾶς **β** | γενέσεως καὶ φθορᾶς (**α**)

(54): 700ᵃ30   αὕτη ἂν αἰτία εἴη **β** | αὕτη αἰτία ἂν εἴη (**α**)

| (55): 700ᵃ30–1 | καὶ τῶν ἄλλων δὲ κινήσεων **β**E \| καὶ τῶν ἄλλων δὴ κινήσεων (coniecit Farquharson) |
| (56): 700ᵇ1 | αὐτὸ αὑτῶι αἴτιον εἶναι **β** \| αὐτὸ αἴτιον εἶναι αὑτῷ (**α**) |

Chapter 6

(57): 700ᵇ9	λοιπὸν δ᾽ ἐστὶν Eb**Γ2** | λοιπόν ἐστι(ν) (BᶜEʳ**γ**)
(58): 700ᵇ14	καὶ γὰρ **β**ECᵃι | καὶ γὰρ καὶ (**θ**)
(59): 700ᵇ16	πάσης αὐτοῖς **β** | αὐτοῖς πάσης (**α**)
(60): 700ᵇ22	ὀρέξεις **βγ** | ὄρεξις (E)
(61): 700ᵇ24	καὶ τὸ **β**ECᵃιλ | καὶ (N)
(62): 700ᵇ24	νοητόν … νοητόν dedi | διανοητόν … διανοητόν (**ω**)
(63): 700ᵇ24	οὐ πᾶν δὲ **β** P | οὐ πᾶν δὲ τὸ (E**εθ**)
(64): 700ᵇ33	καλὸν καὶ dedi | καλὸν καὶ τὸ (**ω**) ἀληθὲς καὶ τὸ πρώτως **β**P | ἀληθῶς καὶ πρώτως (**α**)
(65): 701ᵃ3	κινουμένων **β** | κινήσεων coniecit Nussbaum

Chapter 7

(66): 701ᵃ8	ἔοικε δὲ **β** N G1(x₂) Bᵖ | ἔοικε(ν) (E **λιε**)
(67): 701ᵃ17	ἀγαθὸν δὲ οἰκία **β** | οἰκία δ᾽ ἀγαθόν (**α**)
(68): 701ᵃ19	ἱματίου δὲ δέομαι **β** | ἱματίου δέομαι (**α**)
(69): 701ᵃ19	ἱμάτιον ποιεῖ **β**ECᵃ | ἱμάτιον ποιητέον (**δ**)
(70): 701ᵃ24	δυεῖν ὁδῶν dedi (< δύ᾽ εἰ ποδῶν Bᶜ, Ea.c.?) | δύο εἰδῶν (Ep.c. **γ** Eʳ)
(71): 701ᵃ26	ἐπιστᾶσα **β** | ἐφιστᾶσα (**α**)
(72): 701ᵃ27	οὐκέτι **β** | οὐκ (**α**)
(73): 701ᵃ35	τοῦ κινεῖσθαι **ω** | τῆς κινήσεως Nussbaum (*perperam?*)
(74): 701ᵇ1	διὰ προαίρεσιν ἢ βούλησιν **β** | διὰ βούλησιν coniecit Nussbaum
(75): 701ᵇ3	κρουόντων πρὸς **β** | κρουόντων (**α**)
(76): 701ᵇ3	ἀλλήλας **ω** | ἄλληλα (coniecit Torraca)
(77): 701ᵇ3	<εὐθὺς τῶν ζωιδίων τὰς μαχαίρας> exempli gratia dedi | <τῶν ξύλων> coniecit Nussbaum
(78): 701ᵇ4	ὅπερ **α** | ὁ γὰρ (Richards & Ross)
(79): 701ᵇ4	<ὁ> ὀχούμενος dedi | ὀχούμενος (**β**)
(80): 701ᵇ4	αὐτὸς **β** | αὐτὸ (**α**)
(81): 701ᵇ4–5	<πάλιν> καὶ πάλιν dedi | καὶ πάλιν (**ω**)

(82): 701^{b}5	κύκλωι δὲ **β** | κύκλῳ (**a**)
(83): 701^{b}13–14	ἔλαττον καὶ μεῖζον **β** | μεῖζον καὶ ἔλαττον (**a**)
(84): 701^{b}14–15	αὐξανομένων <καὶ συστελλομένων> τῶν μορίων dedi | αὐξανομένων τῶν μορίων (**ω**)
(85): 701^{b}15–16	πνεῦμα καὶ **β**E | πάλιν συστελλομένων διὰ (**γ**)
(86): 701^{b}20	θερμοῦ ἢ ψυχροῦ ἢ **ω** | seclusit Nussbaum
(87): 701^{b}30	καὶ **β**EιC^a | εἰ καὶ (**θ** < Mich. < Al.)
(88): 701^{b}30	ἐν Al. | κατὰ μέγεθος ἐν (**γ**)

Chapter 8

(89): 701^{b}34	τε καὶ Al. | καὶ (**ω**)
(90): 701^{b}36–7	ἀλλὰ—συμβαῖνον **ω** | post 702^{a}1 θερμότητος transposuit cum Moraux
(91): 702^{a}4	καὶ ψύξεώς **βA** | ἢ ψύξεώς (**a**)
(92): 702^{a}11	καὶ ἐπὶ τοῦ…καὶ ἐπὶ τοῦ **β** | καὶ ἔτι τοῦ…καὶ (**a**)
(93): 702^{a}14	ἀπολείπηι **β**EH^{a}LV^g | ἀπολίπῃ (Xp.c. PB^{p}M^{o}ϵ)
(94): 702^{a}15	διὰ τοῦτο **β** | διὰ τοῦτο δ' (**a**)
(95): 702^{a}18	ἐπιτηδείως ἔχειν **β** | ἐπιτηδείως (**a**)
(96): 702^{a}22	ἐστὶν τοῦ μὲν **β** | τοῦ μέν ἐστιν (Vat. gr. 261 et 266)
(97): 702^{a}29	κινεῖ καὶ κινεῖται **β** | κινεῖται (**a**)
(98): 702^{a}29	ἀλλ' ἀνάγκη **β** | ἀνάγκη (**a** E^r)
(99): 702^{a}29	δ<ἢ> εἶναι dedi | δ' εἶναι (**ω**)
(100): 702^{a}30	ἓν dedi | ἓν εἶναι (**ω**)
(101): 702^{b}4	μόριον **β** | μέρος (**a**)
(102): 702^{b}8	τοῦ ἐσχάτου **β**, quod ante τοῦ μὲν transposuimus | ἐσχάτου (**a**)

Chapter 9

(103): 702^{b}15	ἀνωτέρωι (Dativus) E | ἀνωτέρω (Adverbium) (**βγ**)
(104): 702^{b}17	ἐσχάτων **β** | ἄκρων (**a**)
(105): 702^{b}19	καὶ τὰς N | καὶ πρὸς τὰς X
(106): 702^{b}28–36	Diagramma *ΑΒΓ* **γ** | non habet Nussbaum
(107): 702^{b}30	κινήσεσθαι (passivē) **β**EC^a**λ** | κινεῖσθαι (Nι)
(108): 702^{b}32	ἐνδέχεται καὶ **β** | ἐνδέχεται (**a**)
(109): 702^{b}32	κινεῖσθαι τῶι B **β** | τῷ B κινεῖσθαι (**a**)

Chapter 10

(110): 703ᵃ22   καὶ βία<ι ἑλκ>τική dedi (< βιαστικὴ **ω**) | καὶ ἑλκτικὴ
(Farquharson ex G)

(111): 703ᵃ25–6   κρατεῖται...ὑπ' ἀλλήλων **β** | κρατεῖ...ἀλλήλων (**a**)

Chapter 11

(112): 703ᵇ7   φανέντος μέν τινος **β** | φανέντος τινός (**a**)

(113): 703ᵇ12   αὐξάνεσθαι **β**N | αὔξεσθαι (**a**)

(114): 703ᵇ15–16   καὶ ἐντὸς ὑπάρχουσιν **β** | καὶ αἱ ἐντὸς ὑπάρχουσαι (**a**)

(115): 703ᵇ22–3   τούτου—ζωτικήν **ω** | cum Jaeger seclusit Nussbaum

(116): 703ᵇ28   πρὸς ἄλληλα δὲ **βθ**Cᵃ | πρὸς ἀλλήλας (E)

(117): 703ᵇ29–36   Diagramma *ΑΒΓΔΕ* **βγ** | non habet Nussbaum

(118): 703ᵇ32   ἀρχὴ **ω** | cum Farquharson seclusit Nussbaum

(119): 703ᵇ34   ἀπὸ δὲ τοῦ *E*...ἀπὸ μὲν τοῦ *E* dedi secundum
diagramma | ἀπὸ δὲ τοῦ *B*...ἀπὸ μὲν τοῦ *B* (**ω**)

(120): 704ᵇ1   καὶ περὶ **β**(EʳOᵈSVᵖ) *Γ*2(*et de* G) | περὶ (**a**Bᵉ)

Appendix IV: The Stemmatic Position
of Berolinensis Bᵉ in *De Insomniis*

In order to establish a stemma codicum of *De Insomniis*, Escobar 1990 collated all fifty Greek manuscripts of the work[296] against Bekker's edition (1831), listed their deviations from Bekker's text, and used the way in which these deviations are distributed among the manuscripts as a criterion for the establishment of two hyparchetypes **α** and **β**; further sub-groups are then defined on the basis of shared deviations from **α** and **β**. The *evaluation* of readings, by contrast, is a feature absent from Escobar's work: he nowhere discusses the *strengths* and *weaknesses*, linguistic or philosophical or otherwise, of the readings by which his main ms.-groups differ from each other.[297] Even so, Escobar's stemma of *Insomn.* shares with Nussbaum's stemma of *MA* the basic bipartite structure, as our simplified version of Escobar's stemma shows:

---

[296] Listed by Escobar 1990, 43–4, described p. 44–80.
[297] The excellent textual notes contained in the commentary on *Insomn.* by Philip J. van der Eijk 1994 were a major step forward.

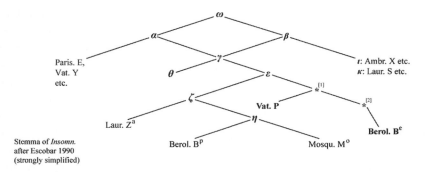

Paris. E,
Vat. Y
etc.

ι: Ambr. X etc.
κ: Laur. S etc.

Vat. P

Laur. Z^a

Berol. B^e

Stemma of *Insomn.*
after Escobar 1990
(strongly simplified)

Berol. B^p

Mosqu. M^o

Escobar's families **α** and **β** are clearly equivalent to Nussbaum's two families *a*[298] and *b*;[299] Escobar's **β**-family, in particular, consists mainly of two sub-groups one of which (*ι*) corresponds to Nussbaum's group b_2+N,[300] whereas the other (*κ*) corresponds to Nussbaum's group b_1 (enlarged).[301] A further group of *Insomn.* manuscripts (*ε*) is equivalent to Nussbaum's group Z^aP (enlarged): Laurentianus Plut. 87.21 (Z^a), Berolinensis Phill. 1507/II (B^p), Mosquensis Sinod. 240 (M^o), and Vaticanus gr. 1339 (P). But unlike Nussbaum, Escobar does not assign this group to his family **β**; instead, he derives it (together with a further group, **θ**, which has no equivalent in the transmission of *MA*) from a third, intermediate prototype **γ** the text of which would have been based, in passages where **α** and **β** disagree with each other, on a preferential choice between these divergent readings.[302] Therefore, Escobar places the **γ**-family (and its progeny **θ** and **ε**) in equidistance from **α** and **β**. Furthermore, he regards Berolinensis Phill. 1507/I (B^e) as a descendant of **γ**, and in particular of **ε**.

We will first review the evidence for the relationship between B^e and P.[303] The two manuscripts share twelve readings against the remaining **γ**-manuscripts.[304] Whereas most of these B^eP-readings are at least defensible, or

---

[298] Escobar's first family (**α**) contains, *inter alia*, the three manuscripts which make up Nussbaum's family *a*: Parisinus E and Vaticani Y and V.

[299] Escobar's second family (**β**) contains, *inter alia*, most of the manuscripts which make up Nussbaum's family *b*: Marcianus O^d, Laurentianus S, Ambrosianus X, Marcianus H^a, and Vaticani L and N.

[300] Escobar's sub-group *ι* contains Ambrosianus X, Marcianus H^a, Vaticanus L, and Vaticanus N.

[301] Escobar's sub-group *κ* contains not only Laurentianus S and Marcianus O^d, but also Vaticanus Palatinus V^p which we have added to Nussbaum's *b_1* in section 9 of the present introduction.

[302] Escobar 1990, 82-8, lists the passages where his **α**-family diverges from a **β**-reading preferred by Bekker 1831, 458^a33–462^b11, and he indicates which of these divergent **α**-readings are shared by **γ**. Likewise, Escobar 1990, 115-22, lists the passages where his **β**-family diverges from an **α**-reading preferred by Bekker, and he indicates which of these divergent **β**-readings are shared by **γ**. See also Escobar 1990, 168-9.

[303] All P and B^e readings mentioned or implied by Escobar 1990 were checked by Christina Prapa, and only minor corrections had to be made.

[304] Escobar 1990, 174-5: 458^b3 ἐπεὶ B^eP : ἤ a : εἰ γβ.– 458^b7 πάντα καὶ καθεύδοντα B^eP : πάντα μύοντα καὶ καθεύδοντα γαβ.– 459^a4-5 ἐγρηγορότες...ἐγρηγορότες B^eP : ἐγρηγορότων...ἐγρηγορότων γ :

even superior to the readings of the other manuscripts,[305] there are also three undisputable errors.[306] On the other hand, P features several separative errors, by which it diverges not only from all other manuscripts but also from Berolinensis B^e: Escobar offered four examples[307] and concluded, plausibly, that B^e, for all the readings it shares exclusively with P, still does not depend on P. This state of affairs might suggest that B^e—being much younger than P—is a descendant not of P itself but of P's lost *model* (★[1] in Escobar's stemma): this model would have been still free of the individual errors of its copy P, but it would have already introduced the twelve readings shared by B^e and P against the other *γ*-manuscripts. In 459ᵃ4 and ᵃ5, however, the B^eP-error ἐγρηγορότες was certainly not derived from *γ*'s ἐγρηγορότων, but clearly from the *αβ*-reading ἐγρηγορότος: B^e's mistake is due to an old majuscule confusion (ο → ε) committed by a scribe who had ἐγρηγορότος in front of him. The error, then, seems to go back to an old source in which the reading known *to us* from Escobar's archetype had already been corrupted before the ninth-century transliteration into minuscule script took place.

The most problematic feature of Escobar's stemma follows from the preceding one: a common ancestor of P and B^e would have to belong, by definition, to P's family *γ* in general and to P's group *ε* in particular. So *if* P's model (★[1]) were also the ancestor of Berolinensis B^e, as indicated by Escobar's stemma, B^e would have to share, by and large, all idiosyncratic readings of both *γ* and *ε*, i.e. all readings by which *γ* and *ε* diverge from both main families *α* and *β*. In this respect, however, Escobar's hypothesis fails to account for his evidence: only three out of eleven *γ*-divergences from *αβ* are shared by B^e;[308] and according to

---

ἐγρηγορότος... ἐγρηγορότος *αβ*.– 459ᵃ25 ἕκαστον τὸ αἰσθητήριον B^eP : ἕκαστον αἰσθητήριον *γαβ*.– 459ᵃ31 ἕτερον οὗτος B^eP : οὗτος κινούμενος ἕτερον *γαβ*.– 459ᵇ8 ἐπειδὴ...αἰσθανόμεθα B^eP : ὅτι...αἰσθανόμεθα *α* : ὅταν...αἰσθανώμεθα *γβ*.– 459ᵇ9 ἔκ τε τοῦ ἡλίου B^ePα : ἐκ τοῦ ἡλίου *γβ*.– 459ᵇ13 ἐφ' ὃ B^eP : ὑφ' ᾧ *α* : ἐφ' ὅπερ *γβ*.– 459ᵇ26 διαπορήσειεν B^ePβ : ἀπορήσειεν *γα*.– 460ᵃ2 ὥσπερ τὰ λαμπρά B^eP : ὥσπερ καὶ τὰ λαμπρά *γαβ*.– 461ᵃ5 διὰ τῶν...γίνεσθαι B^eP : διὰ τό...γίνεσθαι *γαβ*.– 461ᵃ27 αἰσθητῶν B^eP : αἰσθητηρίων *γ* : αἰσθημάτων *α* : αἰσθήσεων *β*.

[305] In 459ᵃ30–1, for instance, the *γαβ*-reading τὸ γὰρ κινῆσαν ἐκίνησεν ἀέρα τινά, καὶ πάλιν οὗτος κινούμενος ἕτερον is a clumsy paraphrase of the crisp B^eP-reading τὸ γὰρ κινῆσαν ἐκίνησεν ἀέρα τινά, καὶ πάλιν ἕτερον οὗτος.

[306] 458ᵇ7 πάντα καὶ καθεύδοντα B^eP : πάντα μύοντα καὶ καθεύδοντα *γαβ*. Cf. van der Eijk 1994, 138: 'Das Nicht-wirksam-Sein des Gesichts während des Schlafes wird von Aristoteles aus der empirisch wahrnehmbaren Tatsache geschlossen, daß die Augen dann geschlossen sind (μύοντα). Hieraus schließt er eine ähnliche Untätigkeit der anderen Sinne.'– 459ᵃ4–5 ἐγρηγορότες (*bis*) B^eP : ἐγρηγορότων (*bis*) *γ* : ἐγρηγορότος (*bis*) *αβ*.– 461ᵃ5 διὰ τῶν ἐκ τῶν ἔξω...γίνεσθαι...παλίρροιαν B^eP : διὰ τὸ ἐκ τῶν ἔξω... γίνεσθαι...παλίρροιαν *γαβ*.

[307] Escobar 1990, 175–6: 458ᵇ5–6 καὶ μέγεθος καὶ τὰ τοιαῦτα P : καὶ μέγεθος καὶ τὰ ἄλλα τὰ τοιαῦτα B^eβ : καὶ μέγεθος καὶ κίνησις καὶ τἆλλα τὰ τοιαῦτα *a*.– 458ᵇ8 οὐδ' ἐν P : οὐδὲν ἐν B^e *γβ* : οὐδὲ ἐν *a*.– 460ᵇ8–9 τρόπον δὲ τὸν αὐτόν P : τὸν αὐτὸν δὲ τρόπον B^e *γαβ*.– 462ᵃ8 ἀλήθειαν λέγομεν P : ἀληθὲς λέγομεν B^pM° : ἀληθῆ λέγομεν B^e *γαβ*.

[308] Escobar 1990, 167, n. 2 admits: 'Die Handschrift weist in textkritischer Hinsicht manche spezifischen Probleme auf...Nur wenige und allerdings nicht sehr bedeutende Stellen aus der folgenden

his own list, only thirteen out of a total of forty-three idiosyncratic ε-readings would be shared by B[e].[309] What is more: Two of the thirteen ε-readings in question are in fact *not* shared by B[e],[310] so that out of forty-three characteristic ε-readings no more than eleven are attested also by B[e].[311] All in all, then, forty out of the total of fifty-four readings by which either the whole γ-family or its ε-group diverge from the two main families *α* and *β*, are *not* shared by B[e], whereas only fourteen of these γ/ε-readings are. By consequence, Escobar had to insert between ms.★[1] and B[e] a further hypothetical lost manuscript ★[2]: the immediate model of B[e], which would have removed, by 'counter-contamination', as it were, forty (!) peculiar γ/ε-readings and replaced them with standard readings.[312] It seems evident, however, that without having recourse to a second source, the forty divergences in question that would have been still present in ms.★[1] could neither have been identified there, nor corrected in ms.★[2].

Among the eleven peculiar readings which B[e] *does* share with ε, there are two clear errors,[313] one of which might be of interest for the history of transmission: In 461[b]16, B[e] and ε offer τοῦ ἅλατος instead of the received reading τοῦ ἁλός. The neuter τὸ ἅλας ('salt') is known to readers of the *Sermon on the Mount* as the *Koine* equivalent of ὁ ἅλς.[314] Since Friedrich Blass rejected the restoration of τὸ ἅλας in book II of the ps.-Hippocratic *On Regimen* (*c*.400 BC),[315] the earliest

---

Liste...sind auch bei ihr zu finden.' Cf. ibid. 167-8: 459[b]25-26 περὶ οὗ κἂν καθ' αὑτό...σκέψαιτό τις B[e]γ : περὶ ὧν κἂν καθ' αὑτόν...σκέψαιτό τις a : περὶ οὗ καὶ αὑτοῦ...σκέψαιτό τις ἂν β.– 462[b]5 παίδων B[e]γ : παιδίων a : παιδίοις β.– 462[b]7–8 ἢ καταφερομένη ποιεῖ B[e]γ : ἢ πάλιν καταφερομένην ποιεῖν a : ἢ πάλιν καταφερομένη ποιεῖ β.

[309] Escobar 1990, 171, puts it mildly: 'Die Fassung I [i.e. B[e]] wird von diesen Lesarten nur zum Teil charakterisiert, wie man auf der folgenden Liste vermerkt hat.' For the list, see pp. 171-4.

[310] In 460[b]6, B[e] shares the correct majority reading πολεμίους, not the εN error πολέμους, as implied by Escobar 1990, 172, and in 462[a]32, B[e] shares the correct majority reading που, not the ε-reading πῃ, as implied by Escobar 1990, 174.

[311] 458[b]4 ὅλως δὲ B[e]ε : καὶ ὅλως δὲ β : καὶ ὅλως a.– 458[b]26 ἐκ τούτων B[e]ε : περὶ τούτων cett.– 459[b]21 ὑπό...ὑπό B[e]ε : ἀπό...ἀπό cett.– 459[b]27 καὶ[1] om. B[e]ε : habent cett.– 460[b]17 κρίνειν τε τὸ κύριον B[e]ε : κρίνειν τὸ κύριον a : κρίνειν τό τε κύριον β.– 460[b]21 κυριωτέρα γὰρ ἑτέρα B[e]ε : κυριωτέρα γὰρ cett.– 461[a]5 εἰς τὰ ἐντός B[e]ε : εἰς τὸ ἐντός cett.– 461[a]28 δοκεῖν B[e]ε : καὶ δοκεῖν cett.– 461[b]16 ἅλατος B[e]ε : ἁλός cett.– 461[b]19 ἔχουσιν B[e]ε : ἔχουσαι cett.– 462[a]30 ὅταν ἐν τῷ καθεύδειν καὶ ᾖ καθεύδει B[e]ε : ὅταν ἐν τῷ καθεύδειν ᾖ, ᾖ καθεύδει cett.

[312] Escobar 1990, 176: 'Die Textgestaltung der Handschrift [i.e. B[e]] (Bindefehler mit ε und P) zwingt uns anzunehmen, daß sie aus einer korrigierten Vorlage geflossen ist'; and ibid. n. 3: 'Dabei wäre sowohl der Wortlaut der Vorlage und damit die meisten der spezifischen Fehler wie auch einige der kontaminierten Lesarten korrigiert worden.'

[313] 460[b]21 κυριωτέρα γὰρ ἑτέρα τῆς ἁφῆς ἡ ὄψις B[e]ε : κυριωτέρα γὰρ τῆς ἁφῆς ἡ ὄψις cett.; the ἑτέρα wrongly inserted in B[e]ε seems to go back to a marginal gloss based on 461[b]4–5 (ἐὰν μὴ ἑτέρα κυριωτέρα— scil. αἴσθησις—ἀντιφῇ) which then made its way into the text.– 461[b]16 τοῦ ἅλατος B[e]ε : τοῦ ἁλός cett.

[314] *Ev.Matt.* 5.13: ὑμεῖς ἐστε τὸ ἅλας τῆς γῆς.

[315] Kühner/Blass 1890-2, I, 424 (§ 122/1): 'b. Hippokr.VI, 564 ist τὸ ἅλας falsche Lesart.' Cf. [Hp.] *Vict.* (Περὶ διαίτης) II, 56, 1; p. 178.14–15 Joly/Byl: 'ἐν ἁλὶ δὲ κρέα ταριχηρὰ τρόφιμα μέν ἧσσον, διὰ τὸ ἅλας τοῦ ὑγροῦ ἀπεστερημένα' (διὰ τὸ ἅλα θ : διὰ τὸ ἅλες M : διὰ τὸ ἅλας recc.). It is true that διὰ τό is common to both independent manuscripts θ and M, so that the archetype must have offered a neuter form.

evidence for τὸ ἅλας seems to be provided by the ps.-Aristotelian *Mirabilia*,[316] and accordingly, we will not assign τοῦ ἅλατος to the Attic Greek of Aristotle himself. But one might wonder whether this form is not more likely to have entered the transmission of our Corpus *before* the establishment of Atticism in the late first century BC than after, especially since the genitive cannot be explained as a Biblical expression spontaneously introduced by a Christian scribe in Byzantium.[317] It seems possible, then, that this *Koine* form was introduced, inadvertently, by Andronicus when he prepared his edition in the first century BC. This form was bound to be corrected in the course of transmission, so that its presence in ε would go back to a contamination with readings from a very early independent source.

The true nature of the relationship between ε and B^e in *Insomn.* is revealed by the transmission of 460^b16–18.[318] Here, only B^e and one ε-manuscript (Z^a) share with α the reading preferred, on philosophical grounds, by van der Eijk:[319] *'the fact that (i) the judging activity of the controlling sense and (ii) the coming to be of mental images do not take place in virtue of the same faculty'* (α: ... τὸ μὴ κατὰ τὴν αὐτὴν δύναμιν (i) κρίνειν τὸ κύριον καὶ (ii) τὰ φαντάσματα γίγνεσθαι). In both B^eZ^a and α there are two infinitives each of which is equipped with its own subject. The only difference is that in α, the link between the two infinitive constructions is provided only by καὶ, whereas in B^eZ^a it is expressed by τε ... καὶ (B^eZ^a: τὸ μὴ κατὰ τὴν αὐτὴν δύναμιν (i) κρίνειν τε τὸ κύριον (ii) καὶ τὰ φαντάσματα γίνεσθαι). In β, by contrast, we get one infinitive with two subjects, the second of which is indicated by a relative clause: *'the fact that (i) the controlling sense and (ii) [that] by which mental images come to be, do not judge by the same faculty'* (β: ...τὸ μὴ κατὰ τὴν αὐτὴν δύναμιν κρίνειν τό τε κύριον καὶ [scil. τοῦτο] ᾧ τὰ φαντάσματα γίνεται). This time, τε ... καὶ provides the link between the two subjects, and accordingly, the τε has been inserted between τό and κύριον here, not after κρίνειν. Now the remaining ε-manuscripts (PB^pM^o) share

---

But in *Koine* Greek, there was also a neuter τὸ ἅλα (Blass/Debrunner/Rehkopf 2001, § 47 n. 5), so that it seems more plausible to accept the θ-reading than to 'correct', with recc., the M-reading to διὰ τὸ ἅλας. In any case, the reading of the archetype seems to go back to a manuscript in which τὸν ἅλα was replaced with a *Koine* neuter form.

[316] [Arist.] *Mir.* 138, 844^b15–16: καὶ γίνεται κάλλιστον ἅλας. Even if the ultimate source for this chapter was the fourth-century BC historian and rhetorician Theopompus of Chios (cf. Flashar 1972, 140–1), the chapter can, of course, still not count as fourth-century BC evidence for τὸ ἅλας.

[317] In Biblical Greek the *genitive* of 'salt' is not ἅλατος but ἁλός; cf. Lust/Eynikel/Hauspie 2015 s.v. ἅλας and ἅλς and Bauer/Aland 1988 s.v. ἅλας, and, in particular, the famous salt-passage in *Ge.* 19, 26 (p. 26 Rahlfs/Hanhart): καὶ ἐπέβλεψεν ἡ γυνὴ αὐτοῦ (scil. τοῦ Λωτ) εἰς τὰ ὀπίσω καὶ ἐγένετο στήλη ἁλός.

[318] 460^b16–18 τὸ μὴ κατὰ τὴν αὐτὴν δύναμιν κρίνειν τε τὸ κύριον καὶ τὰ φαντάσματα γίνεσθαι B^eZ^a : τὸ μὴ κατὰ τὴν αὐτὴν δύναμιν κρίνειν τὸ κύριον καὶ τὰ φαντάσματα γίγνεσθαι α : τὸ μὴ κατὰ τὴν αὐτὴν δύναμιν κρίνειν τό τε κύριον καὶ ᾧ τὰ φαντάσματα γίνεται β : τὸ μὴ κατὰ τὴν αὐτὴν δύναμιν κρίνειν τε τὸ κύριον καὶ ᾧ τὰ φαντάσματα γίνονται ε(PB^pM^o).

[319] Van der Eijk 1994, 198–9.

the overall construction of *β* (one infinitive + two subjects) but conflate it with B[e]'s position of τε ... καί in a quite incompetent manner: τὸ μὴ κατὰ τὴν αὐτὴν δύναμιν κρίνειν <u>τε</u> τὸ κύριον <u>καὶ</u> <u>ᾧ</u> τὰ φαντάσματα γίνονται. Here, the word order makes us expect that τε will provide a link between κρίνειν and a second infinitive, whereas in fact there is no second infinitive.[320] It seems beyond doubt, then, that the position of τε ... καί, though common to B[e] and ε, originated in the context of the B[e] construction,[321] and that it was introduced in ε(PB[p]M[o]) by contamination.

We have seen by now that the error shared by B[e] with P in 459[a]4–5[322] and perhaps also the one shared with ε in 461[b]16[323] seem to go back to an old independent source, and that B[e] has preserved the correct reading of 460[b]16–18, whereas three ε-manuscripts (PB[p]M[o]) have produced an ungrammatical text in that passage by adopting only one element of the B[e]-reading and by conflating this element with the *β*-reading. With regard to these observations, we propose another way of accounting for Escobar's evidence which presupposes less than half as many cases of contamination: We assume that B[e] is a *direct descendant* of a second hyparchetype (*ψ*), i.e. of a source independent of Escobar's two main families *α* and *β*. On our hypothesis, B[e] itself is completely independent of both Escobar's *γ*-family and his ε-group. The shared readings which Escobar explained by postulating B[e]'s dependence on *γ*, ε, and P's model ★[1], are to be explained, rather, by assuming that Vaticanus P, ε, and *γ* were contaminated with readings from a second hyparchetype *ψ*, i.e. from B[e]'s ultimate source: Vaticanus P with twelve such readings, ε with eleven, and *γ* with three.

This assumption accounts for the *absence* of forty *γ*/ε-readings in B[e], and it is strongly supported by Nussbaum's and De Leemans' observation that in the transmission of *MA* both P and its group are contaminated with readings which are also transmitted by William's second Greek model *Γ2* and which go back to an independent source.[324]

---

[320] Cf. van der Eijk 1994, 199: 'diese Fassung ist aber syntaktisch nicht einwandfrei (wegen ... des merkwürdigen τε τό).' It is true that according to Denniston 1954, 518–19, such an early position of τε is justified if the preceding word can be mentally supplied in the second part and if this preceding word is, e.g., a preposition (cf. Aristotle, *Cat.* 5[a]7–8: ὁ γὰρ νῦν χρόνος συνάπτει πρός <u>τε</u> τὸν παρεληλυθότα <u>καὶ</u> [scil. πρὸς] τὸν μέλλοντα) or an article; but in the present case, this justification does not apply.

[321] Escobar missed this point since he overlooked the fact that B[e] and Z[a] do *not* transmit, with PB[p]M[o], ε's relative clause καὶ ᾧ ... γίνονται (γίνονται PB[p]M[o] : γίνεται *β*): In fact, they share with *α* the infinitive construction καὶ ... γίνεσθαι (γίνεσθαι B[e]Z[a] : γίγνεσθαι *α*).

[322] 459[a]4–5 ἐγρηγορότες (*bis*) B[e]P : ἐγρηγορότων (*bis*) *γ* : ἐγρηγορότος (*bis*) *αβ*.

[323] 461[b]16 τοῦ ἅλατος B[e]ε : τοῦ ἁλός cett.

[324] As to P, see Nussbaum 1975a, 104–5 (= 1976, 130): 'There can, however, be no doubt that P has access to an independent source, probably also used by *Γ*' (already quoted). As to PZ[a], see the following passages cited by De Leemans 2011a, CCXIV, n. 215 (already quoted): 698[b]8 αὐτῶι EYV NXH[b]L C[a]O[d]S : αὐτοῖς PZ[a] B[e]E[b]b.– 699[a]26–7 διαπορήσειεν EYV NXH[b]L C[a]O[d]S : ἀπορήσειε(ν) PZ[a] B[e]E[b]b.

It remains to be seen, however, whether our hypothesis can account equally well for the remaining part of Escobar's evidence, which consists in the passages in which Immanuel Bekker's choice among conflicting **α**- and **β**-readings is not confirmed by **γ**. In these cases, **γ** shares the **α**-reading whereas Bekker has opted for **β**, or *vice versa*. Now, out of the thirty-nine **γ**-readings which diverge from Bekker's text in this way, twenty-seven are shared by Bᵉ whereas twelve are not. Escobar (who assumes that Bᵉ is a descendant of **γ**) would have to account for the twelve exceptions by admitting that the number of cases in which a **γ**-reading would have been removed in Bᵉ's immediate model (★[2]), by contamination, rises still further, from the forty cases (already mentioned) to fifty-two. And without *evaluating* the readings in question, the twenty-seven cases where an **α**- or a **β**-reading rejected by Bekker *is* common to **γ** and Bᵉ cannot not be regarded as conjunctive errors on the basis of which one could prove Bᵉ's dependence on **γ**: An agreement against Bekker does not, by itself, prove anything, since even Bekker may have preferred 'wrong' readings once in a while. In this respect, Escobar's method is unsatisfactory since he nowhere discusses the strengths and weaknesses of any of the **α**- or **β**-readings which Bᵉ and **γ** share against Bekker.

On our hypothesis by contrast (according to which Bᵉ goes back to a second hyparchetype **ψ** from which **γ** and its progeny were contaminated), we have to assume that **γ**, not Bekker, succeeded in restoring the text of the first hyparchetype **ω**, by a correct choice among the conflicting **α**- and **β**-readings. In cases where either **α** or **β** introduced an error, the correct reading, i.e. the reading of **ω**, will have corresponded, in most cases, to the reading of its brother **ψ**, so that **γ**'s *correct* choices will have produced a text shared, by and large, by both hyparchetypes **ω** and **ψ**. In such cases Bᵉ, which we assume to be a descendant of **ψ**, can agree with **γ** without depending on **γ** and without there being any contamination in **γ**. Our hypothesis presupposes, however, that the readings in question are, in general, acceptable, or, if erroneous, easy to correct: It is of course true that *some* errors may indeed be common to both hyparchetypes (i.e. go back to the archetype) and that one or two easy ones among these errors may have been corrected by **α** or by **β**. But it would be obviously implausible to assume that both hyparchetypes agreed in a *large* number of errors *all of which* were then corrected either by **α** or by **β**. It follows that our most urgent task was to evaluate the readings in question.

(a) Bᵉ displays eighteen out of the twenty-one **γ**-readings that are in agreement with **α** against a **β**-variant accepted by Bekker.[325] Twelve of these are to

---

[325] Two cases are missing in Escobar's list: Escobar 1990, 84, failed to note that in 459ᵇ22 Bᵉ**γ** share **α**'s correct reading δύσοσμοι τῶν ὁμοίων against **β**'s untenable expansion δύσοσμοι, <καὶ ἐπὶ> τῶν ὁμοίων

be found in the main part of *Insomn.* (458ᵃ33–462ᵃ31),[326] whereas the remaining six are contained in 462ᵃ31–ᵇ11, i.e. in a short appendix on people that have never had a dream or had to reach an advanced age until they had one. The most conspicuous case of an **α**-text both shared by Bᶜ**γ** and superior to Bekker's **β**-text is provided by lines 462ᵃ31–ᵇ7 of the appendix just mentioned. This passage is transmitted in two completely different versions:

Bᶜ**γα** (≈ all editions since Biehl 1898)	**β** (≈ Bekker)[327]
ἤδη δέ τισι συμβέβηκε μηθὲν ἐνύπνιον ἑωρακέναι κατὰ τὸν βίον,	ἤδη δέ τισι συμβέβηκεν <u>ὥστε</u> μηδὲν ἐνύπνιον ἑωρακέναι κατὰ τὸν βίον· <u>σπάνιον μὲν οὖν τὸ τοιοῦτόν ἐστι, συμβαίνει δ' ὅμως. καὶ τοῖς μὲν ὅλως διετέλεσεν,</u>
τοῖς δὲ πόρρω που [πη **ε**] προελθούσης τῆς ἡλικίας ἰδεῖν πρότερον μὴ ἑωρακότας [ἑωρακόσιν **γα**].	<u>ἐνίοις δὲ καὶ προελθοῦσι πολλῷ</u> [πόρρω Bekker] <u>τῆς ἡλικίας ἐγένετο, πρότερον οὐδὲν ἐνύπνιον ἑωρακόσιν.</u>
τὸ δ' αἴτιον τοῦ μὴ γίνεσθαι παραπλήσιον φαίνεται τῷ ἐπὶ τῶν παίδων [παιδίων **α**] καὶ μετὰ τὴν τροφήν.	τὸ δ' αἴτιον τοῦ μὴ γίνεσθαι παραπλήσιόν <u>τι δεῖ νομίζειν ὅτι οὐδὲ μετὰ τὴν τροφὴν καθυπνώσασιν οὐδὲ τοῖς παιδίοις γίνεται ἐνύπνιον.</u>
ὅσοις γὰρ συνέστηκεν ἡ φύσις ὥστε πολλὴν ἀναθυμίασιν πρὸς τὸν ἄνω τόπον ἀναφέρεσθαι...	ὅσοις γὰρ <u>τοῦτον τὸν τρόπον</u> συνέστηκεν ἡ φύσις ὥστε πολλὴν <u>προσπίπτειν</u> ἀναθυμίασιν πρὸς τὸν ἄνω τόπον...

(Bekker) to which we will come back shortly. Similarly, Escobar 1990, 87, failed to note that in 462ᵃ31 Bᶜ**γ** share **α**'s reading συμβέβηκε (c. dat. et inf.) against **β**'s expansion συμβέβηκε <ὥστε> (c. dat. et inf.) which would be more convincing, in prose, if there were no dative (see the examples in Kühner/ Gerth 1898–1904, II, 13, Anmerk. 11).

[326] Cf. Escobar 1990, 82-8. 458ᵇ8 ὥστε Bᶜ**γα** : om. **β** Bekker.– 458ᵇ32-3 οὐ τοῦτο δὲ Bᶜ**γα** : οὐ μέντοι τοῦτο **β** Bekker.– 459ᵇ22 δύσοσμοι τῶν ὁμοίων Bᶜ**γα** : δύσοσμοι, καὶ ἐπὶ τῶν ὁμοίων **β** Bekker.– 459ᵇ22-3 φανερῶς δὲ συμβαίνει ταῦθ' ὡς λέγομεν Bᶜ**γα** : ταῦτά γε δὴ φανερῶς συμβαίνει τοῦτον τὸν τρόπον **β** Bekker.– 459ᵇ25-26 περὶ οὗ κἂν καθ' αὑτό... σκέψαιτό τις Bᶜ**γ** : περὶ ὧν κἂν καθ' αὑτόν... σκέψαιτό τις **α** : περὶ οὗ καὶ αὐτοῦ... σκέψαιτό τις ἂν **β** Bekker.– 460ᵃ15 αἰσθάνεται μάλιστα Bᶜ**γα** XL : μάλιστα αἰσθάνεται **β** Bekker.– 460ᵃ18 ἀπιέναι Bᶜ**γα** : ἐξιέναι **β** Bekker.– 460ᵃ24-5 καὶ ὅτι Bᶜ**γα** : ἔτι δὲ καὶ ὅτι **β** : ἔτι δὲ ὅτι S Bekker.– 460ᵃ28-30 ταχέως γὰρ λαμβάνει τὰς τῶν πλησίων ὀσμὰς καὶ τὸ ἔλαιον παρασκευασθὲν καὶ ὁ οἶνος Bᶜ**γα** : τό τε γὰρ παρασκευασθὲν ἔλαιον ταχέως λαμβάνει τὰς τῶν πλησίον ὀσμάς, καὶ οἱ οἶνοι τὸ αὐτὸ τοῦτο πάσχουσιν **β** Bekker.– 460ᵇ5 ἐν φόβοις Bᶜ**γα** : ἐν φόβῳ **β** Bekker.– 461ᵇ27-8 αἰσθανόμενον Bᶜ**γα** SUX : μὴ αἰσθανόμενον L Bekker.– 462ᵃ7 ἀντιφήσει Bᶜ**γα** : ἀντίφησι **β** Bekker.

[327] The six diverging bits of text have been underlined.

The β-version of this passage, though accepted by Bekker, is a piece of *wholesale rewriting* of Aristotle's text that has been justly dismissed by all editors since Biehl 1898 (except β's ὥστε in 462ᵃ31).[328] Accordingly, γ—by preferring the α-text—has hit the reading of the common ancestor of α and β (i.e., on our hypothesis, of hyparchetype ω); so that the agreements of Bᶜ with $\gamma\alpha$ against β that are contained in this passage are no errors at all and, *a fortiori*, no conjunctive errors. Given that the rewriting of the passage is due only to β, both hyparchetypes will have featured the version known to us from Bᶜ$\gamma\alpha$, so that Bᶜ can agree with $\gamma\alpha$ without depending on γ, let alone on ϵ. The independence of Bᶜ is confirmed by the fact, overlooked by Escobar, that in this passage ϵ displays a separative error absent from Bᶜ.[329]

Further support for our hypothesis is yielded by the main part of *Insomn.* (458ᵃ33–462ᵃ31) which contains another dozen readings shared by Bᶜ, γ, and α against Bekker's β-readings. Among these, there are six cases where there is not much to choose between them,[330] but in two cases the divergence is again to be explained, in the light of the appendix just discussed, as β-rewriting,[331] in two further cases Bekker's β-reading is manifestly inferior;[332] and in the remaining

---

[328]   Biehl 1898, 73–4 (+ ὥστε in 462ᵃ31); Drossaart Lulofs 1947, 15–16 (+ ὥστε in 462ᵃ31); Mugnier 1953, 86–7 (+ ὥστε in 462ᵃ31); Ross 1955; Siwek 1963, 226 (+ ὥστε in 462ᵃ31); Gallop 1996, 104. Cf. also van der Eijk 1994, 249: 'Aber die Unterschiede…sind derartig, daß die Vermutung naheliegt, daß es eine ausführlichere Parallelfassung gegeben hat, welche die knappen und lapidaren Aussagen der ursprünglichen Fassung erläutern sollte.…Ich halte es für angezeigt, die kürzere Fassung…als die bessere zu betrachten.'

[329]   In 462ᵇ2, Bᶜ shares with α the correct adverb που, whereas its supposed ancestor ϵ is marred by the error πη.

[330]   458ᵇ32–3 οὐ τοῦτο δὲ Bᶜ$\gamma\alpha$: οὐ μέντοι τοῦτο β Bekker; but οὐ τοῦτο δὲ is a perfect equivalent of β's οὐ μέντοι τοῦτο (see Denniston 1954, 186–7 and 369–70).– 460ᵃ15 αἰσθάνεται μάλιστα Bᶜ$\gamma\alpha$ XL : μάλιστα αἰσθάνεται β Bekker, but recent editors preferred the α reading.– 460ᵃ18 τοῦ δὲ μὴ ἀπιέναι (scil. τὴν κηλῖδα) ταχέως ἐκ τῶν καινῶν κατόπτρων Bᶜ$\gamma\alpha$: τοῦ δὲ μὴ ἐξιέναι κτλ. β Bekker, but ἀπιέναι was preferred by Ross.– 460ᵃ24-25 καὶ ὅτι…καὶ ὅτι Bᶜ$\gamma\alpha$: καὶ ὅτι…ἔτι δὲ καὶ ὅτι β : καὶ ὅτι…ἔτι δὲ ὅτι S Bekker, but the insertion of ἔτι δὲ was justly deemed superfluous by Ross.– 460ᵇ5 ἐν φόβοις…ἐν ἔρωτι Bᶜ$\gamma\alpha$: ἐν φόβῳ…ἐν ἔρωτι β Bekker, but ἐν φόβῳ seems to be due to secondary assimilation to ἐν ἔρωτι.– 462ᵃ7-8 ἐὰν δὲ λανθάνῃ ὅτι καθεύδει, οὐδὲν (οὐθὲν Bᶜ) ἀντιφήσει τῇ φαντασίᾳ Bᶜ$\gamma\alpha$: ἐὰν δὲ λανθάνῃ ὅτι καθεύδει, οὐδὲν ἀντίφησι κτλ. β Bekker, but Ross preferred the future tense (ἀντιφήσει).

[331]   459ᵇ22-3 φανερῶς δὲ συμβαίνει ταῦθ' ὡς λέγομεν Bᶜ$\gamma\alpha$: ταῦτά γε δὴ φανερῶς συμβαίνει τοῦτον τὸν τρόπον β; but the α version is impeccable, whereas β has tried to make Aristotle's Greek more elegant by introducing four dactyls in a row (ταῦτά γε δὴ φανερῶς συμβαίνει) as van der Eijk 1994, 167, pointed out.– 460ᵃ28-30 ταχέως γὰρ λαμβάνει τὰς τῶν πλησίων ὀσμὰς καὶ τὸ ἔλαιον παρασκευασθὲν καὶ ὁ οἶνος Bᶜ$\gamma\alpha$ (the reports of Ross and Siwek on P are misleading) : τό τε γὰρ παρασκευασθὲν ἔλαιον ταχέως λαμβάνει τὰς τῶν πλησίον ὀσμάς, καὶ οἱ οἶνοι τὸ αὐτὸ τοῦτο πάσχουσιν β, where (i) τὸ παρασκευασθὲν ἔλαιον has been *prepended* to the phrase ταχέως (γὰρ) λαμβάνει τὰς τῶν πλησίων ὀσμὰς (lest the latter be referred to the subject of the preceding sentence), (ii) the second subject (οἶνος) has been pluralized in order to stick to the plural used in the preceding sentence, and (iii) the new plural subject has been provided with a predicate on its own.

[332]   459ᵇ20-2 γίνονται δὲ…ὑπὸ [ἀπὸ $\gamma\alpha$] τῶν ἰσχυρῶν ὀσμῶν δύσοσμοι τῶν ὁμοίων Bᶜ$\gamma\alpha$: γίνονται δὲ…ἀπὸ τῶν ἰσχυρῶν ὀσμῶν δύσοσμοι, καὶ ἐπὶ τῶν ὁμοίων [<ὁμοίως> add. Drossaart Lulofs] β; but the

two cases B^eγ not only share a superior **a**-reading, but present an even better version of it.[333] The only true error shared by B^e, γ, and **a** is a relatively slight one[334] which could easily be corrected by β on occasion of its rewriting of 460^a28-30.

(b) B^e shares nine out of the eighteen γ-readings that are in full or partial agreement with β against an **a**-variant accepted by Bekker.[335] In three cases, there is, once more, not much to choose between them.[336] In one further passage, the B^eγ-reading shares only a minor feature with the β-reading, while being free from its main weakness.[337] An interesting disagreement occurs in 458^b25.[338] Aristotle has claimed that at night our opinion (*doxa*) depends on

β reading is clearly unsatisfactory (hence the emendation; see also van der Eijk 1994, 167), whereas on the B^eγα reading (δύσοσμοι τῶν ὁμοίων) Aristotle would be referring to *partial* anosmia caused by olfactory adaptation.– 461^b27-9 ὥσπερ αἰσθανόμενον τοῦτο κινεῖται B^eγα SUX : ὥσπερ μὴ αἰσθανόμενον κτλ. L Bekker; but L's minority reading has been given up by the recent editors.

[333] 458^b3–8 ἐπεί..., ὥστε δῆλον B^eP vel εἰ..., ὥστε δῆλον γ Siwek : ἤ..., ὥστε δῆλον **a** : εἰ..., δῆλον β Bekker. For Aristotle's characteristic use of apodotic ὥστε, as attested here by B^eγ (whereas in **a**, the ὥστε has lost its apodotic function due to the corruption of εἰ), see Bonitz 1863, 72–90.– 459^b25-26 περὶ οὗ κἂν καθ' αὐτό...σκέψαιτό τις B^eγ : περὶ ὧν κἂν καθ' αὐτὸν...σκέψαιτό τις **a** : περὶ οὗ καὶ αὐτοῦ...σκέψαιτό τις ἂν β Bekker; but Aristotle wants to say that the mirror (ἔνοπτρον, neuter) is a rewarding subject of study *in itself* (καθ' αὐτὸ), so that the B^eγ- reading (which is transmitted by **a** in a corrupted form) is clearly superior to the β-reading.

[334] 460^a29: τὰς τῶν πλησίων ὀσμὰς B^eγα : τὰς τῶν πλησίον ὀσμὰς β M^o. The use of πλησίος as an adjective is alien to Attic prose (LSJ s.v. πλησίος *sub finem*: 'The Adj. is poet. and Ion.; in Att. Prose only the Adv. is found'); here, it seems to be a mere slip of the pen triggered by the preceding τῶν.

[335] See Escobar 1990, 169, with nn. 2-3 and the list pp. 115-18: 458^b4 ὅλως δὲ B^eε : καὶ ὅλως δὲ β : καὶ ὅλως **a** Bekker.– 458^b6 ἢ τὰ ἴδια B^eγβ : ἴδια δ' **a** Bekker.– 458^b25 ὃ ἐννοοῦμεν...ἐδοξάζομεν B^eγ vel ἐννοοῦμεν ἅ...ἐδοξάζομεν β : ὃ ἐννοοῦμεν...δοξάζομεν **a** Bekker.– 459^a21-2 ᾗ φανταστικόν B^eγβ : ᾗ τὸ φανταστικόν **a** Bekker.– 459^b18-19 καὶ ἀπὸ τῶν κινουμένων B^eγβ : καὶ αἱ ἀπὸ τῶν κινουμένων **a** Bekker.– 461^b2 ὥς φαμεν B^eγβ : ὁρᾶν φαμεν **a** Bekker.– 461^b15 ἤδί B^e(ηδει)γβ : ἤδε **a** Bekker.– 461^b22-3 τοῦ ἀληθοῦς B^eγβ : τοῦ αἰσθήματος ἀληθοῦς **a** : τοῦ αἰσθήματος <τοῦ> ἀληθοῦς Bekker.– 461^b29 τὸ ἀληθές·B^eγβ : ἀληθές **a** Bekker.

[336] 458^b4 ὅλως δὲ (vel ὅλως δ') αἰσθήσεως B^eε : καὶ ὅλως δὲ (vel καὶ ὅλως δ') αἰσθήσεως β : καὶ ὅλως αἰσθήσεως **a** Bekker; but the δὲ shared by B^eε with β is impeccable both with an initial καὶ (β) and without it (B^eε).– 461^b2 ὥς φαμεν B^eγβ : ὁρᾶν φαμεν **a** Bekker, but coming immediately after 461^a31–^b1 (καὶ ἐγρηγορὼς δοκεῖ ὁρᾶν καὶ ἀκούειν καὶ αἰσθάνεσθαι κτλ.) a second main clause with ὁρᾶν φαμεν seems to be superfluous.– 461^b15 ἤδί B^e(ηδει)γβ : ἤδε **a** Bekker, but cf. 461^b14 τῃδί.

[337] In 458^b3–6, the **a**-text printed by the editors goes as follows: εἰ δὲ χρῆσις ὄψεως ὅρασις καὶ ἀκοῆς |4| τὸ ἀκούειν καὶ ὅλως αἰσθήσεως τὸ αἰσθάνεσθαι, κοινὰ δέ ἐστιν |5| τῶν αἰσθήσεων οἷον σχῆμα καὶ μέγεθος καὶ |6| τὰ ἄλλα τὰ τοιαῦτα, ἴδια δ' οἷον χρῶμα ψόφος χυμός κτλ. The β-text differs (i) by replacing, at the end of ^b4, κοινὰ δέ ἐστιν with the unfortunate anaphoric reference ταῦτα δ' ἐστὶ τὰ κοινά, and (ii) by reading, in ^b6, ᾗ τὰ ἴδια instead of ἴδια δ'. Now B^eγ do *not* share the problematic β-version of ^b4 but they *do* share the β-version of ^b6, and we submit that κοινὰ δ' ἐστί..., ᾗ τὰ ἴδια...(B^eγ: 'and if/since there are common perceptible objects...or the specific ones') suits the argument as well as κοινὰ δ' ἐστί..., ἴδια δ'...(**a**: 'and if there are common perceptible objects...and specific ones').

[338] 458^b25 ὃ ἐννοοῦμεν τῇ δόξῃ ἐδοξάζομεν B^eγ : ἐννοοῦμεν ἃ τῇ δόξῃ ἐδοξάζομεν β : ὃ ἐννοοῦμεν τῇ δόξῃ δοξάζομεν **a** Bekker.

dream-images just as, at daytime, on sense perceptions (458^{b}10–20). He offers a piece of evidence (458^{b}20–25): People saw dream images hinting at a speech they had to deliver and thereby stimulating them to prepare it by mnemonic exercise. Still asleep, they imagined a set of objects differing from the dream image and corresponding to the points of a speech. Before their inner eye, they put these objects into certain *loci* the order of which they knew by heart. They could do this asleep since the *loci* and the mnemonic method were familiar to them from a diurnal mnemonic exercise, i.e. from an earlier activity of their *doxa*. Thus, we cognize (ἐννοοῦμεν) at sleep what we opinionated before (τῆι δόξηι ἐδοξάζομεν B^{c}βγ). This reading is superior since δοξάζομεν (E) would deprive the nocturnal exercise of its diurnal basis.[339] Last not least, there are four passages in which the B^{c}γβ-reading is clearly superior to the α-reading.[340]

Therefore, the fact that readings rejected by Bekker are shared by both B^c and γ either with α or with β may be plausibly explained by the assumption that the readings in question go back to the true archetype and survived into both hyparchetypes ω and ψ from whence they could reach B^c and γ independently; the few shared errors which we had to register cannot count as counter-evidence since the archetype itself was, by definition, not entirely free of errors. On Escobar's hypothesis, by contrast, we would have to admit an additional dozen 'counter-contaminations' in B^c's immediate model (★[2]), yielding a total of fifty-two cases. This result has to be added to the fact that in 460^{b}16–18 we observed that a correct reading known to us from B^c was adopted in ε in a secondary way, by incompetently conflating it with the β-reading. We conclude that Escobar's hypothesis on the position of B^c is clearly less suitable to account for his own evidence than the assumption according to which B^c is a direct descendant of a second hyparchetype (ψ) from which P and his ancestors ε and γ were contaminated to various degrees.

---

[339] The rejection of ἐδοξάζομεν by van der Eijk 1994, 146 is unconvincing. He assumes that the temporal contrast in ἐννοοῦμεν/ἐδοξάζομεν would have to refer to our remembering (μνημονεύειν), after waking up, what we cognized *before* at sleep (cf. 458^{b}18–20). If so, we would indeed have to reject ἐδοξάζομεν since in the present context ἐννοοῦμεν clearly refers to cognitions during sleep. Yet v. d. Eijk's assumption is unnecessary, since mnemonics at sleep clearly presuppose previous mnemonics at daytime, which in turn yield the point of reference for ἐδοξάζομεν.

[340] 459^{a}21–2 τούτου δ' (scil. τοῦ αἰσθητικοῦ) ᾗ φανταστικόν B^{c}γβ : τούτου δ' ᾗ τὸ φανταστικόν α Bekker, but Aristotle does not normally use ᾗ = *qua* with a following article (cf. *Metaph.* Γ 1, 1003^{a}21 τὸ ὂν ᾗ ὄν, *Ph.* I 4, 187^{b}7–8 τὸ ἄπειρον ᾗ ἄπειρον ἄγνωστον).– 459^{b}18–19 καὶ ἀπὸ τῶν κινουμένων δὲ μεταβάλλουσιν B^{c}γβ : καὶ ἀπὸ τῶν κινουμένων δὲ μεταβάλλουσιν αἱ α Bekker; but αἱ cannot stand, as van der Eijk 1994, 166 has shown.– 461^{b}22–23 καὶ ἀπελθόντος τοῦ ἀληθοῦς B^{c}γβ Ross Siwek : καὶ ἀπελθόντος τοῦ αἰσθήματος ἀληθοῦς α : καὶ ἀπελθόντος τοῦ αἰσθήματος <τοῦ> ἀληθοῦς Bekker : καὶ ἀπελθόντος τοῦ αἰσθήματος {ἀληθοῦς} Waszink, but in fact the textual problem resides in αἰσθήματος (α) since it not only occupies the wrong place (by preceding ἀληθοῦς instead of following it), but also spoils the argument, as van der Eijk 1994, 237–8 has shown. So the B^{c}γβ-reading is clearly correct.– 461^{b}29 τὸ ἀληθές·B^{c}γβ Drossaart Lulofs Ross Siwek : ἀληθές α Bekker, but α's reading was rejected by the more recent editors.

ARISTOTELIS *DE MOTV ANIMALIVM*

Aristotelis *De Motu Animalium*

A New Critical Edition of the Greek Text

by

OLIVER PRIMAVESI

With an English Translation

by

BENJAMIN MORISON

SIGLA

The independent witnesses to the Greek text and their reconstructed sources

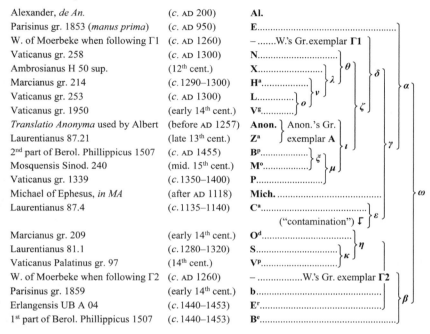

Alexander, *de An.*	(*c.* AD 200)	**Al.**
Parisinus gr. 1853 (*manus prima*)	(*c.* AD 950)	**E**
W. of Moerbeke when following Γ1	(*c.* AD 1260)	− W.'s Gr. exemplar **Γ1**
Vaticanus gr. 258	(*c.* AD 1300)	**N**
Ambrosianus H 50 sup.	(12th cent.)	**X**
Marcianus gr. 214	(*c.* 1290–1300)	**Hᵃ**
Vaticanus gr. 253	(*c.* AD 1300)	**L**
Vaticanus gr. 1950	(early 14th cent.)	**Vᵍ**
Translatio Anonyma used by Albert	(before AD 1257)	**Anon.** Anon.'s Gr.
Laurentianus 87.21	(late 13th cent.)	**Zᵃ** exemplar A
2nd part of Berol. Phillippicus 1507	(*c.* AD 1455)	**Bᵖ**
Mosquensis Sinod. 240	(mid. 15th cent.)	**Mᵒ**
Vaticanus gr. 1339	(*c.* 1350–1400)	**P**
Michael of Ephesus, *in MA*	(after AD 1118)	**Mich.**
Laurentianus 87.4	(*c.* 1135–1140)	**Cᵃ**
		("contamination") Γ
Marcianus gr. 209	(early 14th cent.)	**Oᵈ**
Laurentianus 81.1	(*c.* 1280–1320)	**S**
Vaticanus Palatinus gr. 97	(14th cent.)	**Vᵖ**
W. of Moerbeke when following Γ2	(*c.* AD 1260)	− W.'s Gr. exemplar **Γ2**
Parisinus gr. 1859	(early 14th cent.)	**b**
Erlangensis UB A 04	(*c.* 1440–1453)	**Eʳ**
1st part of Berol. Phillippicus 1507	(*c.* 1440–1453)	**Bᵉ**

*The transmission of the Latin translation by William of Moerbeke
and the 3 stages of its development according to De Leemans 2011a*

The Principal Manuscript Families		Development of W.'s Manuscript
x_1	**x**	**G1**: *W.'s original translation*
x_2		↓
	y	**GR'**: *W.'s 1st Revision*
P¹ (Exemplar "*De historiis animalium*")	**P** (source of	↓
P² (Exemplar "*De motibus animalium, et aliorum parvorum*")	the Parisian Exemplaria)	**GR''**: *W.'s 2nd Revision*
z_1		
z_2	**z**	
z_3		(**G**: Readings common to all three stages)

{Ἀριστοτέλους "Περὶ ζώιων κινήσεως..."}

I

|698ᵃ1| Περὶ δὲ τῆς τῶν ζώιων κινήσεως, ὅσα μὲν αὐτῶν περὶ |2| ἕκαστον ὑπάρχει γένος – καὶ τίνες διαφοραὶ καὶ τίνες αἰτίαι |3| τῶν καθ' ἕκαστον συμβεβηκότων αὐτοῖς –, ἐπέσκεπται περὶ |4| ἁπάντων ἐν ἑτέροις. ὅλως δὲ περὶ τῆς κοινῆς αἰτίας τοῦ κι|5|νεῖσθαι κίνησιν ὁποιανοῦν – τὰ μὲν γὰρ πτήσει κινεῖται τὰ |6| δὲ νεύσει τὰ δὲ πορείαι τῶν ζώιων τὰ δὲ κατ' ἄλλους τρό|7|πους τοιούτους – ἐπισκεπτέον νῦν. ὅτι μὲν οὖν ἀρχὴ τῶν ἄλλων |8| κινήσεων τὸ αὐτὸ αὑτὸ κινοῦν, τούτου δὲ τὸ ἀκίνητον, καὶ ὅτι |9| τὸ πρῶτον κινοῦν ἀναγκαῖον ἀκίνητον εἶναι, διώρισται πρότε|10|ρον, ὅτεπερ καὶ περὶ κινήσεως ἀϊδίου, πότερόν ἐστιν ἢ οὐκ ἔστιν, |11| καὶ εἰ ἔστιν, τίς ἐστιν. δεῖ δὲ τοῦτο μὴ μόνον τῶι λόγωι κα|12|θόλου λαβεῖν, ἀλλὰ καὶ ἐπὶ τῶν καθ' ἕκαστα καὶ τῶν αἰ|13|σθητῶν, δι' ἅπερ καὶ τοὺς καθόλου ζητοῦμεν λόγους καὶ ἐφ' |14| ὧν ἐφαρμόττειν οἰόμεθα δεῖν αὐτούς. φανερὸν γὰρ καὶ ἐπὶ |15| τούτων, ὅτι ἀδύνατον κινεῖσθαι μηδενὸς ἠρεμοῦντος, πρῶτον |16| μὲν ἐν αὐτοῖς τοῖς ζώιοις· ἀεὶ γάρ, ἂν κινῆταί τι τῶν μο|17|ρίων, ἠρεμεῖ τι· καὶ διὰ τοῦτο αἱ καμπαὶ τοῖς ζώιοις εἰσίν. |18| ὥσπερ γὰρ κέντρωι χρῶνται ταῖς καμπαῖς καὶ γίγνεται τὸ |19| ὅλον μέρος, ἐν ὧι ἡ καμπή, καὶ ἓν καὶ δύο καὶ εὐθὺ καὶ |20| κεκαμμένον, μεταβάλλον δυνάμει καὶ ἐνεργείαι διὰ τὴν |21| καμπήν. καμπτομένου δὲ καὶ κινουμένου τὸ μὲν κινεῖται ση|22|μεῖον τὸ δὲ μένει τῶν ἐν ταῖς καμπαῖς, ὥσπερ ἂν εἰ τῆς |23| διαμέτρου ἡ μὲν Α καὶ ἡ Δ μένοι, ἡ δὲ Β κινοῖτο, καὶ |24| γίνοιτο ἡ ΑΓ.

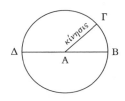

Tituli quem delevi formae duae traduntur. **I** (ζώιων ante κινήσεως): ἀριστοτέλους περὶ ζώιων κινήσεως ω : περὶ ζώιων κινήσεως Appendix Hesychiana, Al., Simp. — **II** (κινήσεως ante ζώιων): qīnīsaʾūs ṭīn zūʾūn Ptolem. al-Ġarīb : περὶ (τῆς) κινήσεως ζώιων Simp., Phlp., Ps.-Simp. *in de An.*

———

698ᵃ4 ἐν ἑτέροις: cf. imprimis *IA*, necnon *HA* II, 1, 498ᵃ3–ᵇ10; IV, 1–7; *PA* IV, 6–14 || **9–10** διώρισται πρότερον: *Ph.*VIII, 5 || **10** ὅτεπερ: *Ph.*VIII, 1–2;VIII, 8

———

698ᵃ1 τῆς τῶν ζώιων κινήσεως β : κινήσεως τῆς τῶν ζώιων α || **1–2** αὐτῶν περὶ ἕκαστον βΕ : περὶ ἕκαστον αὐτῶν γ || **7** οὖν α : om. β || **8** αὐτὸ αὑτὸ βΕ : αὑτὸ ἑαυτὸ γ || **11** τίς βγ : τί Ε || **16** μὲν βγ : μὲν οὖν Ε || **16–17** ἀεὶ...ἠρεμεῖ β : δεῖ...ἠρεμεῖν α || **22–24** diagramma servavit α || **23** καὶ ἡ Δ β : καὶ Δ α || **24** ἡ ΑΓ Ε², cf. Mich.ᴾ 105,5 (ἡ ΑΓ κίνησις) : ἡ Α καὶ Γ ω

{Aristotle: "Concerning movement of animals…"}

|**698ᵃ**1| Concerning the movement of animals, those features which apply to each kind of them—what their differences are, and for what reasons they each have their particular features—have all been investigated elsewhere. |4| What needs investigation now is, quite generally, the common cause of this moving, whatever type of movement it is, for some animals move by flying, some by swimming, some by walking, and some in other such ways. |7| Now, it was already determined that that which moves itself by itself is the origin of the movement of other things, and that the origin of *its* movement is that which is unmoved, i.e. that the first mover must be unmoved—this was determined when it was also determined whether there is everlasting movement or not, and if there is, what kind of movement it is. |11| But we must grasp this not only as applying universally on the basis of that argument, but also as applying to particular cases, i.e. to perceptible things, things which also explain why we seek those general accounts and to which, we think, we should fit those accounts.

|14| For it is clear in these cases too that it is impossible for something to move if nothing is at rest, in the first place, in the animals themselves. |16| For always, if one of the parts moves, something is at rest, and that's why there are joints in animals. |18| For they use their joints like a centre and the whole part with the joint in it becomes both one and two, i.e. straight and bent, changing over potentially and actually because of the joint. |21| When it's bending and moving, one point in the joint moves and another stays still, just as when the geometrical points A and D on the diameter stay still whereas B moves, and AC comes into being.

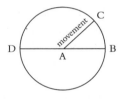

ἀλλ' ἐνταῦθα μὲν δοκεῖ πάντα τρόπον ἀδιαίρε|25|τον εἶναι τὸ κέντρον, καὶ γὰρ τὸ κινεῖσθαι, ὥς φασι, πλάτ|26|τουσιν ἐπ' αὐτῶν, οὐ γὰρ κινεῖσθαι τῶν μαθηματικῶν οὐθέν, |27| τὰ δ' ἐν ταῖς καμπαῖς δυνάμει καὶ ἐνεργείαι γίγνεται ὁτὲ |698ᵇι| μὲν ἕν, ὁτὲ δὲ διαιρεῖται. ἀλλ' οὖν ἀεὶ ἡ ἀρχή γε ἡ πρὸς ὅ, ἧι ἀρχή, ἠρε|2|μεῖ κινουμένου τοῦ μορίου τοῦ κάτωθεν, οἷον τοῦ μὲν βραχίονος |3| κινουμένου τὸ ὠλέκρανον, ὅλου δὲ τοῦ κώλου ὁ ὦμος, καὶ τῆς |4| μὲν κνήμης τὸ γόνυ, ὅλου δὲ τοῦ σκέλους τὸ ἰσχίον. ὅτι μὲν |5| οὖν καὶ ἐν αὐτῶι ἕκαστον δεῖ τι ἔχειν ἠρεμοῦν, ὅθεν ἡ ἀρχὴ |6| τοῦ κινουμένου ἐστίν, καὶ πρὸς ὃ ἀπερειδόμενον καὶ ὅλον ἀθρόον |7| κινηθήσεται καὶ κατὰ μέρος, φανερόν.

2

|8| Ἀλλὰ πᾶσα ἡ ἐν αὑτοῖς ἠρεμία ὅμως ἄκυρος, ἂν μή |9| τι ἔξω ἧι ἁπλῶς ἠρεμοῦν καὶ ἀκίνητον. ἄξιον δὲ ἐπιστή|10|σαντας ἐπισκέψασθαι περὶ τοῦ λεχθέντος· ἔχει γὰρ τὴν |11| θεωρίαν οὐ μόνον ὅσον ἐπὶ τὰ ζῷα συντείνουσαν, ἀλλὰ καὶ |12| πρὸς τὴν τοῦ παντὸς κίνησιν καὶ φοράν. ὥσπερ γὰρ καὶ ἐν |13| αὐτῶι δεῖ τι ἀκίνητον εἶναι, εἰ μέλλει κινεῖσθαι, οὕτως ἔτι |14| μᾶλλον ἔξω δεῖ τι εἶναι τοῦ ζώιου ἀκίνητον, πρὸς ὃ ἀπερει|15|δόμενον κινεῖται τὸ κινούμενον. εἰ γὰρ ὑποδώσει ἀεὶ οἷον τοῖς |16| μυσὶ τοῖς ἐν τῆι πίττηι ἢ τοῖς ἐν τῆι ἄμμωι πορευομένοις, οὐ |17| πρόεισιν· οὐδὲ ἔσται οὔτε πορεία, εἰ μὴ ἡ γῆ μένοι, οὔτε πτῆ|18|σις ἢ νεῦσις, εἰ μὴ ὁ ἀὴρ ἢ ἡ θάλαττα ἀντερείδοι. ἀνάγκη |19| δὲ τοῦτο ἕτερον εἶναι τοῦ κινουμένου, καὶ ὅλον ὅλου, καὶ μόριον |20| μηθὲν εἶναι τοῦ κινουμένου τὸ οὕτως ἀκίνητον· εἰ δὲ μή, οὐ κι|21|νηθήσεται. μαρτύριον δὲ τούτου τὸ ἀπορούμενον, διὰ τί ποτε |22| τὸ πλοῖον ἔξωθεν μὲν ἄν τις ὠθῆι τῶι κοντῶι τὸν ἱστὸν ἤ τι |23| ἄλλο προσβάλλων μόριον κινεῖ ῥαιδίως, ἐὰν δ' ἐπ' αὐτῶι τις |24| ὢν τῶι πλοίωι τοῦτο πειρᾶται πράττειν, οὐκ ἂν κινήσειεν οὐδ' |25| ὁ Τιτυός, οὐδ' ὁ Βορέας πνέων ἔσωθεν ἐκ τοῦ πλοίου, εἰ τύ|26|χοι πλέων τὸν τρόπον τοῦτον ὅνπερ οἱ γραφεῖς ποιοῦσιν· ἐξ |27| αὐτοῦ γὰρ τὸ πνεῦμα ἀφιέντα γράφουσιν. ἐάν τε γὰρ ἠρέμα |699ᵃι| ῥιπτῆι τὸ πνεῦμά τις ἐάν τ' ἰσχυρῶς οὕτως ὥστε ἄνεμον ποιεῖν |2| τὸν μέγιστον, ἐάν τε ἄλλο τι ἧι τὸ ῥιπτούμενον ἢ ὠθούμενον,

698ᵇ15–16 τοῖς μυσὶ τοῖς ἐν τῆι πίττηι: cf. [D.] 50 (i.e. Apollod. Pasionis f.), 26; Theoc. 14, 51; Herod. 2, 62–63; Zen. restitutus e cod. Par. Suppl. 676 (S), Cohn 1887, 69 (= Lucill. Tarrh. fr. IV Linnenk.); Suet. Π. βλασφ. VIII 222 Taillardat; Lib. *Ep.* 192, 6 (X 177.9 Foerster); Nicetas Eugenian. *Drosilla et Charicles* IV, 410 (p. 120 Conca)

698ᵇι διαιρεῖται β : διαιρετά α | γε β : om. α | πρὸς ὅ E : πρόσω β : πρώτη γ || **3** ὠλέκρανον βE CᵃN : ὠλέκρανον cett. || **5** ἕκαστον δεῖ τι β : ἕκαστόν τι δεῖ α || **6** ἐστίν βE : ἔσται γ || **8** ἡ ἐν α : μὲν β | αὑτοῖς β : αὑτῶι α || **9** ἔξω βE : ἔξωθεν γ || **14** τι] non habent E Γι θ Zᵃ || **16** μυσὶ τοῖς α : μυσὶν β | τῆι πίττηι β, E ante rasuram : τῆ γῆ γE² || **17** ἔσται α : ἔστιν β || **23** ἐπ' αὐτῶι β : ἐν αὑτῶι α || **24–25** οὐδ'…οὐδ' β : οὔτ' ἄν…οὔθ' α || **26** πλέων β : πνέων α

|24| But in this case it seems that the centre is in every way indivisible, for, they say, they are fictitiously attributing movement to them given that no mathematical object moves, whereas the points in the joints, potentially and actually, sometimes come to be one and sometimes are divided. |698ᵇ1| But then the origin 'against which', insofar as it is the origin, is always at rest when the lower part moves, such as when the forearm moves the elbow is at rest, when the whole arm moves the shoulder is at rest, when the lower leg moves the knee is at rest, and when the leg moves the thigh is at rest. |4| So then it is clear that each thing must also have something at rest within itself, whence the origin of the moving thing is, and pressing against which it will move both as a collective whole and in its parts.

2

|8| But any rest in them is nonetheless ineffective, unless there is something outside them unqualifiedly at rest and unmoving, and it is worthwhile stopping and considering what has been said, since it makes our study extend not just to animals but also beyond to the motion, i.e. local motion, of the whole. |12| For just as there must also be something unmoving within it, if it is to move, so even more so must there be something unmoving external to the animal, by pressing against which the moving thing moves. |15| For if it always gives way— as it does with the proverbial 'mice in pitch' or with people trying to walk on sand—then the thing will not advance: that is, there will not be any walking, if the ground does not stay still, nor will there be any flying or swimming, if the air or the sea does not push back in turn. |18| But it is necessary that this thing be different from the moving thing, and as a whole different from the whole of it, i.e. the thing which is unmoved in this way must be no part of the moving thing; if not, it will not move. |21| Evidence for this is the difficulty of why it is that one can easily move the boat from outside—if someone were to push it with a pole, striking the mast or some other part of it—whereas if someone who is in the same boat tries to do this, he would not move it, nor would Tityus, and not even Boreas blowing from within the boat, if he happened to be trying to sail in the way that the painters make him: for they depict him expelling the air from within it. |27| For regardless of whether someone expels the air gently or so strongly that they create a very great wind, and regardless of whether what is expelled or pushed out is something other than air,

|3| ἀνάγκη πρῶτον μὲν πρὸς ἠρεμοῦν τι τῶν αὐτοῦ μορίων ἀπε|4|ρειδόμενον ὠθεῖν, εἶτα πάλιν τοῦτο τὸ μόριον, ἢ αὐτὸν οὗ |5| τυγχάνει μόριον ὄν, πρὸς τῶν ἔξωθέν τι ἀποστηριζόμενον μέ|6|νειν. ὁ δὲ τὸ πλοῖον ὠθῶν ἐν τῶι πλοίωι αὐτὸς ὢν καὶ ἀπο|7|στηριζόμενος πρὸς τὸ πλοῖον εὐλόγως οὐ κινεῖ τὸ πλοῖον διὰ |8| τὸ ἀναγκαῖον εἶναι πρὸς ὃ ἀποστηρίζεται μένειν. συμβαίνει |9| δ᾿ αὐτῶι τὸ αὐτὸ ὅ τε κινεῖ καὶ πρὸς ὃ ἀποστηρίζεται. ἔξω|10|θεν δὲ ἕλκων καὶ ὠθῶν κινεῖ· οὐθὲν γὰρ μέρος ἡ γῆ τοῦ |11| πλοίου.

<h1 style="text-align:center">3</h1>

|12| Ἀπορήσειε δ᾿ ἄν τις, ἆρ᾿ εἴ τι κινεῖ τὸν ὅλον οὐρανόν, |13| εἶναί τέ τι δεῖ ἀκίνητον καὶ τοῦτο μηθὲν εἶναι τοῦ οὐρανοῦ |14| μηδ᾿ ἐν τῶι οὐρανῶι. εἴτε γὰρ αὐτὸ κινούμενον κινεῖ αὐτόν, ἀ|15|νάγκη τινὸς ἀκινήτου θιγγάνον κινεῖν καὶ τοῦτο μηθὲν εἶναι |16| μόριον τοῦ κινοῦντος· εἴτ᾿ εὐθὺς ἀκίνητόν ἐστιν τὸ κινοῦν, ὁμοίως |17| οὐθὲν ἔσται τοῦ κινουμένου μόριον. καὶ τοῦτό γ᾿ ὀρθῶς λέγουσιν |18| οἱ λέγοντες ὅτι κύκλωι φερομένης τῆς σφαίρας οὐδ᾿ ὁτιοῦν |19| μένει μόριον· ἢ γὰρ ἂν ὅλην ἀναγκαῖον ἦν μένειν, ἢ δια|20|σπᾶσθαι τὸ συνεχὲς αὐτῆς. ἀλλ᾿ ὅτι τοὺς πόλους οἴονταί τινα |21| δύναμιν ἔχειν, οὐθὲν ἔχοντας μέγεθος ἀλλ᾿ ὄντας ἔσχατα |22| καὶ στιγμάς, οὐ καλῶς. πρὸς γὰρ τῶι μηδεμίαν οὐσίαν εἶναι |23| τῶν τοιούτων μηθενὸς καὶ κινεῖσθαι τὴν μίαν κίνησιν ὑπὸ |24| δυοῖν ἀδύνατον· τοὺς δὲ πόλους δύο ποιοῦσιν. ὅτι μὲν οὖν ἔχει |25| τι καὶ πρὸς τὴν ὅλην φύσιν οὕτως ὥσπερ ἡ γῆ πρὸς τὰ ζῶια |26| τὰ κινούμενα δι᾿ αὐτῶν, ἐκ τῶν τοιούτων ἄν τις διαπορή|27|σειεν. οἱ δὲ μυθικῶς τὸν Ἄτλαντα ποιοῦντες ἐπὶ τῆς γῆς |28| ἔχοντα τοὺς πόδας δόξαιεν ἂν ἀπὸ διανοίας εἰρηκέναι τὸν |29| μῦθον, ὡς τοῦτον ὥσπερ διάμετρον ὄντα καὶ στρέφοντα τὸν |30| οὐρανὸν περὶ τοὺς πόλους· τοῦτο δ᾿ ἂν συμβαίνοι κατὰ λόγον |31| διὰ τὸ τὴν γῆν μένειν. ἀλλὰ τοῖς ταῦτα λέγουσιν ἀναγκαῖον |32| φάναι μηδὲν εἶναι μόριον αὐτὴν τοῦ παντός. πρὸς δὲ τούτοις |33| δεῖ τὴν ἰσχὺν ἰσάζειν τοῦ κινοῦντος καὶ τὴν τοῦ μένοντος. |34| ἔστιν γάρ τι πλῆθος ἰσχύος καὶ δυνάμεως καθ᾿ ἣν μένει τὸ |35| μένον, ὥσπερ καὶ καθ᾿ ἣν κινεῖ τὸ κινοῦν·

699ᵃ17–24 καὶ τοῦτό γ᾿ ὀρθῶς... τοὺς δὲ πόλους δύο ποιοῦσιν: cf. *TrGF* I, iv, 43 (Critias) F 3 Snell/Kannicht ubi δίδυμοι ἄρκτοι ≈ δύο πόλοι (cf. *Mete.* 362ᵃ23, ᵇ4, ᵇ30–32) et Ἀτλάντειος πόλος ≈ διάμετρος || **27–30** οἱ δὲ μυθικῶς τὸν Ἄτλαντα ποιοῦντες... στρέφοντα τὸν οὐρανὸν περὶ τοὺς πόλους: cf. Ennius *Annales* 27 (= lib. I fr. xxiii) Skutsch (unde Vergil. *Aeneis* IV 481–482 ≈ VI 796–797)

699ᵃ4 αὐτὸν **β** : αὐτὸ ἢ **a** || **10** ἕλκων καὶ ὠθῶν **β** : ὠθῶν ἢ ἕλκων **a** || **13** τέ τι δεῖ **β** : τε δεῖ **a** (unde θέλει **γ**) | οὐρανοῦ **β** : οὐρανοῦ μόριον **a** || **17** ἔσται coni. Thomæus (*erit*) : ἔσεσθαι **ω** || **26** τὰ **β** : καὶ τὰ **a** || **26–27** διαπορήσειεν **a** : ἀπορήσειεν **β** || **28** ἄν **a** : om. **β** || **30** ἂν συμβαίνοι **β**E : ἂν συμβαίνει **γ** || **35** καὶ καθ᾿ ἣν **βγ** : καθὴν E

|699ᵃ3| first, he must be pushing while pressing against some one of his own parts which is at rest, and second, that part, or the person himself of whom it happens to be a part, must remain still, fixed against something external. |6| But it's only reasonable that whoever is pushing the boat while he himself is in the boat and is fixed against the boat does not move the boat because of the fact that it is necessary for that against which he is fixed to stay still. |8| And it so happens that for him the thing that he is moving and the thing against which he is fixed are the same! |10| But if from outside he drags and pushes it, he moves it, for the ground is no part of the boat.

3

|12| Someone may raise the difficulty of whether, if something moves the whole universe, there must indeed be something unmoving, where this must be nothing of the universe, and not in the universe. |14| For if it moves the universe while itself moving, it must move it while itself touching something unmoving and this must be no part of the thing moving the universe. |16| And if that which moves the universe is immediately unmoving, similarly it will be no part of the moving thing. |17| And those who say that no part whatsoever of the sphere which moves in a circle stays still, are correct in this proposal, at any rate: for then it would be necessary either for the whole thing to stay still, or for its continuity to be ripped apart. |20| But since they think the poles have a certain power even though they have no magnitude and are instead limits and geometrical points, their proposal is not a good one. |22| For apart from the fact that none of the things of this kind have any substantial being, it is also impossible for there to be movement in a single motion brought about by two things: but they make the poles two things. |24| So then, from such difficulties one might conclude that there is also something which bears the same relation to the whole of nature as the earth does to those animals which move through their own agency. |27| Now those who, in the manner of a story, make Atlas keep his feet on the earth, would seem to have told their story thoughtfully, assuming that he is like an axis and twirls the heaven around the poles. |30| This would be a reasonable suggestion, since the earth remains still. |31| But those who propose these things have to say that it is no part of the whole. |32| And moreover the force of the thing causing the movement and that of the thing that stays still should be equal. |34| For there is a certain amount of force and power on the basis of which the thing that stays still stays still, just as there is also an amount on the basis of which the thing causing the movement causes the movement.

καὶ ἔστιν τις ἀνα|36|λογία ἐξ ἀνάγκης, ὥσπερ τῶν ἐναντίων κινήσεων, οὕτω καὶ |37| τῶν ἠρεμιῶν. καὶ αἱ μὲν ἴσαι ἀπαθεῖς ὑπ' ἀλλήλων, κρα|**699ᵇ**1|τοῦνται δὲ κατὰ τὴν ὑπεροχήν. διόπερ εἴτε Ἄτλας εἴτε τι |2| τοιοῦτον ἕτερόν ἐστιν τὸ κινοῦν τῶν ἐντός, οὐ δεῖ μᾶλλον ἀντερεί|3|δειν τῆς μονῆς ἣν ἡ γῆ τυγχάνει μένουσα· ἢ κινηθήσεται |4| ἡ γῆ ἀπὸ τοῦ μέσου καὶ ἐκ τοῦ αὑτῆς τόπου. ὡς γὰρ τὸ ὠ|5|θοῦν ὠθεῖ, οὕτω τὸ ὠθούμενον ὠθεῖται, καὶ ὁμοίως κατ' ἰσχύν. |6| κινεῖ δὲ τὸ ἠρεμοῦν πρῶτον, ὥστε μᾶλλον καὶ πλείων ἡ ἰσχὺς |7| ἢ ὁμοία καὶ ἴση τῆς ἠρεμίας, ὡσαύτως δὲ καὶ τοῦ κινου|8|μένου μέν, μὴ κινοῦντος δέ. τοσαύτην οὖν δεήσει τὴν δύναμιν |9| εἶναι τῆς γῆς ἐν τῶι ἠρεμεῖν ὅσην ὅ τε πᾶς οὐρανὸς ἔχει καὶ |10| τὸ κινοῦν αὐτόν. εἰ δὲ τοῦτο ἀδύνατον, ἀδύνατον καὶ τὸ κινεῖ|11|σθαι τὸν οὐρανὸν ὑπό τινος τοιούτου τῶν ἐντός.

4

|12| Ἔστιν δέ τις ἀπορία περὶ τὰς κινήσεις τῶν τοῦ οὐρανοῦ μο|13|ρίων, ἣν ὡς οὖσαν οἰκείαν τοῖς εἰρημένοις ἐπισκέψαιτ' ἄν τις. |14| ἐὰν γάρ τις ὑπερβάληι τῆι δυνάμει τῆς κινήσεως τὴν τῆς |15| γῆς ἠρεμίαν, δῆλον ὅτι κινήσει αὐτὴν ἀπὸ τοῦ μέσου. καὶ ἡ |16| ἰσχὺς δὲ ἀφ' ἧς αὕτη ἡ δύναμις, ὅτι οὐκ ἄπειρος, φανερόν· |17| οὐδὲ γὰρ ἡ γῆ ἄπειρος, ὥστ' οὐδὲ τὸ βάρος αὐτῆς. ἐπεὶ δὲ τὸ |18| ἀδύνατον λέγεται πλεοναχῶς (οὐ γὰρ ὡσαύτως τήν τε φω|19|νὴν ἀδύνατον εἶναί φαμεν ὁραθῆναι καὶ τοὺς ἐπὶ τῆς σελήνης |20| ὑφ' ἡμῶν· τὸ μὲν γὰρ ἐξ ἀνάγκης, τὸ δὲ πεφυκὸς ὁρᾶ|21|σθαι οὐκ ὀφθήσεται), τὸν δὲ οὐρανὸν ἄφθαρτον εἶναι καὶ ἀδιά|22|λυτον οἰόμεθα μὲν ἐξ ἀνάγκης, συμβαίνει δὲ κατὰ |23| τοῦτον τὸν λόγον οὐκ ἐξ ἀνάγκης <εἶναι>· πέφυκε γὰρ καὶ ἐνδέχεται |24| εἶναι κίνησιν μείζω καὶ ἀφ' ἧς ἠρεμεῖ ἡ γῆ καὶ ἀφ' ἧς κι|25|νοῦνται τὸ πῦρ καὶ τὸ ἄνω σῶμα. εἰ μὲν οὖν εἰσιν αἱ ὑπερ|26|έχουσαι κινήσεις, διαλυθήσεται ταῦτα ὑπ' ἀλλήλων. εἰ δὲ |27| μὴ εἰσὶν μέν, ἐνδέχεται δὲ εἶναι (ἄπειρον γὰρ οὐκ ἐνδέχεται |28| διὰ τὸ μηδὲ σῶμα ἐνδέχεσθαι ἄπειρον εἶναι), ἐνδέχοιτ' ἂν |29| διαλυθῆναι τὸν οὐρανόν. τί γὰρ κωλύει τοῦτο συμβῆναι, εἴπερ |30| μὴ ἀδύνατον; οὐκ ἀδύνατον δέ, εἴπερ μὴ τὸ ἀντικείμενον ἀναγ|31|καῖον. ἀλλὰ περὶ μὲν τῆς ἀπορίας ταύτης ἕτερος ἔστω λόγος.

699ᵇ2 ἕτερόν ἐστιν **β** : ἔστιν ἕτερον **α** | οὐ δεῖ **β** : οὐδὲν **α** (δεῖ post ἀντερείδειν addidit E) ǁ 6 ἡ **α** : om. **β** ǁ 7 τοῦ **β** : αἱ τοῦ E : τῆς τοῦ **γ** ǁ 13 ὡς **βγ** : om. E ǁ 14 ὑπερβάληι dedi : ὑπερβάλῃ BᶜCᵃL et al. : ὑπερβάλλῃ(ι) ENEʳ et al. ǁ 19 εἶναί φαμεν **β** : φαμὲν εἶναι **α** ǁ 21–23 εἶναι...ἐξ ἀνάγκης,...ἐξ ἀνάγκης εἶναι dedi : εἶναι...ἐξ ἀνάγκης εἶναι,...ἐξ ἀνάγκης **ω** ǁ 25–26 ὑπερέχουσαι **βγ** : περὶ ἔχουσαι E ǁ 28 ἐνδέχοιτ' ἂν **α** : ἐνδέχεται **β** ǁ 30 εἴπερ **β** : εἰ **α**

|35| And just as there must be some proportion for motions which are opposed, so too for states of rest. |37| And equal ones are unaffected by each other, but they are overcome in cases of excess. |699ᵇ1| For this reason, whether the interior thing causing motion is Atlas or some other such thing, it should not press down more than the fixity with which the earth gets to stay still. |3| Otherwise, the earth will be moved from the centre, i.e. from its own place. |4| For as the pusher pushes, so the pushed is pushed—with similar force, that is. |6| And the thing which is first at rest causes movement in such a way that its force is even greater than—rather than similar and equal to—its state of rest, and similarly too in comparison with the thing which is moved but isn't causing motion. |8| Therefore the power of the earth in its state of rest should be just as much as the power that the combination of the whole heaven and the thing that causes motion to it holds. |10| And if this is impossible, then it is impossible also for the heaven to be moved by some such interior thing.

4

|12| But there is a difficulty about the motions of the parts of the universe, which someone might investigate as being related to what has been said. |14| For if someone were to overcome with the power of his motion the state of rest of the earth, it is clear that he would be moving it away from the centre. |15| And that the force from which this very power would come need not be infinite, is clear. |17| For the earth is not infinite and so neither is its weight. |17| But since the impossible is spoken of in many ways—for it is not in the same way that we say both sound and the men in the moon are impossible for us to see, for the one is impossible to see by necessity, but the other is of such a nature as to be seen but will not be seen—we *think* the universe is indestructible and indissoluble by necessity but in fact it follows from this explanation <that it is> not so by necessity. |23| For a motion greater than that from which the earth is at rest and from which fire and the body above is moved, is of such a nature as to exist and can exist. |25| So if these overbearing motions occur, those things would be disbanded by one another. |26| But if they do not occur and it is possible for them to occur (for it is not possible for the required motion to be infinite because it is not possible for a body to be infinite), the universe can indeed be disbanded. |29| For what prevents this from happening, provided that it is not impossible? |30| Yet it is not impossible, provided that its opposite is not necessary. |31| But about this difficulty let there be a different explanation.

|32| ἆρα δὲ δεῖ τι ἀκίνητον εἶναι καὶ ἠρεμοῦν ἔξω τοῦ κινουμένου, |33| μηδὲν ὂν
ἐκείνου μόριον, ἢ οὔ; καὶ τοῦτο πότερον καὶ ἐπὶ τοῦ |34| παντὸς οὕτως ὑπάρχειν
ἀναγκαῖον; ἴσως γὰρ ἂν δόξειεν ἄτο|35|πον εἶναι, εἰ ἡ ἀρχὴ τῆς κινήσεως ἐντός.
διὸ δόξειεν ἂν τοῖς |36| οὕτως ὑπολαμβάνουσιν εὖ εἰρῆσθαι Ὁμήρωι

|37| ἀλλ᾽ οὐκ ἂν ἐρύσαιτ᾽ ἐξ· οὐρανόθεν πεδίονδε
|700ᵃ1| Ζῆν᾽ ὕπατον μήστωρ᾽, οὐδ᾽ εἰ μάλα πολλὰ κάμοιτε·
|2| πάντες δ᾽ ἐξάπτεσθε θεοὶ πᾶσαί τε θέαιναι.

|3| τὸ γὰρ ὅλως ἀκίνητον ὑπ᾽ οὐδενὸς ἐνδέχεται κινηθῆναι· ὅθεν |4| λύεται καὶ
ἡ πάλαι λεχθεῖσα ἀπορία, πότερον ἐνδέχεται |5| ἢ οὐκ ἐνδέχεται διαλυθῆναι
τὴν τοῦ οὐρανοῦ σύστασιν, εἰ ἐξ ἀκι|6|νήτου ἤρτηται ἀρχῆς. ἐπὶ δὲ τῶν ζῴων
οὐ μόνον τὸ οὕτως |7| ἀκίνητον δεῖ ὑπάρχειν, ἀλλὰ καὶ ἐν αὐτοῖς τοῖς
κινουμένοις |8| κατὰ τόπον ὅσα κινεῖ αὐτὰ αὑτά {δεῖ γὰρ αὐτοῦ τὸ μὲν |9| ἠρεμεῖν
τὸ δὲ κινεῖσθαι}, πρὸς ὃ ἀπερειδόμενον τὸ κινούμενον |10| κινήσεται· <δεῖ γὰρ
αὐτοῦ τὸ μὲν ἠρεμεῖν τὸ δὲ κινεῖσθαι>, οἷον ἄν τι κινῇ τῶν μορίων·
ἀπερείδεται γὰρ θά|11|τερον ὡς πρὸς μένον θάτερον. περὶ δὲ τῶν ἀψύχων ὅσα
κι|12|νεῖται ἀπορήσειεν ἄν τις, πότερον ἅπαντα ἔχει ἐν αὐτοῖς |13| καὶ τὸ
ἠρεμοῦν καὶ τὸ κινούμενον, καὶ πρὸς τῶν ἔξωθέν τι ἠρεμοῦν |14| ἀπερείδεσθαι
ἀνάγκη καὶ πάντα ταῦτα, ἢ ἀδύνατον οἷον πῦρ |15| ἢ γῆν ἢ τῶν ἀψύχων τι ἄλλ᾽,
<ἀλλ᾽> ὑφ᾽ ὧν ταῦτα κινεῖται πρώ|16|των. πάντα γὰρ ὑπ᾽ ἄλλου κινεῖται τὰ
ἄψυχα, ἀρχὴ δὲ |17| πάντων ὁμοίως τῶν οὕτως κινουμένων τὰ αὐτὰ αὑτὰ
κινοῦντα. τῶν δὲ |18| τοιούτων περὶ μὲν τῶν ζῴων εἴρηται· τὰ γὰρ τοιαῦτα
πάντα |19| ἀνάγκη καὶ ἐν αὑτοῖς ἔχειν τὸ ἠρεμοῦν καὶ ἔξω πρὸς ὃ |20|
ἀπερείσεται. εἰ δέ τί ἐστιν ἀνωτέρω καὶ πρῶτον κινοῦν, ἄδη|21|λον, καὶ ἄλλος
λόγος περὶ τῆς τοιαύτης ἀρχῆς. τὰ δὲ ζῷα |22| ὅσα κινεῖται, πάντα πρὸς τὰ
ἔξω ἀπερειδόμενα κινεῖται, |23| καὶ ἀναπνέοντα καὶ ἐκπνέοντα. οὐθὲν γὰρ
διαφέρει μέγα |24| ῥῖψαι βάρος ἢ μικρόν, ὅπερ ποιοῦσιν οἱ πτύοντες καὶ
βήτ|25|τοντες καὶ οἱ εἰσπνέοντες καὶ οἱ ἐκπνέοντες.

699ᵇ37–700ᵃ2 *Ilias* VIII, 21–22 + 20 ‖ **700ᵃ1** Cf. Eust. *In Iliadem*, II 518,9–12 v. d. Valk,
unde elucet variam lectionem πάντων (α) ex antiqua verbi ὕπατον explicatione in textum irrepsisse ‖ **4** ἡ πάλαι λεχθεῖσα ἀπορία: cf. supra 699ᵇ12–13 ‖ **6** ἤρτηται: cf. *Metaph.*
Λ 7, 1072ᵇ14 ‖ **18** εἴρηται: supra *MA* 1–2; cf. *IA* 3 ‖ **21** ἄλλος λόγος: *Metaph.* Λ 7

699ᵇ32 τι ἀκίνητον βγ : ἀκίνητόν τι E ‖ **700ᵃ1** μήστωρ᾽ β Hom. : πάντων α | μάλα α Hom. :
πάνυ β ‖ **5** εἰ α : ἢ β ‖ **6** ἤρτηται α : ἤρκται β ‖ **8** αὐτὰ αὑτά βγ : αὐτὰ E ‖ **8–9** δεῖ γὰρ
– κινεῖσθαι] post ᵃ10 (κινήσεται) transpos. Renehan ‖ **12** αὑτοῖς β : ἑαυτοῖς α ‖ **13**
κινούμενον β : κινοῦν α | ἔξωθέν β : ἔξω α | ἠρεμοῦν β : ἠρεμούντων α ‖ **14** πάντα ταῦτα
β : ταῦτα α ‖ **15** ἄλλ᾽, <ἀλλ᾽> dedi : ἀλλ᾽ ω ‖ **15–16** πρώτων α : πρῶτον β ‖ **17** ὁμοίως β :
om. α ‖ **20** πρῶτον βγ : πρώτως E ‖ **24** καὶ βE : καὶ οἱ γ ‖ **25** οἱ ἐκπνέοντες β : οἱ om. α

|32| Well, then, must there be something unmoved and at rest outside the moved thing, which is no part of it, or not? |33| In particular, must this be so in the case of the whole too? |34| For it would seem to be absurd if the origin of its motion were inside it. |35| This is why Homer would seem to those who think in this way to have spoken well [*Iliad* VIII]:

[l. 21]   *But you could not drag from sky to earth*

[l. 22]   *Zeus, the highest counsellor, not even if you toil exceedingly hard.*

[l. 20]   *Take hold, all you gods and all you goddesses!*

|**700ª**3| For that which is wholly unmoved cannot be moved by anything. For this reason, the difficulty mentioned before—whether it is possible or not for the structure of the universe to be disbanded—can also be solved, if it (i.e. this structure) depends on an unmoved origin. |6| Yet in the case of animals not only must there be something unmoving in this way, but also, in those things which move in respect of place, the ones which move themselves by themselves, (there must be) something which the moving thing will press against when it moves. |10| <For it must have within itself something stationary and something in motion>, as when it moves one of its limbs. |10| For the one presses against the other as against something stationary. |11| Concerning those inanimate things which move, someone might raise the difficulty whether they all also have within themselves something stationary and something in motion, and whether all these things too must press against something external to them which is stationary, or whether this is impossible for something such as fire or earth or any other of the inanimate things, but is true instead only for the first things by which these things are moved. |16| For all inanimate things are moved by something else, and the source of all things thus moved alike are the things which move themselves by themselves. |17| And of these we have spoken already of animals. |18| For all such things must have something stationary both in themselves and outside themselves against which they push off. |20| But whether there is something higher and a first mover is unclear, and such an origin is a topic for another discussion. |21| But animals, which move, all move pressing against things exterior to them, even in the case of breathing in and out. |23| For , there is no great difference between throwing out something heavy or something light, which is just what those who spit and cough, and those who breathe in and those who breathe out, do.

5

|26| Πότερον δὲ ἐν τῶι αὐτὸ αὐτὸ κινοῦντι κατὰ τόπον μόνωι δεῖ |27| τι μένειν, ἢ <καὶ> ἐν τῶι ἀλλοιουμένωι αὐτὸ ὑφ' αὑτοῦ καὶ ἐν τῶι |28| αὐξανομένωι; (περὶ δὲ γενέσεως τῆς ἐξ ἀρχῆς καὶ φθορᾶς |29| ἄλλος λόγος.) εἰ γάρ ἐστιν, ἥνπερ φαμέν, πρώτη κίνησις, γε|30|νέσεως μὲν καὶ φθορᾶς αὕτη ἂν αἰτία εἴη, καὶ τῶν ἄλλων δὲ |31| κινήσεων ἴσως πασῶν. ὥσπερ δὲ ἐν τῶι ὅλωι, καὶ ἐν τῶι ζώιωι |32| κίνησις πρώτη αὕτη, ὅταν τελεωθῆι, ὥστε καὶ αὐξήσεως, εἴ |33| ποτε γίγνεται αὐτὸ αὑτῶι αἴτιον, καὶ ἀλλοιώσεως. εἰ δὲ μή, |34| οὐκ ἀνάγκη. αἱ δὲ πρῶται αὐξήσεις καὶ ἀλλοιώσεις ὑπ' |35| ἄλλου γίνονται καὶ δι' ἑτέρων. γενέσεως δὲ καὶ φθορᾶς οὐ|700ᵇ1|δαμῶς οἷόν τε αὐτὸ αὑτῶι αἴτιον εἶναι οὐθέν· προϋπάρχειν |2| γὰρ δεῖ τὸ κινοῦν τοῦ κινουμένου καὶ τὸ γεννῶν τοῦ γεννωμένου· |3| αὐτὸ δὲ αὑτοῦ πρότερον οὐδέν ἐστιν.

6

|4| Περὶ μὲν οὖν ψυχῆς, εἴτε κινεῖται εἴτε μή, καὶ εἰ κινει|5|ται, πῶς κινεῖται, πρότερον εἴρηται ἐν τοῖς διωρισμένοις |6| περὶ αὐτῆς. ἐπεὶ δὲ τὰ ἄψυχα πάντα κινεῖται ὑφ' ἑτέρου, |7| περὶ δὲ τοῦ πρώτου κινουμένου καὶ ἀεὶ κινουμένου, τίνα τρόπον |8| κινεῖται καὶ πῶς κινεῖ τὸ πρῶτον κινοῦν, διώρισται πρότερον |9| ἐν τοῖς περὶ τῆς πρώτης φιλοσοφίας, λοιπὸν δ' ἐστὶν θεωρῆ|10|σαι πῶς ἡ ψυχὴ κινεῖ τὸ σῶμα καὶ τίς ἀρχὴ τῆς τοῦ |11| ζώιου κινήσεως. τῶν γὰρ ἄλλων παρὰ τὴν τοῦ ὅλου κίνησιν τὰ |12| ἔμψυχα αἴτια τῆς κινήσεως, ὅσα μὴ κινεῖται ὑπ' ἀλλή|13|λων διὰ τὸ προσκόπτειν ἀλλήλοις. διὸ καὶ πέρας ἔχουσιν |14| αὐτῶν πᾶσαι αἱ κινήσεις· καὶ γὰρ αἱ τῶν ἐμψύχων. |15| πάντα γὰρ τὰ ζῶια καὶ κινεῖ καὶ κινεῖται ἕνεκά τινος, ὥστε |16| τοῦτ' ἔστιν πάσης αὐτοῖς τῆς κινήσεως πέρας, τὸ οὗ ἕνεκα. |17| ὁρῶμεν δὲ τὰ κινοῦντα τὸ ζῶιον διάνοιαν καὶ φαντασίαν καὶ |18| προαίρεσιν καὶ βούλησιν καὶ ἐπιθυμίαν. ταῦτα δὲ πάντα |19| ἀνάγεται εἰς νοῦν καὶ ὄρεξιν. καὶ γὰρ ἡ φαντασία καὶ ἡ |20| αἴσθησις τὴν αὐτὴν τῶι νῶι χώραν ἔχουσιν·

700ᵃ29 ἄλλος λόγος: cf. et infra 700ᵃ35–ᵇ3 et GA II, 1, 735ᵃ9–14 | ἥνπερ φαμέν Ph. VIII, 7 ‖ **31** ὥσπερ δὲ ἐν τῶι ὅλωι, καὶ ἐν τῶι ζώιωι κτλ.: cf. Ph. VIII, 2, 252ᵇ26–28 ‖ **700ᵇ5–6** ἐν τοῖς διωρισμένοις περὶ αὐτῆς: de An. I, 3–4 ‖ **8–9** διώρισται πρότερον ἐν τοῖς περὶ τῆς πρώτης φιλοσοφίας: Metaph. Λ 7, imprimis 1072ᵇ3–4

700ᵃ27 ἢ <καὶ> γ : ἢ βE | αὐτὸ E : αὐτῶι βγ | καὶ ἐν τῶι β : καὶ α ‖ **30** μὲν β : om. α | ἂν αἰτία β : αἰτία ἂν α | δὲ βE : om. γ ‖ **33** αὐτὸ αὑτῶι βγ : αὐτῶι αὐτῶι E ‖ **35** ἑτέρων α : ἕτερον β ‖ **700ᵇ1** οἷόν τε α : οἴονται β | αὑτῶι αἴτιον εἶναι β : αἴτιον εἶναι αὑτῶι α ‖ **9** δ' βE : om. γ ‖ **11** ὅλου βγ : λόγου E ‖ **16** πάσης αὐτοῖς β : αὐτοῖς πάσης α

5

|26| Must there be something at rest only in something which moves itself by itself in respect of place, or <also> in something which alters itself by itself and in something which grows? |28| (Original generation and destruction are topics of another discussion.) |29| For if the primary kind of motion is the one (i.e. locomotion) which we say it is, then it would be the cause of generation and destruction, but also perhaps of all the other kinds of motion. |31| And just as in the universe, that kind of motion is the primary one also in the animal, when it has come to maturity, with the consequence that it (i.e. locomotion) comes to be the cause both of growth, if ever the animal itself becomes a cause for itself, and of alteration. |33| But if it doesn't (come to maturity), it isn't necessary for something to be at rest. |34| The first instances of growth and alteration come about by the agency of something else and through other things, and nothing can in any way be responsible for its own growth and destruction. |700^{b}1| For the mover must precede the moved thing and the generator the generated. |3| But nothing is itself prior to itself.

6

|4| Well then, soul, whether it is moved or not, and if it is moved, how it is moved, has been discussed previously, in our determinations about it. |6| And since all inanimate things are moved by something else, and it has been previously determined in the works concerning first philosophy how the first moved thing, which is always moved, is moved and how the first mover moves it, it remains to consider how the soul moves the body and which origin belongs to animal motion. |11| For except for the motion of the whole, animate things are responsible for the motion of other things, at least those which are not moved one by another as a result of striking against one another. |13| This is why all the motions of these things also have a limit, since the motions of animate things do too. |15| For all animals both cause movement and are moved for the sake of some goal, so that this is the limit of every one of their motions, the goal. |17| But we see that the things which move animals are discursive thought and appearance and decision and wish and appetite. |18| All of these are reduced to thought (*nous*) and desire—|19| for both appearance and sense-perception hold the same place as thought,

κριτικὰ γὰρ |21| πάντα, διαφέρουσιν δὲ κατὰ τὰς εἰρημένας ἐν ἄλλοις δια|22|φοράς. βούλησις δὲ καὶ θυμὸς καὶ ἐπιθυμία πάντα ὀρέξεις, |23| ἡ δὲ προαίρεσις κοινὸν διανοίας καὶ ὀρέξεως· ὥστε κινεῖ πρῶ|24|τον τὸ ὀρεκτὸν καὶ τὸ νοητόν. οὐ πᾶν δὲ νοητόν, |25| ἀλλὰ τὸ τῶν πρακτῶν τέλος, διὸ τὸ τοιοῦτόν ἐστιν τῶν ἀγα|26|θῶν τὸ κινοῦν, ἀλλ' οὐ πᾶν τὸ καλόν· ᾗ γὰρ ἕνεκα τούτου |27| ἄλλο καὶ ᾗ τέλος ἐστὶν τῶν ἄλλου τινὸς ἕνεκα ὄντων, ταύτηι |28| κινεῖ. δεῖ δὲ τιθέναι καὶ τὸ φαινόμενον ἀγαθὸν ἀγαθοῦ χώ|29|ραν ἔχειν, καὶ τὸ ἡδύ· φαινόμενον γάρ ἐστιν ἀγαθόν. ὥστε |30| δῆλον ὅτι ἔστιν μὲν ᾗ ὁμοίως κινεῖται τὸ ἀεὶ κινούμενον ὑπὸ τοῦ |31| ἀεὶ κινοῦντος καὶ τῶν ζώιων ἕκαστον, ἔστιν δὲ ᾗ ἄλλως, διὸ καὶ |32| τὸ μὲν ἀεὶ κινεῖται, ἡ δὲ τῶν ζώιων κίνησις ἔχει πέρας. τὸ |33| δὲ ἀΐδιον καλὸν καὶ ἀληθὲς καὶ τὸ πρώτως ἀγαθὸν καὶ |34| μὴ ποτὲ μὲν ποτὲ δὲ μὴ θειότερον καὶ τιμιώτερον ἢ ὥστ' |35| εἶναι πρὸς ἕτερον. τὸ μὲν οὖν πρῶτον οὐ κινούμενον κινεῖ, ἡ δὲ |701ᵃ1| ὄρεξις καὶ τὸ ὀρεκτικὸν κινούμενον κινεῖ. τὸ δὲ τελευταῖον τῶν |2| κινουμένων οὐκ ἀνάγκη κινεῖν οὐθέν. φανερὸν δὲ ἐκ τούτων καὶ |3| ὅτι εὐλόγως ἡ φορὰ τελευταία τῶν κινουμένων ἐν τοῖς γιγνο|4|μένοις· κινεῖται γὰρ καὶ πορεύεται τὸ ζῷον ὀρέξει ἢ προ|5|αιρέσει, ἀλλοιωθέντος τινὸς κατὰ τὴν αἴσθησιν ἢ τὴν φαν|6|τασίαν.

7

|7| Πῶς δὲ νοῶν ὁτὲ μὲν πράττει ὁτὲ δὲ οὐ πράττει, καὶ |8| κινεῖται ὁτὲ δ' οὐ κινεῖται; ἔοικε δὲ παραπλησίως συμβαίνειν |9| καὶ περὶ τῶν ἀκινήτων διανοουμένοις καὶ συλλογιζομένοις. |10| ἀλλὰ ἐκεῖ μὲν θεώρημα τὸ τέλος (ὅταν γὰρ τὰς δύο προ|11|τάσεις νοήσηι, τὸ συμπέρασμα ἐνόησεν καὶ συνέθηκεν), ἐν|12|ταῦθα δὲ ἐκ τῶν δύο προτάσεων τὸ συμπέρασμα γίνεται ἡ |13| πρᾶξις,

---

700ᵇ21–22 κατὰ τὰς εἰρημένας ἐν ἄλλοις διαφοράς: de An. II, 5 – III, 8 || 23–24 ὥστε κινεῖ πρῶτον τὸ ὀρεκτὸν καὶ τὸ νοητόν: cf. supra 700ᵇ18–19 ταῦτα δὲ πάντα ἀνάγεται εἰς νοῦν καὶ ὄρεξιν et Metaph. Λ 7, 1072ᵃ26 κινεῖ δὲ ὧδε τὸ ὀρεκτὸν καὶ τὸ νοητόν || 33 ἀΐδιον... ἀληθές: cf. Metaph. Θ 10, 1051ᵇ15–18 et 23–33

700ᵇ22 ὀρέξεις **βγ** : ὄρεξις E || 23–24 κινεῖ πρῶτον τὸ ὀρεκτὸν **β** : om. **α** || 24 τὸ νοητόν. οὐ πᾶν δὲ νοητόν dedi cl. Metaph. Λ 7, 1072ᵃ26 : τὸ διανοητόν. οὐ πᾶν δὲ διανοητόν **ω** | πᾶν δὲ **β** : πᾶν δὲ τὸ **α** || 25 τὸ τοιοῦτον **α** : τοιοῦτόν **β** || 28 κινεῖ **α** : κινεῖν **β** || 32 τὸ μὲν **β** : τὰ μὲν **α** || 33 καλὸν καὶ dedi : καλὸν καὶ τὸ **ω** | ἀληθὲς καὶ τὸ **β** : ἀληθῶς καὶ **α** || 34 ἢ ὥστ' **α** : πως **β** || 35 πρὸς ἕτερον **β** : πρότερον **α** || 701ᵃ3 κινουμένων **β** : γιγνομένων **α** || 4 ὀρέξει **α** : om. **β** || 8 ἔοικε δὲ **β** : ἔοικε(ν) **α**

|20| since they are all apt for making discriminations (but differ in the ways described in other works), but wish and spirit and appetite are all desires, and decision belongs to both discursive thought and desire—, from whence it follows that it is the *object* of desire (*orekton*) and the *object* of thought (*noeton*) that primarily cause movement, though not just any object of thought, but the goal of what is achievable through action. |25| This is why, amongst goods, it is a thing of this sort which is the mover, but not just any fine thing. |26| For it is insofar as something else is for the sake of this, and insofar as it is the goal of things which are for the sake of something else, that it causes movement. |28| (We must lay down that the apparent good too holds the place of the good, and the pleasant, for it is an apparent good.) |29| So it is clear that that which always is moved by that which always causes movement and every animal are moved in one way similarly, but in another way differently, which is why the one is always being moved but the motion of animals has a limit. |32| But the everlasting fine and true thing, i.e. the primarily good thing which is not at one time good and at another time not good, is too divine and worthy of honour to be oriented (in its goodness) towards something else. |35| So then the first thing causes movement without itself being moved, but desire and the faculty of desire cause movement while being moved. |701ᵃ1| But it is not necessary for the last of the moved things itself to cause anything to move. |2| It's clear from these things also that it's reasonable that the local motion of the things moved be the last in the chain of occurrences. |4| For the animal is moved and progresses forward by desire or decision, with something having been altered on the basis of sense-perception or appearance.

7

|7| How is it that when one is thinking sometimes one acts and sometimes one doesn't, and sometimes one is moved and sometimes one isn't? |8| It seems likely that something similar happens too in the case of those who are thinking discursively and reasoning about unchanging objects. |10| But there, the goal is seeing why something is true (for whenever one thinks the two propositions, one thinks the conclusion and puts it together), whereas here the conclusion from the two propositions becomes the action.

οἷον ὅταν νοήσηι ὅτι παντὶ βαδιστέον ἀνθρώπωι, αὐτὸς |14| δὲ ἄνθρωπος, βαδίζει εὐθέως, ἂν δ' ὅτι οὐθενὶ βαδιστέον νῦν |15| ἀνθρώπωι, αὐτὸς δὲ ἄνθρωπος, εὐθὺς ἠρεμεῖ· καὶ ταῦτ' |16| ἄμφω πράττει, ἂν μή τι κωλύηι ἢ ἀναγκάζηι. »ποιητέον |17| μοι ἀγαθόν· ἀγαθὸν δὲ οἰκία«. ποιεῖ οἰκίαν εὐθύς. »σκεπά|18|σματος δέομαι· ἱμάτιον δὲ σκέπασμα· ἱματίου δέομαι. – οὗ |19| δέομαι, ποιητέον· ἱματίου δὲ δέομαι«. ἱμάτιον ποιεῖ. καὶ τὸ |20| συμπέρασμα, τὸ ἱμάτιον ποιητέον, πρᾶξίς ἐστιν. πράττει |21| δὲ ἀπ' ἀρχῆς. »εἰ ἱμάτιον ἔσται, ἀνάγκη τόδε πρῶτον, εἰ |22| δὲ τόδε, τόδε«· καὶ τοῦτο πράττει εὐθύς. ὅτι μὲν οὖν ἡ πρᾶ|23|ξις τὸ συμπέρασμα, φανερόν· αἱ δὲ προτάσεις αἱ ποιητι|24|καὶ διὰ δυεῖν ὁδῶν γίνονται, διά τε τοῦ ἀγαθοῦ καὶ διὰ τοῦ |25| δυνατοῦ. ὥσπερ δὲ τῶν ἐρωτώντων ἔνιοι, οὕτω τὴν ἑτέραν πρό|26|τασιν τὴν δήλην οὐδ' ἡ διάνοια ἐπιστᾶσα σκοπεῖ οὐθέν· οἷον εἰ |27| τὸ βαδίζειν ἀγαθὸν ἀνθρώπωι, ὅτι αὐτὸς ἄνθρωπος, οὐκέτι ἐν|28|διατρίβει. διὸ καὶ ὅσα μὴ λογισάμενοι πράττομεν, ταχὺ |29| πράττομεν. ὅταν ἐνεργήσηι γὰρ ἢ τῆι αἰσθήσει πρὸς τὸ οὗ |30| ἕνεκα ἢ τῆι φαντασίαι ἢ τῶι νῶι, οὗ ὀρέγεται, εὐθὺς ποιεῖ. |31| ἀντ' ἐρωτήσεως γὰρ ἢ νοήσεως ἡ τῆς ὀρέξεως γίνεται ἐνέρ|32|γεια. »ποτέον μοι« ἡ ἐπιθυμία λέγει· »τοδὶ δὲ ποτόν« ἡ αἴ|33|σθησις εἶπεν ἢ ἡ φαντασία ἢ ὁ νοῦς· εὐθὺς πίνει. οὕτω μὲν |34| οὖν ἐπὶ τὸ κινεῖσθαι καὶ πράττειν τὰ ζῶια ὁρμῶσιν, τῆς μὲν |35| ἐσχάτης αἰτίας τοῦ κινεῖσθαι ὀρέξεως οὔσης, ταύτης δὲ γιγνο|36|μένης ἢ δι' αἰσθήσεως ἢ διὰ φαντασίας καὶ νοήσεως. τῶν |37| δὲ ὀρεγομένων πράττειν τὰ μὲν δι' ἐπιθυμίαν ἢ θυμὸν τὰ δὲ |701ᵇ1| διὰ προαίρεσιν ἢ βούλησιν τὰ μὲν ποιοῦσιν, τὰ δὲ πράττουσιν. ὥσ|2|περ δὲ τὰ αὐτόματα κινεῖται μικρᾶς κινήσεως γενομένης – |3| λυομένων τῶν στρεβλῶν καὶ κρουόντων πρὸς ἀλλήλας <εὐθὺς τῶν ζωιδίων τὰς μαχαίρας>, |4| καὶ τὸ ἁμάξιον, ὅπερ <ὁ> ὀχούμενος αὐτὸς κινεῖ εἰς εὐθὺ <πάλιν> καὶ |5| πάλιν, κύκλωι δὲ κινεῖται τῶι ἀνίσους ἔχειν τοὺς τροχούς – ὁ γὰρ |6| ἐλάττων ὥσπερ κέντρον γίγνεται, καθάπερ ἐν τοῖς κυλίνδροις – , |7| οὕτω καὶ τὰ ζῶια κινεῖται.

701ᵇ2 De automatis cf. GA II 1, 734ᵇ10–14; ibid. 5, 741ᵇ7–9; Metaph. A 2, 983ᵃ12–15 ‖ **3** <εὐθὺς> cf. supra 701ᵃ14–15.17.22.30.33 | <τῶν ζωιδίων>: cf. Hero Aut. I, 5 et XXII, 3–4

701ᵃ15–16 ταῦτ' ἄμφω dedi : ταῦτα ἄμφω α : τοῦτ' ἄμφω β ‖ **16** ἀναγκάζηι α : ἀναγκάζει β ‖ **17** ἀγαθὸν δὲ οἰκία β : οἰκία δὲ ἀγαθόν α ‖ **19** δὲ β : om. α | ποιεῖ E Cᵃ : ποιητέον δ ‖ **21** ἔσται α : ἐστὶν β ‖ **22** τόδε, τόδε· καὶ τοῦτο βγ : τόδε, καὶ τόδε E ‖ **24** δυεῖν ὁδῶν dedi : δύ' εἰ ποδῶν Bᶜ : δ[.] ... ὁδῶν Ea.c. ut vid. : δύο εἰδῶν Ep.c. cett. ‖ **26** ἐπιστᾶσα β : ἐφιστᾶσα α ‖ **27** οὐκέτι β : οὐκ α ‖ **32** ποτέον β : ποτόν α ‖ **32–33** ἡ αἴσθησις α : αἴσθησις β ‖ **33** οὕτω β : οὕτως α ‖ **701ᵇ1** διὰ προαίρεσιν β : δι' ὄρεξιν α ‖ **3** πρὸς β : om. α | <εὐθὺς τῶν ζωιδίων τὰς μαχαίρας> exempli gratia dedi : τὰς στρέβλας ω, quod iam Forster delevit ‖ **4** ὅπερ α : ὥσπερ β | <ὁ> inserui : ὀχούμενος αὐτὸς β : ὀχούμενον αὐτὸ α ‖ **4–5** <πάλιν> καὶ πάλιν dedi : καὶ πάλιν ω ‖ **5** δὲ β : om. α

|13| For example, whenever someone thinks that every man should go walking, and that he is a man, immediately he goes walking, whereas if he thinks that no one now should go walking, and that he is a man, he immediately refrains from walking. |15| And he does both these things, unless something prevents him, or forces him, respectively. |16| 'Something good should be made by me, but a house is a good thing'. Immediately, he makes a house. |17| 'I need a covering, but a cloak is a covering. I need a cloak.— |18| That which I need, should be made. But I need a cloak.' He makes a cloak. |19| And the conclusion that a cloak should be made is an action. |20| But his action starts somewhere: 'If there is to be a cloak, necessarily this must happen first; but if this is to happen, this.' And he does that immediately. |22| Now, that the conclusion is the action is clear. |23| But the propositions which are suited for accomplishing something come about through a pair of routes: both through the good and through the possible. |25| Just as some questioners do in the dialectical game, so discursive thought does not settle on and examine the second proposition, the obvious one, in any way. |26| For instance, if going walking is good for a man, he does not dwell any more upon the fact that he is a man. |28| This is why we also do quickly the things we do without calculation. |29| For whenever something has an active perception of the goal, or an appearance or a thought, what it desires it immediately does. |31| For the activity of desire comes about in place of questioning or thinking. |32| 'I should drink', appetite is saying; 'this can be drunk', stated perception or appearance or thought. |33| Immediately he drinks. |33| In this way then animals have impulses to move and act, with desire being the last cause of their movement, and coming about either through perception or through appearance and thought. |36| Of animals who desire to act, some produce or act because of appetite or spirit, others because of choice or wish. |**701**ᵇ1| Just as the automatic theatres are set in motion when only a small movement has happened—when the cables are released and the <figures immediately> strike their <sabres> against one another—and as the little wagon which <the> driver himself tries to move in a straight line <again> and again but which is moved in a circle because it has unequal wheels—for the smaller one comes to function as a centre-point, just as in the case of cylinders—so too are animals moved.

ἔχει γὰρ ὄργανα τοιαῦτα τήν τε |8| τῶν νεύρων φύσιν καὶ τὴν τῶν ὀστῶν, τὰ μὲν ὡς ἐκεῖ τὰ |9| ξύλα καὶ ὁ σίδηρος, τὰ δὲ νεῦρα ὡς αἱ στρέβλαι, ὧν λυο|10|μένων καὶ ἀνιεμένων κινοῦνται. ἐν μὲν οὖν τοῖς αὐτομάτοις |11| καὶ τοῖς ἁμαξίοις οὐκ ἔστιν ἀλλοίωσις, ἐπεὶ εἰ ἐγίγνοντο ἐλάτ|12|τους οἱ ἐντὸς τροχοὶ καὶ πάλιν μείζους, κἂν κύκλωι τὸ αὐτὸ |13| ἐκινεῖτο· ἐν δὲ τῶι ζώιωι δύναται τὸ αὐτὸ καὶ ἔλαττον καὶ |14| μεῖζον γίνεσθαι καὶ τὰ σχήματα μεταβάλλειν αὐξανο|15|μένων <καὶ συστελλομένων> τῶν μορίων διὰ θερμότητα καὶ πνεῦμα καὶ |16| ψῦξιν καὶ ἀλλοιουμένων. ἀλλοιοῦσιν δὲ αἱ φαντασίαι καὶ |17| αἱ αἰσθήσεις καὶ αἱ ἔννοιαι. αἱ μὲν γὰρ αἰσθήσεις εὐθὺς |18| ὑπάρχουσιν ἀλλοιώσεις τινὲς οὖσαι, ἡ δὲ φαντασία καὶ ἡ |19| νόησις τὴν τῶν πραγμάτων ἔχουσιν δύναμιν· τρόπον γάρ τινα |20| τὸ εἶδος τὸ νοούμενον τὸ τοῦ θερμοῦ ἢ ψυχροῦ ἢ ἡδέος ἢ φοβε|21|ροῦ τοιοῦτον τυγχάνει ὂν οἷόν περ καὶ τῶν πραγμάτων ἕκα|22|στον, διὸ καὶ φρίττουσιν καὶ φοβοῦνται νοήσαντες μόνον. ταῦ|23|τα δὲ πάντα πάθη καὶ ἀλλοιώσεις εἰσίν. ἀλλοιουμένων δὲ |24| ἐν τῶι σώματι τὰ μὲν μείζω τὰ δὲ ἐλάττω γίνεται. ὅτι δὲ |25| μικρὰ μεταβολὴ γιγνομένη ἐν ἀρχῆι μεγάλας καὶ πολλὰς |26| ποιεῖ διαφορὰς ἄπωθεν, οὐκ ἄδηλον· οἷον τοῦ οἴακος ἀκαρι|27|αῖόν τι μεθισταμένου πολλὴ ἡ τῆς πρώρας γίνεται μετάστα|28|σις. ἔτι δὲ κατὰ θερμότητα ἢ ψῦξιν ἢ κατ' ἄλλο τι τοι|29|οῦτο πάθος ὅταν γένηται ἀλλοίωσις περὶ τὴν καρδίαν |30| καὶ ἐν ταύτηι ἐν ἀναισθήτωι μορίωι, πολλὴν |31| ποιεῖ τοῦ σώματος διαφορὰν ἐρυθήμασιν καὶ ὠχρότησιν, καὶ |32| φρίκαις καὶ τρόμοις καὶ τοῖς τούτων ἐναντίοις.

8

|33| Ἀρχὴ μὲν οὖν, ὥσπερ εἴρηται, τῆς κινήσεως τὸ ἐν τῶι |34| πρακτῶι διωκτόν τε καὶ φευκτόν· ἐξ ἀνάγκης δὲ ἀκολουθεῖ τῆι |35| νοήσει καὶ τῆι φαντασίαι αὐτῶν θερμότης καὶ ψῦξις· τὸ |36| μὲν γὰρ λυπηρὸν φευκτόν, τὸ δὲ ἡδὺ διωκτόν. ἀλλὰ λαν|37|θάνει περὶ τὰ μικρὰ τοῦτο συμβαῖνον, ἔστιν δὲ τὰ λυπηρὰ |702ᵃ1| καὶ ἡδέα πάντα σχεδὸν μετὰ ψύξεώς τινος καὶ θερμότητος. |2| τοῦτο δὲ δῆλον ἐκ τῶν παθημάτων. θάρρη γὰρ καὶ φόβοι |3| καὶ ἀφροδισιασμοὶ καὶ τὰ ἄλλα τὰ σωματικὰ λυπηρὰ καὶ |4| ἡδέα τὰ μὲν κατὰ μόριον μετὰ θερμότητος καὶ ψύξεώς ἐστιν, |5| τὰ δὲ καθ' ὅλον τὸ σῶμα·

701ᵇ13–702ᵃ10 reddit Al. 76.18–78.2, (unde Mich. 114.27–115.25 et 119.15–120.7)

701ᵇ13–14 ἔλαττον καὶ μεῖζον β : μεῖζον καὶ ἔλαττον α || 14 γίνεσθαι α : γενέσθαι β || 15 <καὶ συστελλομένων> inserui | πνεῦμα καὶ βΕ : πάλιν συστελλομένων διὰ γ || 21 ὂν βΕ : om. γ || 22 μόνον βγ : om. Ε || 27 ἢ βΕ Al. : om. γ || 28–29 τοιοῦτο ΕBᵉ : τοιοῦτον cett. || 30 καὶ] εἰ καὶ Al. | ἐν Al. : κατὰ μέγεθος βΕ : κατὰ μέγεθος ἐν γ || 34 τε Al. : om. ω || 702ᵃ1 ἡδέα α Al. : τὰ ἡδέα β || 3 τὰ ἄλλα τὰ β : τὰ ἄλλα α || 4 καὶ β : ἢ α

|7| For they have organs of that sort, with the nature of sinews and the nature of bones, the ones like the wood and iron in the former case, and the others—sinews—like the cables; they are moved when these things are untied and unfastened. |10| Well, within the automatic theatres and wagons there is no alteration taking place, since if the inside wheels were to become smaller and then greater, then the same thing would still be moved in a circle. |13| But in an animal the same thing can become smaller and bigger and change forms, when the parts grow <and contract>, through heat and pneuma and cold, i.e. by alteration. |16| These alterations are caused by appearances and perceptions and thoughts. |17| For perceptions immediately have their being as alterations of a certain type, but appearance and thought have the power of their objects. |19| For somehow or other, the form of something hot or cold or sweet or frightening, when held in thought, just then is in its being like the things themselves, which is why merely thinking about them makes us shudder and get scared. |22| All these are affections and alterations. |23| Of the things which are altered in the body, some get bigger and some get smaller. |24| But that a small change at the beginning makes several big differences down the line is no mystery; for instance, with a somewhat fleeting shift of the rudder comes a big shift of the prow. |28| Again, whenever there is an alteration on the basis of heating or cooling or some other such affection around the heart and in some imperceptible part within it, it makes a considerable difference to the body, causing blushings and palings, and shiverings and shudderings and their opposites.

8

|33| So then, the thing to be pursued or avoided in the domain of what is achievable in action is an origin of motion, as has been said. |34| But warming and cooling necessarily follow the thought and appearance of those things, for the painful is to be avoided and the pleasant to be pursued. |36| But this happens around the small parts without the subject noticing, and, roughly speaking, painful and pleasant things are all accompanied by some cooling and warming. |702ᵃ2| This is clear from affections. For feelings of boldness and fear and sexual arousal and the other painful and pleasant bodily things occur sometimes in some particular part accompanied by warming and chilling, and sometimes in the whole body.

μνῆμαι δὲ καὶ ἐλπίδες, οἷον |6| εἰδώλοις χρώμεναι τοῖς τοιούτοις, ὁτὲ μὲν ἧττον ὁτὲ δὲ |7| μᾶλλον αἴτιαι τῶν αὐτῶν εἰσιν. ὥστε εὐλόγως ἤδη δημιουρ|8|γεῖται τὰ ἐντὸς καὶ τὰ περὶ τὰς ἀρχὰς τῶν ὀργανικῶν μο|9|ρίων μεταβάλλοντα ἐκ πεπηγότων ὑγρὰ καὶ ἐξ ὑγρῶν |10| πεπηγότα καὶ μαλακὰ καὶ σκληρὰ ἐξ ἀλλήλων. τούτων |11| δὲ συμβαινόντων τὸν τρόπον τοῦτον καὶ ἐπὶ τοῦ παθητικοῦ καὶ ἐπὶ τοῦ |12| ποιητικοῦ τοιαύτην ἐχόντων τὴν φύσιν οἵαν πολλαχῆι εἰρή|13|καμεν, ὁπόταν συμβῆι ὥστ' εἶναι τὸ μὲν ποιητικὸν τὸ δὲ |14| παθητικόν, καὶ μηθὲν ἀπολείπηι αὐτῶν ἑκάτερον τῶν ἐν τῶι |15| λόγωι, εὐθὺς τὸ μὲν ποιεῖ τὸ δὲ πάσχει. διὰ τοῦτο ἅμα |16| ὡς εἰπεῖν νοεῖ ὅτι πορευτέον καὶ πορεύεται, ἐὰν μή τι ἐμ|17|ποδίζηι ἕτερον. τὰ μὲν γὰρ ὀργανικὰ μέρη παρασκευάζει |18| ἐπιτηδείως ἔχειν τὰ πάθη, ἡ δὲ ὄρεξις τὰ πάθη, τὴν δὲ ὄρεξιν ἡ |19| φαντασία· αὕτη δὲ γίγνεται ἢ διὰ νοήσεως ἢ δι' αἰσθήσεως. |20| ἅμα δὲ καὶ ταχὺ διὰ τὸ <τὸ> ποιητικὸν καὶ παθητικὸν τῶν πρὸς |21| ἄλληλα εἶναι τὴν φύσιν.

τὸ δὲ κινοῦν πρῶτον τὸ ζῶιον ἀν|22|άγκη εἶναι ἔν τινι ἀρχῆι. ἡ δὲ καμπὴ ὅτι ἐστὶν τοῦ μὲν |23| ἀρχὴ τοῦ δὲ τελευτή, εἴρηται. διὸ καὶ ἔστιν μὲν ὡς ἑνί, ἔστιν |24| δὲ ὡς δυσὶ χρῆται ἡ φύσις αὐτῆι. ὅταν γὰρ κινῆται ἐντεῦ|25|θεν, ἀνάγκη τὸ μὲν ἠρεμεῖν τῶν σημείων τῶν ἐσχάτων, τὸ |26| δὲ κινεῖσθαι· ὅτι γὰρ πρὸς ἠρεμοῦν δεῖ ἀπερείδεσθαι τὸ κι|27|νοῦν, εἴρηται πρότερον. κινεῖται μὲν οὖν καὶ οὐ κινεῖ τὸ ἔσχα|28|τον τοῦ βραχίονος. τῆς δ' ἐν τῶι ὠλεκράνωι κάμψεως τὸ μὲν |29| κινεῖ καὶ κινεῖται τὸ ἐν αὐτῶι τῶι ὅλωι κινουμένωι, ἀλλ' ἀνάγκη δ<ὴ> εἶναί τι |30| καὶ ἀκίνητον, ὃ δή φαμεν δυνάμει μὲν ἓν σημεῖον |31| ἐνεργείαι δὲ γίνεσθαι δύο· ὥστ' εἰ τὸ ζῶιον ἦν ὁ βραχίων, ἐν|32|ταῦθα ἄν που ἦν ἡ ἀρχὴ τῆς ψυχῆς ἡ κινοῦσα. ἐπεὶ δὲ ἐνδέ|33|χεται καὶ πρὸς τὴν χεῖρα ἔχειν τι οὕτως τῶν ἀψύχων – οἷον |34| εἰ κινοίη τὴν βακτηρίαν ἐν τῆι χειρί –, φανερὸν ὅτι οὐκ ἂν εἴη |35| ἐν οὐδετέρωι ἡ ψυχὴ τῶν ἐσχάτων, οὔτ' ἐν τῶι ἐσχάτωι τοῦ |36| κινουμένου οὔτ' ἐν τῆι ἑτέραι ἀρχῆι. καὶ γὰρ τὸ ξύλον ἔχει καὶ |702ᵇ1| ἀρχὴν καὶ τέλος πρὸς τὴν χεῖρα. ὥστε διά γε τοῦτο, εἰ μὴ καὶ |2| ἐν τῆι βακτηρίαι ἡ κινοῦσα ἀπὸ τῆς ψυχῆς ἀρχὴ ἔνεστιν, οὐδ' |3| ἐν τῆι χειρί· ὁμοίως γὰρ ἔχει καὶ τὸ ἄκρον τῆς χειρὸς πρὸς |4| τὸν καρπόν, καὶ τοῦτο τὸ μόριον πρὸς τὸ ὠλέκρανον.

702ᵃ12–13 πολλαχῆι εἰρήκαμεν: cf. imprimis *Metaph.* Θ 5, *GC* I, 7–9

702ᵃ11 καὶ ἐπὶ τοῦ… καὶ ἐπὶ τοῦ β : καὶ ἔτι τοῦ… καὶ α || 12 πολλαχῆι β : πολλαχοῦ α || 13 ὥστ' εἶναι α : ὡς τείνει β || 14 ἑκάτερον α : ἑκατέρω β || 15 τοῦτο β : τοῦτο δὲ α || 18 ἔχειν β : om. α || 20 τὸ <τὸ> θ, Bonitz : τὸ cett. || 22 ἐστὶν τοῦ μὲν β : μέν ἐστι τοῦ μὲν α (unde μέν ἐστιν E) || 28 ὠλεκράνωι βE NLCᵃ : ὠλεκράνω cett. || 29 κινεῖ καὶ κινεῖται β : κινεῖται α | ἀλλ' β : om. α | δ<ὴ> εἶναί τι dedi : δ' εἶναί τι γβ : δ' εἶναι τινὰ E || 30 καὶ α : om. β | ἓν dedi : ἓν εἶναι ω || 31 ὁ β : om. α || 702ᵇ1 εἰ μὴ καὶ β : εἰ μὴ α || 4 μόριον β : μέρος α | ὠλέκρανον βE NCᵃ : ὠλέκρανον cett.

|5| But memories and anticipations, using such things as images, are causes of them, sometimes to a lesser extent and sometimes to a greater. |7| So it stands to reason that the interior regions and the ones around the origins of the parts which are suited to be instruments, are made as they are, so as to change from solidified to liquid and from liquid to solidified, alternating between soft and hard. |11| Since these things happen in this way both in the active and in the passive thing, both having such a nature as we have said in many places, whenever it comes about that there is something active and something passive, and neither of them falls short in any way of what is in their definition, immediately the one acts and the other is acted upon. |15| Because of this, something thinks that it should move forwards, and actually moves forwards, simultaneously, so to speak, so long as nothing else gets in the way. |17| For the affections prepare the parts suited to be instruments to be in an appropriate condition, desire prepares the affections, and appearance desire. |19| But appearance comes about either through thought or through perception. |20| And this happens simultaneously and swiftly because of the fact that <the> active and passive are among the things related to each other by nature.

|21| But that which primarily moves the animal must be located in some origin. |22| But it has already been stated that the joint is of one thing the origin and of something else the end-point. |23| That's also why nature uses it in a way as one thing, in a way as two. |24| For whenever the animal is moved from the joint, one of these two end-points must remain still and the other must be moved. |26| For the thing that causes motion should press against something at rest, as has been stated before. |27| Now, the extremity of the forearm [i.e. the wrist] is moved but does not cause motion. |28| Rather, one part of the joint in the elbow causes motion and is moved, namely the part in the whole which is moved. |29| And of course, there has to be at least *something* unmoved, too, and accordingly we say the elbow becomes something which is potentially one point, but in actuality two. |31| So if the animal were the forearm, the motion-causing origin of the soul would be in the elbow. |32| But since in fact it is possible for something inanimate to be related in just this way to the hand, e.g. if someone were to cause motion to the stick in his hand, |34| it is clear that the soul would be in neither of the end-points, neither in the [touched] end of the moved thing nor in the [touching] end-point of the hand. |36| For the wood too has both an origin in the hand and an end-point touching the hand. |$702^{b}1$| The result is that, on this account at any rate, if the motion-causing origin from the soul is not located in the stick, it is not located in the hand either. |3| For the main part of the hand has a similar relationship to the wrist as does that part to the elbow.

οὐθὲν γὰρ |5| διαφέρει τὰ προσπεφυκότα τῶν μή· γίγνεται γὰρ ὥσπερ |6| ἀφαιρετὸν μέρος ἡ βακτηρία. ἀνάγκη ἄρα ἐν μηδεμιᾶι εἶ|7|ναι ἀρχῆι ἤ ἐστιν ἄλλου τελευτή, μηδὲ εἴ τί ἐστιν ἕτερον |8| ἐκείνου ἐξωτέρω, οἷον τοῦ ἐσχάτου τοῦ μὲν τῆς βακτηρίας ἐν τῆι |9| χειρὶ ἡ ἀρχή, τούτου δὲ ἐν τῶι καρπῶι. εἰ δὲ μηδ' ἐν τῆι |10| χειρί, ὅτι ἀνωτέρω ἔτι, ἡ ἀρχὴ οὐδ' ἐνταῦθα· ἔτι γὰρ τοῦ |11| ὀλεκράνου μένοντος κινεῖται ἅπαν τὸ κάτω συνεχές.

9

|12| Ἐπεὶ δὲ ὁμοίως ἔχει ἀπὸ τῶν ἀριστερῶν καὶ ἀπὸ τῶν |13| δεξιῶν, καὶ ἅμα τὰ ἐναντία κινεῖται, ὥστε μὴ εἶναι τῶι ἠρε|14|μεῖν τὸ δεξιὸν κινεῖσθαι τὸ ἀριστερὸν μηδ' αὖ τῶι τοῦτο ἐκεῖνο, |15| ἀεὶ δ' ἐν τῶι ἀνωτέρωι ἀμφοτέρων ἡ ἀρχή, ἀνάγκη ἐν τῶι |16| μέσωι εἶναι τὴν ἀρχὴν τῆς ψυχῆς τῆς κινούσης· ἀμφοτέρων |17| γὰρ τῶν ἐσχάτων τὸ μέσον ἔσχατον. ὁμοίως δ' ἔχει πρὸς τὰς |18| κινήσεις τοῦτο καὶ τὰς ἀπὸ τοῦ ἄνω καὶ κάτω οἷον τὰς |19| ἀπὸ τῆς κεφαλῆς, <καὶ> τὰς ἀπὸ τῆς ῥάχεως τοῖς ἔχουσιν |20| ῥάχιν. καὶ εὐλόγως δὲ τοῦτο συμβέβηκεν· καὶ γὰρ τὸ αἰ|21|σθητικὸν ἐνταῦθα εἶναί φαμεν ὥστε ἀλλοιουμένου διὰ τὴν αἴ|22|σθησιν τοῦ τόπου τοῦ περὶ τὴν ἀρχὴν καὶ μεταβάλλοντος τὰ |23| ἐχόμενα συμμεταβάλλει ἐκτεινόμενά τε καὶ συναγόμενα |24| τὰ μόρια, ὥστ' ἐξ ἀνάγκης διὰ ταῦτα γίγνεσθαι τὴν κίνησιν |25| τοῖς ζώιοις. τὸ δὲ μέσον τοῦ σώματος μέρος δυνάμει μὲν ἕν |26| ἐνεργείαι δὲ ἀνάγκη γίνεσθαι πλείω· καὶ γὰρ ἅμα κινεῖται |27| τὰ κῶλα ἀπὸ τῆς ἀρχῆς, καὶ θατέρου ἠρεμοῦντος θάτερον |28| κινεῖται. λέγω δὲ οἷον ἐπὶ τῆς ΑΒΓ τὸ Β κινεῖται, κινεῖ |29| δὲ τὸ Α. ἀλλὰ μὴν δεῖ γέ τι ἠρεμεῖν, εἰ μέλλει τὸ μὲν |30| κινήσεσθαι τὸ δὲ κινεῖν. ἐν ἄρα δυνάμει ὂν τὸ Α ἐνεργείαι δύο |31| ἔσται, ὥστε ἀνάγκη μὴ στιγμὴν ἀλλὰ μέγεθός τι εἶναι. |32| ἀλλὰ μὴν ἐνδέχεται καὶ τὸ Γ ἅμα κινεῖσθαι τῶι Β, ὥστε ἀν|33|άγκη ἀμφοτέρας τὰς ἀρχὰς τὰς ἐν τῶι Α κινουμένας κινεῖν.

702ᵇ12–20 respicit Al. 97,25–98,1 Bruns

702ᵇ8 τοῦ ἐσχάτου τοῦ μὲν τῆς βακτηρίας dedi : τοῦ μὲν τῆς βακτηρίας τοῦ ἐσχάτου **β** : τοῦ μὲν τῆς βακτηρίας ἐσχάτου **a** ‖ **11** ὀλεκράνου **βE** Na.c.Cᵃ : ὠλεκράνου cett. ‖ **14** μηδ' αὖ **a** : μὴ δὲ **β** ‖ **15** τῶι ἀνωτέρωι E : iota utrumque codices reliqui fere omnes more suo omittunt | ἡ ἀρχή **βγ** : ἀρχή E ‖ **17** ἐσχάτων **β** : ἄκρων **a** ‖ **19** καὶ coni. **θ** : πρὸς **ω** | τὰς **βγ** : τὰ E ‖ **23** συμμεταβάλλει **βγ** : συμμεταβάλλειν E ‖ **25** ἕν **a** : om. **β** ‖ **28–36** diagramma servavit **γ**(CᵃOᵈZᵃ) ‖ **29** ἠρεμεῖν **a** : ἠρεμοῦν **β** ‖ **30** ὂν τὸ Α **βE** : ὄντα τὰ ΑΕ **γ** ‖ **31** ἔσται **a** : ἐστίν **β** ‖ **32** καὶ **β** : om. **a** | κινεῖσθαι τῶι Β **β** : τῶι Β κινεῖσθαι **a**

|4| For appendages grown from the body aren't in any way different from those which aren't; for the stick gets to be like a part of the body, albeit separate. |6| And so, necessarily, the motion-causing origin is in no origin which is the end of something else, not even if there is something other than it more external to it, as if, for instance, the end of the stick has its origin in the hand, and the end of the latter has it in the wrist. |9| But if the origin is not in the hand, because it is still higher up, nor will it be in the wrist, for when the elbow is stationary all of what is below it, and continuous with it, is still moved.

9

|12| But since things are the same with the right-hand parts and the left-hand parts, and since the opposite sides are moved simultaneously—so that it is not possible for the left to be moved in virtue of the right staying still, nor vice versa—and since at every step the origin is in the upper one of both end-points [in the joints], it is necessary that the origin of the motion-causing soul must be in the middle. |16| For the middle serves as an end-point for the end-points on either side. |17| This is also the same with motions both from above and below (for instance the ones from the head), and with the ones from the backbone (in the case of those which have a backbone). |20| And it is reasonable that this be so. |20| For we say that the organ of perception is also there, so that when the area around the origin is altered because of sense-perception, and changes, the neighbouring parts change along with it, and get both stretched out and compressed, so that by necessity motion comes about in animals because of these things. |25| And the middle part of the body necessarily comes to be something which is potentially one and in actuality many. |26| For it is both the case that the limbs are simultaneously moved from the origin, and also the case that when one is moved the other is at rest. |28| I mean for example in the case of the figure ABC, B is moved but A causes the motion. |29| But now there must be something at rest, if one is to be moved and the other cause movement. |30| And so A, while being one potentially, will be two in actuality, so that necessarily it is not a geometrical point but some magnitude. |32| But now C too can be moved at the same time as B, so that necessarily both origins in A are moved and cause movement.

|34| δεῖ τι ἄρα εἶναι παρὰ ταύτας ἕτερον, τὸ κινοῦν καὶ μὴ κινού|35|μενον· ἀπερείδοιντο μὲν γὰρ ἂν τὰ ἄκρα καὶ αἱ ἀρχαὶ αἱ |36| ἐν τῶι Α πρὸς ἀλλήλας κινουμένων, ὥσπερ ἂν εἴ τινες τὰ |703ᵃ1| νῶτα ἀντερείδοντες κινοῖεν τὰ σκέλη. ἀλλὰ τὸ κινοῦν ἄμ|2|φω ἀναγκαῖον <ἓν> εἶναι, τοῦτο δέ ἐστιν ἡ ψυχή, ἕτερον μὲν οὖσα |3| τοῦ μεγέθους τοῦ τοιούτου, ἐν τούτωι δ' οὖσα.

10

|4| Κατὰ μὲν οὖν τὸν λόγον τὸν λέγοντα τὴν αἰτίαν τῆς |5| κινήσεως ἐστὶν ἡ ὄρεξις τὸ μέσον, ὃ κινεῖ κινούμενον· ἐν δὲ |6| τοῖς ἐμψύχοις σώμασιν δεῖ τι εἶναι σῶμα τοιοῦτον. τὸ μὲν |7| οὖν κινούμενον μὲν μὴ πεφυκὸς δὲ κινεῖν δύναται πάσχειν |8| κατ' ἀλλοτρίαν δύναμιν· τὸ δὲ κινοῦν ἀναγκαῖον ἔχειν τινὰ |9| δύναμιν καὶ ἰσχύν. πάντα δὲ φαίνεται τὰ ζῷα καὶ ἔχοντα |10| πνεῦμα σύμφυτον καὶ ἰσχύοντα τούτωι. τίς μὲν οὖν ἡ σωτη|11|ρία τοῦ συμφύτου πνεύματος, εἴρηται ἐν ἄλλοις. τοῦτο δὲ |12| πρὸς τὴν ἀρχὴν τὴν ψυχικὴν ἔοικεν ὁμοίως ἔχειν ὥσπερ τὸ |13| ἐν ταῖς καμπαῖς σημεῖον, τὸ κινοῦν καὶ κινούμενον, πρὸς τὸ |14| ἀκίνητον. ἐπεὶ δ' ἡ ἀρχὴ τοῖς μὲν ἐν τῆι καρδίαι τοῖς δ' ἐν |15| τῶι ἀνάλογον, διὰ τοῦτο καὶ τὸ πνεῦμα τὸ σύμφυτον ἐν|16|ταῦθα φαίνεται ὄν. πότερον μὲν οὖν ταὐτόν ἐστι τὸ πνεῦμα |17| ἀεὶ ἢ γίγνεται ἀεὶ ἕτερον, ἔστω ἄλλος λόγος· (ὁ αὐτὸς γὰρ |18| ἐστιν καὶ περὶ τῶν ἄλλων μορίων)· φαίνεται δ' εὐφυῶς ἔχον |19| πρὸς τὸ κινητικὸν εἶναι καὶ παρέχειν ἰσχύν. τὰ δὲ ἔργα τῆς |20| κινήσεως ὦσις καὶ ἕλξις, ὥστε δεῖ τὸ ὄργανον αὐξάνεσθαί |21| τε δύνασθαι καὶ συστέλλεσθαι. τοιαύτη δέ ἐστιν ἡ τοῦ πνεύ|22|ματος φύσις· καὶ γὰρ ἀβίαστος συστελλομένη <τε καὶ ἐκτεινομένη> καὶ βίαι <ἑλκ>τικὴ |23| καὶ ὠστικὴ διὰ τὴν αὐτὴν αἰτίαν· καὶ ἔχει βάρος πρὸς |24| τὰ πυρώδη καὶ κουφότητα πρὸς τὰ ἐναντία.

703ᵃ10–11 τίς μὲν—ἄλλοις] haec verba ad librum περὶ τροφῆς spectant secundum Mich. et Rose; ad librum De respiratione secundum cod. Vat. V², ad incerti auctoris librum De spiritu secundum Zeller et Bonitz || **14–16** respicit Al. 77,10–13 Bruns || **19–22** respicit Al. 77,5–6 Bruns

---

703ᵃ2 ἀναγκαῖον <ἓν> εἶναι Γ1 Α : ἀναγκαῖον εἶναι ω || **10–11** τίς μὲν—ἄλλοις] num genuina sint dubitat Jaeger cl. ᵃ16–17 (πότερον—λόγος) || **17** ἕτερον, ἔστω ἄλλος λόγος a : ἕτερος λόγος, ἄλλος β || **22** συστελλομένη <τε καὶ ἐκτεινομένη> Farquharson : συστελλομένη ω | βίαι <ἑλκ>τικὴ dedi : βιαστικὴ ω : tractiva G, unde ἑλκτικὴ Farquharson || **23** βάρος β : καὶ βάρος a

|34| And so there must be something else over and above these, something which causes movement yet isn't moved. |35| For the limbs and, in particular, their origins in A, when movement takes place, would press one against the other, just as if some people were pressing their backs together and moving their legs. |**703**ª1| But it is necessary that the thing which moves both things is <one>, and that is the soul, which is different from a magnitude of that sort, but is in it.

10

|4| Now on the basis of the account which states the cause of motion, desire is the intermediate item, the one which causes movement while being moved. |5| But in animate bodies, there should be some body of that sort. |6| Well, that which is moved but is not of such a nature as to cause movement can be affected on the basis of a different kind of power. |8| But that which causes movement must have some power and strength. |9| But all animals clearly both have some connate pneuma and are strong because of it. |10| Well, what it takes to preserve the connate pneuma has already been stated in other works. |11| But it is likely that this stands in a similar relation to the psychic origin as the point in the joints, the one which causes movement and is moved, does to the unmoved. |14| But since the origin for some animals is in the heart, and for others is in something merely analogous, for this reason the connate pneuma clearly is there too. |16| Now let the question of whether the pneuma is always the same or is constantly being regenerated be the subject of another enquiry. |17| For it is the same enquiry as for the other parts too. |18| But clearly it is disposed to be naturally suited to causing motion and conferring strength. |19| The effects of this motion are pushing and pulling, whence it follows that the organ must be capable both of being increased and of being contracted. |21| Such is the nature of the pneuma. |22| For it is being both contracted <and expanded> without force, and capable of pulling and pushing by force because of the same cause. |23| And it is both heavy compared to fiery things and light compared to the opposite things.

δεῖ δὲ τὸ μέλ|25|λον κινεῖν μὴ ἀλλοιώσει τοιοῦτον εἶναι· κρατεῖται γὰρ κατὰ |26| τὴν ὑπεροχὴν τὰ φυσικὰ σώματα ὑπ' ἀλλήλων, τὸ μὲν κοῦ|27|φον κάτω ὑπὸ τοῦ βαρυτέρου ἀπονικώμενον, τὸ δὲ βαρὺ |28| ἄνω ὑπὸ τοῦ κουφοτέρου. ὧι μὲν οὖν κινεῖ κινουμένωι μορίωι ἡ |29| ψυχή, εἴρηται, καὶ δι' ἣν αἰτίαν. ὑποληπτέον δὲ συνεστά|30|ναι τὸ ζῶιον ὥσπερ πόλιν εὐνομουμένην. ἔν τε γὰρ τῆι πό|31|λει ὅταν ἅπαξ στῆι ἡ τάξις, οὐθὲν δεῖ κεχωρισμένου μο|32|νάρχου, ὃν δεῖ παρεῖναι παρ' ἕκαστον τῶν γινομένων, ἀλλ' |33| αὐτὸς ἕκαστος ποιεῖ τὰ αὑτοῦ ὡς τέτακται, καὶ γίνεται |34| τόδε μετὰ τόδε διὰ τὸ ἔθος· ἔν τε τοῖς ζώιοις τὸ αὐτὸ τοῦτο |35| διὰ τὴν φύσιν γίνεται καὶ τῶι πεφυκέναι ἕκαστον, οὕτω συ|36|στάντων, ποιεῖν τὸ αὑτοῦ ἔργον, ὥστε μηδὲν δεῖν ἐν ἑκάστωι |37| εἶναι ψυχήν, ἀλλ' ἔν τινι ἀρχῆι τοῦ σώματος οὔσης τὰ ἄλλα |703ᵇ1| ζῆν μὲν τῶι προσπεφυκέναι, ποιεῖν δὲ τὸ ἔργον τὸ ἑαυτῶν |2| διὰ τὴν φύσιν.

II

|3| Πῶς μὲν οὖν κινεῖται τὰς ἑκουσίους κινήσεις τὰ ζῶια, |4| καὶ διὰ τίνας αἰτίας, εἴρηται. κινεῖται δέ τινας καὶ ἀκου|5|σίους ἔνια τῶν μερῶν, τὰς δὲ πλείστας οὐχ ἑκουσίους. λέγω |6| δὲ ἀκουσίους μὲν οἷον τὴν τῆς καρδίας τε καὶ τὴν τοῦ αἰδοίου· |7| πολλάκις γὰρ φανέντος μέν τινος οὐ μέντοι κελεύσαντος τοῦ |8| νοῦ κινοῦνται. οὐχ ἑκουσίους δὲ οἷον ὕπνον καὶ ἐγρήγορ|9|σιν καὶ ἀναπνοήν, καὶ ὅσαι ἄλλαι τοιαῦταί εἰσιν· οὐθε|10|νὸς γὰρ τούτων κυρία ἁπλῶς ἐστιν οὔθ' ἡ φαντασία οὔθ' ἡ |11| ὄρεξις. ἀλλ' ἐπειδὴ ἀνάγκη ἀλλοιοῦσθαι τὰ ζῶια φυσικὴν |12| ἀλλοίωσιν, ἀλλοιουμένων δὲ τῶν μορίων τὰ μὲν αὐξάνεσθαι |13| τὰ δὲ φθίνειν, ὥστ' ἤδη κινεῖσθαι καὶ μεταβάλλειν τὰς |14| πεφυκυίας ἔχεσθαι μεταβολὰς ἀλλήλων, (αἰτίαι δὲ τῶν |15| κινήσεων θερμότητες καὶ ψύξεις αἵ τε θύραθεν καὶ |16| ἐντὸς ὑπάρχουσιν φυσικαί), καὶ αἱ παρὰ τὸν λόγον δὴ γι|17|νόμεναι κινήσεις τῶν ῥηθέντων μορίων ἀλλοιώσεως συμπε|18|σούσης γίγνονται. ἡ γὰρ νόησις καὶ ἡ φαντασία, ὥσπερ εἴ|19|ρηται πρότερον, τὰ ποιητικὰ τῶν παθημάτων προσφέρουσιν· |20| τὰ γὰρ εἴδη τῶν ποιητικῶν προσφέρουσιν. μάλιστα δὲ τῶν |21| μορίων ταῦτα ποιεῖ ἐπιδήλως διὰ τὸ ὥσπερ ζῶιον κεχω|22|ρισμένον ἑκάτερον εἶναι τῶν μορίων.

703ᵃ25–26 κρατεῖται... ὑπ' ἀλλήλων β : κρατεῖ... ἀλλήλων α ‖ 28 τοῦ α : om. β ‖ 36 ποιεῖν α : ποιεῖ β ‖ 703ᵇ1 ἑαυτῶν β : αὑτῶν α ‖ 7 μέν... οὐ μέντοι β : μέν om. α ‖ 8 ἑκουσίους βγ : ἑκουσίως E ‖ 8–9 καὶ ἐγρήγορσιν α : ἐγρήγορσιν β ‖ 12 αὐξάνεσθαι β : αὔξεσθαι α ‖ 15 θερμότητες καὶ β : θερμότητές τε καὶ | αἵ τε (relat.)... καὶ β : αἵ τε (artic.)... καὶ αἱ α ‖ 16 ὑπάρχουσιν β : ὑπάρχουσαι α | φυσικαί α : αἱ φυσικαί β

|24| Anything which is going to cause motion without alteration must be like this. |25| For natural bodies are overcome by one another on the basis of which one predominates, the light being overpowered downwards by the heavier, and the heavy overpowered upwards by the lighter. |28| It has now been stated what the part is through whose movement the soul causes motion, and through what cause. |29| But the animal must be supposed to be constituted like a well-governed city. |30| For in the city, as soon as order is established, there is no need for a separate monarch who must be present at all the goings-on, but each part itself does its own thing as instructed, and this follows that because of habit. |34| In animals, the same thing comes about because of their nature and the fact that each of the parts is constituted so as to be naturally suited to performing its own task, with the result that there is no need of soul in each part, but it resides in some bodily origin and the other parts live by being naturally attached to that, and perform their own work because of nature.

II

|703^{b}3| It has been stated, then, how animals are moved in voluntary motions, and by what causes. |4| Some of their parts, however, are also moved in certain motions against their will, as well as, in most cases, non-voluntary motions. |5| I call 'against their will' motions such as that of the heart and private parts. |7| For often when something appears to the subject, they are moved although thought has forbidden action. |8| But I call 'non-voluntary' such motions as sleep and waking up and breathing, and any others like this. |9| For none of these is straightforwardly controlled by appearance or desire. |11| But since animals must undergo natural alteration, and some of those altered parts grow and some shrink, with the result that already they are moved and change with changes that naturally are continuous with one another (the causes of these changes are heatings and chillings which naturally occur both from outside and within), also the motions of the aforementioned parts which come about against reason come about when alteration has occurred. |18| For thought and appearance, as previously stated, bring along things which produce affections. |20| For they bring along the forms of things which produce them. |20| Most prominently amongst the parts, those previously mentioned clearly produce motions because each of the parts is like a separate animal.

τούτου δ' αἴτιον ὅτι ἔχου|23|σιν ὑγρότητα ζωτικήν. ἡ μὲν οὖν καρδία φανερὸν δι' ἣν αἰ|24|τίαν· τὰς γὰρ ἀρχὰς ἔχει τῶν αἰσθήσεων· τὸ δὲ μόριον τὸ γεν|25|νητικὸν ὅτι τοιοῦτόν ἐστιν, σημεῖον· καὶ γὰρ ἐξέρχεται ἐξ |26| αὐτοῦ ὥσπερ ζῶιόν τι ἡ τοῦ σπέρματος δύναμις. αἱ δὲ κι|27|νήσεις τῆι τε ἀρχῆι ἀπὸ τῶν μορίων καὶ τοῖς μορίοις ἀπὸ |28| τῆς ἀρχῆς εὐλόγως συμβαίνουσιν. καὶ πρὸς ἄλληλα δὲ οὕτως |29| ἀφικνοῦνται· δεῖ γὰρ νοῆσαι τὸ Α ἀρχήν. αἱ οὖν κινήσεις |30| καθ' ἕκαστον στοιχεῖον τῶν ἐπιγεγραμμένων ἐπὶ τὴν ἀρχὴν |31| ἀφικνοῦνται καὶ ἀπὸ τῆς ἀρχῆς κινουμένης καὶ μεταβαλ|32|λούσης, ἐπειδὴ πολλὰ δυνάμει ἐστίν· ἡ μὲν τοῦ Β ἀρχὴ |33| ἐπὶ τὸ Β, ἡ δὲ τοῦ Γ ἐπὶ τὸ Γ, ἡ δὲ ἀμφοῖν ἐπ' ἄμφω. |34| ἀπὸ δὲ τοῦ Ε ἐπὶ τὸ Γ τῶι ἀπὸ μὲν τοῦ Ε ἐπὶ τὸ Α |35| ἐλθεῖν ὡς ἐπ' ἀρχήν, ἀπὸ δὲ τοῦ Α ἐπὶ τὸ Γ ὡς ἀπ' ἀρ|36|χῆς. ὅτι δὲ ὁτὲ μὲν τὰ αὐτὰ νοησάντων γίνεται ἡ κίνησις ἡ |37| παρὰ τὸν λόγον ἐν τοῖς μορίοις, ὁτὲ δ' οὔ, αἴτιον τὸ ὁτὲ |704ᵃ1| μὲν ἐνυπάρχειν τὴν παθητικὴν ὕλην ὁτὲ δὲ μὴ τοσαύτην ἢ |2| τοιαύτην. |3| περὶ μὲν οὖν τῶν μορίων ἑκάστου τῶν ζώιων, καὶ περὶ |704ᵇ1| ψυχῆς, ἔτι δὲ καὶ περὶ αἰσθήσεως καὶ ὕπνου καὶ μνήμης καὶ |2| τῆς κοινῆς κινήσεως, εἰρήκαμεν τὰς αἰτίας· λοιπὸν δὲ περὶ |3| γενέσεως εἰπεῖν.

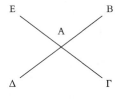

704ᵃ3 περὶ μὲν οὖν τῶν μορίων ἑκάστου τῶν ζώιων: PA ‖ **ᵃ3–ᵇ1** καὶ περὶ ψυχῆς: de An. ‖ **ᵇ1** περὶ αἰσθήσεως: Sens. | καὶ ὕπνου: Somn. Vig., Insomn., Div. Somn. | καὶ μνήμης: Mem. ‖ **1–2** καὶ τῆς κοινῆς κινήσεως: MA ‖ **2–3** λοιπὸν δὲ περὶ γενέσεως εἰπεῖν: GA

703ᵇ22 τούτου **βγ** : τοῦτο Ε ‖ **24** τὰς γὰρ **βγ** : τὰς Ε ‖ **28** ἄλληλα δὲ **βγ** : ἀλλήλας Ε ‖ **29–36** diagramma servaverunt et **β**(Eʳ) et **γ**(A[ZᵃAnon.]CᵃOᵈ) ‖ **34** ἀπὸ δὲ τοῦ Ε dedi secundum diagramma : ἀπὸ δὲ τοῦ Β **ω** | τῶι **β**E : τὸ δ' **γ** | ἀπὸ μὲν τοῦ Ε dedi secundum diagramma : ἀπὸ μὲν τοῦ Β **ω** ‖ **36** ὅτι **βγ** : ἔτι Ε | τὰ αὐτὰ **β** : ταῦτα **α** ‖ **704ᵇ1** καὶ περὶ **β** : καὶ om. **α**

|22| The cause of this is that they have vital moisture. |23| Why the heart is like an animal is clear: for it holds the origins of sense-perceptions. |24| But there is also evidence that the reproductive part is of this kind. |25| For the potentiality which is seed also comes out of it, like some kind of animal. |26| Now it is reasonable that movements occur in the origin caused by the parts and in the parts caused by the origin. |28| Yet in this way the parts also reach one another: |29| For one should regard A as an origin. |29| Then with reference to each of the letters of the diagram, the movements come *to* the origin, and—when this is moved and changes—they proceed *from* the origin, since the latter is potentially many: the origin of B towards B, the origin of C towards C, and the origin of both towards both. |34| By contrast, the movement from E to C proceeds by going from E towards A *as* to an origin, and from A to C *as* from an origin. |36| And the cause of the fact that sometimes, even though you are thinking the same things, movement contrary to reason comes about in the parts, and sometimes not, is that sometimes the receptive matter is present in the right quantity or quality and sometimes not. |704ª3| So then, concerning the parts of each animal, and concerning soul, and again also concerning perception and sleep and memory and motion in general, we have stated the causes. |704ᵇ2| What remains is to speak about generation.

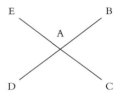

APPARATVS PLENIOR

TITVLVS

Tituli spurii a me deleti quem Andronicus ab operis initio derivasse videtur formae duae traduntur:

I

(ζώιων ante κινήσεως): ἀριστοτέλους περὶ ζώιων κινήσεως ω (ἀριστοτέλους περὶ τῆς τῶν ζώιων κινήσεως EʳOᵈS : περὶ ζώιων κινήσεως πρῶτον N² : ἀριστοτέλους περὶ ζώιων κινήσεων A[ZᵃAnon.(*Aristotelis de motibus animalium*)] : nil habent N¹Vᵖ¹) : Περὶ ζώιων κινήσεως γ' App. Hesych. (*Vita Hesych.* l. 178, p. 101 Dorandi) : ἐν τοῖς Περὶ ζώων κινήσεως Al. 97.26–27 Bruns : ἐν τῷ Περὶ ζώων κινήσεως Simp. *in Ph.* 1191.6–7 Diels : Περὶ ζώων κινήσεως edd.

II

(κινήσεως ante ζώιων): <περὶ> κινήσεως τῶν ζῴων <α'> / Ἀνατομῶν ζ' Ptolemaeus al-Ġarīb apud Ibn al-Qiftī 45.1–2 Lippert (كتابه فى حركة الحيوانات وتشريحها) ويسمّى قينيساوس طين زوأون أناطومن ٧ مقالات 'Liber eius de motu animalium et sectione eorum, et apellatur *qīnīsaʾūs ṭīn zūʾūn ʾanāṭūmun* 7 tractatūs') : Περὶ κινήσεως ζῴων Simp. *in Cael.* 398.20 Heiberg; *in Ph.* 670.1 Diels; Simp. (?) *in de An.* 301.18; 303.15 et 22 Hayduck; Phlp. *in Ph.* 2.9 Vitelli : Περὶ τῆς κινήσεως ζῴων Phlp. *in de An.* 157.21–22 Hayduck.

TEXTVS

Caput 1

698ᵃ1 τῆς τῶν ζώων κινήσεως β(BᵉEʳ OᵈSVᵖ) : κινήσεως τῆς τῶν ζώ(ι)ων E Cᵃ Mich.¹⁽ˢ⁾ 104.6 cf. G(*de motu autem eo qui animalium*) : κινήσεως τῶν ζώων ζ(NXHᵃLVᵍ ZᵃPBᵖMᵒ) : τῆς κινήσεως τῶν ζώων b | ζώιων E, qui iota adscriptum passim conservat : ζώων cett.; iota subscriptum hic illic praebent Cᵃ, Vᵖ, N, L, b || **1–2** αὐτῶν περὶ ἔκαστον β(BᵉEʳb) E : περὶ ἔκαστον αὐτῶν cett. (Mich.¹ 104.6–7) || **4–5** κινεῖσθαι] κινεῖσθε E : κοινεῖσθαι Bᵖ || **6** τῶν ζώιων] τῶν ζώντων κ(SVᵖ) : τὰ δὲ ἔρψει Mich.ᵖ 104.14–15 (ad librum *De incessu* spectans) ι(**A**[Anon.(cf. *reptilia*); deficit Zᵃ]PBᵖMᵒ) ‖ **7** οὖν] om. **β**(BᶜEʳ) ‖ **8** αὐτὸ αὐτὸ **β**(BᶜEʳb) : αὐτὸ αυτὸ E : αὐτὸ ἑαυτὸ cett., edd. ‖ **11** τίς] τί E ‖ **11–12** καθόλου] om. Mich.¹ 104.18 **μ**(PBᵖMᵒ) Jaeger ‖ **13–14** καὶ ἐφ' ὧν ἐφαρμόττειν οἰόμεθα δεῖν αὐτούς] cf. οὓς εἰ μὲν εὑρήσομεν ἐφαρμόζοντας τοῖς μερικοῖς, πιστεύομεν, εἰ δὲ μή, ἀποσειόμεθα Mich.ᴾ 104.25–26, unde *eas que conveniunt particularibus acceptamus et eas que non conveniunt particularibus abicimus* Alb. in marg. (cf. De Leemans 2011b LXXII) ‖ **14** ἐφαρμόττειν] ἐναρμόττειν Ea.c. ‖ **16** μὲν] μὲν οὖν E Bᵖ (cf. *igitur* Anon.) Jaeger Torraca Nussbaum ‖ **16–17** ἀεὶ . . . ἠρεμεῖ **β**(BᶜEʳb) : δεῖ . . . ἠρεμεῖν cett., edd. ‖ **22–24** diagramma servaverunt E Mich.(ORP) NL Zᵃ CᵃOᵈ necnon Bodl. Can. 107 (Bᵒ) aut ex Γ2 aut ex κ | diagrammatis formae traduntur tres, quarum primam et NCᵃZᵃOᵈ Mich.(P) praebent et Michael ante oculos habuit (cf. Mich.ᴾ 105.5: ἡ ΑΓ κίνησις), alteram E¹, tertiam Mich.(OR) L (tria tentamina) Bᵒ:

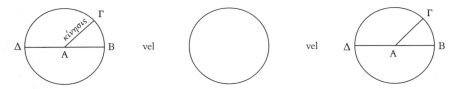

23 ἡ μὲν Α (scil. στιγμὴ) καὶ ἡ Δ (scil. στιγμή) **β**(BᶜEʳb OᵈSVᵖ) : ἡ μὲν Α καὶ Δ **α**(E NXHᵃLVᵍ ZᵃPBᵖMᵒ) : ἡ μὲν Α καὶ ἡ δέλτα Cᵃ, qui ἡ δέλτα post correcturam scripsit, ante correcturam autem ἡ Α scripsisse videtur (ad ᵃ23–24 καὶ . . . ἡ Α saliens ubi γίνοιτο omiserat iam ε) : ἡ μὲν ΑΔ Nussbaum ‖ **24** ἡ ΑΓ (scil. εὐθεῖα) fecit E² in supplendis lineis ᵃ24–25 (ubi καὶ Γ – εἶναι omiserat E¹), edd., cf. ἡ ΑΓ κίνησις Mich.ᴾ 105.5 : ἡ Α καὶ Γ ω : ἡ ΔΑΓ Wilson 1913, 137 ‖ **26** κινεῖσθαι] ἂν κινῆσθαι b : κινεῖται ι(**A**[ZᵃAnon.]PBᵖMᵒ) Bekker Nussbaum ‖ **27–698ᵇ1** δυνάμει καὶ ἐνεργείαι . . . διαιρεῖται **β**(BᶜEʳb Γ2[*dividitur* GR"]), *virtute et accidente . . . dividitur* Anon., cf. 698ᵃ20 μεταβάλλον δυνάμει καὶ ἐνεργείαι : δυνάμει καὶ ἐνεργείαι . . . διαιρετά **α** (> *potentia et actu . . . divisibile* G1 GR') edd. ‖ **698ᵇ1** γε **β**(BᶜEʳb) : om. cett., edd. | ἡ πρὸς ὃ E² (ἡ προς ὃ E¹) Jaeger Forster Louis Nussbaum : ἡ πρόσω **β**(BᶜEʳ) **μ**(PBᵖMᵒ), qui error a scriptione continua ΠΡΟΣΟ ortus esse videtur, cf. 698ᵇ14, 699ᵃ8, 700ᵃ19 : ἡ πρώτη **γ**(Γ1[*primum* scil. *principium* G] OᵈSVᵖ[ἡ om. et πρώτη ante ἀρχὴ¹ transp. Cᵃ]b) Torraca, unde ἡ ᾱ **ζ**(**A**[ZᵃAnon.(cf. *designatum per* Α Alb., scil. *principium*)]), quod in ἡ πρώτω corrupit **θ**(N) et om. **λ**(XHᵃLVᵍ) Bekker ‖ **3** ὀλέκρανον **β**(Eʳ[ὀλ. Bᶜb]) E Cᵃ N(ὀλ.), cf. Aristoph. *Pax* 443 (ἐκ τῶν ὀλεκράνων ἀκίδας ἐξαιρούμενον) : ὠλέκρανον cett., edd. ‖ **4** τὸ γόνυ] τοῦ γόνυ E ‖ **5** ἕκαστον δεῖ τι **β**(BᶜEʳb) : ἕκαστόν τι δεῖ (vel ἕκαστον τί δεῖ) cett., edd. ‖ **6** ἐστίν **β**(BᶜEʳ OᵈSVᵖ) E : ἔσται cett., edd.

Caput 2

698ᵇ8 ἡ ἐν] μὲν **β**(BᶜEʳ) | αὐτοῖς **β**(BᶜEʳb) **ι**(**A**[Zᵃ(cf. *in membris* Alb.)] P[ἡ ἐν αὐτῇ
Bᵖ]Mᵒ) : αὐτῶι **α**(E *Γ*ɪ NXHᵃLVᵍ CᵃOᵈSVᵖ) edd. ‖ **9** ἔξω **β**(BᶜEʳb *Γ*2) E :
ἔξωθεν cett., edd. ‖ **13–14** εἶναι – ἀκίνητον] om. Vᵍ ‖ **14** τι (vel τί) **β**(BᶜEʳb
OᵈSVᵖ) Cᵃ **ι**(**A**[*aliquid* Anon.] PBᵖMᵒ) : om. E *Γ*ɪ(G) **θ**(NXHᵃL[deficit Vᵍ]) Zᵃ |
πρὸς ὅ] προσὸ E; de hac scriptione cf. 698ᵇ1, 699ᵃ8, 700ᵃ19 ‖ **15–16** τοῖς μυσὶ
τοῖς ἐν τῆι πίττηι dedi : τοῖς μυσὶν ἐν τῆι πίττηι **β**(BᶜEʳ) : τοῖς ποσὶ τοῖς ἐν τῆι
πίττηι E ante rasuram : τοῖς μυσὶ τοῖς ἐν τῇ γῇ **γ**(*Γ*ɪ N ZᵃPBᵖMᵒ) E² Bekker
Forster Torraca Louis (unde τοῖς μυσὶ ἐν τῇ ζειᾷ Farquharson n. 2, τοῖς ἐμύσι
τοῖς ἐν τῇ γῇ Diels ap. Jaeger, τοῖς μυσὶ ['shellfish'] τοῖς ἐν πηλῷ Nussbaum
1975a, τοῖς ἐμύσι τοῖς ἐν πηλῷ Nussbaum 1978) : τοῖς μυσὶ τοῖς ἐν γῇ **λ**(XHᵃLVᵍ) :
τοῖς ἐν τῇ ἐν τῇ γῇ b | textum a **γ** traditum (τοῖς μυσὶ τοῖς ἐν τῇ γῇ ἢ τοῖς ἐν τῇ
ἄμμῳ πορευομένοις) in τοῖς ἐν τῇ γῇ πορευομένοις μυσὶν contraxit Mich.ᵖ
105.25, unde verbis a **γ** traditis novum ordinem τοῖς ἐν τῇ γῇ πορευομένοις
μυσὶν ἢ τοῖς ἐν τῇ ἄμμῳ imposuit **ε**(CᵃOᵈSVᵖ) : τοῖς ποσὶ τοῖς ἐν τῇ ἄμμῳ
πορευομένοις Platt 1913, 295 : τοῖς μυσὶ τοῖς ἐν τῇ ἅλῳ πορευομένοις Barnes ‖
17 πρόεισιν] πρόισιν E | ἔσται] ἔστιν **β**(BᶜEʳ) | εἰ] ἢ E ‖ **17–18** πτῆσις ἢ νεῦσις
(πτῆσις ἢ νῆσις Eʳ : νεῦσις ἢ πτῆσις b)] πτῆσις ἢ πλεύσις E : (πτῆσις ἢ) πλεῦσις
in ras. scr. Zᵃ² (πτῆσις ἢ...^...Zᵃ¹) : *volatus... nec natatio* Anon. ‖ **23** ἐπ' αὐτῶι
β(BᶜEʳb OᵈSVᵖ) : ἐν αὐτῶι cett. ‖ **24–25** οὐδ'...οὐδ' **β**(BᶜEʳ), cf. Kühner/Gerth
1904, 294 (§ 535/5.a) : οὔτ' ἂν...οὔθ' **α**(E *Γ*ɪ[*neque... neque* G]NXHᵃLVᵍ
PBᵖMᵒ**A**[o...οὔθ' Zᵃ : *neque... aut* Alb.] CᵃOᵈ)b Bekker Forster Torraca Louis :
οὔτ' ἂν...οὐδ' **κ**(SVᵖ) : οὐδ' ἂν...οὔθ' Jaeger Nussbaum ‖ **25** Τιτυός...Βορέας]
Boreas...Zephirus Alb. : *Circius...Boreas* GɪGR" (*Circinus...Boreas* GR'), unde
Κίρκιος...Βορέας Torraca ‖ **26** πλέων **β**(BᶜEʳb SVᵖ¹) : πνέων cett., edd. ‖ **27**
αὐτοῦ (scil. τοῦ πλοίου)] αὐτοῦ HᵃLVᵍ Mᵒ Cᵃ edd. ‖ **699ᵃ4** αὐτὸν **β**(Bᶜ[αὐτὸ Eʳ :
αὐτοῦ b]) : αὐτὸ ἢ cett., edd. ‖ **8** πρὸς ὅ] προσὸ E; de hac scriptione cf. 698ᵇ1
et 14, 700ᵃ19 ‖ **10** ἕλκων καὶ ὠθῶν κινεῖ **β**(BᶜEʳ) : ὠθῶν ἢ ἕλκων κινεῖ **α**(E *Γ*ɪ
NXHᵃLVᵍ PBᵖMᵒ Cᵃ)b : ἕλκων ἢ ὠθῶν κινεῖ **η**(OᵈSVᵖ) : ὠθῶν ἐκκινεῖν fecit ex
ὠθῶν ἐκκινεῖ Zᵃ, cf. *impellit* Anon.

Caput 3

699ᵃ13 τι a Barnes 1980, 244 temptatum et a Manuwald 1989, 118 postulatum
servavit **β**(εἶναί τε τι δεῖ Bᶜ : εἶναί τι δεῖ Eʳ : εἶναι δεῖ τι b) : om. **α**(εἶναί τε δεῖ
E [cf. *oportet* Anon.] Bekker Farquharson Forster Louis Nussbaum : εἶναι θέλει **γ**
[*vult esse* G] Mich.¹ 107.8 Jaeger Torraca, quod ab εἰναιτελει ortum esse videtur)
| καὶ τοῦτο] καὶ τοῦτο <καὶ> Farquharson n. 2 Nussbaum : τοῦτο καὶ Forster |
οὐρανοῦ **β**(BᶜEʳ) : οὐρανοῦ μόριον cett., edd. ‖ **14** αὐτόν] αὐτὸ E ‖ **15** θιγγάνον
κινεῖν] θιγγάνειν E : θιγγάνον κινεῖ N : θιγγάνειν κινεῖν Zᵃ ‖ **17** ἔσται coni.

Thomæus 1523 CXXXIIv (*erit*), Jaeger Forster : ἔσεσθαι ω Bekker Torraca Louis Nussbaum, sed a priore apodosi (ᵃ14–16) alteram (ᵃ16–17) propter varietatem et temporum (ᵃ14–15: ἀνάγκη... εἶναι / ᵃ16–17: ὁμοίως... ἔσεσθαι codd.) et negationum (ᵃ15: μηθὲν / ᵃ17: οὐθὲν) praedicandi quoque modo differre oportet (ᵃ14–15: ἀνάγκη...μηθὲν εἶναι / ᵃ16–17: ὁμοίως οὐθὲν ἔσται); cf. Renehan 1996, 226–227 ‖ 25–26 πρὸς τὰ ζῶια τὰ (scil. κινούμενα δι' αὑτῶν) β(Bᶜ [καὶ τὰ ζῶια τὰ Eʳ]b OᵈSVᵖ) ι(PBᵖMᵒ[*ad animalia que moventur per se ipsa* Anon.]) Platt 1913, 295 : πρὸς τὰ ζῶια καὶ τὰ (scil. κινούμενα δι' αὑτῶν) α(E ΓιNHᵃVᵍ Zᵃ Cᵃ) edd. : πρὸς τὰ ζῶια καὶ τὰ (scil. κινούμενα δι' αὑτῶν) XL, Thomæus 1523 CXXXIIIr (*ad animalia / & ad ea quæ per se mouentur*), Barnes 1980, 224, cf. iam Forster 448, note a) ‖ 26–27 διαπορήσειεν] ἀπορήσειεν β(BᶜEʳb) ι(Zᵃ[ἀπορήσειε]PBᵖMᵒ) ‖ 28 ἂν] om. β(BᶜEʳb) ‖ 30 ἂν συμβαίνοι β(BᶜEʳb) E Mᵒ Bekker Forster Torraca Louis Nussbaum : ἂν συμβαίνει γ(Γι[*utique accidit* G]NCᵃZᵃ), unde ἂν συμβαίνη (= ἐὰν συμβαίνηι) η(OᵈSVᵖ) λ(XHᵃLVᵍ) PBᵖ Jaeger | κατὰ λόγον] καὶ κατὰ λόγον ι(ZᵃPBᵖMᵒ) Jaeger Torraca Louis ‖ 35 καὶ καθ' ἣν] καθ' ἣν E Zᵃ ‖ 37 ὑπ' ἀλλήλων] ὑπ' ἀλλήλον ex ὑπ' ἀλλήλου E : ἀπ' ἀλλήλων Bᵖ ‖ 699ᵇ2 τοιοῦτον ἕτερόν ἐστιν β(BᶜEʳ)P vel τοιοῦτον ἕτερον ἐστὶ η(OᵈSVᵖ) : τοιοῦτόν ἐστιν ἕτερον E, edd. vel τοιοῦτον ἐστιν ἕτερον γ(NXHᵃLVᵍ Cᵃ) : τοιοῦτον ἕτερον ι(ZᵃBᵖMᵒ) ‖ 2–3 οὐ δεῖ μᾶλλον ἀντερείδειν β(BᶜEʳ Γ2[*non oportet magis contratendere* GR"]) : οὐδὲν μᾶλλον ἀντερείδειν γ(Γι[*nichil magis contratendere* GιGR'] NXHᵃLVᵍ ZᵃPBᵖMᵒ CᵃOᵈSVᵖ)b : οὐδὲν μᾶλλον ἀντερείδειν δεῖ E, edd. ‖ 6 ἤ] om. β(BᶜEʳb OᵈSVᵖ) ‖ 7 ὡσαύτως] ὢ αὕτως E ‖ 7–8 τοῦ κινουμένου (gen. comp.!) β(BᶜEʳb Γ2[*et moti* G]) : αἰ (i.e. αἱ) τοῦ κινουμένου E : τῆς τοῦ κινουμένου γ(HᵃLVᵍ ZᵃPBᵖMᵒ CᵃOᵈS) Forster Torraca Nussbaum : ἡ τοῦ κινουμένου N Aldina Bekker Jaeger Louis : ἡ τῆς τοῦ κινουμένου XVᵖ : ἡ τοῦ κινουμένου <καὶ κινοῦντος τῆς τοῦ κινουμένου> Farquharson n. 3.

Caput 4

699ᵇ13 ὡς] om. E Zᵃ : καὶ Cᵃ ‖ **14** τις] της E | ὑπερβάληι dedi : ὑπερβάλη Bᶜ CᵃOᵈ ZᵃMᵒ LVᵍ : ὑπερβάλληι E edd. : ὑπερβάλλη NXHᵃ P(ὑπερβάλλει Bᵖ) SVᵖ Eʳb ‖ **19** ἀδύνατον εἶναι φαμεν β(BᶜEʳb Γ2[*dicimus esse impossibile* G]) : ἀδύνατον φαμέν εἶναι EN edd. : εἶναι om. γ(ZᵃPBᵖMᵒ CᵃOᵈSVᵖ [φαμὲν ἀδύνατον transp. λ]) ‖ **21–23** εἶναι... ἐξ ἀνάγκης,... ἐξ ἀνάγκης <εἶναι> dedi : εἶναι... ἐξ ἀνάγκης εἶναι,... ἐξ ἀνάγκης ω Bekker : εἶναι... ἐξ ἀνάγκης,... ἐξ ἀνάγκης Eʳp.c. in marg. (in supplendo lineam ᵇ22, ubi οἰόμεθα μὲν ἐξ ἀνάγκης εἶναι omiserat Eʳa.c.) Bonitz 1863, 50 (= 180) Jaeger Torraca Louis Nussbaum ‖ **24** μείζω] μήζω E ‖ **25** αἱ] om. Mich.ᶜ 110.11–12 Cᵃ ι(ZᵃPBᵖMᵒ) Jaeger Nussbaum ‖ **25–26** ὑπερέχουσαι] περὶ ἔχουσαι E : ὑπάρχουσαι Eʳ : ὑπερβάλλουσαι ι(PBᵖMᵒ), cf Alb. qui et *excellit* et *superhabet* praebet ‖ **26** ὑπ’ ἀλλήλων] ἀπ’ αλλήλων E ‖ **28** ἐνδέχοιτ’ ἄν **α**(E *Γ*ι NXHᵃLVᵍ PBᵖMᵒ CᵃOᵈSVᵖ) edd. : οὐδὲ ἐνδέχοιτ’ ἄν **A**(Zᵃ Anon.[… *autem*… *non contingit*]) : ἐνδέχεται **β**(BᶜEʳb) ‖ **29–30** εἴπερ… εἴπερ **β**(BᶜEʳb) : εἴπερ… εἰ cett., edd. ‖ **32** τι ἀκίνητον **β**(BᶜEʳb OᵈSVᵖ) **γ** Mich.¹ ιιι.8 Jaeger Nussbaum : ἀκίνητόν τι E(ἀκινητόν τι) Bekker Forster Louis ‖ **37** ἐρύσαιτ’ (ἐρύσαιτε b)] ἐρύσετ’ E vel ἐρύσετε **ε**(CᵃOᵈS[ἐρύσεται Vᵖ]) ‖ **700ᵃι** ὕπατον μήστωρ’ **β**(BᶜEʳb) Homeri vulgata : ὕπατον πάντων **α**(E *Γι*[*infimum omnium* G1 vel *suppremum omnium* GR’GR”] **ε**[CᵃOᵈSVᵖ]) edd., quae lectio a vetere explicatione verbi ὕπατον (‘ἢ γὰρ ἁπλῶς πάντων ὕπατον, ἢ τῶν ἀρχόντων [scil. ὕπατον]’) ab Eustathio laudata (*In Iliadem*, II 518.11 v. d. Valk) orta esse videtur : ὕπατον μήστορα πάντων **ζ**(NA[ZᵃAnon.(*magistrum omnium*)]PBᵖMᵒ) : ὕπατον μήστωρα **λ**(XHᵃLVᵍ) ‖ μάλα **α**(μάλλα **κ**[SVᵖ] : om. **A**[ZᵃAnon.]) Homeri vulgata, edd. : πάνυ **β**(BᶜEʳ *Γ*2[*valde* GR’GR”; cf. De Leemans 2011a CLXXXVII]) ‖ **2** ἐξάπτεσθε (ἐξάπτοισθε X)] ἐξάπτεσθαι E ZᵃP vel ἐξάπτεσθαι Bᶜ ‖ **5** διαλυθῆναι] διλυθῆναι E ‖ εἰ] ἢ **β**(BᶜEʳ[ἤ]) ‖ **5–6** ἀκινήτου] ἀκίνητον Bekker Jaeger Forster ‖ **6** ἤρτηται] ἤρκται **β**(BᶜEʳb *Γ*2[*ortum est* G]) ‖ **8** ὅσα κινεῖ αὐτὰ αὐτά] ὅσα κινεῖ αὐτὰ E **ι**(**A**[ZᵃAnon.(*quot*… *moventia*)]BᵖMᵒ) Vᵖa.c. : ὅσα αὐτὰ κινεῖ αὐτά Cᵃ(ex ὅσα αὐτὰ κινεῖ αὐτά) ‖ αὐτοῦ τὸ] αὐτῶν τὸ **θ**(NXHᵃLVᵍ) Nussbaum : αὐτοῖς τοῦτο **ι**(**A**[ZᵃAnon.(cf. *in omnibus*… *talibus*… *hoc* Alb.)] PBᵖMᵒ) Platt 1913, 295 ‖ **8–9** δεῖ γὰρ – κινεῖσθαι] post ᵃ10 (κινήσεται) transposuit Renehan 1996, 234 ‖ **9** ἠρεμεῖν… κινεῖσθαι **ω** : κινεῖσθαι… ἠρεμεῖν Thomæus 1523 CXXXVIr (*moueri*… *quiescere*) Moraux 1959, 364 ‖ **12** αὐτοῖς EʳbOᵈ Cᵃ(ex αὐτοῖς) PMᵒp.c. ut vid. vel αὐτοῖς Bᶜ CᵃSVᵖ Bᵖ **A**(ZᵃAnon.[*ipsis*]) : ἑαυτοῖς E **θ**(NXHᵃLVᵍ) ‖ **13** κινούμενον **β**(BᶜEʳb) : κινοῦν cett., edd. ‖ πρὸς τῶν] πρὸς τὸν E : πρῶτον **A**(ZᵃAnon.[*primum*]) : πρός τι Eʳ ‖ ἔξωθέν **β**(BᶜEʳb OᵈSVᵖ), *extrinsecorum* G : ἔξω cett. (ἐξ’ ὧν **A**[ZᵃAnon.(*a quibus*)]), edd. ‖ ἠρεμοῦν **β**(BᶜEʳb) : ἠρεμούντων cett., edd. ‖ **14** πάντα ταῦτα **β**(BᶜEʳb) : ταῦτα **α** edd. : πάντα post ταῦτα inseruit P ‖ **15** ἀλλ’, <ἀλλ’> scripsi, de accentu in ἀλλ’ (< ἀλλά) omittendo cf. Kühner/Blass 1890, 332 (§ 85/4) : ἀλλ’ **ω**(E NXHᵃL **A**[Zᵃ Anon.] Cᵃ BᵉbOᵈSVᵖ) Farquharson Jaeger Forster Torraca Nussbaum : ἄλλο Eʳ (ἀλλ’ iam Bekker Louis) : ἀλλὰ PBᵖMᵒ : ἀλ’ Vᵍ ‖ **15–16** πρώτων] πρῶτον **β**(BᶜEʳb Sa.c.) BᵖA(Zᵃ Anon.[*primitus*]) ‖ **17** ὁμοίως **β**(BᶜEʳb *Γ*2[*similiter* GR”(BvFa z)]) : om. cett., edd. ‖ αὐτὰ αὐτά] αὐτὰ **ι**(**A**[*se ipsa* Anon.]PMᵒ [αὐτὰ ZᵃBᵖ]) ‖ **19** αὐτοῖς Cᵃa.c. L PMᵒ Eʳb, cf. G1(*se ipsis* Di) Anon., Bekker Jaeger Forster Torraca Louis : αὐτοῖς cett., Nussbaum ‖ **20** πρῶτον] πρώτως E **ι**([πρώτω Zᵃ]PBᵖMᵒ) edd. : πρώτων fecit Es.l. : et *primitus* et *primum* Anon. (De Leemans 2011b 17.393) ‖ **24** καὶ **β**(Bᶜb OᵈSVᵖ) E edd. : om. Eʳ : καὶ οἱ **γ**(NXHᵃLVᵍ ZᵃPBᵖMᵒ Cᵃ) ‖ **25** οἱ ἐκπνέοντες **β**(BᶜEʳb OᵈSVᵖ) Cᵃ : ἐκπνέοντες cett. (ἐμπνέοντες Zᵃ), edd.

Caput 5

700ᵃ26 αὐτὸ αὐτό] αὐτῷ αὐτὸ λ(XHᵃLVᵍ) ba.c., quod iam Jaeger coniecerat, Torraca Louis Nussbaum : αὐτὸ κ(SVᵖ) Zᵃa.c. Bᵖp.c.(ex αὐτῷ) : αὐτὸ E² Bekker Platt 1913, 295 Forster : αὐτῷ Zᵃ p.c.(ex αὐτὸ) cf. Anon. (*eodem*) ‖ **27** ἢ <καὶ> γ(Γ1[*aut etiam* G1GR"] NXHᵃLVᵍ A[ZᵃAnon.(*etiam*)]PBᵖMᵒ CᵃOᵈSVᵖ) b Mich.¹ 112.22–24 (cf. 26 μόνωι) edd. : ἢ β(BᵉEʳ Γ2[*aut* GR']) E | αὐτὸ ὑφ' αὐτοῦ E A(ZᵃAnon.) vel αὐτὸ ὑφ' ἑαυτοῦ μ(PBᵖ) : αὐτῷ ὑφ' αὐτοῦ β(BᵉEʳb OᵈSVᵖ) θ(NXHᵃLVᵍ) edd. : αὐτῷ ὑφ' ἑαυτοῦ Mᵒ : αὐτοῦ ὑφ' αὐτοῦ (sic!) Cᵃ | καὶ ἐν β(BᵉEʳb OᵈSVᵖ) : καὶ cett., edd. | τῶι² β(BᵉEʳb) : om. cett. ‖ **28–30** τῆς ἐξ ἀρχῆς − μὲν] om. Bᵖ ‖ **29** ἤνπερ] ἦν λ(XHᵃLVᵍ) : ἤπερ (sic!) Nussbaum | πρώτη κίνησις] πρώτως (vel πρῶτον) κίνησις Γ1(G1GR') : πρώτην κίνησιν Mich.ᶜ 113.4 ι(A[Zᵃp.c.(πρώτην τὴν κίνησιν Zᵃa.c.) Anon.(*primum motum*)]PMᵒ) (deficit Bᵖ) Jaeger ‖ **30** μὲν β(BᵉEʳb), de μὲν ... καὶ ... δὲ cf. Denniston *Greek Particles* 203 : om. cett., edd. | αὕτη ἂν αἰτία εἴη β(BᵉEʳb) : αὕτη ἂν εἴη αἰτία ν(HᵃLVᵍ) : αὕτη αἰτία ἂν εἴη cett., edd. | δὲ β(BᵉEʳb OᵈSVᵖ) E Bekker Jaeger Forster Torraca Louis, unde δὴ Farquharson n. 6 Nussbaum : om. γ(NXHᵃLVᵍ ZᵃPBᵖMᵒ Cᵃ) ‖ **32–33** ὥστε καὶ αὐξήσεως (scil. αἰτία ἡ κατὰ τόπον κίνησις), εἴ ποτε γίγνεται αὐτὸ αὑτῶι αἴτιον (scil. αὐτῆς), καὶ ἀλλοιώσεως: sic interpunxit Farquharson n. 8 ‖ **33** αὐτὸ αὑτῶι] αὐτῷ αὑτῶι E vel αὐτῷ αὑτῷ Na.c. Zᵃa.c. : αὐτῷ αὐτὸ Zᵃp.c. ‖ **33–35** εἰ − ἑτέρων] secl. Torraca, sed cf. Moraux 1959, 364 ‖ **35** ἑτέρων] ἕτερον β(BᵉEʳb) : ἑτέρου Cᵃ ‖ **700ᵇ1** οἷόν τε] οἴονται β(BᵉEʳ) PBᵖ | αὐτὸ αὑτῶι αἴτιον εἶναι β(BᵉEʳb) : αὐτὸ αἴτιον αὐτῷ εἶναι Oᵈ : αὐτὸ αἴτιον εἶναι αὑτῶι (vel αὐτὸ αἴτιον εἶναι αὑτῶι) cett., edd.

Caput 6

700ᵇ7 δέ] μὲν Pachymeres (Y) unde Bekker : om. N b ‖ **9** λοιπὸν δ' β (b Γ2[Ap(*reliquium autem*) Dt(*reliquum autem est*)]) E Bekker Forster, cf. Denniston *Greek Particles* 177-181 et supra 699ᵇ21 : λοιπόν γ BᵉEʳ Jaeger Torraca Louis Nussbaum ‖ **10** ἀρχῇ] ἡ ἀρχὴ ι(ZᵃPBᵖMᵒ) Cᵃ, Eʳ in margine, Jaeger (ex P), Louis ‖ **11** ὅλου] λόγου E ‖ **14** καὶ γὰρ] καὶ γὰρ καὶ θ(NXHᵃLVᵍ Aldina) edd. (Bekker ex Aldina 278.18, ut vid.) ‖ **16** πάσης αὐτοῖς β(BᵉEʳb OᵈSa.c.), unde πάσης αὐτῆς κ(Sp.c.Vᵖ) : αὐτοῖς πάσης α edd., unde αὐτοῖς πᾶσι ι(A[ZᵃAnon.(*omnium ipsorum*)]PMᵒ) | τῆς κινήσεως] καὶ τῆς κινήσεως κ(SVᵖ) ‖ **17** φαντασίαν] αἴσθησιν καὶ φαντασίαν λ(XHᵃLVᵍ) Torraca ‖ **18** ἐπιθυμίαν] θυμὸν καὶ ἐπιθυμίαν λ(XHᵃLVᵍ) Torraca ‖ **22** ὀρέξεις βγ : ὄρεξις E edd. ‖ **23–24** ὥστε κινεῖ πρῶτον τὸ ὀρεκτὸν καὶ τὸ νοητόν. οὐ πᾶν δὲ νοητόν dedi (cl. supra 700ᵇ18–19 ταῦτα δὲ πάντα ἀνάγεται εἰς νοῦν καὶ ὄρεξιν et Metaph. Λ 7, 1072ᵃ26 κινεῖ δὲ ὧδε τὸ

ὀρεκτὸν καὶ τὸ νοητόν) : ὥστε κινεῖ πρῶτον τὸ ὀρεκτὸν καὶ τὸ διανοητόν. οὐ πᾶν
δὲ διανοητόν β(BᶜEʳb Γ2[Quare movet primum quod appetibile et quod intellectuale
GR'GR"])P : ὥστε καὶ τὸ διανοητόν. οὐ πᾶν δὲ τὸ διανοητόν a(E Γ1[Quare et
intellectuale G1] CᵃOᵈSVᵖ), quem locum sane lacunosum Mich.ᴾ 113.22–24 hoc
modo interpretatus est: καὶ ἐπεὶ ἡ προαίρεσις κίνησις διανοίας καὶ ὀρέξεως,
ἔσται καί τι διανοητὸν προαιρετόν· οὐ γὰρ πᾶν διανοητόν (scil. προαιρετόν),
unde ζ vocem προαιρετόν in margine adiecisse videtur, ut ex eius progenie (θι)
elucet: ὥστε καὶ τὸ προαιρετόν. οὐ πᾶν δὲ τὸ διανοητὸν προαιρετόν θ(NXHᵃLVᵍ)
et ὥστε καὶ τὸ διανοητὸν (διανοητικὸν Zᵃ) οὐ πᾶν προαιρετόν ι(A[ZᵃAnon.]
BᵖMᵒ) ‖ 24 καὶ τὸ] τὸ om. N Nussbaum | οὐ πᾶν δὲ] οὐ πᾶν δὲ τὸ a(E NXHᵃLVᵍ
CᵃOᵈSVᵖ) : οὐ πᾶν ι(ZᵃBᵖMᵒ) | post οὐ πᾶν δὲ διανοητόν supra lineam προαιρετόν
add. b (ex N, ut vid.) ‖ 25 τὸ τοιοῦτον] τοιοῦτόν β(BᶜEʳb OᵈSVᵖ)P : τῶν τοιούτων
A(ZᵃAnon.[huiusmodi... bonorum]) ‖ 28 κινεῖ] κινεῖν β(BᶜEʳ) : κινεῖσθαι Vᵖ ‖
28–29 ἀγαθοῦ – ἀγαθόν] om. propter homoeoteleuton E ‖ 30 ὁμοίως] ὁμοίος E
‖ 31 κινοῦντος] κινοῦντων E ‖ 32 τὸ μὲν β(BᶜEʳb Γ2[hoc quidem GR"]) Zᵃ, quod
iam Farquharson n. 6 coniecerat, Nussbaum : τὰ μὲν cett., Bekker Jaeger Forster
Torraca Louis ‖ 32–33 τὸ δὲ ἀΐδιον καλὸν καὶ ἀληθὲς καὶ τὸ πρώτως ἀγαθὸν
dedi : τὸ δὲ ἀΐδιον καλὸν καὶ τὸ ἀληθὲς καὶ τὸ πρώτως ἀγαθὸν β(BᶜEʳb)P :
bonum aeternum et verax et primum bonum Alb. : τὸ δὲ ἀΐδιον καλὸν καὶ τὸ ἀληθῶς
καὶ πρώτως (πρῶτον HᵃZᵃ) ἀγαθὸν a(E G1[xᵢ]GR" NXHᵃLVᵍ Zᵃ CᵃOᵈSVᵖ)
Bekker Forster Torraca Louis Nussbaum : τὸ δὲ ἀΐδιον καλὸν καὶ τὸ ἀληθῶς καὶ
τὸ πρώτως ἀγαθὸν Mich.ᶜ 114.9–10 G1(x₂) GR' Jaeger : τὸ δὲ ἀΐδιον καλὸν καὶ
τὸ πρώτως ἀγαθὸν καὶ ἀληθῶς ξ(BᵖMᵒ) ‖ 34 ἢ ὥστ'] πως β(BᶜEʳ Γ2[aliqualiter])
P ‖ 35 πρὸς ἕτερον β(BᶜEʳ Γ2[ad alterum GR'GR"])P Bekker Torraca Nussbaum
: πρότερον cett. (Mich.ᶜ 114.14), quod alii aliis remediis sanare conati sunt:
πρότερόν τι Mich.ᴾ 114.15 Jaeger Forster Louis; ita quod ante ipsum non est aliud
bonum Alb.; <ἕτερον> πρότερον Renehan 1996, 237 ‖ 701ᵃ3 κινουμένων β(BᶜEʳb)
Pp.c., unde κινήσεως Nussbaum : γι(γ)νομένων a Bekker Jaeger Forster Torraca
Louis ‖ 3–4 ἡ φορὰ τελευταία τῶν κινουμένων ἐν τοῖς γιγνομένοις ≈ ἡ φορὰ τῶν
κινουμένων τελευταία ἐν τοῖς γιγνομένοις, cf. Newman 1904, 580 | γι(γ)νομένοις]
κινουμένοις Jaeger Forster ‖ 4–5 ὀρέξει ἢ προαιρέσει] ἢ προαιρέσει β(BᶜEʳ) :
ὀρέγον ἢ προαιροῦν A(Zᵃ Anon.[desiderans...aut eligens]).

Caput 7

701ᵃ7 νοῶν] νῦν E ‖ 8 ἔοικε δὲ β(BᶜEʳb Γ2[videtur autem G1(x₂)]) N Bᵖ : ἔοικεν
E : ἔοικε cett., edd. ‖ 15–16 ταῦτ' ἄμφω dedi : ταῦτα ἄμφω a edd. : τοῦτ' ἄμφω
β(BᶜEʳ), unde τοῦτ' εὐθὺς b ‖ 16 ἀναγκάζηι] ἀναγκάζει β(Bᶜ SVᵖ) Bᵖp.c. ‖ 17
ἀγαθὸν δὲ οἰκία β(BᶜEʳb) : οἰκία δὲ ἀγαθόν cett., edd. | ἀγαθὸν δὲ οἰκία. ποιεῖ]
οἰκία δὲ ποιεῖ ἀγαθὸν κ(SVᵖ) ‖ 18–19 οὗ δέομαι, ποιητέον· ἱματίου δὲ δέομαι]
om. propter homoeoteleuton Cᵃ ι(A[Zᵃ Anon.]PBᵖMᵒ), sed οὗ δέομαι ποιητέον

ex altero fonte (*β*) ante ᵃ19 καὶ τὸ inseruit P ‖ **19** δὲ *β*(BᶜEʳb) : om. cett., edd. |
ποιεῖ *β*(BᶜEʳ OᵈSVᵖ) E Cᵃ Farquharson n. 4 : ποιητέον δ(*Γ*1[*faciendum* G]
NXHᵃLVᵍ ZᵃPBᵖMᵒ) b edd. ‖ **21** ἔσται] ἐστὶν *β*(BᶜEʳ) : om. Zᵃ ‖ **22** τόδε, τόδε·
καὶ τοῦτο *β*(Bᶜb OᵈSVᵖ) *γ*(NXHᵃLVᵍ ZᵃPBᵖMᵒ) : τόδε, καὶ τόδε· καὶ τοῦτο Eʳ
*Γ*2(*hoc et hoc et hoc* GR'GR") : τόδε, καὶ τόδε E vel τόδε, καὶ τοῦτο Cᵃ, cf. *hoc, et
hoc* G1 et *hoc…etiam illud* Anon. ‖ **24** δυεῖν ὁδῶν dedi : δύ᾽ εἰ ποδῶν Bᶜ :
δ[.] …οδῶν Ea.c. ut vid. : δύο εἰδῶν Ep.c. (currente calamo post rasuram), cett.
Mich.ᵖ 117.1, edd. ‖ **26** ἐπιστᾶσα *β*(BᶜEʳ) : ἐφιστᾶσα cett. (ὑφιστᾶσα Zᵃ), edd. :
ἐφεστῶσα Pachymeres (Y) ‖ **27** οὐκέτι *β*(BᶜEʳb *Γ*2[*non iam* G]) : οὐκ cett., edd. ‖
27–28 ἐνδιατρίβει] ἐνδιατρίβῃ E ‖ **29** ἐνεργήσηι γάρ] γὰρ ἐνεργήσῃ transp.
ι([γὰρ ἐγγίσαι Zᵃ] P[γὰρ ἐνεργ(ήσῃ) Bᵖ]Mᵒ) N Bekker Forster ‖ **30** οὗ ὀρέγεται]
οὐέγεται Ea.c. : ὀρέγειν Zᵃa.c. : ὀρέγεται A(Zᵃp.c. Anon.[*desierat*]) ‖ **32** ποτέον
β(ποτὲ ὄν Bᶜ vel ποτὲ εἰ Eʳ) *ν*(HᵃLVᵍ), Pachymeres (Y), edd. : ποτῶ A(ZᵃAnon.
[*in potu*]) : ποτόν cett. (ποντόν Ea.c.) ‖ **32–33** ἡ αἴσθησις] αἴσθησις *β*(BᶜEʳ) ‖ **33**
οὕτω *β*(BᶜEʳb OᵈSVᵖ) Mᵒ : οὕτως cett., edd. ‖ **35** τοῦ κινεῖσθαι **ω** : τῆς κινήσεως
Nussbaum sine ulla adnotatione ‖ **37** πράττειν **ω** : delendum esse censet
Corcilius ‖ **701ᵇ1** διὰ προαίρεσιν ἢ βούλησιν *β*(BᶜEʳb) (cf. supra 700ᵇ15–ᵇ18 et
ᵇ22–ᵇ25) : δι᾽ ὄρεξιν ἢ βούλησιν cett., Bekker Jaeger Forster Torraca Louis : διὰ
βούλησιν Nussbaum ‖ **2** γενομένης] γινομένης Mich.¹ 117.18–19 *ζ*(NXHᵃLVᵍ
ZᵃPBᵖMᵒ) b Aldina Bekker Jaeger Forster Torraca Louis ‖ **3** στρεβλῶν (στρέβλων
Vᵖ : στρεβῶν Cᵃ : στεβλῶν b)] ξύλων Farquharson n. 4 | κρουόντων] post
ἀλλήλας transp. Bᶜ : κροόντων Eʳa.c. : κρουουσῶν Forster | πρὸς *β*(BᶜEʳb) : om.
cett., edd. | ἀλλήλας] ἀλλήλαις Farquharson n. 4 : ἄλληλα Torraca Nussbaum |
<εὐθὺς τῶν ζῳδίων τὰς μαχαίρας> exempli gratia dedi (εὐθὺς suadente
Shields) : τὰς στρέβλας **ω**, quod iam Forster et Torraca deleverunt : τῶν ξύλων
Nussbaum ‖ **4** ὅπερ **α** (Mich.ᶜ 118.16) Bekker Jaeger Forster Torraca Louis : ὁ
γὰρ Richards & Ross apud Farquharson n. 1, Nussbaum : ὥσπερ *β*(BᶜEʳb Vᵖ)
μ(PBᵖMᵒ) | <ὁ> inserui : <τὸ> Forster | ὀχούμενος αὐτὸς *β*(BᶜEʳ) : ὀχούμενον
αὐτὸ **α** Bekker Jaeger Forster Torraca Louis : ὀχούμενος αὐτὸ *η*(OᵈSVᵖ) Richards
& Ross apud Farquharson n. 1, Nussbaum : ὀχούμενον αὐτὸς b ‖ **4–5** <πάλιν>
καὶ πάλιν dedi cl. *Ph. Θ* 10, 267ᵇ10–11 (τὸ ὠθοῦν πάλιν καὶ πάλιν) : καὶ πάλιν
ω edd. ‖ **5** δὲ *β*(BᶜEʳb) : om. cett., edd. ‖ **7** οὕτω καί] οὕτως καὶ E vel οὕτως καὶ
Cᵃ ‖ **9–10** λυομένων] συστελλομένων Farquharson n. 3 ‖ **13** τὸ αὐτό] τὸ αὐτῶ E
‖ **13–14** ἔλαττον καὶ μεῖζον *β*(BᶜEʳb OᵈSVᵖ) : μεῖζον καὶ ἔλαττον cett., edd. ‖ **14**
γίνεσθαι] γενέσθαι *β*(BᶜEʳb) ‖ **15** <καὶ συστελλομένων> inserui cl. 703ᵃ20–21
δεῖ τὸ ὄργανον αὐξάνεσθαί τε δύνασθαι καὶ συστέλλεσθαι | πνεῦμα καὶ *β*(BᶜEʳb
*Γ*2[*spiritum et* G]) E : πάλιν συστελλομένων διὰ cett. (cf. Mich.ᵖ 119.7 πάλιν
συστέλλονται), edd. ‖ **16** ψῦξιν dedi (cf. ad ᵇ28 et ᵇ35, LSJ 1996, 2026, Frisk 1970,
1141, Chantraine 1968–1980, 1295) : ψύξιν codd. (om. N), edd. ‖ **19** νόησις] νόσις
E ‖ **20** θερμοῦ ἢ ψυχροῦ ἢ] secl. Nussbaum, sed cf. Barnes 1980, 225 et Kollesch
1985, 51 ‖ **21** ὂν *β*(BᶜEʳb) E edd. : om. cett. ‖ **22** μόνον] om. E ‖ **26** ἄπωθεν Bᶜ N :

ἄποθεν cett., edd. ‖ 27 ἡ β(BᶜEʳb) E P Al. 77.10 edd. : om. γ ‖ 28 ψῦξιν Al. cod.
Marc. 258 : ψύξιν codd., edd. ‖ 28–29 τοιοῦτο EBᶜ : τοιοῦτον cett., edd. ‖ 30 καὶ]
εἰ καὶ Al. 77.12 > Mich.ᴾ 115.20 > (ζ >) θ(NXHᵃLVᵍ) > Nussbaum | ἐν ταύτηι]
ἐκ ταύτης Platt 1913, 296 | ἐν ἀναισθήτωι Al. 77.12 : κατὰ μέγεθος ἀναισθήτωι
β(BᶜEʳb Γ2[secundum magnitudinem insensibili G]) E Vᴾ : κατὰ μέγεθος ἐν
ἀναισθήτω γ(NXHᵃLVᵍ Zᵃp.c.PBᴾMᵒ CᵃOᵈS) edd. : κατὰ μέγεθος ἐν αἰσθητικῷ
Platt 1913, 296 ‖ 31 ποιεῖ] ποιεῖται Mich.ᴾ 115.21 ι(ZᵃPBᴾMᵒ).

Caput 8

701ᵇ34 διωκτόν τε καὶ φευκτόν Al. 77.16 : διωκτὸν καὶ φευκτόν ω (φευκτὸν καὶ
διωκτὸν transp. Hᵃ) ‖ 35 θερμότης] θερμώτης E | ψῦξις Al. cod. Marc. 258 :
ψύξις codd. (ψυχρότης ι[ZᵃPBᴾMᵒ]) ‖ 36–37 ἀλλὰ λανθάνει περὶ τὰ μικρὰ
τοῦτο συμβαῖνον] post 702ᵃ1 θερμότητος transp. Moraux 1959, 365, Nussbaum
‖ 702ᵃ1 ἡδέα α Al. 77.19, cf. ᵃ3–4 : τὰ ἡδέα β(BᶜEʳb) ‖ 3 τὰ ἄλλα τὰ β(BᶜEʳb)
μ(PBᴾMᵒ) Bekker Forster Nussbaum (cf. Kühner/Gerth 1898, 635 [§ 464/9]) :
τὰ ἄλλα cett., Jaeger Torraca Louis ‖ 4 καὶ β(BᶜEʳb Γ2[et GɪGR']) A(ZᵃAnon.
[et]) : ἢ cett., edd. ‖ 11 καὶ ἐπὶ τοῦ…καὶ ἐπὶ τοῦ β(BᶜEʳ) vel καὶ ἐπὶ τοῦ…καὶ
τοῦ b vel καὶ ἐπὶ τοῦ…καὶ η(OᵈSVᴾ) Mich.ᴾ(S) 120.10 : καὶ ἔτι τοῦ…καὶ cett.
(καὶ ἔστι τοῦ…καὶ L) Mich.ᴾ(CPR) edd. ‖ 12 πολλαχῇι β(πολλαχῇ Eʳb :
πολλαχοὶ Bᶜ) : πολλαχοῦ cett., edd. ‖ 13 ὥστ᾽ εἶναι] ὡς τείνει β(Bᶜ [ὥστ᾽ εἶνει
S]), quod in γίνεσθαι correxit Eʳ ‖ 14 ἀπολείπηι (ἀπολείπει Mich.ᶜ 120.15, N :
ἀπολείπειν Zᵃ)] ἀπολίπη Xp.c. μ(PBᴾM) ε(CᵃOᵈSVᴾ) edd. | ἑκάτερον] ἑκατέρω
(dat.) β(BᶜEʳb), sed cf. Classen/Steup ad Thuc.VIII 22, 1 (οὐδὲν ἀπολείποντες
προθυμίας) ‖ 15 τοῦτο β(BᶜEʳb) : τοῦτο δὲ cett., edd.; sed cf. Kühner/Gerth
1904, 343–344 (§ 546/5.a.γ), Schwyzer/Debrunner 1950, 702, Kassel ad Rh. B
6, 1384ᵃ36 ‖ 16 ἐὰν β(BᶜEʳb SVᴾ) : ἂν cett., edd. ‖ 18 ἔχειν β(BᶜEʳb) : om. cett.,
edd. ‖ 20 διὰ τὸ <τὸ> θ(NXHᵃLVᵍ), quod coniecerat iam Bonitz 1866, 360 [=
253], Jaeger Forster Torraca Louis Nussbaum, cf. Bywater ad Po. 1459ᵃ8 : διὰ τὸ
cett., Bekker ‖ 22 ἐστὶν τοῦ μὲν β(BᶜEʳb) : μέν ἐστι τοῦ μὲν γ (τοῦ μὲν post [23]
ἀρχὴ transp. Zᵃ) Bekker Forster Torraca Louis : μέν ἐστιν E¹(μέν ἔστιν) Jaeger :
<τοῦ> μέν ἐστιν E² Farquharson n. 4, Nussbaum ‖ 27 εἴρηται] εἴρετε E ‖ 28
ὀλεκράνω Cᵃ L Eʳ vel ὀλεκράνωι E N Bᶜ (cf. supra ad 698ᵇ3) : ὠλεκράνω cett.,
edd. ‖ 29 κινεῖ καὶ κινεῖται β(BᶜEʳb Γ2[movet et movetur GR'GR"]) Farquharson
n. 6 (cl. 703ᵃ12–14 : ὥσπερ τὸ ἐν ταῖς καμπαῖς σημεῖον, τὸ κινοῦν καὶ κινούμενον,
πρὸς τὸ ἀκίνητον scil. ἔχει, cf. et 702ᵃ26–27 ὅτι γὰρ πρὸς ἠρεμοῦν δεῖ
ἀπερείδεσθαι τὸ κινοῦν, εἴρηται πρότερον) Torraca : κινεῖται α (per haplograph-
iam) Bekker Jaeger Forster Louis Nussbaum : κινεῖται καὶ κινεῖ P : κινεῖ A(movet
Anon.), unde κινοῦν Zᵃ | ἀλλ᾽ β(Bᶜb OᵈSVᴾ) : om. α Eʳ edd. | δ<ἡ> εἶναί τι dedi;
de particulis δὴ et δὲ in mss. confusis cf. Bonitz 1863, 95 (= 225) : δ᾽ εἶναί τι γEʳ
edd. : δὲ εἶναί τι Bᶜ : εἶναί τι b : δ᾽ εἶναι τινὰ E ‖ 30 καὶ ἀκίνητον α edd. :

ἀκίνητον **β**(BᶜEʳb *Γ*2[*immobile* G]) | ὅ] ὃ 'quapropter' cf. Kühner/Gerth 1898, 310 (§ 410 Anmerk. 6), Schwyzer/Debrunner 1950, 77 | ἐν dedi : ἐν εἶναι **ω** cl. 702ᵇ25–26 (τὸ δὲ μέσον τοῦ σώματος μέρος δυνάμει μὲν ἓν ἐνεργείαι δὲ ἀνάγκη γίνεσθαι πλείω) ‖ **31** ὁ **β**(BᶜEʳb SVᵖ)P Jaeger Torraca Nussbaum : om. cett., Bekker Forster Louis ‖ **32** ἡ κινοῦσα] κινοῦσα E ‖ **34** τὴν] τις Farquharson n. 1 ‖ **702ᵇ1** εἰ μὴ καὶ (εἰ καὶ μὴ Vᵖ)] εἰ μὴ **a**(E NCᵃ) Eʳ, cf. *si non est in virga* Anon. ‖ **4** μόριον **β**(BᶜEʳb) : μέρος cett., edd. | ὀλέκρανον **β**(BᶜEʳ) E NCᵃ, cf. ad 698ᵇ3 : ὠλέκρανον cett., edd. ‖ **7** ἐστιν] ἐστην E | ἄλλου] ἀλλ' οὐ Bᶜ ‖ **8** ἐξωτέρω] ἐξωτέρωι E, cf. ᵇ10 : ἐξοτέρου Zᵃp.c. (ἐξατέρω a.c. ut vid.) : ἐξώτερον (abbr.) **ξ**(BᵖMᵒ) | τοῦ ἐσχάτου **β**(BᶜEʳb)P, quod ante τοῦ μὲν transposuimus : ἐσχάτου cett. ‖ **10** ἀνωτέρω] ἀνωτέρωι E, cf. ᵇ8 : ἀνώτερον (abbr.) **λ**(XHᵃVᵍ) ZᵃMᵒ : ανωτέρα (sic!) L ‖ **11** ὀλεκράνου E Cᵃ(ex ὀλεκράνου) Eʳ vel ὀλεκράνου Na.c. Bᶜ (cf. ad 698ᵇ3) : ὠλεκράνου cett., edd.

Caput 9

702ᵇ13–14 τῶι ἠρεμεῖν τὸ δεξιὸν] *in quiescendo semper dextrum* G, cf. Mich.ᵖ 124.1–2 τῷ ἀεὶ ἠρεμεῖν τὸ ἀριστερόν ‖ **14** μηδ' αὖ τῶι (μὴ δ' αὐτὸ Zᵃ)] μὴ δὲ τῶ **β**(BᶜEʳb *Γ*2[*neque in eo quod hoc illud* GR'GR'']) ‖ **15** ἐν τῶι ἀνωτέρωι E vel ἐν τῶ ἀνωτέρω (dat.) codd. plerique vel ἐν τῷ ἀνωτέρω (Vᵖ) : αὐτῶν ἀνωτέρω (adv.) Eʳ : ἐν τῷ ἀνωτέρω (adv.) edd. | ἡ ἀρχή] ἀρχή E ‖ **17** ἐσχάτων **β**(BᶜEʳb) : ἄκρων cett. | τὰς] <ταύτας> τὰς Platt 1913, 296 ‖ **18** καὶ κάτω] secl. Farquharson n. 5, Torraca ‖ **19** καὶ τὰς N (καὶ in margine apposuit **θ**, ut vid.), coni. Forster : καὶ πρὸς τὰς X (καὶ ex **θ**) Torraca Nussbaum : πρὸς τὰς **β**(BᶜEʳ OᵈSVᵖ)P **γ**(HᵃLVᵍ Cᵃ) Bekker Louis : πρὸς τὰ Eb Jaeger : καὶ πρὸς τὰ Farquharson n. 5 : τὰς **ι**(ZᵃMᵒ) (cf. Mich.ᶜ 123.25) : om. Bᵖ | τοῖς] τοῖ E ‖ **20–21** αἰσθητικὸν] ἐσθητικὸν E ‖ **21–23** ὥστε...συμμεταβάλλει] ὥστε...συμμεταβάλλειν E **ξ**(BᵖMᵒ) ‖ **24** γίγνεσθαι **η**(OᵈSVᵖ) (γί- s.l. Bᶜ) vel γίνεσθαι cett. : γίνεσθε E : γίνεσθαι ante διὰ ταῦτα transp. N ‖ **25** ἐν] om. **β**(BᶜEʳ SVᵖ) (ἐνεργείαι ᵇ26 duplicat Eʳ : deficit Oᵈ : ὦ s.l. S) ‖ **28–36** diagramma servavit **γ**(CᵃOᵈZᵃ) | diagrammatis formae fuerunt tres, quarum primam servant CᵃOᵈ, alterius et Mich. 125.25 et **δ** mentionem faciunt (vide infra ad ᵇ30) ut a **γ** adiecta esse videatur, tertiam praebet Zᵃ:

 vel vel

28 ἐπὶ] ἔπει E : ἀπὸ Bᵖ ‖ **29** τι ἠρεμεῖν ⟨τι ἠρεμήν Bᵖ⟩] τι ἠρεμοῦν β(Bᶜ[τι εἶναι ἠρεμοῦν Eʳ]) ‖ **30** κινήσεσθαι ⟨κινήσησθαι E⟩] κινεῖσθαι N μ(PBᵖMᵒ) Aldina edd., sed cf. Bonitz s.v. κινεῖν, 391ᵃ22–32 ('tempus futurum passivae significationis et κινηθήσεται et κινήσεται exhibetur') | ἐν ἄρα δυνάμει] ἄρα δυνάμει ἐν E : ἔστι δὲ, δυνάμει Eʳ : ἐν ἄρα δυνάμει ὂν δυνάμει b | ὂν τὸ A β(BᶜEʳb Γ2[existens, ipsum A GR"])E ι(PBᵖMᵒ) : ὄντα τὰ AE γ(Mich.ᵖ 125.25 et Mich.ᶜ 125.30 δ[Γı(existentia AE Gı) NXLHᵃa.c.Vᵍ]) : ὄντα τὰ AB ϵ(CᵃOᵈSVᵖ) Hᵃp.c., cf. existentia AB GR' : ὄντα τὸ AB τὸ AΓ A(ZᵃAnon.[cf. tam AB quam AC Alb.]) ‖ **31** ἔσται ⟨ἔστε E⟩ ⟨erunt Gı GR' : erit GR"⟩] ἔστιν β(BᶜEʳ) ‖ **32** καὶ β(BᶜEʳb Γ2[et G]) : om. cett., edd. | κινεῖσθαι τῶι B β(BᶜEʳ OᵈSVᵖ) : κινεῖσθαι τό B b : τῶι B κινεῖσθαι cett. (τὸ B κινεῖσθαι Hᵃa.c. : τῶ A κινεῖσθαι A[ZᵃAnon.(A simul moveri)]), edd. ‖ **36** κινουμένων (gen. absol., κινούμεναι Zᵃp.c. : κινουμένας Bᵖ)] secl. Platt 1913, 296 ‖ **703ᵃ1–2** ἀλλὰ τὸ κινοῦν ἄμφω ἀναγκαῖον ⟨ἐν⟩ εἶναι Farquharson n. 4 ex G (vide infra ad ᵃ2) : ἀλλὰ τὸ κινοῦν ἄμφω ἀναγκαῖον εἶναι ω : ἀλλὰ τὸ κινοῦν ἄμφω ⟨ἀκίνητον⟩ ἀναγκαῖον εἶναι Jaeger : ἀλλ᾽ ἀ⟨κίνητον⟩ τὸ κινοῦν ἄμφω ἀναγκαῖον εἶναι Barnes 1980, 226 ‖ **2** ἀναγκαῖον ⟨ἐν⟩ εἶναι Γı(necesse unum esse Gı[x₂]GR' vel necesse esse unum Gı[x₁]GR", unde ἐν Vindobonensis Wʷ man. alt. in marg.) A(ἀναγκαῖον μὲν εἶναι Zᵃ : oportet… unum… sit Anon.) : ἀναγκαῖον εἶναι ω (εἶναι om. N).

Caput 10

703ᵃ4 τὸν λόγον τὸν λέγοντα] Mich.ᵖ 126.28 τὸν λόγον τὸν λέγοντα καὶ δεικνύντα, cf. rationem demonstrativam que dicit Alb. ‖ **7** κινούμενον μὲν] κινούμενον Mich.ˡ 127.11 ϵ(CᵃOᵈSVᵖ) N : κινούμενον σῶμα A(Zᵃp.c.[κινοῦν σῶμα Zᵃa.c.] Anon.[cf. corpus quod quidem est mobile Alb.]) | δύναται] δύνατε E ‖ **10–11** τίς μὲν—ἄλλοις] haec verba ad librum περὶ τροφῆς spectant secundum Mich. 127.16–17 (item Rose 1854, 166–167); ad librum De respiratione secundum Vat.V²; ad incerti auctoris librum De spiritu (481ᵃ1–2 τίς ἡ τοῦ ἐμφύτου πνεύματος διαμονή, καὶ τίς ἡ αὔξησις) secundum Zeller ³1879, 96 (n. 1 ad p. 94) et Bonitz Index s.v. Ἀριστοτέλης 100ᵃ52–54; num genuina sint dubitat Jaeger 1913b, 48 (cl. 703ᵃ16–17 πότερον μὲν οὖν ταὐτόν ἐστιν τὸ πνεῦμα ἀεὶ ἢ γίγνεται ἀεὶ ἕτερον, ἔστω ἄλλος λόγος); cf. Farquharson n. 4 ‖ **17** ἕτερον a EʳbOᵈ : ἕτερος β(Bᶜ SVᵖ) | ἔστω (sit GıGR')] om. β(BᶜEʳb Γ2[sit om. GR"]) | ἄλλος λόγος a edd. : λόγος, ἄλλος β(BᶜEʳb OᵈSVᵖ) N Aldina ‖ **18** δ' εὐφυῶς (vel δὲ εὐφυῶς)] δὲ ὑφ' ὣ ὥς Bᶜ vel δὲ ὑφ' ὣ ὡς Eʳ ‖ **22** ἀβίαστος] ἀβιάστως Bᵖ, coni. iam Farquharson n. 4, Torraca : ἄβυσσος N (> Aldina) | συστελλομένη ⟨τε καὶ ἐκτεινομένη⟩ Farquharson n. 4 cl. Mich. in PA 88.35–36 (τοῦ ἐν τῇ καρδίᾳ πνεύματος ἐκτεινομένου καὶ συστελλομένου, ὡς ἐν τῇ Περὶ ζῴων κινήσεως δέδεικται),

cf. Mich.ᵖ ad loc. 128.5–6, Torraca Nussbaum : συστελλομένη **ω** (στελλομένη Bᶜ)
Bekker Jaeger Forster Louis | βίαι ἑλκτικὴ dedi : βιαστικὴ **ω** Bekker Jaeger
Louis : ἑλκτικὴ *Γ*ι(*tractiva* G, cf. *retractatum* Anon.) Iuntina (i.e. Thomæus qui
iam in versione latina [1523 CLIr] *attractiua* dederat) Farquharson n. 4 ex G,
Torraca Nussbaum || **23–24** καὶ ἔχει βάρος...καὶ κουφότητα **β**(BᶜEʳb), cf. *et
habet gravitatem... et levitatem* G : καὶ ἔχει καὶ βάρος... καὶ κουφότητα cett., edd.
|| **25–26** κρατεῖται...ὑπ᾽ ἀλλήλων **β**(BᶜEʳb), cf. *tenentur in se invicem* Anon. :
κρατεῖ...ἀλλήλων **a** edd. : κρατεῖται...ἀλλήλων **η**(OᵈSVᵖ) || **28** τοῦ] om.
β(BᶜEʳ) || **29** εἴρηται] εἴρηται τὸ πνεῦμα **A**(Zᵃ[cf. *dictum igitur... cuius est spiritus
movens* scil. *anima* Alb.]), cf. Mich.ᵖ 128.7–8 τοιοῦτον δὲ τὸ πνεῦμα | ὑποληπτέον]
ὑποληπτέων E || **35–36** οὕτω συστάντων (absol., scil. τῶν ζῴων) **ω**, cf. ᵃ34 τοῖς
ζῴοις et Kühner/Gerth 1904, 81–82 (§ 486 Anmerk. 2) : <τῶν> οὕτω
συστάντων Farquharson n. 2 vel <μόριον τῶν> οὕτω συστάντων Barnes 1980,
226 || **36** ποιεῖν] ποιεῖ **β**(BᶜEʳb) || **703ᵇ1** ἑαυτῶν **β**(BᶜEʳb) : αὑτῶν **a** (αὑτοῦ PMᵒ :
αὑτῷ Zᵃa.c.) : αὐτῶν edd.

Caput 11

703ᵇ5 πλείστας] πλείστους E L Vᵖ | οὐχ] om. E || **7** πολλάκις] πολλάκι E |
μέν... οὐ μέντοι **β**(BᶜEʳb) (cf. Denniston *Greek Particles* 370) : μέν om. cett, edd.
|| **8** οὐχ ἑκουσίους] οὐχ ἑκουσίως E(ἑκουσίως) ZᵃBᵖ || **8–9** ὕπνον καὶ ἐγρήγορσιν
καὶ ἀναπνοήν] ὕπνον ἐγρήγορσιν καὶ ἀναπνοήν **β**(BᶜEʳ) **μ**(PBᵖMᵒ) : ὕπνον καὶ
ἐγρήγορσιν ἀναπνοήν **θ**(NXHᵃLVᵍ) : ὕπνον καὶ ἐγρήγορσιν **A**(ZᵃAnon.) || **9**
ἄλλαι] ἄλλα E || **12** αὐξάνεσθαι **β**(BᶜEʳb)N : αὔξεσθαι cett., edd. || **13** ὥστ᾽ ἤδη
(ὥστε ἤδη b)] ὥστε μη ἤδη E : ὥστ᾽ ἤδη καὶ **μ**(PBᵖMᵒ) || **15** θερμότητες καὶ
ψύξεις] θερμότητές τε καὶ ψύξεις E **λ**(XHᵃLVᵍ) : θερμότης καὶ ψύξις *Γ*ι(*caliditas
et frigiditas* G)N | θύραθεν καὶ] θύραθεν καὶ αἱ E **δ**(*Γ*ι[Gιz] NXLVᵍ)b (αἱ ex
archetypi margine, ut vid.), edd. || **16** ὑπάρχουσιν φυσικαί dedi : ὑπάρχουσιν αἱ
φυσικαί **β**(BᶜEʳ) (αἱ ex archetypi margine, ut vid.) : ὑπάρχουσαι αἱ φυσικαί b :
ὑπάρχουσαι φυσικαί cett. (**a** participium fecit duorum articulorum αἵ τε... καὶ
αἱ causa, ut vid.) | τὸν λόγον] τῶν λόγον E || **22–23** τούτου δ᾽—ζωτικήν) 'ut
interpolamentum' del. Jaeger Forster Nussbaum (cf. Nussbaum 1975, 602–603,
quae paginae in Nussbaum 1978 exciderunt), sed cf. Barnes 1980, 226 || **22**
τούτου] τοῦτο (sic!) E vel τοῦτο Zᵃ, cf. *Po*. 4, 1448ᵇ13 || **24** τὰς γὰρ] τὰς E N Eʳ
Bekker || **28** ἄλληλα δὲ] ἀλλήλας E(ἀλλήλας) edd. : *autem* om. GR' : ἄλληλα
ι(ZᵃPBᵖMᵒ); de καὶ... δὲ cf. supra 700ᵃ30 et Denniston *Greek Particles* 200–201
|| **29–36** diagramma servaverunt et **β**(Eʳ) et **γ**(**A**[ZᵃAnon.]CᵃOᵈ) | diagrammatis
formae traduntur tres, quarum primam servant ZᵃCᵃOᵈ, alteram praebet Eʳ,
tertiam manu propria fecit Alb. (autographon Coloniense fol. 348r = p. 71

Geyer) qui ingenii quo erat acumine varietatem litterarum ad textum traditum adaptavit:

32 ἀρχή] del. Farquharson n. 3 Nussbaum (sed cf. ᵇ26–28) ‖ **34** ἀπὸ δὲ τοῦ E dedi secundum diagramma : ἀπὸ δὲ τοῦ B ω | ἐπὶ τὸ Γ (Mich.ᶜ 130.22)] Mich. 130.23 λείπει τὸ 'οὐκέτι', ἵν' ᾖ 'ἀπὸ δὲ τοῦ B ἐπὶ τὸ Γ οὐκέτι' : *ad G non adhuc* GI GR' : ἐπὶ τοῦ Γ λείπει τὸ 'οὐκ ἀφικνοῦνται' Zᵃ, cf. *et etiam aliquando non deficit venire ex B in C* Alb. | τῶι β(BᶜEʳb) P E, cf. *propter G* Farquharson n. 4, Jaeger Forster Torraca Louis Nussbaum : τὸ δ' cett., Aldina : τῷ δ' Bekker | ἀπὸ μὲν τοῦ E dedi secundum diagramma : ἀπὸ μὲν τοῦ B ω ‖ **36** ὅτι] ἔτι E Farquharson n. 5 | τὰ αὐτὰ β(BᶜEʳb Γ2[*eadem* GR"])P, unde ταὐτὰ Farquharson n. 6, Jaeger Forster Torraca Louis Nussbaum : ταῦτα cett. (*hec* GI GR') (τοῦτο ξ[BᵖMᵒ] : om.Vᵍ), Bekker ‖ **37** τὸ] om. E ‖ **704ᵃ1** ἐνυπάρχειν] ἐνυπάρχ (abbr.) ι(Zᵃ[ἐνυπάρχην P Mᵒa.c. ut vid. vel ἐν ὑπάρχειν Bᵖ]) : ὑπάρχειν N Aldina Bekker Forster Louis ‖ **704ᵃ3–ᵇ3** non habet b ‖ **704ᵇ1** ἔτι δὲ καὶ περὶ β(Eʳ Γ2[*adhuc autem et de* G] OᵈSVᵖ), cf. *HA* III 519ᵇ22–23 : ἔτι δὲ περὶ cett., edd.

BIBLIOGRAPHY

Accattino/Donini 1996: *Alessandro di Afrodisia, L'Anima*. Traduzione, intro-
duzione e commento a cura di Paolo Accattino e Pierluigi Donini. Roma/
Bari.

Allan 1955: D.J. Allan. 'The Practical Syllogism', *Autour d'Aristote. Recueil
d'études de philosophie ancienne et médiévale offert à Monseigneur A.
Mansion*. Louvain, 325–40.

Argyropoulos/Caras 1980: Roxane D. Argyropoulos and Iannis Caras.
*Inventaire des manuscrits grecs d'Aristote et des ses Commentateurs.
Contribution à l'histoire du texte d'Aristote. Supplément*. Paris.

Bagnall/Worp 2004: Roger S. Bagnall and Klaas A. Worp. *Chronological
Systems of Byzantine Egypt*. Second Edition. Leiden/Boston.

Balme 1987: David M. Balme. 'The Place of Biology in Aristotle's Philosophy',
in *Philosophical Issues in Aristotle's Biology*, ed. Allan Gotthelf and
James G. Lennox. Cambridge, 9–20.

Balme 1992: *Aristotle, De Partibus Animalium I and De Generatione Animalium I*.
Ed. and transl. with notes by David M. Balme. With a report on recent work
and an additional bibliography by Allan Gotthelf. Oxford.

Barnes 1971/2: Jonathan Barnes. 'Aristotle's Concept of Mind', *Proceedings of
the Aristotelian Society* 72, 101–14.

Barnes 1980: Jonathan Barnes. 'Review of Nussbaum 1978', *The Classical Review*
30/2, 222–26.

Barthélemy-Saint-Hilaire 1846: Jules Barthélemy-Saint-Hilaire. *Psychologie
d'Aristote*. Paris.

Bauer/Aland 1988: Walter Bauer. *Griechisch–deutsches Wörterbuch zu den
Schriften des Neuen Testaments und der frühchristlichen Literatur*. 6., völlig
neu bearbeitete Auflage, herausgegeben von Kurt und Barbara Aland.
Berlin/New York.

Beare 1908: John I. Beare. *Greek Theories of Elementary Cognition from
Alcmaeon to Aristotle*. Oxford.

Bekker 1831: *Aristoteles Graece ex recensione Immanuelis Bekkeri*. Edidit
Academia Regia Borussica. Volumen prius. Berlin.

Bénatouïl 2004: Thomas Bénatouïl. 'L'usage des analogies dans le *De Motu
Animalium*', in Laks/Rashed 2004, 81–114.

Berger 2005: Friederike Berger. *Die Textgeschichte der* Historia Animalium *des
Aristoteles*. Serta Graeca 21. Wiesbaden.

Berryman 2002: Sylvia Berryman. 'Aristotle on *Pneuma* and Animal Self-Motion', *Oxford Studies in Ancient Philosophy* 23, 85–97.

Berryman 2003: Sylvia Berryman. 'Ancient Automata and Mechanical Explanation', *Phronesis* 48, 344–69.

Berryman 2009: Sylvia Berryman. *The Mechanical Hypothesis in Ancient Greek Natural Philosophy*. Cambridge.

Biehl 1898: *Aristotelis Parva Naturalia*. Recognovit Guilelmus Biehl. Leipzig.

Blass/Debrunner/Rehkopf 2001: Friedrich Blass/Albert Debrunner. *Grammatik des neutestamentlichen Griechisch*. Bearbeitet von Friedrich Rehkopf. 18. Auflage. Göttingen.

Bloch 2003: David Bloch. 'Alexander of Aphrodisias as a Textual Witness: The Commentary on the *De Sensu*', *Cahiers de l'institut du moyen-âge grec et latin* 74, 21–38.

Bloch 2008: David Bloch. 'The Text of Aristotle's *De sensu* and *De memoria*', *Revue d'histoire des textes*, n.s. 3, 1–58.

Block 1961: Irving Block. 'The Order of Aristotle's Psychological Writings', *American Journal of Philology* 82, 50–77.

Bodnár 2004: István Bodnár. 'The Mechanical Principles of Animal Motion', in Laks/Rashed 2004, 137–48.

Bonitz 1863: Hermann Bonitz. 'Aristotelische Studien. 3', in *Sitzungsberichte der Philosophisch-Historischen Classe der Kaiserlichen Akademie der Wissenschaften*. Zweiundvierzigster Band. Wien, 25–109 (reprinted in Bonitz 1969, 155–239).

Bonitz 1866: Hermann Bonitz. 'Aristotelische Studien. IV', in *Sitzungsberichte der Philosophisch-Historischen Classe der Kaiserlichen Akademie der Wissenschaften*. Zweiundfünfzigster Band. Wien, 347–423 (reprinted in Bonitz 1969, 240–316).

Bonitz 1867: Hermann Bonitz. 'Aristotelische Studien. V', in *Sitzungsberichte der Philosophisch-Historischen Classe der Kaiserlichen Akademie der Wissenschaften*. Fünfundfünfzigster Band. Wien, 13–55 (reprinted in Bonitz 1969, 317–59).

Bonitz 1870: 'Index Aristotelicus. Edidit Hermann Bonitz', in *Aristotelis Opera*. Edidit Academia Regia Borussica. Volumen Quintum. *Aristotelis qui ferebantur librorum fragmenta. Scholiorum in Aristotelem supplementum. Index Aristotelicus*. Berlin.

Bonitz 1969: Hermann Bonitz. *Aristotelische Studien*. Fünf Teile in einem Band. Reprografischer Nachdruck der Ausgaben Wien 1862–1867. Hildesheim.

Bos/Ferwerda 2008: *Aristotle on the Life-Bearing Spirit* (De Spiritu): *A Discussion with Plato and His Predecessors on* Pneuma *as the Instrumental Body of the Soul*, ed. Abraham P. Bos and Rein Ferwerda. Leiden.

Brandis 1857: Christian A. Brandis. *Aristoteles und seine akademischen Zeitgenossen*. Handbuch der Geschichte der Griechisch-Römischen Philosophie, zweiter Teil, zweite Abhandlung, zweite Hälfte. Berlin.

Browning 1962: Robert Browning. 'An Unpublished Funeral Oration on Anna Comnena', *Proceedings of the Cambridge Philological Society* n.s. 8, 1–12.

Bruns 1887: *Alexandri Aphrodisiensis praeter commentaria scripta minora. De anima cum Mantissa*. Consilio et auctoritate Academiae Litterarum Regiae Borussicae. Ed. Ivo Bruns. Supplementum Aristotelicum II, I. Berlin.

Buddensiek 2009: Friedemann Buddensiek. 'Aristoteles' Zirbeldrüse? Zum Verhältnis von Seele und *pneuma* in Aristoteles' Theorie der Ortsbewegung der Lebewesen', in *Body and Soul in Ancient Philosophy*, ed. Dorothea Frede and Burkhard Reis. Berlin/New York, 309–29.

Bywater 1909: Ἀριστοτέλους περὶ ποιητικῆς. *Aristotle on the Art of Poetry*, revised text with critical introduction, transl., and commentary by Ingram Bywater. Oxford.

Canart 1980: Paul Canart. *Lezioni di paleografia e di codicologia greca*. Città del Vaticano (http://pyle.it/wp-content/uploads/2014/08/Canart_Lezioni_L. pdf; 20/12/18).

Canart 2008: Paul Canart. 'Additions et corrections au Repertorium der Griechischen Kopisten *800–1600*, 3', in *Vaticana et Medievalia. Études en l'honneur de Louis Duval-Arnould*, ed. Jean Marie Martin, Bernadette Martin-Hisard, and Agostino Paravicini Bagliani. Millennio medievale 71. Firenze, 41–63.

Carlini 1972: Antonio Carlini. *Studi sulla tradizione antica e medievale del Fedone*. Roma.

Carter 2018: Jason Carter. 'Does the Soul Weave? Reconsidering *De Anima* 1.4, 408a29–b18' *Phronesis* 63, 25–63.

Caston 1996: Victor Caston. 'Why Aristotle Needs Imagination', *Phronesis* 41/1, 20–55.

Caston 2006: Victor Caston. 'Aristotle's Psychology', in *A Companion to Ancient Philosophy*, ed. Mary Louise Gill and Pierre Pellegrin. Malden, 316–46.

Cavallo 2000: Guglielmo Cavallo. 'Scritture informali, cambio grafico e pratiche librarie a Bisanzio tra i secoli XI e XII', in *I manoscritti greci tra riflessione e dibattito*. Atti del V Colloquio Internazionale di Paleografia Greca (Cremona, 4–10 ottobre 1998), ed. Giancarlo Prato. Papyrologica Florentina 31. Vol. 1. Firenze, 219–38.

Chaniotis 2004: Angelos Chaniotis. 'Epigraphic Evidence for the Philosopher Alexander of Aphrodisias', *Bulletin of the Institute of Classical Studies* 47, 79–81.

Chantraine 1968–1980: Pierre Chantraine, *Dictionnaire étymologique de la langue grecque. Histoire des mots.* 4 Vols., Paris.

Charles 1984: David Charles. *Aristotle's Philosophy of Action.* London.

Charles 2009a: David Charles. 'Aristotle on Desire and Action', in *Body and Soul in Ancient Philosophy*, ed. Dorothea Frede and Burkhard Reis, Berlin/New York, 291–307.

Charles 2009b: David Charles. '*Nicomachean Ethics* VII.3: Varieties of *akrasia*', in *Aristotle:* Nicomachean Ethics *Book VII. Symposium Aristotelicum*, ed. Carlo Natali, Oxford, 41–71.

Charles 2011: David Charles. 'Desire in Action: Aristotle's Move', in *Moral Psychology and Human Action in Aristotle*, ed. Michael Pakaluk and Giles Pearson, Cambridge, 75–94.

Classen/Steup 1922: *Thukydides*. Erklärt von J. Classen. Achter Band. *Achtes Buch*. Dritte Auflage. Neugestaltet von J. Steup. Berlin.

Cohn 1887: Leopold Cohn. *Zu den Paroemiographen*. Mitteilungen aus Handschriften. Breslauer philologische Abhandlungen II 2. Breslau.

Conca 1990: *Nicetas Eugenianus, De Drosillae et Chariclis amoribus*. Edidit Fabricius Conca. Amsterdam.

Coope 2015: Ursula Coope. 'Self-Motion as Other-Motion in Aristotle's *Physics*', in *Aristotle's Physics: A Critical Guide*, ed. Mariska Leunissen. Cambridge, 245–64.

Coope 2020: Ursula Coope. 'Animal and Celestial Motion: The Role of an External Springboard MA 2–3', in Rapp/Primavesi 2020, 240–72.

Cooper 1975: John M. Cooper. *Reason and Human Good in Aristotle*. Cambridge, Mass.

Cooper 2020: John M. Cooper. 'The Role of Thought in Animal Voluntary Self-Locomotion MA 7 (through 701b1)', in Rapp/Primavesi 2020, 345–86.

Corcilius 2008a: Klaus Corcilius. *Streben und Bewegen. Aristoteles' Theorie der animalischen Ortsbewegung.* Quellen und Studien zur Philosophie 79. Berlin/New York.

Corcilius 2008b: Klaus Corcilius. 'Two-Jobs for Aristotle's Practical Syllogism?', in Rapp/Brüllmann 2008, 163–84.

Corcilius 2008c: Klaus Corcilius. 'Praktische Syllogismen bei Aristoteles', *Archiv für Geschichte der Philosophie* 90/3, 247–97.

Corcilius 2008d: Klaus Corcilius. 'Aristoteles' praktische Syllogismen in der zweiten Hälfte des 20. Jahrhunderts', in Rapp/Brüllmann 2008, 101–32.

Corcilius 2020: Klaus Corcilius. 'Resuming Discussion of the Common Cause of Animal Self-Motion: How Does the Soul Move the Body? MA 6', in Rapp/Primavesi 2020, 299–344.

Corcilius/Gregoric 2010: Klaus Corcilius and Pavel Gregoric. 'Separability vs. Difference: Parts and Capacities of the Soul in Aristotle', *Oxford Studies in Ancient Philosophy* 39, 81–119.

Corcilius/Gregoric 2013: Klaus Corcilius and Pavel Gregoric. 'Aristotle's Model of Animal Motion', *Phronesis* 58, 52–97.

Coren 2022: Daniel Coren. 'Review of Rapp/Primavesi 2020', *Rhizomata* 10/1, 153–63.

Coughlin/Leith/Lewis 2020: *The Concept of Pneuma after Aristotle*, ed. Sean Coughlin, David Leith, and Orly Lewis. Berlin.

Coxe 1854: Henry O. Coxe. *Catalogi codicum manuscriptorum Bibliothecæ Bodleianæ pars tertia codices Græcos et Latinos Canonicianos complectens.* Oxford.

Crawford 1953: *Averroes Cordubensis, Commentarium Magnum in Aristotelis De Anima Libros*, ed. F. Stuart Crawford. Cambridge, Mass.

Crubellier 2004: Michel Crubellier. 'Le "syllogisme pratique", ou Comment la pensée meut le corps', in Laks/Rashed 2004, 9–26.

Darrouzès 1970: Jean Darrouzès. *Georges et Dèmètrios Tornikès, Lettres et Discours*. Introduction, texte, analyses, traduction et notes. Paris.

De Andrés 1987: Gregorio de Andrés. *Catalogo de los codices griegos de la biblioteca nacional.* Madrid.

De Groot 2008: Jean De Groot. '*Dunamis* and the Science of Mechanics: Aristotle on Animal Motion', *Journal of the History of Philosophy* 46, 43–68.

De Groot 2014: Jean De Groot. *Aristotle's Empiricism. Experience and Mechanics in the 4th Century BC.* Las Vegas/Zürich/Athína.

De Leemans 2011a: *Aristoteles, De Progressu Animalium, De Motu Animalium. Translatio Guillelmi de Morbeka*, ed. Pieter de Leemans. Aristoteles Latinus XVII 2.II–III. Turnhout.

De Leemans 2011b: *Aristoteles, De Motu Animalium. Fragmenta translationis anonymae.* Ed. Pieter de Leemans. Aristoteles Latinus XVII 1.III. Turnhout.

Denniston 1954: John D. Denniston. *The Greek Particles*. Second edition revised by Kenneth J. Dover. Oxford (first edition 1934).

Diels 1882: *Simplicii In Aristotelis Physicorum libros quattuor priores commentaria*. Consilio et auctoritate Academiae Litterarum Regiae Borussicae ed. Hermannus Diels. Berlin.

Diels 1895: *Simplicii In Aristotelis Physicorum libros quattuor posteriores commentaria*. Consilio et auctoritate Academiae Litterarum Regiae Borussicae ed. Hermannus Diels. Berlin.

Donini 1968: Pier Luigi Donini. 'Il *De Anima* di Alessandro di Afrodisia e Michele Efesio', *Rivista di Filologia e di Istruzione Classica* 96, 316–23.

Dorandi 2006: 'La *Vita Hesychii* d'Aristote', *Studi Classici e Orientali* 52, 87–106.

Drachmann 1963: Aage G. Drachmann. *The Mechanical Technology of Greek and Roman Antiquity: A Study of the Literary Sources.* København/Madison/London.

Drossaart Lulofs 1947: *Aristotelis De Insomniis et De Divinatione per Somnum: A new Edition of the Greek Text with the Latin Translation. By Hendrik J. Drossaart Lulofs.* Philosophia Antiqua II. Vol 1: *Preface, Greek Text.* Leiden.

Düring 1957: Ingemar Düring. *Aristotle in the Ancient Biographical Tradition.* Studia Graeca et Latina Gothoburgensia V. Gothenburg.

Düring 1959: Ingemar Düring. 'Review of Torraca 1958a', *Gnomon* 31/5, 415–18.

Düring 1966: Ingemar Düring. *Aristoteles. Darstellung und Interpretation seines Denkens.* Heidelberg (reprinted 2005).

Emonds 1941: Hilarius Emonds. *Zweite Auflage im Altertum.* Kulturgeschichtliche Studien zur Überlieferung der antiken Literatur. Klassisch-Philologische Studien Heft 14. Leipzig.

Escobar 1990: Angel Escobar. *Die Textgeschichte der Aristotelischen Schrift ΠΕΡΙ ΕΝΥΠΝΙΩΝ. Ein Beitrag zur Überlieferungsgeschichte der* Parva Naturalia. Inauguraldissertation zur Erlangung des Doktorgrades am Fachbereich Altertumswissenschaften der Freien Universität Berlin. Berlin (unpublished).

Everson 1997: Stephen Everson. *Aristotle on Perception.* Oxford.

Falcon 2017: Andrea Falcon. 'The Place of the *De Motu Animalium* in Aristotle's Natural Philosophy', in Wians/Polansky 2017, 215–35.

Falcon 2021: Andrea Falcon. 'Review of Rapp/Primavesi 2020', *Mind* (forthcoming; preprint published online: https://doi.org/10.1093/mind/fzab018).

Farquharson 1912: Arthur S.L. Farquharson. 'De Motu Animalium, De Incessu Animalium', in *The Works of Aristotle*, transl. into English under the editorship of John A. Smith and William D. Ross. Vol. V. Oxford.

Fazzo 2004: Silvia Fazzo. 'Sur la composition du traité dit *de motu animalium.* Contribution à l'analyse de la théorie aristotélicienne du premier moteur', in Laks/Rashed 2004, 203–29.

Fernandez 2014: Patricio Fernandez. 'Reasoning and the Unity of Aristotle's Account of Animal Motion', *Oxford Studies in Ancient Philosophy* 47, 151–203.

Ferro 2021: Antonio Ferro. *Aristotle on Self-Motion: The Criticism of Plato in De Anima and Physics VIII.* Basel.

Flashar 1972: *Aristoteles. Mirabilia.* Übersetzt von Hellmut Flashar. Aristoteles, Werke in deutscher Übersetzung 18: *Opuscula, Teil II / Teil III.* Berlin.

Foerster 1921: *Libanii Opera.* Vol. X. *Epistulae 1–839.* Recensuit Richard Foerster. Leipzig.

Förstel 1999: Christian Förstel, 'Manuel le Rhéteur et Origène. Note sur deux manuscrits parisiens', *Revue des études byzantines* 57, 245–54.

Formentin 2008: Maria R. Formentin, 'Uno *Scriptorium* a Palazzo Farnese?', *Scripta* 1, 77–102.

Forster 1937: 'Aristotle, Movement of Animals', in *Aristotle, Parts of Animals*, with an English transl. by Arthur L. Peck. *Movement of Animals, Progression of Animals*, with an English transl. by Edward S. Forster. London/Cambridge, Mass., 435–79 (second edition 1961).

Franceschini 1958: Ezio Franceschini. 'Review of Torraca 1958a', *Aevum* 32/3, 294–95.

Freely 2012: John Freely. *The Flame of Miletus: The Story of Greek Science from Antiquity to the Renaissance*. London.

Freudenthal 1995: Gad Freudenthal. *Aristotle's Theory of Material Substance: Heat and Pneuma, Form and Soul*. Oxford.

Freudenthal 1869: Jacob Freudenthal. 'Zur Kritik und Exegese von Aristoteles' περὶ τῶν κοινῶν σώματος καὶ ψυχῆς ἔργων (parva naturalia)', *Rheinisches Museum* 24, 81–93 and 392–419.

Frisk 1970: Hjalmar Frisk, *Griechisches etymologisches Wörterbuch*. Band II: Κρ–Ω. Heidelberg.

Furley 1967: David Furley. *Two Studies in the Greek Atomists*. Princeton, NJ.

Furley 1978: David Furley. 'Self-Movers', in Lloyd/Owen 1978, 165–79 (reprinted in Gill/Lennox 1994, 3–14).

Furley 1994: *See* Furley 1978.

Gallop 1996: *Aristotle on Sleep and Dreams*. A text and transl. with introduction, notes and glossary by David Gallop. Warminster.

Gamillscheg 1997: Ernst Gamillscheg. *Repertorium der Griechischen Kopisten 800–1600*. 3. Teil: *Handschriften aus Bibliotheken Roms mit dem Vatikan*. A. *Verzeichnis der Kopisten*. Unter Mitarbeit von Dieter Harlfinger und Paolo Eleuteri. Wien.

Geyer 1955: 'Alberti Magni Liber de principiis motus processivi. Ad fidem autographi edidit Bernhardus Geyer', in *Sancti doctoris Ecclesiae Alberti Magni Ordinis Fratrum Praedicatorum Episcopi Opera omnia*, ad fidem codicum manuscriptorum edenda apparatu critico notis prolegomenis indicibus instruenda curavit Institutum Alberti Magni Coloniense Bernhardo Geyer praeside, tomus XII. Münster, XXI–XXXII and 47–76.

Gill/Lennox 1994: *Self-Motion: From Aristotle to Newton*, ed. Mary Louise Gill and James G. Lennox. Princeton.

Golitsis 2011: Pantelis Golitsis. 'Copistes, élèves et érudits. La production de manuscrits philosophiques autour de Georges Pachymère', in *The Legacy of Bernard de Montfaucon: Three Hundred Years of Studies on Greek Handwriting*. Proceedings of the Seventh International Colloquium of Greek Palaeography (Madrid–Salamanca, 15–20 September 2008), ed. A. Bravo García, I. Pérez Martín. 2 vols. Turnhout 2010, 157–70 and 757–68.

Gottlieb 2008: Paula Gottlieb. 'The Ethical Syllogism', in Rapp/Brüllmann 2008, 197–212.

Goulet 1989: Richard Goulet. 'Aristote de Stagire. Prosopographie—L'Œuvre d'Aristote', in *Dictionnaire des philosophes antiques*, ed. Richard Goulet. Vol. 1: *Abam(m)on à Axiothéa*. Paris, 413–43.

Gourinat 2004: Jean-Baptiste Gourinat. 'Syllogisme pratique et logique déontique,' in Laks/Rashed 2004, Villeneuve d'Ascq, 27–66.

Gourinat 2008: Jean-Baptiste Gourinat. 'Is there Anything Logically Distinctive about Practical Syllogism?', in Rapp/Brüllmann 2008, 133–150.

Gregoric 2020a: Pavel Gregoric. 'Soul and *Pneuma* in *De Spiritu*', in Coughlin/Leith/Lewis 2020, 17–35.

Gregoric 2020b: Pavel Gregoric. 'The Origin and the Instrument of Animal Motion MA 9–10', in Rapp/Primavesi 2020, 416–44.

Gregoric/Kuhar 2014: Pavel Gregoric and Martin Kuhar. 'Aristotle's Physiology of Animal Motion: On Neura and Muscles', *Apeiron* 47/1, 94–115.

Gregoric/Lewis 2015: Pavel Gregoric and Orly Lewis. 'Pseudo-Aristotelian *De Spiritu*: A New Case Against Authenticity', *Classical Philology* 110, 159–67.

Gutas 1986: Dimitri Gutas. 'The Spurious and the Authentic in the Arabic Lives of Aristotle', in *Pseudo-Aristotle in the Middle Ages: The* Theology *and Other Texts*, ed. Jill Kraye, William F. Ryan, and Charles B. Schmitt. London, 15–36.

Hankinson 2020: R.J. Hankinson. 'Aristotle and the Mechanics of Desire MA 7 (from 701b2)–8', in Rapp/Primavesi 2020, 387–415.

Hardie 1964: William F.R. Hardie. 'Aristotle's Treatment of the Relation Between the Soul and the Body', *The Philosophical Quarterly* 14, 53–72.

Hardie 1968: William F.R. Hardie. *Aristotle's Ethical Theory.* Oxford.

Harlfinger 1971: Dieter Harlfinger. *Die Textgeschichte der pseudo-Aristotelischen Schrift* Περὶ ἀτόμων γραμμῶν. *Ein kodikologisch-kulturgeschichtlicher Beitrag zur Klärung der Überlieferungsverhältnisse im Corpus Aristotelicum.* Amsterdam.

Harlfinger/Wiesner 1964: Dieter Harlfinger and Jürgen Wiesner. 'Die griechischen Handschriften des Aristoteles und seiner Kommentatoren. Ergänzungen und Berichtigungen zum *Inventaire* von A. Wartelle', *Scriptorium* 18, 238–57.

Hayduck 1882: *Simplicii In libros Aristotelis* De Anima *Commentaria.* Consilio et auctoritate Academiae Litterarum Regiae Borussicae, ed. Michael Hayduck. Berlin.

Hayduck 1897: *Ioannis Philoponi In Aristotelis* De Anima *libros Commentaria.* Consilio et auctoritate Academiae Litterarum Regiae Borussicae, ed. Michael Hayduck. Berlin.

Hayduck 1899: *Alexander Aphrodisiensis In Aristotelis* metereologicorum *libros commentarium.* Consilio et auctoritate Academiae Litterarum Regiae Borussicae, ed. Michael Hayduck. Berlin.

Hayduck 1904: *Michaeli Ephesii In libros* De Partibus Animalium, De Animalium Motione, De Animalium Incessu *Commentaria.* Consilio et auctoritate Academiae Litterarum Regiae Borussicae, ed. Michael Hayduck. Berlin.

Hecquet-Devienne 2000: Myriam Hecquet-Devienne. 'Les mains du *Parisinus Graecus* 1853', *Scrittura e Civiltà* 24, 103–71.

Heiberg 1894: *Simplicii In Aristotelis De caelos commentaria.* Consilio et auctoritate Academiae Litterarum Regiae Borussicae ed. I.L. Heiberg. Berlin.

Hein 1985: Christel Hein. *Definition und Einteilung der Philosophie. Von der spätantiken Einleitungsliteratur zur arabischen Enzyklopädie.* Frankfurt am Main.

Heinze 1899: *Themistii In libros Aristotelis De Anima Paraphrasis.* Consilio et auctoritate Academiae Litterarum Regiae Borussicae, ed. Richard Heinze. Berlin.

Henry/Schwyzer 1964: *Plotini Opera.* Tomus I: *Porphyrii vita Plotini, Enneades I–III,* ed. Paul Henry and Hans-Rudolf Schwyzer. Oxford.

Hicks 1907: Robert D. Hicks. *Aristotle, De Anima,* with transl., introductions, and notes. Cambridge.

Hunger 1961: Herbert Hunger. *Katalog der griechischen Handschriften der Österreichischen Nationalbibliothek.* Teil 1: *Codices Historici. Codices Philosophici et Philologici.* Wien.

Irmischer 1852: Johann C. Irmischer. *Handschriften-Katalog der Königlichen Universitäts-Bibliothek zu Erlangen.* Frankfurt am Main/Erlangen.

Isépy 2016: Peter Isépy. *Zur mittelalterlichen Überlieferung von Aristoteles' De Motu Animalium. Die Bedeutung der Übersetzung Wilhelms von Moerbeke und der Paraphrase Alberts des Großen für die griechische Texttradition.* Serta Graeca 31. Wiesbaden.

Isépy/Prapa 2018: Peter Isépy and Christina Prapa. 'Der Codex *Berolinensis Phillippicus* 1507. Nachfahre eines unabhängigen Zweiges der Aristoteles-Überlieferung? Eine kodikologisch-paläographische, stemmatische und textkritische Untersuchung am Beispiel von Aristoteles, *Sens.* und *Mem.*', *Revue d'histoire des textes* n.s. 13, 1–58.

Isépy/Primavesi 2014: Peter Isépy and Oliver Primavesi. 'Helladios und Hesychios. Neues zum Text der *Bibliotheke* des Photios (Cod. 279)', *Zeitschrift für Papyrologie und Epigraphik* 192, 121–42.

Jaeger 1913a: Werner Jaeger. 'Das Pneuma im Lykeion', *Hermes* 48/1, 29–74.

Jaeger 1913b: *Aristotelis De Animalium Motione et De Animalium Incessu, Ps-Aristotelis De spiritu libellus,* ed. Vernerus Guilelmus Jaeger. Leipzig.

Johansen 2012: Thomas Kjeller Johansen. *The Powers of Aristotle's Soul.* Oxford.

Joly/Byl 1984: *Hippocratis De diaeta,* ed. in linguam francogallicam vertit, commentatus est Robert Joly adiuvante Simon Byl, editio altera lucis ope expressa addendis et corrigendis aucta curatis a Simon Byl. Corpus Medicorum Graecorum I/2,4. Berlin.

Judson 1994: Lindsay Judson. 'Heavenly Motion and the Unmoved Mover', in Gill/Lennox 1994, 155–71.

Kassel 1965: *Aristotelis de arte poetica liber*. Recognovit brevique adnotatione critica instruxit Rudolf Kassel. Oxford.

Kassel 1971: Rudolf Kassel. *Der Text der Aristotelischen Rhetorik. Prolegomena zu einer kritischen Ausgabe*. Peripatoi 3. Berlin/New York.

Kassel 1976: *Aristotelis ars rhetorica*, ed. Rudolfus Kassel. Berlin/New York.

Keßler 1995: *Aristoteles Latine interpretibus variis*. Ed. Academia Regia Borussica. Berlin 1831. Nachdruck herausgegeben und eingeleitet von Eckhard Keßler. Humanistische Bibliothek II 30. München.

Koch 2017: Lutz Koch. τὸ τῆς λέξεως συνεχές. *Michael von Ephesos und die Rezeption der Aristotelischen Schrift* De Motu Animalium *in Byzanz*. Diss., Universität Hamburg 2015; published online (http://ediss.sub.uni-hamburg. de/volltexte/2017/8647/; 09/11/17).

Kollesch 1960: Jutta Kollesch. 'Aristoteles, De motu anim. 701b2–9', *Philologus* 104, 143–4.

Kollesch 1985: Jutta Kollesch. *Aristoteles, Über die Bewegung der Lebewesen, Über die Fortbewegung der Lebewesen*. Übersetzt und erläutert von Jutta Kollesch. Aristoteles, Werke in deutscher Übersetzung 17/II–III. Darmstadt.

Kühner/Blass 1890–2: Raphael Kühner. *Ausführliche Grammatik der Griechischen Sprache*. Erster Teil: *Elementar- und Formenlehre*. Dritte Auflage in zwei Bänden. In neuer Bearbeitung besorgt von Dr. Friedrich Blass. Hannover (reprinted Darmstadt 2015).

Kühner/Gerth 1898–1904: Raphael Kühner. *Ausführliche Grammatik der Griechischen Sprache*. Zweiter Teil. *Satzlehre*. Dritte Auflage in zwei Bänden. In neuer Bearbeitung besorgt von Bernhard Gerth. Hannover (reprinted Darmstadt 2015).

Kung 1982: Joan Kung. 'Aristotle's *De Motu Animalium* and the Separability of the Sciences', *Journal of the History of Philosophy* 20, 65–76.

Labarrière 2004: Jean-Louis Labarrière. *Langage, vie politique et mouvement des animaux*. Études aristotéliciennes. Paris.

Laks 2020: André Laks. 'Articulating the De Motu Animalium. The Place of the Treatise within the Corpus Aristotelicum', in Rapp/Primavesi 2020, 472–95.

Laks 2000: André Laks. 'Metaphysics Λ 7', in *Aristotle's Metaphysics Lambda*, ed. Michael Frede and David Charles. Oxford, 207–44.

Laks 2013: André Laks. *Los motores inmóviles de Aristóteles: una introducción sencilla a un problema complejo*. Cátedra Tópicos 2012. Mexico.

Laks/Rashed 2004: *Aristote et le mouvement des animaux. Dix études sur le De Motu Animalium*, ed. André Laks and Marwan Rashed. Villeneuve d'Ascq.

Landauer 1902: *Themistii in libros Aristotelis de caelo paraphrasis Hebraice et Latine. Consilio et auctoritate Academiae Litterarum Regiae Borussicae*, ed. Samuel Landauer. Berlin.

Lemerle 1971: Paul Lemerle. *Le premier humanisme byzantin. Notes et remarques sur enseignement et culture à Byzance des origines au Xe siècle*. Bibliothèque Byzantine, Études 6. Paris.

Lennox 2010: James G. Lennox. 'Aristotle's Natural Science: The Many and the One', *Apeiron* 43/2–3, 1–23.

Linnenkugel 1926: Albert Linnenkugel. *De Lucillo Tarrhaeo epigrammatum poeta, grammatico, rhetore*. Rhetorische Studien 13. Paderborn.

Lippert 1903: *Ibn Al-Qifṭī's Taʾrīḫ al-ḥukamāʾ*. Auf Grund der Vorarbeiten Aug. Müller's herausgegeben von Julius Lippert. Leipzig.

Lloyd/Owen 1978: *Aristotle on Mind and the Senses*. Proceedings of the Seventh Symposium Aristotelicum, ed. Geoffrey E.R. Lloyd, and Gwilym E.L. Owen. Cambridge.

Loening 1903: Richard Loening. *Die Zurechnungslehre des Aristoteles*. Jena.

Lorenz 2006: Hendrik Lorenz. *The Brute Within: Appetive Desire in Plato and Aristotle*. Oxford.

Lorenz 2008: Hendrik Lorenz. 'Zur Bewegung der Lebewesen bei Aristoteles', in Rapp/Corcilius 2008, 53–64.

Louis 1973: *Aristote, Marche des Animaux, Mouvement des Animaux, Index des traités biologiques*, texte établi et traduit par Pierre Louis. Paris.

LSJ 1996: Henry G. Liddell, Robert Scott, and Henry S. Jones. *A Greek–English Lexicon*, with a revised supplement. Oxford.

Luna/Segonds 2007: *Proclus, Commentaire sur le Parménide de Platon*, texte établi et traduit par Concetta Luna et Alain Ph. Segonds. Tome I, 1ère partie: *Introduction générale*. Paris.

Lust/Eynikel/Hauspie 2015: Johan Lust, Erik Eynikel, and Katrin Hauspie. *Greek–English Lexicon of the Septuagint*. Third corrected edition. Stuttgart.

Maas 1937: Paul Maas. 'Leitfehler und stemmatische Typen', *Byzantinische Zeitschrift* 37, 289–94.

Maas/Flower 1958: Paul Maas. *Textual Criticism*, transl. from the German by Barbara Flower. Oxford.

Manuwald 1989: Bernd Manuwald. *Studien zum Unbewegten Beweger in der Naturphilosophie des Aristoteles*. Akademie der Wissenschaften und der Literatur, Abhandlungen der geistes- und sozialwissenschaftlichen Klasse 1989/9. Stuttgart.

Mayhew 2014: *The Aristotelian* Problemata Physica: *Philosophical and Scientific Investigations*, ed. Robert Mayhew. Leiden/Boston.

Mayhew 2021: Robert Mayhew. 'Review of Rapp/Primavesi 2020', *Bryn Mawr Classical Review* (https://bmcr.brynmawr.edu/2021/2021.12.46/; 21/11/2022).

Menn 2002: Stephen Menn. 'Aristotle's Definition of Soul and the Program of the *De Anima*', *Oxford Studies in Ancient Philosophy* 22, 83–109.

Meyer 1993: Susan Sauvé Meyer. *Aristotle on Moral Responsibility*. Cambridge, Mass./Oxford.

Meyer 1994: Susan Sauvé Meyer. 'Self-Movement and External Causation', in Gill/Lennox 1994, 65–80.

Mioni 1958: *Aristotelis codices graeci qui in bibliothecis Venetis adservantur*, recognovit adnotatione critica instruxit Elpidius Mioni. Padova.

Mioni 1981: Elpidius Mioni. *Bibliothecae Divi Marci Venetiarum codices graeci manuscripti*. Volumen I. *Thesaurus Antiquus, Codices 1–299*. Roma.

Mondrain 2005: Brigitte Mondrain. 'Traces et mémoire dans la lecture des textes. Les *marginalia* dans les manuscrits scientifiques byzantins', in *Scientia in margine. Études sur les* marginalia *dans les manuscrits scientifiques du Moyen Âge à la Renaissance*, ed. Danielle Jacquart and Charles Burnett. Genève, 1–25.

Mondrain 2011: Brigitte Mondrain. 'Copier et lire des manuscrits théologiques et philosophiques à Byzance', in *Byzantine Theology and its Philosophical Background*, ed. Antonio Rigo. Byzantios. Studies in Byzantine History and Civilization 4. Turnhout, 87–107.

Moraux 1951: Paul Moraux. *Les listes anciennes des ouvrages d'Aristote*. Louvain.

Moraux 1959: Paul Moraux. 'Review of Torraca 1958a', *L'antiquité classique* 28, 363–66.

Moraux 1967: Paul Moraux. 'Le parisinus graecus 1853 (ms. E)', *Scriptorium* 21, 17–41.

Moraux 1973: Paul Moraux. 'Wiederentdeckung des Corpus Aristotelicum. Erste Ausgaben', in *Der Aristotelismus bei den Griechen. Von Andronikos bis Alexander von Aphrodisias*. Erster Band: *Die Renaissance des Aristotelismus im I. Jh. v. Chr.*, ed. Paul Moraux. Peripatoi 5. Berlin/New York, 1–94.

Moraux et al. 1976: Paul Moraux, Dieter Harlfinger, Diether Reinsch and Jürgen Wiesner. *Aristoteles Graecus. Die griechischen Manuskripte des Aristoteles*. Band 1: *Alexandrien–London*. Berlin/New York.

Morel 2007: Pierre-Marie Morel. *De la matière à l'action. Aristote et le problème du vivant*. Paris.

Morel 2013: Pierre-Marie Morel. *Aristote. Le mouvement des animaux*, suivi de *La locomotion des animaux*, traduction et présentation par Pierre-Marie Morel. Paris.

Morel 2016: Pierre-Marie Morel. 'La physiologie des passions dans le *De Motu Animalium* d'Aristote', in *L'Homme et ses Passions*. Actes du XVIIᵉ Congrès International de l'Association Guillaume Budé, organisé à Lyon du 26 au 29 août 2013, ed. Isabelle Boehm, Jean-Louis Ferrary, and Sylvie Franchet d'Espèrey. Paris, 291–301.

Morel 2020: Pierre-Marie Morel. 'Voluntary or Not? The Physiological Perspective MA 11', in Rapp/Primavesi 2020, 445–71.

Morison 2004: Benjamin Morison. 'Self-Motion in *Physics* VIII', in Laks/ Rashed 2004, 67–80.

Morison 2020: Benjamin Morison. 'Completing the Argument that Locomotion Requires an External and Unmoved Mover MA 4–5', in Rapp/Primavesi 2020, 273–98.

Moss 2012: Jessica Moss. *Aristotle on the Apparent Good: Perception*, Phantasia, *Thought, and Desire*. Oxford.

Mugnier 1953: *Aristote. Petits traités d'histoire naturelle*, text établi et traduit par René Mugnier. Paris.

Müller 2008: Anselm Müller. 'Formal and Material Goodness in Action: Reflections on an Aristotelian Analogy between Cognitive and Practical Teleology', in Rapp/Brüllmann 2008, 213–28.

Newman 1902: *The Politics of Aristotle*, with an introduction, two prefatory essays and notes critical and explanatory by W.L. Newman. Volume III: *Two Essays*. Books III, IV, and V—Text and Notes. Oxford.

Nussbaum 1975a: Martha C. Nussbaum. *Aristotle's De Motu Animalium*. A thesis presented by Martha Louise Craven Nussbaum to The Department of the Classics in partial fulfillment of the requirements for the degree of Doctor of Philosophy in the subject of Classical Philology, Harvard University. Cambridge, Mass.

Nussbaum 1975b: Martha C. Nussbaum. 'Review of Louis 1973', *The Journal of Hellenic Studies* 95, 207–8.

Nussbaum 1976: Martha C. Nussbaum. 'The Text of Aristotle's *De Motu Animalium*', *Harvard Studies in Classical Philology* 80, 111–59.

Nussbaum 1978: Martha C. Nussbaum. *Aristotle's De Motu Animalium*, text with transl., commentary, and interpretive essays. Princeton, NJ (corrected paperback edition 1985).

Nussbaum 1983: Martha C. Nussbaum. 'The "Common Explanation" of Animal Motion', in *Zweifelhaftes im Corpus Aristotelicum*. Akten des 9. Symposium Aristotelicum, ed. Paul Moraux and Jürgen Wiesner. Berlin, 116–56.

Nussbaum 1985: *See* Nussbaum 1978.

Nussbaum 1986: Martha C. Nussbaum. *The Fragility of Goodness: Luck and Ethics in Greek Tragedy and Philosophy*. Cambridge.

Nuyens 1948: François J.C.J. Nuyens. *L'évolution de la psychologie d'Aristote*. Louvain (reprinted 1973).

Oehler 1962: Klaus Oehler. *Die Lehre vom noetischen und dianoetischen Denken bei Platon und Aristoteles. Ein Beitrag zur Erforschung der Geschichte des Bewusstseinsproblems in der Antike*. München.

Omont 1892: Henri Omont. 'Les manuscrits grecs datés des XVe & XVIe siècles de la Bibliothèque Nationale et des autres bibliothèques de France', *Revue des Bibliothèques* 2, 1–87.

Orlandi 2017: Luigi Orlandi. *ANDRONIKOS KALLISTOS: Manuscripts, Activities, Texts.* Diss., Universität Hamburg. Hamburg (unpublished).

Pappa 2002: *Georgios Pachymeres, Philosophia.* Buch 10. *Kommentar zur Metaphysik des Aristoteles*, Editio princeps. Einleitung, Text, Indices von Eleni Pappa. Corpus Philosophorum Medii Aevi 2. Athína.

Pearson 2012: Giles Pearson. *Aristotle on Desire.* Cambridge.

Peck 1943: Arthur L. Peck. 'Appendix B', in *Aristotle, Generation of Animals.* With an English transl. London/Cambridge, Mass., 576–93.

Peck 1953: Arthur L. Peck, 'The Connate *Pneuma*: An Essential Factor in Aristotle's Solutions to the Problems of Reproduction and Sensation', in *Science, Medicine, and History.* Vol. 1, ed. Edgar A. Underwood. London, 111–21.

Platt 1913: Arthur Platt. 'Notes on Aristotle', *The Journal of Philology* 32, 274–99.

Polansky 2007: Roland Polansky. *Aristotle's De Anima.* Cambridge.

Poppelreuter 1891: Hans Poppelreuter. *Zur Psychologie des Aristoteles, Theophrast, Strato.* Leipzig.

Preus 1981: *Aristotle and Michael of Ephesus: On the Movement and Progression of Animals*, transl., with introduction and notes by Anthony Preus. Hildesheim/New York.

Price 2008: Anthony W. Price. 'The Practical Syllogism in Aristotle: A New Interpretation', in Rapp/Brüllmann 2008, 151–162a.

Primavesi 2007: Oliver Primavesi. 'Ein Blick in den Stollen von Skepsis. Vier Kapitel zur frühen Überlieferung des *Corpus Aristotelicum*', *Philologus* 151, 51–77.

Primavesi 2008: Oliver Primavesi. 'Two Notes on the Platonic Text', in *Plato's Theaetetus.* Proceedings of the Sixth Symposium Platonicum Pragense, ed. by Aleš Havlíček, Filip Karfík, and Štěpán Špinka. Praha, 331–71.

Primavesi 2018: O. Primavesi. 'Philologische Einleitung', in Primavesi/Corcilius 2018, xi–cxliv.

Primavesi 2022: Oliver Primavesi. 'Zitatfragment und Textkritik. Empedokles' Theorie der Augenfunktion und der Text des Laternengleichnisses', in *Lachmanns Erbe.* Editionsmethoden in klassischer Philologie und germanistischer Mediävistik, ed. Anna Kathrin Bleuler and Oliver Primavesi. *Beihefte zur Zeitschrift für Deutsche Philologie* 19. Berlin, 427–572.

Primavesi/Corcilius 2018: *Aristoteles. De Motu Animalium. Über die Bewegung der Lebewesen.* Historisch-kritische Edition des griechischen Textes und philologische Einleitung von Oliver Primavesi. Deutsche Übersetzung, philosophische Einleitung und erklärende Anmerkungen von Klaus Corcilius. Hamburg.

Rahlfs/Hanhart 2006: *Septuaginta. Id est Vetus Testamentum graece iuxta LXX interpretes*, ed. Alfred Rahlfs, editio altera quam recognovit et emendavit Robert Hanhart. Duo volumina in uno. Stuttgart.

Rapp 2020a: Christof Rapp. 'The Inner Resting Point and the Common Cause of Animal Motion', in Rapp/Primavesi 2020, 203–39.

Rapp 2020b: Christof Rapp. 'Joints and Movers in the Cliffhanger Passage at the end of Aristotle, De Anima III.10', in *Aristote et l'âme humaine. Lectures de 'De Anima' III offertes à Michel Crubellier*, ed. Gweltaz Guyomarc'h, Claire Louguet, Charlotte Murgier. Louvain-la-Neuve, 273–302.

Rapp 2022: Christof Rapp. "Heart and Soul in Aristotle's De Generatione II", in *Aristotle's* Generation of Animals. A *Comprehensive Approach*. Berlin/Boston, 269–318.

Rapp/Brüllmann 2008: *The Practical Syllogism*, ed. Christof Rapp and Philipp Brüllmann. Logical Analysis and History of Philosophy 11. Paderborn.

Rapp/Corcilius 2008: *Beiträge zur Aristotelischen Handlungstheorie*, ed. Christof Rapp and Klaus Corcilius. Stuttgart.

Rapp/Primavesi 2020: *Aristotle's De Motu Animalium. Symposium Aristotelicum*, ed. Christof Rapp and Oliver Primavesi. Oxford.

Rashed 2001: Marwan Rashed. *Die Überlieferungsgeschichte der aristotelischen Schrift* De generatione et corruptione. Serta Graeca 12. Wiesbaden.

Rashed 2002: Marwan Rashed. 'Nicolas d'Otrante, Guillaume de Moerbeke et la "Collection philosophique"', *Studi Medievali* 43, 693–717.

Rashed 2004: Marwan Rashed. 'Agrégat de parties ou *vinculum substantiale*? Sur une hésitation conceptuelle et textuelle du *corpus* aristotélicien', in Laks/Rashed 2004, 185–202.

Rashed 2021: Ptolémée « al-gharīb ». Épître à Gallus sur la vie, le testament et les écrits d'Aristote. Texte établi et traduit par Marwan Rashed. Paris.

Rebenich/Franke 2012: *Theodor Mommsen und Friedrich Althoff. Briefwechsel 1882–1903.* Herausgegeben und eingeleitet von Stefan Rebenich und Gisa Franke. Deutsche Geschichtsquellen des 19. und 20. Jahrhunderts 67. München.

Renehan 1994: Robert Renehan. 'Of Mice and Men in Aristotle', *Classical Philology* 89/3, 245–55.

Renehan 1996: Robert Renehan. 'Aristotelian Explications and Emendations, II: Passages from the *De Anima, De Partibus Animalium, De Generatione Animalium, De Motu Animalium, Politics*, and *Nicomachean Ethics*', *Classical Philology* 91/3, 223–46.

Romero 2001: Fernando G. Romero. 'Varia Paroemiographica Graeca', *Cuadernos de filología clásica. Estudios griegos e indoeuropeos* 11, 241–54.

Rose 1854: Valentini Rose *De Aristotelis librorum ordine et auctoritate commentatio*. Berlin.

Rose 1893: Valentin Rose. *Verzeichniss der lateinischen Handschriften der Königlichen Bibliothek zu Berlin*. Erster Band. *Die Meerman-Handschriften des Sir Thomas Phillipps*. Berlin.

Ross 1955: Sir David Ross. *Aristotle, Parva Naturalia*, revised text with introduction and commentary by Sir David Ross. Oxford.

Ross 1957: Sir David Ross. 'The Development of Aristotle's Thought', *Proceedings of the British Academy* 43, 63–78 (reprinted in *Articles on Aristotle*. Vol. 1: *Science*, ed. Jonathan Barnes, Malcolm Schofield, and Richard Sorabji. London 1975, 1–13).

Ross 1961: Sir David Ross. *Aristotle, De Anima*, ed. with introduction and commentary by Sir David Ross. Oxford.

Rüsche 1930: Franz Rüsche. *Blut, Leben und Seele. Ihr Verhältnis nach der Auffassung der griechischen und hellenistischen Antike, der Bibel und der alten Alexandrinischen Theologen*. Paderborn.

Santas 1969: Gerasimos Santas. 'Aristotle on Practical Inference, the Explanation of Action, and Akrasia', *Phronesis* 14, 162–91.

Schmidt 1899: 'Heronis Alexandrini De automatis', in *Heronis Alexandrini Opera quae supersunt omnia*. Vol. 1. *Pneumatica et automata*. Recensuit Guilelmus Schmidt. Leipzig, 335–453.

Schofield 2011: Malcolm Schofield. '*Phantasia* in *De Motu Animalium*', in *Moral Psychology and Human Action in Aristotle*, ed. Michael Pakaluk and Giles Pearson, Cambridge, 119–34.

Schwyzer/Debrunner 1950: Eduard Schwyzer. *Griechische Grammatik*. Auf der Grundlage von Karl Brugmanns Griechischer Grammatik. Zweiter Band: *Syntax und Syntaktische Stilistik*. Vervollständigt und herausgegeben von Albert Debrunner. München.

Seeck 1992: Gustav A. Seeck. 'Review of Manuwald 1989', *Anzeiger für die Altertumswissenschaft* 14, 3/4, col. 190–2.

Semler 1765: Johann S. Semler. *Hermenevtische Vorbereitung*. Drittes Stück, Erste Abtheilung, *worin von dem griechischen Text, und Handschriften der Evangelien Beobachtungen vorkommen*. Halle im Magdeburgischen.

Shailor 1984: Barbara A. Shailor. *Catalogue of Medieval and Renaissance Manuscripts in the Beinecke Rare Book and Manuscript Library, Yale University*. Vol. 1: *MSS 1–250*. Binghamton (New York).

Shields 2007: Christopher Shields. 'The Peculiar Motion of Aristotelian Souls', *Proceedings of the Aristotelian Society Supplementary Volume* 81, 139–61.

Shields 2009: Christopher Shields. 'The Priority of Soul in Aristotle's *De Anima*: Mistaking Categories?', in *Body and Soul in Ancient Philosophy*, ed. Dorothea Frede and Burkhard Reis. Berlin/New York, 267–90.

Shields 2016: *Aristotle, De Anima*, transl. with an introduction and commentary by Christopher Shields. Oxford.

Siwek 1963: *Aristotelis Parva naturalia Graece et Latine*, edidit, versione auxit, notis illustravit Paul Siwek. S.J. Collectio Philosophica Lateranensis 5. Roma.

Skutsch 1985: *The Annals of Quintus Ennius*, ed. with introduction and commentary by Otto Skutsch. Oxford.

Snell/Kannicht 1986: *Tragicorum Graecorum Fragmenta (TrGF)*. Vol 1. *Didascaliae Tragicae, Catalogi Tragicorum et Tragoediarum, Testimonia et Fragmenta Tragicorum Minorum*, edidit Bruno Snell. Editio correctior et addendis aucta. Curavit Richard Kannicht. Göttingen.

Solmsen 1957: Friedrich Solmsen. 'The Vital Heat, the Inborn Pneuma and the Aether', *Journal of Hellenic Studies* 57, 119–23.

Spengel 1849: Leonhard Spengel. *Ueber die Reihenfolge der naturwissenschaftlichen Schriften des Aristoteles*. München.

Speranzi 2012/17: David Speranzi. 'Scheda manoscritto: Firenze, Biblioteca Riccardiana, Riccardiano, Ricc.14', in *Manus online* (http://manus.iccu.sbn.it//opac_SchedaScheda. php?ID=202044; 14/12/18).

Stadler 1909: *Alberti Magni liber de principiis motus processivi ad fidem Coloniensis archetypi*, ed. Hermann Stadler. Programm des Könglichen Maximilians-Gymnasiums für das Schuljahr 1908/1909. München.

Stefec 2012: Rudolf S. Stefec. 'Die griechische Bibliothek des Angelo Vadio da Rimini', *Römische Historische Mitteilungen* 54, 95–184.

Stevenson 1888: *Codices manuscripti graeci Reginae Suecorum et Pii Pp. II Bibliothecae Vaticanae, descripti Praeside I. B. Cardinali Pitra episcopo Port uensi S. R. E. Bibliothecario*, recensuit et digessit Henricus Stevenson Senior, eiusdem Bibliothecae Scriptor. Roma.

Studemund/Cohn 1890: *Verzeichniss der griechischen Handschriften der Königlichen Bibliothek zu Berlin. I. Codices ex bibliotheca Meermanniana Phillippici Graeci nunc Berolinenses descripserunt Guilelmus Studemund et Leopoldus Cohn*. Die Handschriften-Verzeichnisses der Königlichen Bibliothek zu Berlin, Elfter Band. Berlin.

Taillardat 1967: *Suétone, Περὶ βλασφημιῶν. Περὶ παιδιῶν (extraits byzantins)*, ed. Jean Taillardat. Paris.

Thielscher 1948: Paul Thielscher. 'Die relative Chronologie der erhaltenen Schriften des Aristoteles nach den bestimmten Selbstzitaten', *Philologus* 97, 229–65.

Thomæus 1523: *ARISTOTELIS STAGIRITAE PARVA NATURALIA: De Sensu & sensili. De Memoria & reminiscentia. De Somno & uigilia. De Insomniis. De Diuinatione per somnia. De Animalium Motione. De Animalium Incessu. De Extensione & breuitate vitæ. De Iuuentute & Senectute, Morte & Vita, & de Spiratione*. Omnia in latinum conuersa & antiquorum more explicata. á.N. Leonico Thomaeo. Venice (Thomæus' transl. of *MA* is reprinted in Keßler 1995, 342–5).

Thurn 1980: Hans Thurn. *Die griechischen Handschriften der Universitätsbibliothek Erlangen*. Wiesbaden.

Torraca 1958a: *Aristotele, De Motu Animalium*, ed. Luigi Torraca. Collana di studi Greci XXX. Napoli.

Torraca 1958b: Luigi Torraca. 'Sull' autenticità del *De Motu Animalium* di Aristotele', *Maia* 10, 220–33.

Torraca 1959: Luigi Torraca. 'Contributi alla storia del testo greco e del testo moerbekiano del *"De Motu Animalium"*', in *Ricerche sull'Aristotele minore*, ed. Luigi Torraca. Padova, 7–26.

Torstrik 1857: Adolf Torstrik. 'XXIV. Die authentica der Berliner ausgabe des Aristoteles', *Philologus* 12, 494–530.

Torstrik 1858: Adolf Torstrik. '3. Die authentica der Berliner ausgabe des Aristoteles. (Nachtrag zu Philologus XII, p. 494 flgg.)', *Philologus* 13, 204–6.

Tracy 1983: Theodore Tracy. 'Heart and Soul in Aristotle', in *Essays in Ancient Greek Philosophy*, ed. John P. Anton and Anthony Preus. Vol. 2. Albany, 321–39.

Trendelenburg 1833: *Aristotelis De Anima libri tres*, ad interpretum Graecorum auctoritatem et codicum fidem recognovit commentariis illustravit Frider. A. Trendelenburg. Jena.

Trovato 2017. Paolo Trovato. *Everything You Always Wanted to Know about Lachmann's Method: A Non-Standard Handbook of Genealogical Textual Criticism in the Age of Post-Structuralism, Cladistics, and Copy-Text*. Revised edition. Padova (first edition 2014).

van der Eijk 1994: *Aristoteles. De Insomniis. De Divinatione per Somnum*. Übersetzt und erläutert von Philip van der Eijk. Aristoteles, Werke in deutscher Übersetzung 14/ III. Berlin.

van der Valk 1976: *Eustathii Archiepiscopi Thessalonicensis commentarii ad Homeri Iliadem pertinentes*. Ad fidem codicis Laurentiani editi. Curavit Marchinus van der Valk. Vol. II: *Praefationem et commentarios ad libros E–I complectens*. Leiden.

van Leeuwen 2016: Joyce van Leeuwen. *The Aristotelian* Mechanics: *Text and Diagrams*. Boston Studies in the Philosophy and History of Science 316. Cham/Heidelberg/New York/Dordrecht/London.

Vendruscolo 2008: Fabio Vendruscolo, 'Codici dell'Argiropulo tra gli *Utinenses Graeci*', *Incontri triestini di filologia classica* 6 (2006/07), 289–97.

Verbeke 1978: Gérard Verbeke. 'Doctrine du pneuma et entéléchisme chez Aristote', in Lloyd/Owen 1978, 191–214.

Vitelli 1887: *Ioannis Philoponi In Aristotelis Physicorum libros tres priores commentaria*. Consilio et auctoritate Academiae Litterarum Regiae Borussicae, ed. Hieronymus Vitelli. Berlin.

Vladimir 1894: Archimandrite Vladimir. *Sistematičeskoe opisanie rukopisej Moskovskoj sinodalnoj (patriarsej) biblioteki*. Vol. 1. Moskwa.

Vuillemin-Diem/Rashed 1997: Gudrun Vuillemin-Diem and Marwan Rashed. 'Burgundio de Pise et ses manuscrits grecs d'Aristote: Laur. 87.7 et Laur. 81.18', *Recherches de Théologie et Philosophie médiévales* 64, 136–98.

Wartelle 1963: André Wartelle. *Inventaire des manuscrits grecs d'Aristote et de ses Commentateurs. Contribution à l' histoire du texte d'Aristote*. Paris.

Wedin 1988: Michael Wedin. *Mind and Imagination in Aristotle*. New Haven/London.

Wendland 1901: *Alexandri in librum De sensu commentarium*. Consilio et auctoritate Academiae Litterarum Regiae Borussicae, ed. Paulus Wendland. Berlin.

Whiting 2002: Jennifer E. Whiting. 'Locomotive Soul: The Parts of Soul in Aristotle's Scientific Works', *Oxford Studies in Ancient Philosophy* 22, 141–200.

Wians 1996: *Aristotle's Philosophical Development: Problem and Prospects*, ed. William Wians. Lanham.

Wians/Polansky 2017: *Reading Aristotle: Argument and Exposition*, ed. William Wians and Ronald Polansky. Leiden.

Wiesner 1981: Jürgen Wiesner. 'Zu den Scholien der Parva Naturalia des Aristoteles', in *Proceedings of the World Congress on Aristotle, Thessaloniki August 7–14, 1978*. Vol. 1. Athína, 233–7.

Wiggins 1975: David Wiggins. 'Deliberation and Practical Reason', *Proceedings of the Aristotelian Society* 76, 29–51 (reprinted in *Essays on Aristotle's Ethics*, ed. Amely O. Rorty. Berkeley/Los Angeles/London 1980, 221–40).

Wilson 1913: J. Cook Wilson. 'Difficulties in the Text of Aristotle', *The Journal of Philology* 32, 137–65.

Wilson 1983: Nigel Wilson. 'A Mysterious Byzantine Scriptorium: Ioannikios and his Colleagues', *Scrittura e Civiltà* 7, 161–76.

Zeller 1879: Eduard Zeller. *Philosophie der Griechen in ihrer Geschichtlichen Entwicklung. Zweiter Theil, zweite Abtheilung: Aristoteles und die alten Peripatetiker*. Dritte Auflage. Leipzig.

Zingano 2022: Marco Zingano. 'Review of Rapp/Primavesi 2020', *Classical Review* 72/2, 72–5.

Zucca 2022: Diego Zucca. 'Review of Rapp/Primavesi 2020', *Elenchos* 43/2, 377–84.

INDEX LOCORUM

INDEX OF NAMES